Management and Organisations

Second Edition

A Pearson Custom Publication

Management and Organisations

Second Edition

Compiled from:

Management: An Introduction
Fifth Edition
David Boddy with Steve Paton

PEARSON
Custom Publishing

Pearson Education Limited
Edinburgh Gate
Harlow
Essex CM20 2JE

And associated companies throughout the world

Visit us on the World Wide Web at:
www.pearsoned.co.uk

First published 2010

This Custom Book Edition © 2011 Published by Pearson Education Limited

Compiled from:

Management: An Introduction Fifth Edition
by David Boddy with Steve Paton
ISBN 978 0 273 73896 1
Copyright © Prentice Hall Europe 1998
Copyright © Pearson Education Limited 2002, 2011

ISBN 978 0 85776 488 1

Printed and bound in Great Britain by Antony Rowe

Contents

The following chapters are from:

Management: An Introduction
Fifth Edition
by David Boddy with Steve Paton

Chapter 1	Managing in organisations	1
Chapter 2	Models of management	31
Chapter 3	Organisation cultures and contexts	64
Chapter 6	Planning	92
Chapter 7	Decision making	116
Chapter 10	Organisation structure	148
Chapter 12	Information systems and e-business	181
Chapter 13	Managing change and innovation	210
Chapter 18	Managing operations and quality	240
	Glossary	269

CHAPTER 1
MANAGING IN ORGANISATIONS

Case study   Ryanair www.ryanair.com

In 2010 Ryanair, based in Dublin, was Europe's largest low-fare airline and, despite the recession, it carried almost 66 million passengers in the 12 months to the end of February: a record for that period. In 1985 the company began offering services between Dublin and London, in competition with the established national carrier, Aer Lingus. In the early years the airline changed its business several times – initially a conventional competitor for Aer Lingus, then a charter company, at times offering a cargo service. The Gulf War in 1990 discouraged air travel and deepened the company's financial problems. In 1991 senior managers decided to focus the airline as a 'no-frills' operator, in which many traditional features of air travel (free food, drink, newspapers and allocated seats) were no longer available. It aimed to serve a group of flyers who wanted a functional and efficient service, not luxury.

In 1997 changes in European Union regulations enabled new airlines to enter markets previously dominated by established national carriers such as Air France and British Airways. Ryanair quickly took advantage of this, opening new routes between Dublin and continental Europe. Although based in Ireland, 80 per cent of its routes are between airports in other countries – in contrast with established carriers that depend heavily on passengers travelling to and from the airline's home country (Barrett, 2009, p. 80).

Managers were quick to spot the potential of the internet, and in 2000 opened Ryanair.com, a booking site. Within a year it sold 75 per cent of seats online and now sells almost all seats this way. It also made a long-term deal with Boeing to purchase 150 new aircraft over the next eight years.

Several factors enable Ryanair to offer low fares:

- Simple fleet – using a single aircraft type (Boeing 737 – most of which are quite new) simplifies maintenance, training and crew scheduling.
- Secondary airports – using airports away from major cities keeps landing charges low, sometimes as little as £1 per passenger against £10 at

© Thierry Tronnel/Corbis

a major airport; it also avoids the delays and costs caused by congestion at major airports.

- Fast turnrounds – staff typically turn an aircraft round between flights in 25 minutes, compared with an hour for older airlines. This enables aircraft to spend more time in the air, earning revenue (11 hours compared with seven at British Airways).
- Simplified operations – not assigning seats at check-in simplifies ticketing and administrative processes, and also ensures that passengers arrive early to get their preferred seat.
- Flying directly between cities avoids transferring passengers and baggage between flights, where mistakes and delays are common.
- Cabin staff collect rubbish before and after landing, saving the cost of cleaning crews which established carriers choose to use.

Source: *Economist*, 10 July 2004; O'Connell and Williams (2005); Doganis (2006); and other published information.

Case questions 1.1

- What did 'management' contribute to the growth of the airline?
- Give examples of three points at which managers changed what the organisation does and how it works.

1.1 Introduction

The Ryanair case illustrates several aspects of management. A group of **entrepreneurs** saw an opportunity in the market, and created an organisation to take advantage of it. They bring resources together and transform them into a service which they sell to customers. They differ from their competitors by using different resources (e.g. secondary airports) and different ways to transform these into outputs (e.g. short turnrounds). They have been innovative in the way they run the business, such as in identifying what some customers valued in a flight – cost rather than luxury – and carried a record 65 million passengers in 2009.

Entrepreneurs such as Michael O'Leary of Ryanair are always looking for ways to **innovate** and make the most of new opportunities. Other managers face a different challenge – more demand with less resources. Those managing the United Nations World Food Programme struggle to raise funds from donor countries – aid is falling while hunger is increasing. In almost every public healthcare organisation, managers face a growing demand for treatment, but have fewer resources with which to provide it.

Organisations of all kinds – from rapidly growing operations such as Facebook to established businesses such as Royal Dutch Shell or Marks & Spencer – depend on people at all levels who can run the current business efficiently and also innovate. This book is about the knowledge and skills that enable people to meet these expectations, and so build a satisfying and rewarding management career.

Figure 1.1 illustrates the themes of this chapter. It represents the fact that people draw resources from the external environment and manage their transformation into outputs that they hope are of greater value. They pass these back to the environment, and the value they obtain in return (money, reputation, goodwill, etc.) enables them to attract new resources to continue in business (shown by the feedback arrow from output to input). If the outputs do not attract sufficient resources, the enterprise will fail.

The chapter begins by examining the significance of managed organisations in our world. It then outlines what management means, and introduces theories about the nature of managerial work. Finally, it introduces ideas on studying management.

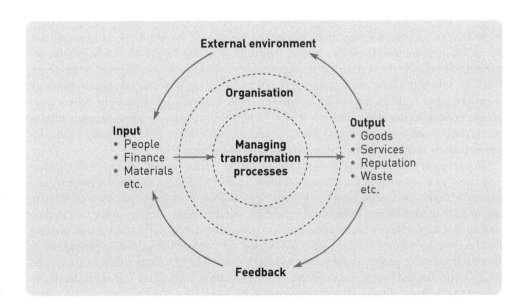

Figure 1.1
Managing organisation and environment

Activity 1.1   **What is management?**

Write a few notes summarising what you think 'management' means.

- You may find it helpful to think of instances in which you have encountered 'management' – such as when you have been managed in your school or university.
- Alternatively, reflect on an occasion when you have managed something, such as a study project. Keep the notes so you can refer to them.

1.2   Managing to add value to resources

We live in a world of managed **organisations**. We experience many every day – domestic arrangements (family or flatmates), large public organisations (the postal service), small businesses (the newsagent), well-known private companies (the jar of coffee) or a voluntary group (the club we attended). They affect us and we judge their performance. Did the transaction work smoothly or was it chaotic? Was the service good, reasonable or poor? Will you go there again?

An **organisation** is a social arrangement for achieving controlled performance towards goals that create value.

Key ideas   **Joan Magretta on the innovation of management**

What were the most important innovations of the past century? Antibiotics and vaccines that doubled, or even tripled, human life spans? Automobiles and aeroplanes that redefined our idea of distance? New agents of communication, such as the telephone, or the chips, computers and networks that are propelling us into a new economy?

All of these innovations transformed our lives, yet none of them could have taken hold so rapidly or spread so widely without another. That innovation is the discipline of management, the accumulating body of thought and practice that makes organisations work. When we take stock of the productivity gains that drive our prosperity, technology gets all of the credit. In fact, management is doing a lot of the heavy lifting.

Source: Magretta (2002), p. 1.

As human societies become more specialised, we depend more on others to satisfy our needs. We meet some of these by acting individually or within family and social groups: organisations provide the rest. Good managers make things work – so that aid is delivered, roads are safe, shops have stock, hospitals function and all the rest. They do not do the work themselves, but build an organisation with the resources *and* competences to deliver what people need (Johnson *et al.*, 2008, pp. 95–6). **Tangible resources** are physical assets such as plant, people and finance – things you can see and touch. **Intangible resources** are non-physical assets such as information, reputation and knowledge.

To transform these resources into valuable goods and services people need to work together. They need to know what to do, understand their customers, deal with enquiries properly and generally make the transaction work well. Beyond that, they look for opportunities to improve, be innovative and learn from experience. Good managers bring out the best in their staff so that they willingly 'go the extra mile': together they develop effective ways of working that become second nature. These 'ways of working' are **competences** – skills, procedures or systems that enable people to use resources productively. The managers role is to secure and retain resources and competences so that the organisation adds **value** – it is producing an output that is more valuable than the resources it has used.

Tangible resources are the physical assets of an organisation such as plant, people and finance.

Intangible resources are non-physical assets such as information, reputation and knowledge.

Competences are the skills and abilities by which resources are deployed effectively – systems, procedures and ways of working.

Value is added to resources when they are transformed into goods or services that are worth more than their original cost plus the cost of transformation.

Well-managed organisations create value in many ways. If you buy a ticket from Ryanair, you can easily measure the tangible value of a cheap flight. In other purchases the value is intangible, as people judge a product by its appearance, what it feels or smells like, how trendy it is or whether it fits their image. Others value good service, or a clear set of instructions. Good managers understand what customers value and build an organisation to satisfy them.

Management in practice   **Creating value at DavyMarkham** www.davymarkham.com

Kevin Parkin is Managing Director (and part-owner) of DavyMarkham, a small engineering company. Although the company has a long history, by the mid-1990s it was making regular losses, and its survival was in doubt. Since Mr Parkin joined the company he has returned it to profit, and in 2009 was predicting a 10 per cent increase in sales the following year. He has concentrated on identifying what the company is good at, and then using tough management and financial discipline to make sure staff follow the recipe for success. Mr Parkin has removed poor managers, walks the shop floor twice a day to check on progress, and engages with the workforce.

It's been essential to tell people the truth about the business, whether it's good or bad, and giving them the enthusiasm they require to make them want to succeed . . . I also ask [my 'mentors' – people I have known in previous jobs] about key strategic decisions, people issues, market penetration, capital spending and general business solutions.

Source: From an article by Peter Marsh and Andrew Bounds, *Financial Times*, 27 May 2009.

Commercial organisations of all kinds (business start-ups, small and medium-sized enterprises (SMEs), online firms and international enterprises) aim to add value and create wealth. So do voluntary and not-for-profit organisations – by educating people, counselling the troubled or caring for the sick. There are about 190,000 charities in England and Wales, with annual incoming resources of over £50 billion (equal to about 3 per cent of gross domestic product), and employing over 660,000 staff (Charities Commission Annual Report for 2008–9, at **www.charitycommission.gov.uk**). Managing a large charity is at least as demanding a job as managing a commercial business, facing similar challenges of adding value to limited resources. Donors and recipients expect them to manage resources well so that they add value to them.

Theatres, orchestras, museums and art galleries create value by offering inspiration, new perspectives or unexpected insights. Other organisations add value by serving particular interests – such as Unison, a trade union that represents workers in the UK public sector, or the Law Society, which defends the interests of lawyers. Firms in most industries create trade organisations to protect their interests by lobbying or public relations work.

While organisations aim to add value, many do not do so. If people work inefficiently they will use more resources than customers will pay for. They may create pollution and waste, and so destroy wealth. Motorway builders create value for drivers, residents of by-passed villages, and shareholders – but destroy value for some people if the route damages an ancient woodland rich in history and wildlife. The idea of creating value is subjective and relative.

Managers face some issues that are unique to the setting in which they operate (charities need to maintain the support of donors) and others which arise in most organisations (business planning or ensuring quality). Table 1.1 illustrates some of these diverse settings, and their (relatively) unique management challenges – which are in addition to challenges that are common to all.

Table 1.1 Where people manage

Setting – industry or type	Examples in this book	'Unique' challenges
Business start-ups	Innocent Drinks in the early days – Part 1 case	Securing funding to launch and enough sales of an unknown product to sustain cash-flow. Building credibility
Small and medium-sized enterprises (SMEs)	DavyMarkham – MIP feature above	Generating enough funds to survive, innovate and enter new markets
Professional business services	Hiscox (insurance) – MIP feature in Chapter 11	Managing highly-qualified staff delivering customised, innovative services
Voluntary, not-for-profit organisations and charities	Eden Project – Chapter 15 case	Providing an experience which encourages visitors to return, raising funds for educational work, fulfilling mission
Public sector organisations	Crossrail – Chapter 6 case	Managing high-profile political and commercial interests
Large private businesses	Virgin Media – Part 4 case	Controlling diverse activities
Online firms	Google – Chapter 12 case; Apple – Chapter 14 case	Maintaining constant innovation in rapidly changing market
International businesses	Starbucks – Chapter 4 case Zara – Chapter 19 case	Managing diverse activities across many cultures; balancing central control and local initiative

Note: MIP = Management in Practice

Whatever its nature, the value an organisation creates depends on how well those who work there develops its capabilities.

Activity 1.2   **Focus on management settings**

Choose ONE of the settings in Table 1.1 which interests you. Gather information about an organisation of that type (using, for example, case studies in this book or someone you know who works in that setting) so you can:

- Name one organisation in that setting.
- Identify how it adds value to resources, and the main management challenges it faces.
- Collect evidence about the managing in that setting.
- Compare your evidence with someone who has gathered data about a different setting, and summarise similarities or differences in the management challenges.

1.3　Meanings of management

Management as a universal human activity

Management as a universal human activity occurs whenever people take responsibility for an activity and consciously try to shape its progress and outcome.

As individuals we run our lives and careers: in this respect we are managing. Family members manage children, elderly dependants and households. Management is both a **universal human activity** and a distinct occupation. In the first sense, people manage an infinite range of activities:

> When human beings 'manage' their work, they take responsibility for its purpose, progress and outcome by exercising the quintessentially human capacity to stand back from experience and to regard it prospectively, in terms of what will happen; reflectively, in terms of what is happening; and retrospectively, in terms of what has happened. Thus management is an expression of human agency, the capacity actively to shape and direct the world, rather than simply react to it. (Hales, 2001, p. 2)

A manager is someone who gets things done with the aid of people and other resources.

Management is the activity of getting things done with the aid of people and other resources.

Rosemary Stewart (1967) expressed this idea when she described a **manager** as someone who gets things done with the aid of people and other resources, which defines **management** as the activity of getting things done with the aid of people and other resources. So described, management is a universal human activity – domestic, social and political – as well as in formally established organisations.

In pre-industrial societies people typically work alone or in family units, controlling their time and resources. They decide what to make, how to make it and where to sell it, combining work and management to create value. Self-employed craftworkers, professionals in small practices, and those in a one-person business do this every day. We all do it in household tasks or voluntary activities in which we do the work (planting trees or selling tickets for a prize draw) and the management activities (planning the winter programme).

Activity 1.3　Think about the definition

Choose a domestic, community or business activity you have undertaken.

- What, specifically, did you do to 'get things done with the aid of people and other resources'?
- Decide if the definition accurately describes 'management'.
- If not, how would you change it?

Management as a distinct role

Management as a distinct role develops when activities previously embedded in the work itself become the responsibility not of the employee but of owners or their agents.

Human action can also separate the 'management' element of a task from the 'work' element, thus creating 'managers' who are in some degree apart from those doing the work. **Management as a distinct role** emerges when external parties, such as a private owner of capital, or the state, gain control of a work process that a person used to complete themselves. These parties may then dictate what to make, how to make it and where to sell it. Workers become employees selling their labour, not the results of their labour. During industrialisation in Western economies, factory owners took control of the physical and financial means of production. They also tried to control the time, behaviour and skills of those who were now employees rather than autonomous workers.

The same evolution occurs when someone starts an enterprise, initially performing the *technical* aspects of the work itself – writing software, designing clothes – and also more *conceptual* tasks such as planning which markets to serve or deciding how to raise money.

If the business grows and the entrepreneur engages staff, he or she will need to spend time on *interpersonal* tasks such as training and supervising their work. The founder progressively takes on more management roles – a **role** being the expectations that others have of someone occupying a position. It expresses the specific responsibilities and requirements of the job, and what someone holding it should (or should not) do.

> A role is the sum of the expectations that other people have of a person occupying a position.

This separation of management and non-management work is not inevitable or permanent. People deliberately separate the roles, and they can also bring them together. As Henri Fayol (1949) (of whom you will read more in Chapter 2) observed:

> Management . . . is neither an exclusive privilege nor a particular responsibility of the head or senior members of a business; it is an activity spread, like all other activities, between head and members of the body corporate. (p. 6)

Key ideas   **Tony Watson on separating roles**

All humans are managers in some way. But some of them also take on the formal occupational work of being managers. They take on a role of shaping . . . work organisations. Managers' work involves a double . . . task: managing others and managing themselves. But the very notion of 'managers' being separate people from the 'managed', at the heart of traditional management thinking, undermines a capacity to handle this. Managers are pressured to be technical experts, devising rational and emotionally neutral systems and corporate structures to 'solve problems', 'make decisions', 'run the business'. These 'scientific' and rational–analytic practices give reassurance but can leave managers so distanced from the 'managed' that their capacity to control events is undermined. This can mean that their own emotional and security needs are not handled, with the effect that they retreat into all kinds of defensive, backbiting and ritualistic behaviour which further undermines their effectiveness.

Source: Watson (1994), pp. 12–13.

Someone in charge of part of, say, a production department will usually be treated as a manager and referred to as one. The people who operate the machines will be called something else. In a growing business such as Ryanair, the boundary between 'managers' and 'non-managers' is likely to be very fluid, with all staff being ready to perform a range of tasks, irrespective of their title. Hales' (2006) research shows how first-line managers now hold some responsibilities traditionally associated with middle managers. They are still responsible for supervising subordinates, but often also have to deal with costs and customer satisfaction – previously a middle manager's job.

1.4   **Specialisation between areas of management**

As an organisation grows, senior managers usually create separate functions and a hierarchy, so that management itself becomes divided (there are exceptions such as W.L. Gore Associates – see Chapter 17 – but these are still a small minority).

Functional specialisation

General managers typically head a complete unit of the organisation, such as a division or subsidiary, within which there will be several functions. The general manager is responsible for the unit's performance, and relies on the managers in charge of each function. A small

> General managers are responsible for the performance of a distinct unit of the organisation.

Functional managers are responsible for the performance of an area of technical or professional work.

Line managers are responsible for the performance of activities that directly meet customers' needs.

organisation will have only one or two general managers, who will also manage the functions. At Shell UK the most senior general manager in 2010 was James Smith, the Chairman.

Functional managers are responsible for an area of work – either as line managers or staff managers. **Line managers** are in charge of a function that creates value directly by supplying products or services to customers: they could be in charge of a retail store, a group of nurses, a social work department or a manufacturing area. Their performance significantly affects business performance and image, as they and their staff are in direct contact with customers or clients. At Shell, Mike Hogg was (in 2010) the General Manager of Shell Gas Direct, while Melanie Lane was General Manager, UK Retail.

Management in practice   The store manager – fundamental to success

A manager with extensive experience of retailing commented:

The store manager's job is far more complex that it may at first appear. Staff management is an important element and financial skills are required to manage a budget and the costs involved in running a store. Managers must understand what is going on behind the scenes – in terms of logistics and the supply chain – as well as what is happening on the shop floor. They must also be good with customers and increasingly they need outward-looking skills as they are encouraged to take high-profile roles in the community.

Source: Private communication from the manager.

Staff managers are responsible for the performance of activities that support line managers.

Staff managers are in charge of activities such as finance, personnel, purchasing or legal affairs which support the line managers, who are their customers. Staff in support departments are not usually in direct contact with external customers, and so do not earn income directly for the organisation. Managers of staff departments operate as line managers within their unit. At Shell, in 2010 Bob Henderson was Head of Legal, and Kate Smith was Head of UK Government Relations.

Project managers are responsible for managing a project, usually intended to change some element of an organisation or its context.

Project managers are responsible for a temporary team created to plan and implement a change, such as a new product or system. Mike Buckingham, an engineer, managed a project to implement a new manufacturing system in a van plant. He still had line responsibilities for aspects of manufacturing, but worked for most of the time on the project, helped by a team of technical specialists. When the change was complete he returned to full-time work on his line job.

Entrepreneurs are people who are able to see opportunities in a market which others have overlooked. They quickly secure the resources they need, and use them to build a profitable business. John Scott (Managing Director of Scott Timber, now the UK's largest manufacturer of wooden pallets – **www.scott-timber.co.uk**) recalls the early days – 'I went from not really knowing what I wanted to do . . . to getting thrown into having to make a plant work, employ men, lead by example. We didn't have an office – it was in my mum's house, and she did the invoicing. The house was at the top of the yard, and the saw mill was at the bottom' (*Financial Times*, 11 July 2007, p. 18).

Management hierarchies

As organisations grow, senior managers usually create a hierarchy of positions. The amount of 'management' and 'non-management' work within these positions varies, and the boundaries between them are fluid (Hales, 2006).

Performing direct operations

People who perform direct operations do the manual and mental work to make and deliver products or services. These range from low-paid cleaners or shop workers to highly-paid pilots or lawyers. The activity is likely to contain some aspects of management work, although in lower-level jobs this will be limited. People running a small business combine management work with direct work to meet customer requirements.

Supervising staff on direct operations

Sometimes called supervisors or first-line managers, they typically direct and control the daily work of a group or process,

> framed by the requirement to monitor, report and improve work performance. (Hales 2005, p. 484)

They allocate and co-ordinate work, monitor the pace and help with problems. Sometimes they become involved with middle managers in making operational decisions on staff or work methods. Examples include the supervisor of a production team, the head chef in a hotel, a nurse in charge of a hospital ward or the manager of a bank branch. They may continue to perform some direct operations, but they will spend less time on them than subordinates.

> **Management in practice**   Leading an army platoon
>
> In the British Army an officer in charge of a platoon is responsible for 30 soldiers. Captain Matt Woodward, a platoon commander, describes the job:
>
> As a platoon commander at a regiment you're looking after up to 30 soldiers, all of whom will have a variety of problems you'll have to deal with – helping them [sort out financial difficulties], one of them might need to go to court for something, and you might go and represent them in court, try and give them a character reference, help them as best you can. Or a soldier who has got a girl pregnant, or a soldier who has just got family problems and needs some help. Somebody else may want to take a posting back to England if they're based in Germany, or indeed if they're in England they might want to go to Germany. That's your job to try and help them out as best you can, to help manage their career to find them the best job they can but also in the place they want to be. And obviously as well as welfare and family and discipline problems we lead soldiers in the field and on operations.
>
> Source: Based on an interview with Matt Woodward.

Managing supervisors or first-line managers

Usually referred to as middle managers, they – such as an engineering manager at Ryanair – are expected to ensure that first-line managers work in line with company policies. They translate strategy into operational tasks, mediating between senior management vision and operational reality. They may help to develop strategy by presenting information about customer expectations or suggesting alternative strategies to senior managers (Floyd and Wooldridge, 2000; Currie and Proctor, 2005). They provide a communication link – telling first-line managers what they expect, and briefing senior managers about current issues. Others face the challenge of managing volunteers. Charities depend on their time and effort, yet commonly face problems when they don't turn up, or work ineffectively – but cannot draw on the systems commonly used to reward and retain paid staff (Boezeman and Ellemers, 2007).

Managing the business

Managing the business is the work of a small group, usually called the board of directors. They establish policy and have a particular responsibility for managing relations with people and institutions in the world outside, such as shareholders, media or elected representatives. They need to know broadly about internal matters, but spend most of their time looking to the future or dealing with external affairs. Depending on local company law, the board usually includes non-executive directors – senior managers from other companies who should bring a wider, independent view to discussions. Such non-executive directors can enhance the effectiveness of the board, and give investors confidence that the board is acting in their interests. They can

> both support the executives in their leadership of the business and monitor and control executive conduct. (Roberts *et al.*, 2005, p. S6)

by challenging, questioning, discussing and debating issues with the executive members. The board will not consider operational issues.

1.5 Influencing through the process of managing

Stakeholders are individuals, groups or organisations with an interest in, or who are affected by, what the organisation does.

Whatever their role, people add value to resources by influencing others, including internal and external **stakeholders** – those parties who affect, or who are affected by, an organisation's actions and policies. The challenge is that stakeholders will have different priorities, so managers need to influence them to act in ways they believe will add value.

They do this directly and indirectly. Direct methods are the interpersonal skills (see Chapter 14) which managers use – persuading a boss to support a proposal, a subordinate to do more work, or a customer to change a delivery date. Managers also influence others indirectly through:

- the process of managing;
- the tasks of managing (Section 1.6); and
- shaping the context (Section 1.7).

Key ideas   Rosemary Stewart – how managers spend their time

What are managers' jobs like? Do they resemble an orderly, methodical process – or a constant rush from one problem to the next? One of the best-known studies was conducted by Rosemary Stewart (1967) of Oxford University, who asked 160 senior and middle managers to keep a diary for four weeks. This showed that they typically worked in a fragmented, interrupted fashion. Over the four weeks they had, on average, only nine periods of 30 minutes or more alone, with 12 brief contacts each day. They spent 36 per cent of their time on paperwork (writing, dictating, reading, calculating) and 43 per cent in informal discussion. They spent the remainder on formal meetings, telephoning and social activities.

The research team also found great variety between managers, identifying five distinct profiles based not on level or function but on how they spent their time:

- **Emissaries** spent most time out of the organisation, meeting customers, suppliers or contractors.
- **Writers** spent most time alone reading and writing, and had the fewest contacts with other managers.
- **Discussers** spent most time with other people and with their colleagues.
- **Troubleshooters** had the most fragmented work pattern, with many brief contacts, especially with subordinates.
- **Committee members** had a wide range of internal contacts, and spent much time in formal meetings.

Source: Stewart (1967).

Henry Mintzberg – ten management roles

Mintzberg (1973) observed how (five) chief executives spent their time, and used this data to create a frequently quoted model of management roles. Like Stewart he noted that managers' work was varied and fragmented (see Key Ideas), and contained ten roles in three categories – informational, interpersonal and decisional. Managers can use these roles to influence other people. Table 1.2 describes them, and illustrates each with a contemporary example provided by the manager of a school nutrition project.

Informational roles

Managing depends on obtaining information about external and internal events, and passing it to others. The *monitor role* involves seeking out, receiving and screening information to understand the organisation and its context. It comes from websites and reports, and especially from chance conversations – such as with customers or new contacts at conferences

Table 1.2 Mintzberg's ten management roles

Category	Role	Activity	Examples from a school nutrition project
Informational	Monitor	Seek and receive information, scan reports, maintain interpersonal contacts	Collect and review funding applications; set up database to monitor application process
	Disseminator	Forward information to others, send memos, make phone calls	Share content of applications with team members by email
	Spokesperson	Represent the unit to outsiders in speeches and reports	Present application process at internal and external events
Interpersonal	Figurehead	Perform ceremonial and symbolic duties, receive visitors	Sign letters of award to successful applicants
	Leader	Direct and motivate subordinates, train, advise and influence	Design and co-ordinate process with team and other managers
	Liaison	Maintain information links in and beyond the organisation	Become link person for government bodies to contact for progress reports
Decisional	Entrepreneur	Initiate new projects, spot opportunities, identify areas of business development	Use initiative to revise application process and to introduce electronic communication
	Disturbance handler	Take corrective action during crises, resolve conflicts among staff, adapt to changes	Holding face-to-face meetings with applicants when the outcome was negative; handling staff grievances
	Resource allocator	Decide who gets resources, schedule, budget, set priorities	Ensure fair distribution of grants nationally
	Negotiator	Represent unit during negotiations with unions, suppliers, and generally defend interests	Working with sponsors and government to ensure consensus during decision making

Source: Based on Mintzberg (1973) and private communication from the project manager.

and exhibitions. Much of this information is oral (gossip as well as formal meetings), or building on personal contacts. In the *disseminator role* the manager shares information by forwarding reports, passing on rumours or briefing staff. As a *spokesperson* the manager transmits information to people outside the organisation – speaking at a conference, briefing the media or giving the department's view at a company meeting. Michael O'Leary at Ryanair is renowned for flamboyant statements to the media about competitors or officials in the European Commission with whose policies he disagrees.

Interpersonal roles

Interpersonal roles arise directly from a manager's formal authority and status, and shape relationships with people within and beyond the organisation. In the *figurehead role* the manager is a symbol, representing the unit in legal and ceremonial duties such as greeting a visitor, signing legal documents, presenting retirement gifts or receiving a quality award. The *leader role* defines the manager's relationship with other people (not just subordinates), including motivating, communicating and developing their skills and confidence – as one commented:

> I am conscious that I am unable to spend as much time interacting with staff members as I would like. I try to overcome this by leaving my door open whenever I am alone, as an invitation to staff to come in and interrupt me, and encourage them to discuss any problems.

The *liaison role* focuses on contacts with people outside the immediate unit. Managers maintain a network in which they trade information and favours for mutual benefit with clients, government officials, customers and suppliers. For some managers, particularly chief executives and sales managers, the liaison role takes a high proportion of their time and energy.

Management in practice   **Strengthening interpersonal roles**

A company restructured its regional operations, closed a sales office in Bordeaux and transferred the work to Paris. The sales manager responsible for south-west France was now geographically distant from her immediate boss and the rest of the team. This caused severe problems of communication and loss of teamwork. She concluded that the interpersonal aspects of the role were vital as a basis for the informational and decisional roles. The decision to close the office had broken these links.

She and her boss agreed to try the following solutions:

- A 'one-to-one' session of quality time to discuss key issues during monthly visits to head office.
- Daily telephone contact to ensure speed of response and that respective communication needs were met,
- Use of fax and email at home to speed up communications.

These overcame the break in interpersonal roles caused by the location change.

Source: Private communication.

Decisional roles

Creativity is the ability to combine ideas in a unique way or to make unusual associations between ideas.

In the *entrepreneurial role* managers demonstrate **creativity** and initiate change. They see opportunities and create projects to deal with them. Managers play this role when they introduce a new product or create a major change programme – as when Lars Kolind became chief executive of Oticon (Chapter 10 case), determined to change an established and inflexible business, unable to deal with new competition. Managers play the *disturbance-handler role* when they deal with problems and changes that are unexpected.

The *resource-allocator role* involves choosing among competing demands for money, equipment, personnel and other resources. How much of her budget should the housing manager, quoted on page 22, spend on different types of project? What proportion of the budget should a company spend on advertising a product? The manager of an ambulance service regularly decides between paying overtime to staff to replace an absent team member, or letting service quality decline until a new shift starts. This is close to the *negotiator role*, in which managers seek agreement with other parties on whom they depend. Managers at Ryanair regularly negotiate with airport owners to agree on the services and fees for a subsequent period.

Activity 1.4   Gather evidence about Mintzberg's model

Recall a time when you were responsible for managing an activity. Alternatively draw on your experience of being managed, and use your then manager as the focus for the activity.

- Do the ten roles cover all of the roles you performed, or did you do things that are not included in his list? What were they?
- Give examples of what you did under (say) five of the roles.
- Were there any of these roles to which you should have given more time? Or less?
- If possible compare your results with other members of your course.
- Decide if the evidence you have collected supports or contradicts Mintzberg's theory.

Mintzberg proposed that every manager's job combines these roles, with their relative importance depending on the manager's level and type of business. Managers usually recognise that they use many of the roles as they influence others.

Case study   Ryanair – the case continues www.ryanair.com

The company has continued to grow rapidly, announcing that it had carried almost 66 million passengers in the 12 months to the end of February. It now referred to itself as 'the world's largest international scheduled airline', and continued to seek new bases from which to operate its growing European network.

The airline's success depends on balancing low costs, fare levels and load factors (Malighetti *et al.*, 2009). Airline seats are what is known as a perishable good – they have no value if they are not used on the flight, so companies aim to maximise the proportion of seats sold on a flight. Ryanair uses a technique known as dynamic pricing, which means that prices

▶

change with circumstances. Typically, fares rise the nearer the passenger is to the departure date, although if a flight is under-booked, the company encourages late sales by very low fares.

Ryanair also earns a growing proportion of revenue from charges and services such as refreshments, and in 2009 it sharply increased the cost of checked-in bags: it prefers customers to carry hand baggage into the cabin. Each time a passenger rents a car or books a hotel room on the Ryanair website, it earns a commission. It sells scratch cards on board, offers in-flight gambling and online gaming over its website: the chief executive thinks that gambling could double Ryanair's profits over the next decade. The company expects revenue from ancillary activities will continue to grow more rapidly than passenger revenue.

Sources: *Economist*, 10 July 2004; *Independent*, 7 October 2006; *Financial Times*, 7 June 2006; Kumar (2006); Malighetti *et al.* (2009); and company website.

Case questions 1.2

- Which of Mintzberg's management roles can you identify being exercised in the latest stage of the Ryanair case?
- Decide which two of these roles are likely to be most critical in the next stage of the company's development, and explain why.

Managers often highlight two roles missing from Mintzberg's list – manager as subordinate and manager as worker. Most managers have subordinates but, except for those at the very top, they are subordinates themselves. Part of their role is to advise, assist and influence their boss – over whom they have no formal authority. Managers often need to persuade people higher up the organisation of a proposal's value or urgency. A project manager recalled:

> This is the second time we have been back to the management team, to propose how we wish to move forward, and to try and get the resources that are required. It is worth taking the time up front to get all members fully supportive of what we are trying to do. Although it takes a bit longer we should, by pressure and by other individuals demonstrating the benefits of what we are proposing, eventually move the [top team] forward.

Many managers spend time doing the work of the organisation. A director of a small property company helps with sales visits, or an engineering director helps with difficult technical problems. A lawyer running a small practice performs both professional and managerial roles.

Key ideas	Managerial work in small businesses

O'Gorman *et al.* (2005) studied the work of ten owner-managers of small growth-oriented businesses to establish empirically if the nature of their work differs from those in the large businesses studied by Mintzberg. They concluded that managerial work in these businesses is in some ways similar to that in large organisations, finding brevity, fragmentation and variety; mainly verbal communication; and an unrelenting pace.

Another observation was that managers moved frequently between roles, switching from, say, reviewing financial results to negotiating prices with a customer. They were constantly receiving, reviewing and giving information, usually by telephone or in unscheduled meetings. They reacted immediately to live information by redirecting their attention to the most pressing issues, so that their days were largely unplanned, with frequent interruptions. They spent only a quarter of their time in scheduled meetings compared with Mintzberg's finding that managers in large organisations spent almost 60 per cent of their time in this way. Finally, the owners of these small businesses spent 8 per cent of their time in non-managerial activities – twice that of those in Mintzberg's study.

The research shows that the nature of managerial work in small growth-oriented businesses is in some ways similar to, and in others different from, that in large organisations. There is the same brevity and fragmentation, but more informal communication.

Source: O'Gorman *et al.* (2005).

Managers as networkers

Does the focus of a manager's influencing activities affect performance? Mintzberg's study gave no evidence on this point, but work by Luthans (1988) showed that the relative amount of time spent on specific roles did affect outcomes. The team observed 292 managers in four organisations for two weeks, recording their behaviours in four categories – communicating, 'traditional management', networking, and human resource management. They also distinguished between levels of 'success' (relatively rapid promotion) and 'effectiveness' (work-unit performance and subordinates' satisfaction). They concluded that *successful* managers spent much more time networking (socialising, politicking, interacting with outsiders) than the less successful. *Effective* managers spent most time on communication and human resource management.

Wolff and Moser (2009) confirmed the link between **networking** and career success, showing building, maintaining and using internal and external contacts was associated with current salary, and with salary growth. Effective networkers seek out useful connections and contacts, and use the information and ideas they gather to create something valuable. They also look critically at their networks – are they dealing too often with people like themselves and with a similar professional background? And a network that is too extensive may take more time and energy than it is worth.

> **Networking** refers to behaviours that aim to build, maintain and use informal relationships (internal and external) that may help work-related activities.

1.6   Influencing through the tasks of managing

A second way in which managers influence others is when they manage the transformation of resources into more valuable outputs. Building on Figure 1.1, this involves the **management tasks** of planning, organising, leading and controlling the transformation of resources. The amount of each varies with the job and the person, and they do not perform them in sequence: they do them simultaneously, switching as the situation requires.

Figure 1.2 illustrates the elements of this definition. It expands the central 'transforming' circle of Figure 1.1 to show the tasks that together make up the transformation process.

> **Management tasks** are those of planning, organising, leading and controlling the use of resources to add value to them.

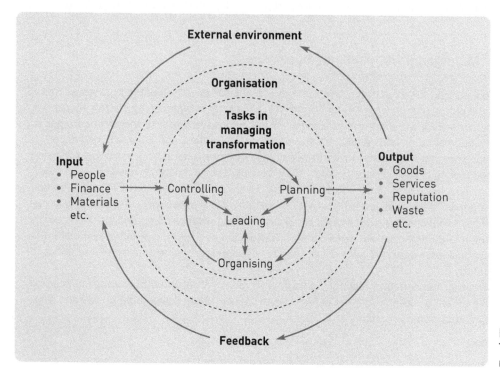

Figure 1.2
The tasks of managing

People draw inputs (resources) from the environment and transform them through the tasks of planning, organising, leading and controlling. This results in goods and services that they pass as output into the environment. The feedback loop indicates that this output is the source of future resources.

External environment

Organisations depend on the external environment for the tangible and intangible resources they need to do their work. So they depend on people in that environment being willing to buy or otherwise value their outputs. Commercial firms sell goods and services, and use the revenue to buy resources. Public bodies depend on their sponsors being sufficiently satisfied with their performance to provide their budget. Most managers are now facing the challenge of how they manage their organisations to ensure that they use natural resources not just efficiently but also sustainably. Part 2 of the book deals with the external environment.

Planning

Planning sets out the overall direction of the work to be done. It includes forecasting future trends, assessing resources and developing performance objectives. It means deciding on the scope and direction of the business, the areas of work in which to engage and how to use resources. Managers invest time and effort in developing a sense of direction for the organisation, or their part of it, and express this in a set of objective. Part 3 deals with planning.

Management in practice   **Planning major rail projects**   www.networkrail.co.uk

More than most civil engineering projects, rail projects depend on extensive and detailed advance planning. In 2010 the UK government announced the preferred route for the first stage of a high-speed West Coast railway line. The first stage will run from London to Birmingham, but construction is not expected to begin until 2015 at the earliest, with completion about four years later. The Crossrail project in London (see Chapter 6 case) also illustrates the scale and complexity of the planning required to build a large railway through (and below) the centre of London.

Source: Company website.

Organising

Organising moves abstract plans closer to reality by deciding how to allocate time and effort. It includes creating a structure for the enterprise, developing policies for human resource management (HRM), deciding what equipment people need, and how to implement change. Part 4 deals with organising.

Management in practice   **Chris Thompson, serial entrepreneur** www.express-group.co.uk

Chris Thompson's grandfather was a shipyard worker on Tyneside and his father a draughtsman who set up Express Engineering, an engineering business, in the 1970s. While working as an apprentice toolmaker in the company, Chris Thompson also sold jeans on a market stall, and turned oil drums into barbecues in his spare time. He took over Express Engineering in 1986, and since then has created more than 40 new businesses. He has sold some to management or third parties, while remaining closely involved with about 20 of them as an investor, director or chairman, many grouped under the brand name Express Group.

The companies are in manufacturing, product development, consultancy, training and property, with many customers in relatively resilient economic sectors such as oil and gas, aerospace and defence. A senior colleague from another company says of Mr Thompson:

He is clear and decisive. He is very considered; doesn't jump to conclusions but makes decisions very quickly. He could have simply continued with the business his father started and been very successful: he is a great example, a great role model.

As well as being closely involved with about 20 of the companies he has founded, he also takes on public sector roles, notably as deputy chair of the regional development agency:

I enjoy the good things in life, but I'm conscious of the disparity between the haves and the have-nots.

Source: From an article by Chris Tighe and Peter March, *Financial Times*, 17 June 2009, p.12.

Leading

Leading is the activity of generating effort and commitment – influencing people of all kinds, generating commitment and motivation, and communicating – whether with individuals or in teams. These activities are directed at all of the other tasks – planning, organising and controlling – so they are placed in the middle of Figure 1.2. Part 5 deals with this topic.

Controlling

Control is the task of monitoring progress, comparing it with plan and taking corrective action. For example, managers set a budget for a housing department, an outpatients' clinic or for business travel. They then ensure that there is a system to collect information regularly on expenditure or performance – to check that they are keeping to budget. If not, they need to decide how to bring actual costs back into line with budgeted costs. Are the outcomes consistent with the objectives? If so, they can leave things alone. But if by Wednesday it is clear that staff will not meet the week's production target, then managers need to act. They may deal with the deviation by a short-term response – such as authorising overtime. Control is equally important in creative organisations. Ed Catmull, cofounder of Pixar comments:

Because we're a creative organization, people [think that what we do can't be measured]. That's wrong. Most of our processes involve activities and deliverables that can be quantified. We keep track of the rates at which things happen, how often something had to be reworked, whether a piece of work was completely finished or not when it was sent to another department . . . Data can show things in a neutral way, which can stimulate discussion. (Catmull, 2008, p. 72)

The discussion to which Catmull refers is the way to learn from experience – an essential contributor to performance. Good managers create and use opportunities to learn from what they are doing, as the Management in Practice feature on a charity illustrates. Part 6 deals with control.

Management in practice   **A charity which encourages learning**

The organisation is a national charity that runs residential homes for people with severe learning disabilities. It has a high reputation for the quality of the care it gives and for the way it treats the carers. Managers take whatever opportunities they can to help staff gain confidence in the difficult and often stressful work. An example:

Staff in one area described how their manager supported their studies by creating a file for them containing information on relevant policies and legislation. The same manager recognised that a night shift worker doing a qualification was not getting the range of experience necessary to complete college assessments: 'So she took me to a review last week and also took me to a referral for a service user. I'd never seen that side before – but now I can relate to the stuff that will come up at college. It's about giving you the fuller picture, because sometimes the night shift can be quite isolating.'

Source: Unpublished research.

The tasks in practice

Managers typically switch between tasks many times a day. They deal with them intermittently and in parallel, touching on many different parts of the job, as this manager in a not-for-profit housing association explains:

My role involves each of these functions. Planning is an important element as I am part of a team with a budget of £8 million to spend on promoting particular forms of housing. So planning where we will spend the money is very important. Organising and leading are important too, as staff have to be clear on which projects to take forward, as well as being clear on objectives and deadlines. Controlling is also there – I have to compare the actual money spent with the planned budget and take corrective action as necessary.

And a manager in a professional services firm:

As a manager in a professional firm, each assignment involves all the elements to ensure we carry it out properly. For example, I have to set clear objectives for the assignment, organise the necessary staff and information to perform the work, supervise staff and counsel them if necessary, and evaluate the results. All the roles interrelate and there are no clear stages for each one.

Activity 1.5   Gather evidence about the tasks of managing

- Do the four tasks of managing cover all of your work, or did you do things that are not included? What were they?
- Give an example of something which you did in each of the tasks.
- Were there any of these to which you should have given more time? Or less?
- If possible, compare your results with other members of your course.

1.7   Influencing through shaping the context

A third way in which managers influence others is through changing aspects of the context in which they work. Changing an office layout, people's reporting relationships, or the rewards they obtain, alter their context and perhaps their actions. The context is both an influence on the manager and a tool with which to influence others (Johns, 2006):

It is impossible to understand human intentions by ignoring the settings in which they make sense. Such settings may be institutions, sets of practices, or some other contexts created by humans – contexts which have a history, within which both particular deeds and whole histories of individual actors can and have to be situated in order to be intelligible. (Czarniawska, 2004, p. 4)

Managers continually aim to create contexts that they hope will influence others to act in ways that meet their objectives.

Dimensions of context

Internal context

Figures 1.1 and 1.2 show the links between managers, their organisation and the external environment. Figure 1.3 enlarges the 'organisation' circle to show more fully the elements that make up the internal environment within which managers work. Any organisation contains these elements – they represent the immediate context of the manager's work. For example, as Jorma Ollila built Nokia into a major business, he and his team made many changes to technology, business processes – and, indeed, to all the elements shown in the figure (Steinbock, 2001), which later chapters examine:

- **culture** (Chapter 3) – norms, beliefs and underlying values of a unit;
- **objectives** (Chapters 6 and 8) – a desired future state of an organisation or unit;
- **structure** (Chapter 10) – how tasks are divided and co-ordinated to meet objectives;
- **technology** (Chapter 12) – facilities and equipment to turn inputs into outputs;
- **power** (Chapter 14) – the amount and distribution of power with which to influence others;
- **people** (Chapter 15) – their knowledge, skills, attitudes and goals;
- **business processes** (Chapter 18) – activities to transform materials and information; and
- **finance** (Chapter 20) – the financial resources available;

Models such as this show that managers work within constraints – they are to some degree helped or hindered by the elements in Figure 1.3. Effective managers do not accept their context passively – they initiate change to create the combination of elements to meet their objectives (Chapter 13).

Historical context

Managing takes place within the flow of history, as what people do now reflects past events and future uncertainties. Managers typically focus on current issues, ensuring that things

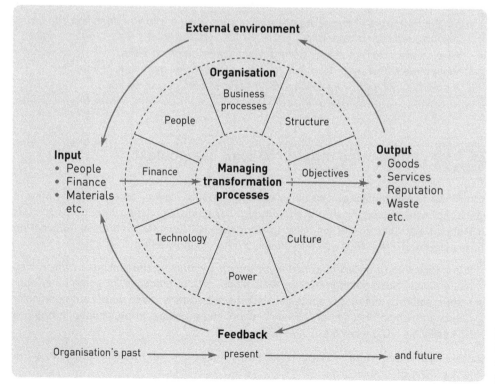

Figure 1.3 The internal and external context of management

run properly, and that the organisation works. At the same time, history influences them through the structure and culture they work within, and which affects how people respond to proposals.

Effective managers also look to the future, questioning present systems and observing external changes. Are we wasting resources? What are others doing? The arrow at the foot of Figure 1.3 represents the historical context.

External context

Chapter 3 shows that the external context includes an immediate competitive (micro) environment and a general (or macro) environment. These affect performance and part of the manager's work is to identify, and adapt to, external changes. Managers in the public sector are expected to deliver improved services with fewer resources, so they seek to influence people to change the internal context (such as how staff work) in order to meet external expectations. They also seek to influence those in the external context about both expectations and resources.

Table 1.3 summarises the last two sections and illustrates how managers can influence others as they perform tasks affecting internal, micro and macro contexts.

Managers and their context

Managers use one of three theories (even if subconsciously) of the link between their context and their action – determinism, choice or interaction.

Determinism

This describes the assumption that factors in the external context determine an organisation's performance – micro and macro factors such as the industry a company is in, the amount of competition, or the country's laws and regulations. Managers adapt to external changes and have little independent influence on the direction of the business. On this view, the context is an independent variable, as shown in Figure 1.4(a).

Table 1.3 Examples of managing tasks in each context

	Internal (organisational)	Micro (competitive)	Macro (general)
Planning	Clarifying the objectives of a business unit and communicating them clearly to all staff	Reducing prices in the hope of discouraging a potential competitor from entering the market	Lobbying for a change in a trade agreement to make it easier to enter an overseas market
Organising	Changing the role of a business unit	Reducing the number of suppliers in exchange for improved terms	Lobbying government to change planning laws to enable longer trading hours
Leading	Redesigning tasks and training staff to higher levels to improve motivation	Arranging for staff to visit customers so that they understand more fully what the customer's need	Sending staff to work in an overseas subsidiary to raise awareness of different markets
Controlling	Ensuring the information system keeps an accurate output record	Implementing an information system directly linked to customers and suppliers	Lobbying for tighter procedures to ensure all countries abide by trade agreements

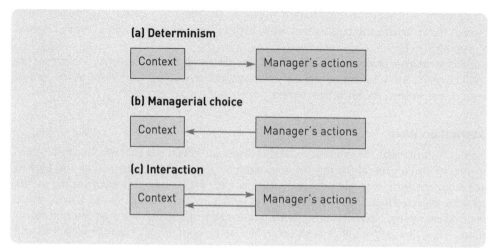

Figure 1.4
Alternative models
of managers and
their context

Choice

An alternative assumption is that people are able to influence events and shape their context. Those in powerful positions choose which businesses to enter or leave, and in which countries they will operate. Managers in major companies lobby to influence taxation, regulations and policy generally, in order to serve their interests. On this view, the context is a dependent variable, as shown in Figure 1.4(b).

Interaction

The interaction approach expresses the idea that people are influenced by, and themselves influence, the context. They interpret the existing context and act to change it to promote personal, local or organisational objectives. A manager may see a change in the company's external environment, and respond by advocating that it responds by entering the market with a product that meets a perceived demand. Others interpret this proposal in the light of *their* perspective – existing suppliers may lobby government to alter some regulations to protect them from this new competitor – the players try to influence decisions in a way that best suits their interests. The outcomes from these interactions affect the context (the company enters the market or the regulations deter them from doing so) – which now provides the historical background to future action. The essential idea is that the relation between the manager and the context works both ways, as shown in Figure 1.4(c). People shape the context, and the context shapes people. Throughout the book there are examples of managers interacting with their context.

Case study   Ryanair – the case continues   www.ryanair.com

The company depends on securing agreements with airport operators, and also approvals from aviation authorities in the countries to which it flies. This often leads it into public disputes with airport operators and/or with the European Commission over subsidies.

In 2009 it withdrew its flights from Manchester airport when it was unable to reach agreement with the airport's owners over landing charges. Michael

O'Leary takes a deliberately aggressive stance to these controversies, believing that:

> as long as its not safety-related, there's no such thing as bad publicity.

He is dismissive of traditional high-cost airlines, the European Commission, airport operators, travel agents and governments that try to protect established airlines from competition.

The Open Skies agreement reached between the European Union and the US in 2008 is intended to increase the number of flights between Europe and the US (Barrett, 2009). This offers new possibilities for Ryanair to extend the successful model from short to long flights – especially given the many people of Irish descent who live in the US.

Sources: *Business Week*, 8 May 2006; *Independent*, 7 October 2006; and other sources.

Case questions 1.3

- Which aspects of the external general environment have affected the company?
- How has the company affected these environments?
- In 2010 the company faced a strategic decision on whether to offer flights to the US. Evaluate the extent to which the factors that have supported its success would be present on these new routes.

1.8   Critical thinking

Managers continually receive data, information and knowledge – but they cannot take what they receive at face value. They must test it by questioning the underlying assumptions, relating it to context, considering alternatives and recognising limitations. These are the skills of critical thinking.

Critical thinking

Brookfield (1987) stresses the benefits of thinking critically, in that it:

> involves our recognizing the assumptions underlying our beliefs and behaviors. It means we can give justifications for our ideas and actions. Most important, perhaps, it means we try to judge the rationality of these justifications . . . by comparing them to a range of varying interpretations and perspectives. (p. 13)

Critical thinking identifies the assumptions behind ideas, relates them to their context, imagines alternatives and recognises limitations.

Critical thinking is positive activity that enables people to see more possibilities, rather than a single path. Critical thinkers 'are self-confident about their potential for changing aspects of their worlds, both as individuals and through collective action' (Brookfield, 1987, p. 5). He identifies four components of critical thinking.

Identifying and challenging assumptions

Critical thinkers look for the assumptions that underlie taken-for-granted ideas, beliefs and values, and question their accuracy and validity. They are ready to discard those that no longer seem valid guides to action, in favour of more suitable ones. Managers who present a well-supported challenge to a theory of marketing that seems unsuitable to their business, or who question the need for a new business division, are engaging in this aspect of critical thinking.

Recognising the importance of context

Critical thinkers are aware that context influences thought and action. Thinking uncritically means assuming that ideas and methods that work in one context will work equally well in others. What we regard as an appropriate way to deal with staff reflects a specific culture: people in another culture – working in another place or at a different time – will have other expectations. Critical thinkers look for such approaches suitable for the relevant context.

Imagining and exploring alternatives

Critical thinkers develop the skill of imagining and exploring alternative ways of managing. They ask how others have dealt with a situation, and seek evidence about the effectiveness of different approaches. This makes them aware of realistic alternatives, and so increases the range of ideas which they can adapt and use.

Seeing limitations

Critical thinking alerts people to the limitations of knowledge and proposals. Critical thinkers recognise that because a practice works well in one situation it does not ensure it will work in another. They are sceptical about research whose claims seem over-sold, asking about the sample or the analysis. They are open to new ideas, but only when supported by convincing evidence and reasoning.

Key ideas   **Techniques to help develop your ability to think critically**

1. Identifying and challenging assumptions:
   - Reflect on recent events which worked well or not-so-well; describing what happened and your reactions to it may help to identify assumptions that were confirmed or challenged by events.
   - Do the same for an achievement of which you are most proud.
   - Imagine that you have decided to leave your job and are advising the committee who will appoint your replacement: list the qualities they should look for in that person. That may indicate the assumptions you hold about the nature of your job, and what it takes to do it well.

2. Recognising the importance of context:
   - Select a practice which people in your organisation take for granted; ask people in other organisations how they deal with the matter, and see if the differences relate to context.
   - Repeat that with people who have worked in other countries.

3. Imagining and exploring alternatives:
   - Brainstorming – trying to think of as many solutions to a problem as you can in a short period, by temporarily suspending habitual judgements.
   - Gather evidence about how other businesses deal with an aspect of management that interest you: the more alternatives you find, the easier it may become to think of alternatives that could work for you.

4. Seeing limitations:
   - Acknowledging the limited evidence behind a theory or prescription.
   - Asking if it has been tested in different settings or circumstances.

Source: Based on Brookfield (1987) and Thomas (2003), p. 7.

Thinking critically will deepen your understanding of management. It does not imply a 'do-nothing' cynicism, 'treating everything and everyone with suspicion and doubt' (Thomas, 2003, p. 7). Critical thinking lays the foundation for a successful career, as it helps to ensure that proposals are supported by convincing evidence and reasoning.

Managing your studies

Studying management is itself a task to manage. Each chapter sets out some learning objectives. The text, including the activities and case questions, help you work towards these objectives, and you can check your progress by using the review questions at the end of each chapter. The questions reflect objectives of varying levels of difficulty (Anderson and Krathwohl, 2001), which Table 1.4 illustrates. Working on these will help develop your confidence to think critically in your studies and as a manager.

Table 1.4 Types of Learning Objective in the Text

Type of objective	Typical words associated with each	Examples
Remember – retrieve relevant knowledge from memory	Recognise, recall	State or write the main elements and relationships in a theory
Understand – construct meaning from information	Interpret, give examples, summarise, compare, explain, contrast	Compare two theories of motivation; contrast two strategies, and explain which theory each reflects
Apply – use a procedure in a specified situation	Demonstrate, calculate, show, experiment, illustrate, modify	Use (named theory) to show the issues which managers in the case should consider
Analyse – break material into parts, showing relation to each other and to wider purpose	Classify, separate, order, organise, differentiate, infer, connect, compare, divide	Collect evidence to support or contradict (named theory); which theory is reflected in (example of practice)?
Evaluate – make judgements based on criteria and standards	Decide, compare, check, judge	Decide if the evidence presented supports the conclusion; should the company do A or B?
Create – put parts together into a coherent whole; reorganise elements	Plan, make, present, generate, produce, design, compose	Present a marketing plan for the company; design a project proposal

Source: Adapted from Anderson and Krathwohl (2001), p. 31.

Studying is an opportunity to practice managing. You can plan what you want to achieve, organise the resources you need, generate personal commitment and check your progress. The book provides opportunities to improve your skills of literacy, reflection (analysing and evaluating evidence before acting), critical thinking, communicating, problem solving and teamwork.

The most accessible sources of ideas and theory are this book, (including the 'further reading' and websites mentioned), your lectures and tutorials. Draw on the experience of friends and relatives to help with some of the activities and questions. As you go about your educational and social lives you are experiencing organisations, and in some cases helping to manage them. Actively reflecting on these experiences will support your studies.

1.9 Integrating themes

Each chapter concludes with a section relating the topic to three integrating themes:

- achieving environmentally sustainable performance;
- meeting expectations about standards of governance and control;
- working in an increasingly international economy.

Sustainable performance

'Sustainability' features regularly in media discussion, is on the legislative agenda of most national governments, and is the subject of the Kyoto Agreement which aims to secure international action to avert climate change. Most managers are aware of the issues, and consider how changes in public opinion and legislation will affect their organisation – what are the implications for the competitive landscape, what threats and opportunities are arising, what should they do to deal with issues of sustainability so that they enhance performance? Managers in the public sector face similar pressures, being expected to provide better services with the same or fewer resources. The interest in **sustainable performance** is driven mainly by legislation, consumer concerns and employees' interest, while barriers include a lack of information on what to do, perceived difficulty in making the business case for such expenditure, and poor implementation of such proposals as are agreed (Hopkins, 2009).

Amory Lovins (Hawken *et al.*, 1999) is an influential advocate of running organisations in a sustainable way, believing that it is wrong to see it as a cost that business will need to bear. Drawing on years of advisory experience at the Rocky Mountain Institute which he helped to found, he maintains that companies who make productive use, not only of financial and physical resources but also of human and natural ones, do well. They turn waste into profit – for example, by taking a radical approach to energy efficiency in buildings, processes and vehicles, and by designing products and services so that they avoid waste.

He also acknowledges that 'turning waste into profit' does not happen easily – it needs thought and careful planning, and will change the way people throughout the organisation do things. It is no different, he suggests, from any other management innovation – people have to pay attention to the problem to find and implement a workable solution. This is likely to involve new capabilities such as being able to work on a whole system, rather than isolated parts; working with colleagues in other units; developing a culture which encourages long-term thinking; and engaging with external stakeholders. These are all part of the work of managing in organisations.

> **Sustainable performance** refers to economic activities that meet the needs of the present population while preserving the environment for the needs of future generations.

Governance and control

The shareholders of commercial companies expect to receive a return on the investment they have made in the business: unless they can be reasonably sure that a business is financially sound they will not lend money or buy shares. They can find some basic information relevant to this in the published Annual Reports, but these are inherently historical documents and cannot cover all aspects of the business. High-profile corporate collapses (see Table 5.1 on page 137 for more details) have occurred despite their Annual Reports giving the impression that all was well. There has also been widespread criticism over the pay and pensions of senior executives, especially in banks. These scandals have damaged investors and employees – and public confidence in the way managers were running these and other large companies.

Many questioned how such things could happen. Why could such apparently successful businesses get into such difficulties so quickly? Were there any warning signals that were ignored? What can be done to prevent similar events happening again? How can public confidence in these businesses be restored? These questions are all linked to corporate governance:

> a lack of effective corporate governance meant that such collapses could occur; good corporate governance can help prevent [them] happening again. (Mallin, 2007, p. 1)

Corporate governance is also relevant in the public sector. There too have been scandals about the poor delivery of service, losses of personal data, failures by staff supposed to be protecting vulnerable people, and examples of dubious expense claims and criminal charges when people award public contracts to business associates. Again people ask how this could happen, who was in charge and what can be done to put things right?

A narrow definition of corporate governance expresses it in essentially financial terms – such that it deals with the ways in which the suppliers of finance to corporations assure themselves of getting a return on their investment. Many now interpret the topic more broadly, to cover the interests of people other than shareholders, and also to include public and not-for-profit organisations. A broader view of the topic is that it is concerned with ensuring that internal controls adequately balance the needs of those with a financial interest in the organisation, and that these are balanced with the interests of other stakeholders.

Governance is an essential mechanism helping the organisation to meet its objectives, by monitoring performance towards them. It does so by:

- helping to ensure there are adequate systems of control to safeguard assets;
- preventing any single individual from becoming too powerful;
- reviewing relationships between managers, directors, shareholders and other stakeholders; and
- ensuring transparency and accountability in transactions.

Internationalisation

Developments in communications technology and changes in the regulations governing international trade have helped to steadily increase the amount of trade that crosses national borders. Managing the international activities of an organisation has become a common feature of the work of many managers – whether working as an expatriate manager in another country, being part of an international team with colleagues from many countries, or managing in an international business which works in many countries.

The international dimension is a pervasive theme of management, with implications for each of the tasks of managing – how to lead in an international environment, and the implications of an increasingly dispersed business for planning, organising and controlling the organisation. These issues will be explored not just in Chapter 4 but also as an integrating theme throughout the book.

Summary

1 **Explain that the role of management is to add value to resources in diverse settings**

- Managers create value by transforming inputs into outputs of greater value: they do this by developing competences within the organisation which, by constantly adding value (however measured) to resources, is able to survive and prosper. The concept of creating value is subjective and open to different interpretations. Managers work in an infinite variety of settings, and Table 1.1 suggests how each setting raises relatively unique challenges.

2 **Give examples of management as a universal human activity and as a distinct role**

- Management is an activity that everyone undertakes to some extent as they manage their daily lives. In another sense, management is an activity within organisations, conducted in varying degrees by a wide variety of people. It is not exclusive to people called 'managers'. People create the distinct role when they separate the management of work from the work itself and allocate the tasks to different people. The distinction between management and non-management work is fluid and is the result of human action.

3 **Compare the roles of general, functional, line, staff and project managers, and of entrepreneurs**

- General managers are responsible for a complete business or a unit within it. They depend on functional managers who can be either in charge of line departments meeting customer needs, such as manufacturing and sales, or in staff departments such as finance which provide advice or services to line managers. Project managers are in charge of temporary activities usually directed at implementing change. Entrepreneurs are those who create new businesses to exploit opportunities they have seen in a market

4 **Explain how managers influence others to add value to resources**

- The processes of managing. Rosemary Stewart drew attention to the fragmented and interrupted nature of management work, while Mintzberg identified ten management roles in three groups which he labelled informational, interpersonal and decisional. Luthans, and more recently Moser, have observed that successful managers were likely to be those who engaged in networking with people inside and outside of the organisation.

- The tasks (or content) of managing. Planning is the activity of developing the broad direction of an organisation's work, to meet customer expectations, taking into account internal capabilities. Organising is the activity of deciding how to deploy resources to meet plans, while leading seeks to ensure that people work with commitment to achieve plans. Control monitors activity against plans, so that people can adjust either if required.

- Contexts within which they and others work. The organisational context consists of eight elements which help or hinder the manager's work – objectives, technology, business processes, finance, structure, culture, power and people. The historical context also influences events, as does the external context made up from the competitive and general environments.

5 **Explain the elements of critical thinking and use some techniques to develop this skill**

- Critical thinking is a positive approach to studying, as it encourages people to develop the skills of identifying and challenging assumptions; recognising the importance of context; imagining and exploring alternatives; and seeing the limitations of any idea or proposal.

6 **Evaluate a manager's approach to the role by analysing how they influence others**

- You can achieve this objective by arranging with a manager to discus their role, and organise your questions or discussion around the theories of the processes, contents and contexts of managerial work outlined in the chapter. If possible, compare your results with others on your course and try to explain any differences which you find.

7 **Current themes and issues**

Managers are expected to:
- achieve environmentally sustainable performance;
- meet expectations about governance and control;
- work in an increasingly international economy.

Review questions

1 Apart from delivering goods and services, what other functions do organisations perform?

2 What is the difference between management as a general human activity and management as a specialised occupation? How has this division happened and what are some of its effects?

3 What examples are there in the chapter of this boundary between 'management' and 'non-management' work being changed and what were the effects?

4 Describe, with examples, the differences between general, functional, line, staff and project managers.

5 Give examples from your experience or observation of each of the four tasks of management.

6 How does Mintzberg's theory of management roles complement that which identifies the tasks of management?

7 What is the significance to someone starting a career in management of Luthans' theory about roles and performance?

8 How can thinking critically help managers do their job more effectively?

9 Review and revise the definition of management that you gave in Activity 1.1.

Concluding critical reflection

Think about the way managers in your company, or one with which you are familiar, go about their work. If you are a full-time student, draw on any jobs you have held, or on the management of your studies at school or university. Review the material in the chapter and make notes on the following questions:

- Which of the issues discussed in this chapter are most relevant to the way you and your colleagues manage?
- What **assumptions** about the role of management appear to guide the way you, or others, manage? Are these assumptions supported by the evidence of recent events – have they worked or not? Which aspects of the content and process of managing are you expected to focus on – or are you unsure? Does your observation support, or contradict, Luthans' theory?
- What aspects of the historical or current **context** of the company appear to influence how you, and others, interpret your management role? Do people have different interpretations?
- Can you compare and contrast your role with that of colleagues on your course? Does this suggest any plausible **alternative** ways of constructing your management role, in terms of where you devote your time and energy? How much scope do you have to change it?
- What **limitations** can you see in the theories and evidence presented in the chapter? For example, how valid might Mintzberg's theory (developed in large commercial firms) be for those managing in a small business or in the public sector? Can you think of ways of improving the model – e.g. by adding elements to it, or being more precise about the circumstance to which it applies?

Further reading

Alvesson, M. and Wilmott, H. (1996), *Making Sense of Management*, Sage, London.

> Discusses management from a critical perspective.

Currie, G. and Proctor, S.J. (2005), 'The Antecedents of Middle Managers' Strategic Contribution: The Case of a Professional Bureaucracy', *Journal of Management Studies*, vol. 42, no. 7, pp. 1325–1356.

> An empirical study comparing how middle managers contributed to strategy in three hospitals, showing the ambiguities in their changing roles, and how contextual factors affected performance.

Drucker, P. (1999), *Management Challenges for the 21st Century,* Butterworth/Heinemann, London.

> Worth reading as a collection of insightful observations from the enquiring mind of this great management theorist.

Finkelstein, S. (2003), *Why Smart Executives Fail: And what you can learn from their mistakes*, Penguin, New York.

> Analysis of failure, giving valuable insights into the complexities of managing.

Hales, C. (2006), 'Moving down the line? The shifting boundary between middle and first-line management', *Journal of General Management*, vol. 32, no. 2, pp. 31–55.

> Reviews the growing pressure on managers as additional responsibilities are added to their role.

Handy, C. (1988), *Understanding Voluntary Organisations,* Penguin, Harmondsworth.

> A valuable perspective on management in the voluntary sector.

Hopkins, M.S. (2009), 'What Executives Don't Get About Sustainability', *MIT Sloan Management Review,* vol. 51, no. 1, pp. 35–40.

Brief introduction to sustainability from a manager's perspective, including an interview with one of the authors of *Natural Capitalism* (Hawken *et al.,* 1999).

Magretta, J. (2002), *What Management Is (and Why it is Everyone's Business),* Profile Books, London.

This small book by a former editor at the *Harvard Business Review* offers a brief, readable and jargon-free account of the work of general management.

Weblinks

These websites have appeared in the chapter:

www.ryanair.com
www.charitycommission.gov.uk
www.davymarkham.com
www.shell.co.uk
www.scott-timber.co.uk
www.networkrail.co.uk
www.express-group.co.uk

Visit two of the business sites in the list, or those of other organisations in which you are interested, and navigate to the pages dealing with recent news, press or investor relations.

- What are the main issues which the organisation appears to be facing?
- Compare and contrast the issues you identify on the two sites.
- What challenges may they imply for those working in, and managing, these organisations?

For video case studies, audio summaries, flashcards, exercises and annotated weblinks related to this chapter, visit **www.pearsoned.co.uk/mymanagementlab**

CHAPTER 2
MODELS OF MANAGEMENT

Aim

To present the main theoretical perspectives on management and to show how they relate to each other.

Objectives

By the end of your work on this chapter you should be able to outline the concepts below in your own terms and:

1 Explain the value of models of management, and compare unitary, pluralist and critical perspectives

2 State the structure of the competing values framework and evaluate its contribution to our understanding of management

3 Summarise the rational goal, internal process, human relations and open systems models, and evaluate what each can contribute to managers' understanding of their role

4 Use the model to classify the dominant form in two or more business units, and to gather evidence about the way this affects the roles of managing in those units

5 Show how ideas from the chapter add to your understanding of the integrating themes

Key terms

This chapter introduces the following ideas:

model (or theory)
metaphor
scientific management
operational research
bureaucracy
administrative management
human relations approach
system

open system
system boundary
feedback
subsystem
socio-technical system
complexity theory
non-linear systems

Each is a term defined within the text, as well as in the Glossary at the end of the book.

Case study
Robert Owen – an early management innovator www.newlanark.org.uk

Robert Owen (1771–1856) was a successful manufacturer of textiles, who ran mills in England and at New Lanark, about 24 miles from Glasgow, in Scotland. David Dale built the cotton-spinning mills at New Lanark in 1785 – which were then the largest in Scotland. Since they depended on water power Dale had built them below the Falls of Clyde – a well-known tourist attraction throughout the eighteenth century. Many people continued to visit both the Falls and New Lanark, which combined both manufacturing and social innovations.

Creating such a large industrial enterprise in the countryside meant that Dale (and Owen after him) had to attract and retain labour – which involved building not only the mill but also houses, shops, schools and churches for the workers. By 1793 the mill employed about 1,200 people, of whom almost 800 were children, aged from 6 to 17: 200 were under 10 (McLaren, 1990). Dale provided the children with food, education and clothing in return for working 12 hours each day: visitors were impressed by these facilities.

One visitor was Robert Owen, who shared Dale's views on the benefits to both labour and owner of good working conditions. By 1801 Dale wanted to sell New Lanark to someone who shared his principles and concluded that Owen (who had married his daughter) was such a man. Owen had built a reputation for management skills while running mills in England, and did not approve of employing children in them.

Having bought the very large business of New Lanark, Owen quickly introduced new management and production control techniques. These included daily and weekly measurements of stocks, output and productivity; a system of labour costing; and measures of work-in-progress. He used a novel control technique: a small, four-sided piece of wood, with a different colour on each side, hung beside every worker. The colour set to the front indicated the previous day's standard of work – black indicating bad. Everyone could see this measure of the worker's performance, which overseers recorded to identify any trends in a person's work:

> Every process in the factory was closely watched, checked and recorded to increase labour productivity and to keep costs down. (Royle, 1998, p. 13)

Reproduced with kind permission of New Lanark Conservation Trust. www.newlanark.org

Most adult employees, at this stage of the Industrial Revolution, had no experience of factory work, or of living in a large community such as New Lanark. Owen found that many 'were idle, intemperate, dishonest [and] devoid of truth' (quoted in Butt, 1971). Evening patrols were introduced to stop drunkenness, and there were rules about keeping the residential areas clean and free of rubbish. He also had 'to deal with slack managers who had tolerated widespread theft and embezzlement, immorality and drunkenness' (Butt, 1971).

During Owen's time at the mill it usually employed about 1,500 people, and soon after taking over he stopped employing children under 10. He introduced other social innovations: a store at which employees could buy goods more cheaply than elsewhere (a model for the Co-operative Movement), and a school which looked after children from the age of one – enabling their mothers to work in the mills.

Sources: Butt (1971); McLaren (1990); Donachie (2000).

Case questions 2.1

- What management issues was Owen dealing with at New Lanark?
- What assumptions guided his management practices?

2.1   Introduction

The brief sketch of Robert Owen illustrates three themes that run through this book. First, he devised management systems to control the workforce and improve mill performance. Second, Owen engaged with the wider social system: he criticised the effects of industrialisation and tried to influence local and national policy to end the use of child labour. Third, he was managing at a time of transition from an agricultural to an industrial economy, and many of the practices he invented were attempts to resolve the tensions between those systems – as we now face tensions between industrial and post-industrial systems.

Owen was an entrepreneur. His attempts to change worker behaviour were innovative, and he was equally creative in devising management systems and new ways of working. Managers today cope with similar issues. HMV needs to recruit willing and capable people for its stores, and ensure that their work creates value. Many share Owen's commitment to responsible business practice: Cooperative Financial Services make a point of stating, and working to, clear ethical principles throughout its business, and doing so in a way that still brings healthy profits. Most see that working conditions affect family life – and try to balance the two by subsidising child care and offering flexible hours to those with family responsibilities.

They also operate in a world experiencing changes equal to those facing Owen. In the newer industrial countries of Eastern Europe and Asia the transition is again from agriculture to industry. Everywhere the internet is enabling people to organise economic activity in new ways, equivalent to the industrial revolution of which Owen was part. Sustainability is now on the agendas of most management teams, as is the move to a more connected international economy.

In coping with such changes, managers, such as Owen before them, search for ways to manage their enterprises to add value. They make assumptions about the best way to do things – and through trial and error develop methods for their circumstances. Managers today can build on these methods when deciding how to deal with their problems. No single approach will suit all conditions – managers need to draw critically and selectively on several perspectives.

The next section introduces the idea of management models, and why they are useful. Section 2.3 presents the competing values framework – a way of seeing the contrasts and complementarities between four theoretical perspectives – and the following sections outline the major ideas within each approach. The final section indicates some of the issues facing managers today – and new models that may represent these conditions.

2.2   Why study models of management?

A model (or theory) represents a complex phenomenon by identifying the major elements and relationships.

A **model (or theory)** represents a more complex reality. Focusing on the essential elements and their relationship helps to understand that complexity, and how change may affect it. Most management problems can only be understood by examining them from several perspectives, so no model offers a complete solution. Those managing a globally competitive business require flexibility, quality and low-cost production. Managers at Ford or Daimler-Chrysler want models of the production process that help them to organise it efficiently from a technical perspective. They also want models of human behaviour that will help them to organise production in a way that encourages enthusiasm and commitment. The management task is to combine both approaches into an acceptable solution.

Managers act in accordance with their model (or theory) of the task. To understand management action we need to know the models available and how people use them, although Pfeffer and Sutton (2006) suggest why people frequently ignore such evidence: see Key Ideas.

> ### Key ideas Pfeffer and Sutton on why managers ignore evidence
>
> In a paper making the case for evidence-based management Pfeffer and Sutton (2006) observe that experienced managers frequently ignore new evidence relevant to a decision and suggest that they:
>
> - trust personal experience more than they trust research;
> - prefer to use a method or solution which has worked before;
> - are susceptible to consultants who vigorously promote their solutions;
> - rely on dogma and myth – even when there is no evidence to support their value;
> - uncritically imitate practices that appear to have worked well for famous companies.
>
> Their paper outlines the benefits of basing practice on sound evidence – similar to the ideas of critical thinking presented in Chapter 1.
>
> Source: Pfeffer and Sutton (2006).

Models identify the variables

Models (theories) aim to identify the main variables in a situation, and the relationships between them: the more accurately they do so, the more useful they are. Since every situation is unique, many experienced managers doubt the value of theory. Magretta's answer is that:

> without a theory of some sort it's hard to make sense of what's happening in the world around you. If you want to know whether you work for a well-managed organization – as opposed to whether you like your boss – you need a working theory of management. (Magretta, 2002, p. 10)

We all use theory, acting on (perhaps implicit) assumptions about the relationships between cause and effect. Good theories help to identify variables and relationships, providing a mental toolkit to deal consciously with a situation. The perspective we take reflects the assumptions we use to interpret, organise and makes sense of events – see Alan Fox in Key Ideas.

> ### Key ideas Alan Fox and a manager's frame of reference
>
> Alan Fox (1974) distinguished between unitary, pluralist or radical perspectives on the relationship between managers and employees. Which assumption a person holds affects how they interpret the tasks of managing. Fox argued that those who take a:
>
> - **unitary perspective** believe that organisations aim to develop rational ways of achieving common interests. Managerial work arises from a technical division of labour, and managers work to achieve objectives shared by all members.
> - **pluralist perspective** believe that the complex division of labour in modern organisations creates groups with distinctive interests. Some conflict over ends and/or means is inevitable, and managerial work involves gaining sufficient consent to meet all interests in some mutually acceptable way.
> - **radical perspective** challenge both unitary and pluralist models, arguing that they ignore the fact that the horizontal and vertical division of labour sustains unequal social relations within capitalist society. As long as these exist managers and employees will be in conflict.
>
> Source: Fox (1974).

As managers influence others to add value they use their mental model of the situation to decide where to focus effort. Figure 2.1 develops Figure 1.3 (the internal context within which managers work) to show some variables within each element: 'structure' could include more specific variables such as roles, teams or control systems. In 2010 Willie Walsh, Chief Executive

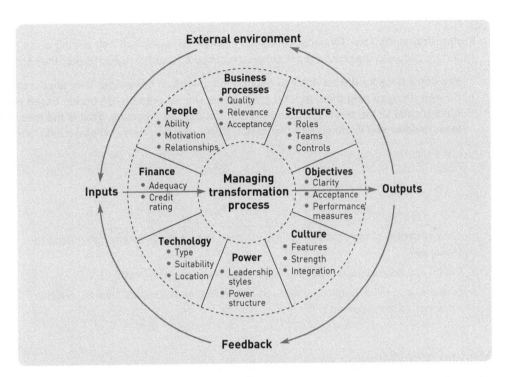

Figure 2.1
Some variables within the internal context of management

of British Airways, was continuing with one of his objectives (set by his predecessor) to raise operating profits to 10 per cent of sales. Figure 2.1 suggests ways of meeting this:

- *objectives* – retaining a reputation for premium travel (a different market than Ryanair);
- *people* – continuing to reduce the number of employees;
- *technology* – reducing capacity at London City Airport, and focusing more flights on Terminal 5 at Heathrow;
- *business processes* – negotiating new working practices with cabin staff.

In each area there are theories about the variables and their relationships – and about which changes will best add value. A change in one element affects others – reducing staff risks hindering the aim of providing a premium service. Any change would depend on available *finance* – and on the chief executive's *power* to get things done. External events (Chapter 3) such as rising fuel prices or changes in economic conditions shape all of these.

Managers need to influence people to add value: people who are aware, thinking beings, with unique experiences, interests and objectives. This affects what information they attend to, the significance they attach to it and how they act. There is an example in Chapter 3 of a retail business in which senior managers, store managers and shop-floor staff attached different meanings to the culture in which they worked. People interpret information subjectively, which makes it hard to predict how they will react: the following MIP feature illustrates two managers' contrasting assumptions about how to deal with subordinates.

Management in practice   **Practice reflects managers' theories**

These examples illustrate contrasting theories about motivation.

Motivating managers: Tim O'Toole, who became Chief Executive of London Underground in 2003, put in a new management structure, appointing a general manager for each line to improve accountability.

> Now there's a human being who is judged on how that line is performing and I want them to feel that kind of intense anxiety in the stomach that comes when there's a stalled train and they realise that it's their stalled train.

Source: From an article by Simon London, *Financial Times*, 20 February 2004.

Supporting staff: John Timpson, Chairman of the shoe repair and key cutting chain, believes the most important people in the company are those who cut customers' keys and re-heel their shoes:

> You come back for the service you get from the people in the shops. They are the stars . . . we need to do everything to help them to look after you as well as possible. [A bonus based on shop takings] is fundamental to the service culture I want. It creates the adrenalin. That is the reason why people are keen to serve you if you go into one of our shops. And why they don't take long lunch breaks.

Source: *Financial Times*, 3 August 2006.

Case questions 2.2

- Give examples of the variables in Figure 2.1 which Robert Owen was attempting to influence?
- Which of the variables were influencing the performance of his mill?
- Is there a conflict between the need to control workers and Owen's creative approach to management?

Models reflect their context

People look for models to deal with the most pressing issues they face. In the nineteenth century, skilled labour was scarce and unskilled labour plentiful: managers were hiring workers unfamiliar with factories to meet growing demand, so wanted ideas on how to produce more efficiently. They looked for ways to simplify tasks so that they could use less-skilled employees, and early management theories gave priority to these issues. People often refer to this focus on efficiency as a manufacturing mindset.

Peter Drucker (1954) observed that customers do not buy products, but the satisfaction of needs: what they value may be different from what producers think they are selling. Manufacturing efficiency is necessary but not sufficient. Managers, Drucker argued, should develop a marketing mindset, focused on what customers want and how much they will pay. Now, as managers try to meet changing customer needs quickly and cheaply, they seek models of flexible working. As business becomes more global, they seek theories about managing across the world.

A **metaphor** is an image used to signify the essential characteristics of a phenomenon.

Key ideas Gareth Morgan's images of organisation

Since organisations are complex creations, no single theory can explain them adequately. We need to see them from several viewpoints, each of which will illuminate one aspect or feature – while also obscuring others. Gareth Morgan (1997) shows how alternative mental images and **metaphors** can represent organisations. Metaphors are a way of thinking about a phenomenon, attaching labels which vividly indicate the image being used. Images help understanding – but also obscure or distort understanding if we use the wrong image. Morgan explores eight ways of seeing organisations as:

- **Machines** – mechanical thinking and the rise of the bureaucracies.
- **Organisms** – recognising how the environment affects their health.
- **Brains** – an information-processing, learning perspective.
- **Cultures** – a focus on beliefs and values.
- **Political systems** – a view on conflicts and power.
- **Psychic prisons** – how people can become trapped by habitual ways of thinking.
- **Flux and transformation** – a focus on change and renewal.
- **Instruments of domination** – over members, nations and environments.

Critical thinking helps improve our mental models

The ideas on critical thinking in Chapter 1 suggest that working effectively depends on being able and willing to test the validity of any theory, and to revise it in the light of experience by:

- identifying and challenging assumptions;
- recognising the importance of context;
- imagining and exploring alternatives;
- seeing limitations.

As you work through this chapter, there will be opportunities to practise these components of critical thinking.

2.3	The competing values framework

Quinn *et al.* (2003) believe that successive models of management (which they group according to four underlying philosophies – 'rational goal', 'internal process', 'human relations' and 'open systems') complement, rather than contradict, each other. They are all:

> symptoms of a larger problem – the need to achieve organizational effectiveness in a highly dynamic environment. In such a complex and fast-changing world, simple solutions become suspect . . . Sometimes we needed stability, sometimes we needed change. Often we needed both at the same time. (p. 11)

While each adds to our knowledge, none is sufficient. The 'competing values' framework integrates them by highlighting their underlying values – see Figure 2.2.

The vertical axis represents the tension between flexibility and control. Managers seek flexibility to cope with rapid change. Others try to increase control – apparently the opposite of flexibility. The horizontal axis distinguishes an internal focus from an external one. Some managers focus on internal issues, while others focus on the world outside. Successive models of management relate to the four segments.

The labels within the circle indicate the criteria of effectiveness which are the focus of models in that segment, shown around the outside. The human relations model, upper left in the figure, stresses the human criteria of commitment, participation and openness. The open systems model (upper right) stresses criteria of innovation, adaptation and growth. The rational goal model in the lower right focuses on productivity, direction and goal clarity. The internal process model stresses stability, documentation and control, within a hierarchical structure. Finally, the outer ring indicates the values associated with each model – the dominant value in the rational goal model is that of maximising output, while in human relations it is developing people. Successive sections of the chapter outline theories associated with each segment.

Management in practice   Competing values at IMI? www.imiplc.com

When Martin Lamb took control of IMI (a UK engineering group which in 2010 employed 14,000 staff in 30 countries) he introduced significant changes to make the company profitable. He decided to concentrate the business on five sectors of engineering, each associated with high-value products and a strong chance of growth in the next few years. He moved much of the manufacturing to low-cost countries, encouraged close links with key customers and aimed to boost innovation. Mr Lamb says:

This is a fundamental transition, aimed at moving IMI away from an old-established manufacturing enterprise to a company focused on product development and applications of knowledge.

Someone who knew the company well commented:

> I always had the feeling . . . that IMI was a bit introverted and anything that (makes) the company more aggressive on the sales side is to be applauded.

The IMI Academy is a forum within which Key Account Managers (staff responsible for major customers) develop their skills of managing customer relationships within an entrepreneurial, customer-focused culture. It includes cross-company courses and web-based discussions, enabling staff to share knowledge, strategy and tactics.

Source: Extracts from an article in *Financial Times*, 4 February 2004; company website.

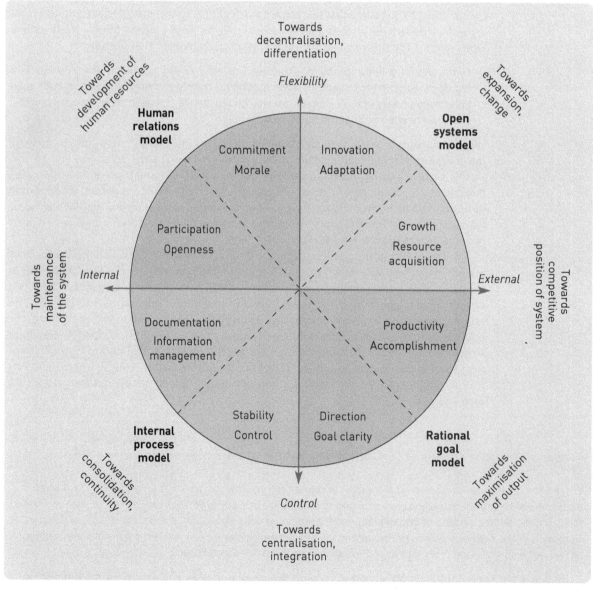

Figure 2.2 Competing values framework

Source: Quinn *et al.* (2003), p. 13.

2.4   Rational goal models

Adam Smith (1776), the Scottish economist, had written enthusiastically about how a pin manufacturer in Glasgow had broken a job previously done by one man into several small steps. A single worker now performed one of these steps repetitively, and this greatly increased the output. Smith believed that this was one of the main ways in which the new industrial system was increasing the wealth of the country.

The availability of powered machinery during the Industrial Revolution enabled business owners to transform manufacturing and mining processes. These technical innovations encouraged, but were not the only reason for, the growth of the factory system. The earlier 'putting-out' system of manufacture, in which people worked at home on materials supplied and collected by entrepreneurs, allowed great freedom over hours, pace and methods of work, and agents had little control over the quantity and quality of output. Emerging capitalist entrepreneurs found that they could secure more control if they brought workers together in a factory. Having all workers on a single site meant that:

> coercive authority could be more easily applied, including systems of fines, supervision . . . the paraphernalia of bells and clocks, and incentive payments. The employer could dictate the general conditions of work, time and space; including the division of labour, overall organisational layout and design, rules governing movement, shouting, singing and other forms of disobedience. (Thompson and McHugh, 2002, p. 22)

This still left entrepreneurs across Europe and later the US (and now China – see following Management in Practice) with the problem of how to manage these new factories profitably. Although domestic and export demand for manufactured goods was high, so was the risk of business failure.

Management in practice   **Incentives at TCL, China** www.tcl.com

TCL Corporation is one of the top producers of electronics products in China, and management is proud of the long hours that employees work. Signs posted next to production lines encourage workers to push themselves to do even more. 'If you don't diligently work today', one warns ominously, 'you'll diligently look for work tomorrow.' The company is growing rapidly and has won many awards for design and quality.

Source: Based on 'Bursting out of China', *Business Week*, 17 November 2003, pp. 24–25; company website.

> **Key ideas**   **Charles Babbage**
>
> Charles Babbage supported and developed Adam Smith's observations. He was an English mathematician better known as the inventor of the first calculating engine. During his work on that project he visited many workshops and factories in England and on the Continent. He then published his reflections on 'the many curious processes and interesting facts' that had come to his attention (Babbage, 1835). He believed that 'perhaps the most important principle on which the economy of a manufacture depends is the division of labour amongst the persons who perform the work' (p. 169).
>
> Babbage also observed that employers in the mining industry had applied the idea to what he called 'mental labour'. 'Great improvements have resulted . . . from the judicious distribution of duties . . . amongst those responsible for the whole system of the mine and its government' (p. 202). He also recommended that managers should know the precise expense of every stage in production. Factories should also be large enough to secure the economies made possible by the division of labour and the new machinery.
>
> Source: Babbage (1835).

Frederick Taylor

The fullest answer to the problems of factory organisation came in the work of Frederick W. Taylor (1856–1915), always associated with the ideas of **scientific management**. An American mechanical engineer, Taylor focused on the relationship between the worker and the machine-based production systems that were in widespread use:

> the principal object of management should be to secure the maximum prosperity for the employer, coupled with the maximum prosperity for each employee. The words 'maximum prosperity' . . . mean the development of every branch of the business to its highest state of excellence, so that the prosperity may be permanent. (Taylor, 1917, p. 9)

He believed that the way to achieve this was to ensure that all workers reached their state of maximum efficiency, so that each was doing 'the highest grade of work for which his natural abilities fit him' (p. 9). This would follow from detailed control of the process, which would become the managers' primary responsibility: they should concentrate on understanding the production systems, and use this to specify every aspect of the operation. In terms of Morgan's images, the appropriate image would be the machine. Taylor advocated five principles:

- use scientific methods to determine the one best way of doing a task, rather than rely on the older 'rule of thumb' methods;
- select the best person to do the job so defined, ensuring that their physical and mental qualities were appropriate for the task;
- train, teach and develop the worker to follow the defined procedures precisely;
- provide financial incentives to ensure people work to the prescribed method; and
- move responsibility for planning and organising from the worker to the manager.

Taylor's underlying philosophy was that scientific analysis and fact, not guesswork, should inform management. Like Smith and Babbage before him, he believed that efficiency rose if tasks were routine and predictable. He advocated techniques such as time and motion studies, standardised tools and individual incentives. Breaking work into small, specific tasks would increase control. Specialist managerial staff would design these tasks and organise the workers:

> The work of every workman is fully planned out by the management at least one day in advance, and each man receives in most cases complete written instructions, describing in detail the task which he is to accomplish, as well as the means to be used in doing the work . . . This task specifies not only what is to be done but how it is to be done and the exact time allowed for doing it. (Taylor, 1917, p. 39)

Scientific management: the school of management called 'scientific' attempted to create a science of factory production.

Taylor also influenced the development of administrative systems such as record keeping and stock control to support manufacturing.

Management in practice   Using work study in the 1990s

Oswald Jones recalls his experience as a work study engineer in the 1990s, where he and his colleagues were deeply committed to the principles of scientific management:

Jobs were designed to be done in a mechanical fashion by removing opportunities for worker discretion. This had dual benefits: very simple jobs could be measured accurately (so causing less disputes) and meant that operators were much more interchangeable which was an important feature in improving overall efficiency levels. (Jones, 2000, p. 647)

Managers in industrialised economies adopted Taylor's ideas widely: Henry Ford was an enthusiastic advocate. When he introduced the assembly line in 1914, the time taken to assemble a car fell from over 700 hours to 93 minutes. Ford also developed systems of materials flow and plant layout, a significant contribution to scientific management (Biggs, 1996; Williams *et al.*, 1992).

Increased productivity often came at human cost (Thompson and McHugh, 2002). Trade unions believed that Taylor's methods increased unemployment, and vigorously opposed them. Many people find that work on an assembly line is boring and alienating, devoid of much meaning. In extreme cases, the time taken to complete an operation is less than a minute, and uses few human abilities.

Management in practice   Ford's Highland Park plant

Ford's plant at Highland Park, completed in 1914, introduced predictability and order 'that eliminates all questions of how work is to be done, who will do it, and when it will be done. The rational factory, then, is a factory that runs like a machine' (Biggs, 1996, p. 6). Biggs provides abundant evidence of the effects of applying rational production methods:

The advances made in Ford's New Shop allowed the engineers to control work better. The most obvious and startling change in the entire factory was, of course, the constant movement, and the speed of that movement, not only the speed of the assembly line, but the speed of every moving person or object in the plant. When workers moved from one place to another, they were instructed to move fast. Laborers who moved parts were ordered to go faster. And everyone on a moving line worked as fast as the line dictated. Not only were workers expected to produce at a certain rate in order to earn a day's wages but they also had no choice but to work at the pace dictated by the machine. By 1914 the company employed supervisors called pushers (not the materials handlers) to 'push' the men to work faster.

The 1914 jobs of most Ford workers bore little resemblance to what they had been just four years earlier, and few liked the transformation. . . . As early as 1912, job restructuring sought an 'exceptionally specialized division of labor [to bring] the human element into [the] condition of performing automatically with machine-like regularity and speed'. (Biggs, 1996, p. 132)

Frank and Lillian Gilbreth

Frank and Lillian Gilbreth (1868–1924 and 1878–1972) worked as a husband and wife team, and were advocates for scientific management. Frank Gilbreth had been a bricklayer, and knew why work was slow and output unpredictable. He filmed men laying bricks and used this to set out the most economical movements for each task. He specified exactly what the employer should provide, such as trestles at the right height and materials at the right time. Supplies of mortar and bricks (arranged the right way up) should arrive at a time that did not interrupt work. An influential book (Gilbreth, 1911) gave precise guidance on how to reduce unnecessary actions (from 18 to 5) and hence fatigue. The rules and charts would help apprentices:

> [They] will enable the apprentice to earn large wages immediately, because he has . . . a series of instructions that show each and every motion in the proper sequence. They eliminate the 'wrong' way [and] all experimenting. (Quoted in Spriegel and Myers, 1953, p. 57)

Lillian Gilbreth focused on the psychological aspects of management, and on the welfare of workers. She also advocated scientific management, believing that, properly applied, it would enable individuals to reach their full potential. Through careful development of systems, careful selection, clearly planned training and proper equipment, workers would build their self-respect and pride. In *The Psychology of Management* (1914) she argued that if workers did something well, and that was made public, they would develop pride in their work and in themselves. She believed workers had enquiring minds, and that management should explain the reasons for work processes:

> Unless the man knows why he is doing the thing, his judgment will never reinforce his work . . . His work will not enlist his zeal unless he knows exactly why he is made to work in the particular manner prescribed. (Quoted in Spriegel and Myers, 1953, p. 431)

Activity 2.2   **What assumptions did they make?**

What assumptions did Frederick Taylor and Lillian Gilbreth make about the interests and abilities of industrial workers?

Operational research

Another practice within the rational goal model is **operational research** (OR). This originated in the early 1940s, when the UK War Department faced severe management problems – such as the most effective distribution of radar-linked anti-aircraft gun emplacements, or the safest speed at which convoys of merchant ships should cross the Atlantic (see Kirby (2003) for a non-technical introduction to the topic). To solve these it formed operational research teams, which pooled the expertise of scientific disciplines such as mathematics and physics. These produced significant results: Kirby points out that while at the start of the London Blitz 20,000 rounds of ammunition were fired for each enemy aircraft destroyed:

Operational research is a scientific method of providing (managers) with a quantitative basis for decisions regarding the operations under their control.

> by the summer of 1941 the number had fallen . . . to 4,000 as a result of the operational research (teams) improving the accuracy of radar-based gun-laying. (Kirby 2003, p. 94)

After the war, managers in industry and government saw that operational research techniques could also help to run complex civil organisations. The scale and complexity of business were increasing, and required new techniques to analyse the many interrelated variables. Mathematical models could help, and computing developments supported increasingly sophisticated models. In the 1950s, the steel industry needed to cut the cost of transporting iron ore: staff used OR techniques to analyse the most efficient procedures for shipping, unloading and transferring it to steelworks.

The method is widely used in both business and public sectors, where it helps planning in areas as diverse as maintenance, cash flow, inventory and staff scheduling in call centres (e.g. Taylor, 2008). Willoughby and Zappe (2006) illustrate how a university used OR techniques to help allocate students to seminar groups.

Table 2.1 Modern applications of the rational goal model

Principles of the rational goal model	Current applications
Systematic work methods	Work study and process engineering departments develop precise specifications for processes
Detailed division of labour	Where staff focus on one type of work or customer in manufacturing or service operations
Centralised planning and control	Modern information systems increase the scope for central control of worldwide operations
Low-involvement employment relationship	Using temporary staff as required, rather than permanent employees

OR cannot take into account human and social uncertainties, and the assumptions built into the models may be invalid, especially if they involve political interests. The technique clearly contributes to the analysis of management problems, but it is only part of the solution.

Current status

Table 2.1 summarises principles common to rational goal models and their modern application.

Examples of aspects of the rational goal approaches are common in manufacturing and service organisations – but note that companies will often use only one of the principles that suits their business. The following Management in Practice feature gives an example from a very successful service business with highly committed and involved members of staff – which wishes to give the same high-quality experience wherever the customer is. It uses the principle of systematic work methods to achieve this.

Management in practice   **Making a sandwich at Pret a Manger** www.pret.com

It is very important to make sure the same standards are adhered to in every single shop, whether you're in Crown Passage in London, Sauchiehall Street in Glasgow, or in New York. The way we do that is by very, very detailed training. So, for example, how to make an egg mayonnaise sandwich is all written down on a card that has to be followed, and that is absolutely non-negotiable.

When somebody joins Pret they have a 10-day training plan, and on every single day there is a list of things that they have to be shown, from how to spread the filling of a sandwich right to the edges (that is key to us), how to cut a sandwich from corner to corner, how to make sure that the sandwiches look great in the box and on the shelves. So every single detail is covered on a 10-day training plan. At the end of that 10-days the new team member has to pass a quiz, it's called the big scary quiz, it is quite big and it is quite scary, and they have to achieve 90 per cent on that in order to progress.

Source: Interview with a senior manager at the company.

Case questions 2.3

- Which of the ideas in the rational goal model was Owen experimenting with at New Lanark?
- Would you describe Owen's approach to management as low involvement?
- What assumptions did he make about the motivation of workers?

The methods are also widely used in the mass production industries of newly industrialised economies such as China and Malaysia. Gamble *et al.* (2004) found that in such plants:

> Work organization tended to be fragmented (on Taylorist lines) and routinised, with considerable surveillance and control over production volumes and quality. (p. 403)

Human resource management policies were consistent with this approach – the recruitment of operators in Chinese electronics plants was:

> often of young workers, generally female and from rural areas. One firm said its operators had to be 'young farmers within cycling distance of the factory, with good eyesight. Education is not important'. (p. 404)

Activity 2.3   **Finding current examples**

Try to find an original example of work that has been designed on rational goal principles. There are examples in office and service areas as well as in factories. Compare your examples with those of colleagues.

2.5   **Internal process models**

Max Weber

Max Weber (1864–1920) was a German social historian who drew attention to the significance of large organisations, noting that, as societies became more complex, they concentrated responsibility for core activities in large specialised units. These government departments and large industrial or transport businesses were hard to manage, a difficulty which those in charge overcame by creating systems ('institutionalising the management process') – rules and regulations, hierarchy, precise division of labour and detailed procedures. Weber observed that **bureaucracy** brought routine to office operations just as machines had to production.

Bureaucratic management has the characteristics shown in the following Key Ideas box.

> **Bureaucracy** is a system in which people are expected to follow precisely defined rules and procedures rather than to use personal judgement.

Key ideas   **The characteristics of bureaucratic management**

- **Rules and regulations:** the formal guidelines that define and control the behaviour of employees. Following these ensures uniform procedures and operations, regardless of an individual's wishes. They enable top managers to co-ordinate middle managers and, through them, first-line managers and employees. Managers leave, so rules bring stability.
- **Impersonality:** rules lead to impersonality, which protects employees from the whims of managers. Although the term has negative connotations, Weber believed it ensured fairness, by evaluating subordinates objectively on performance rather than subjectively on personal considerations. It limits favouritism.
- **Division of labour:** managers and employees work on specialised tasks, with the benefits originally noted by Adam Smith – such as that jobs are relatively easy to learn and control.
- **Hierarchical structure:** Weber advocated a clear hierarchy in which jobs were ranked vertically by the amount of authority to make decisions. Each lower position is under the control of a higher position.
- **Authority structure:** a system of rules, impersonality, division of labour and hierarchy forms an authority structure – the right to make decisions of varying importance at different levels within the organisation.
- **Rationality:** this refers to using the most efficient means to achieve objectives. Managers should run their organisations logically and 'scientifically' so that all decisions help to achieve the objectives.

> **Activity 2.4   Bureaucratic management in education?**
>
> Reflect on your role as a student and how rules have affected the experience. Try to identify one example of your own to add to those below or that illustrates the point specifically within your institution:
>
> - Rules and regulations – the number of courses you need to pass for a degree.
> - Impersonality – admission criteria, emphasising previous exam performance, not friendship.
> - Division of labour – chemists not teaching management and vice versa.
> - Hierarchical structure – to whom your lecturer reports and to whom they report.
> - Authority structure – who decides whether to recruit an additional lecturer.
> - Rationality – appointing new staff to departments that have the highest ratio of students to staff.
>
> Compare your examples with those of other students and consider the effects of these features of bureaucracy on the institution and its students.

Weber was aware that, as well as creating bureaucratic structures, managers were using scientific management techniques to control production and impose discipline on factory work. The two systems complemented each other. Formal structures of management centralise power, while hierarchical organisation aids functional specialisation. Fragmenting tasks, imposing close discipline on employees and minimising their discretion ensures controlled, predictable performance (Thompson and McHugh, 2002).

Weber stressed the importance of a career structure clearly linked to a person's position. This allowed him/her to move up the hierarchy in a predictable and open way, which would increase his/her commitment to the organisation. Rules about selection and promotion brought fairness at a time when favouritism was common. Weber also believed that officials should work within a framework of rules. The right to give instructions was based on a person's position in the hierarchy, and a rational analysis of how staff should work. This worked well in large public and private organisations, such as government departments and banks.

While recognising the material benefits of these methods, Weber saw their costs:

> Bureaucratic rationalization instigates a system of control that traps the individual within an 'iron cage' of subjugation and constraint . . . For Weber, it is instrumental rationality, accompanied by the rise of measurement and quantification, regulations and procedures, accounting, efficiency that entraps us all in a world of ever-increasing material standards, but vanishing magic, fantasy, meaning and emotion. (Gabriel, 2005, p. 11)

> **Activity 2.5   Gathering evidence on bureaucracy**
>
> Rules often receive bad publicity, and we are all sometimes frustrated by rules that seem obstructive. To evaluate bureaucracy, collect some evidence. Think of a job that you or a friend has held, or of the place in which you work.
>
> - Do the supervisors appear to operate within a framework of rules, or do they do as they wish? What are the effects?
> - Do clear rules guide selection and promotion procedures? What are the effects?
> - As a customer of an organisation, how have rules and regulations affected your experience?
> - Check what you have found, preferably combining it with that prepared by other people on your course. Does the evidence support the advantages, or the disadvantages, of bureaucracy?

Henri Fayol

Managers were also able to draw on the ideas of **administrative management** developed by Henri Fayol (1841–1925). While Taylor focused on production systems, Fayol devised management principles that would apply to the whole organisation. Like Taylor, Fayol was an engineer, who in 1860 joined Commentry–Fourchambault–Decazeville, a coal mining and iron foundry company combine. He rose rapidly through the company and became managing director in 1888 (Parker and Ritson, 2005). When he retired in 1918 it was one of the success stories of French industry. Throughout his career he kept detailed diaries and notes, which in retirement he used to stimulate debate about management in both private and public sectors. His book *Administration, industrielle et générale* became available in English in 1949 (Fayol, 1949).

> Administrative management is the use of institutions and order rather than relying on personal qualities to get things done.

Fayol credited his success to the methods he used, not to his personal qualities. He believed that managers should use certain principles in their work – listed in the following Key Ideas box. The term 'principles' did not imply they were rigid or absolute:

> It is all a question of proportion . . . allowance must be made for different changing circumstances . . . the principles are flexible and capable of adaptation to every need; it is a matter of knowing how to make use of them, which is a difficult art requiring intelligence, experience, decision and proportion. (Fayol, 1949, p. 14)

In using terms such as 'changing circumstances' and 'adaptation to every need' in setting out the principles, Fayol anticipated the contingency theories which were developed in the 1960s (see Chapter 10). He was also an early advocate of management education:

> Elementary in the primary schools, somewhat wider in the post-primary schools, and quite advanced in higher education establishments. (Fayol, 1949, p. 16)

Key ideas Fayol's principles of management

1 **Division of work:** if people specialise, they improve their skill and accuracy, which increases output. However, 'it has its limits which experience teaches us may not be exceeded'.

2 **Authority and responsibility:** the right to give orders derived from a manager's official authority or his/her personal authority. 'Wherever authority is exercised, responsibility arises.'

3 **Discipline:** 'Essential for the smooth running of business . . . without discipline no enterprise could prosper.'

4 **Unity of command:** 'For any action whatsoever, an employee should receive orders from one superior only' – to avoid conflicting instructions and resulting confusion.

5 **Unity of direction:** 'One head and one plan for a group of activities having the same objective . . . essential to unity of action, co-ordination of strength and focusing of effort.'

6 **Subordination of individual interest to general interest:** 'The interests of one employee or group of employees should not prevail over that of the concern.'

7 **Remuneration of personnel:** 'Should be fair and, as far as possible, afford satisfaction both to personnel and firm.'

8 **Centralisation:** 'The question of centralisation or decentralisation is a simple question of proportion . . . [the] share of initiative to be left to [subordinates] depends on the character of the manager, the reliability of the subordinates and the condition of the business. The degree of centralisation must vary according to different cases.'

9 **Scalar chain:** 'The chain of superiors from the ultimate authority to the lowest ranks . . . is at times disastrously lengthy in large concerns, especially governmental ones.' If a speedy decision were needed, it was appropriate for people at the same level of the chain to communicate directly. 'It provides for the usual exercise of some measure of initiative at all levels of authority.'

10 **Order:** materials should be in the right place to avoid loss, and the posts essential for the smooth running of the business filled by capable people.

▶

11 **Equity:** managers should be both friendly and fair to their subordinates – 'equity requires much good sense, experience and good nature'.

12 **Stability of tenure of personnel:** a high employee turnover is not efficient – 'Instability of tenure is at one and the same time cause and effect of bad running.'

13 **Initiative:** 'The initiative of all represents a great source of strength for businesses . . . and . . . it is essential to encourage and develop this capacity to the full. The manager must be able to sacrifice some personal vanity in order to grant this satisfaction to subordinates . . . a manager able to do so is infinitely superior to one who cannot.'

14 **Esprit de corps:** 'Harmony, union among the personnel of a concern is a great strength in that concern. Effort, then, should be made to establish it.' Fayol suggested doing so by avoiding sowing dissension among subordinates, and using verbal rather than written communication when appropriate.

Source: Fayol (1949).

Current status

Table 2.2 summarises some principles common to the internal process models of management and indicates their modern application.

'Bureaucracy' has had many critics, who believe that it stifles creativity, fosters dissatisfaction and hinders motivation. Others credit it with bringing fairness and certainty to the workplace, where it clarifies roles and responsibilities, makes work effective – and so helps motivation. Adler and Borys (1996) sought to reconcile this by distinguishing between bureaucracy which is:

- enabling – designed to enable employees to master their tasks; and that which is
- coercive – designed to force employees into effort and compliance.

Table 2.2 Modern applications of the internal process model

Some principles of the internal process model	Current applications
Rules and regulations	All organisations have these, covering areas such as expenditure, safety, recruitment and confidentiality
Impersonality	Appraisal processes based on objective criteria or team assessments, not personal preference
Division of labour	Setting narrow limits to employees' areas of responsibility – found in many organisations
Hierarchical structure	Most company organisation charts show managers in a hierarchy – with subordinates below them
Authority structure	Holders of a particular post have authority over matters relating to that post, but not over other matters
Centralisation	Organisations balance central control of (say) finance or online services with local control of (say) pricing or recruitment
Initiative	Current practice in many firms to increase the responsibility of operating staff
Rationality	Managers are expected to assess issues on the basis of evidence, not personal preference

They studied one aspect of bureaucracy – workflow formalisation (the extent to which an employee's tasks are governed by written rules, etc) – in companies such as Ford, Toyota and Xerox. They concluded that if employees helped to design and implement a procedure, it was likely that they would accept the new rules, and that these would help them to work effectively. This 'enabling bureaucracy' had a positive effect on motivation, while rules that were imposed by management (coercive bureaucracy) had a negative effect. There is a similar example in the W.L. Gore case in Part 5.

Bureaucratic methods are widely used (Walton, 2005) especially in the public sector, and in commercial businesses with geographically dispersed outlets – such as hotels, stores and banks. Customers expect a predictable service wherever they are, so management design centrally controlled procedures and manuals – how to recruit and train staff, what the premises must look like and how to treat customers. If managers work in situations that require a degree of change and innovation that even an enabling bureaucracy will have trouble delivering, they need other models.

2.6   Human relations models

In the early twentieth century, several writers such as Follett and Mayo recognised the limitations of the scientific management perspective as a complete answer.

Mary Parker Follett

Mary Parker Follett (1868–1933) graduated with distinction from Radcliffe College (now part of Harvard University) in 1898, having studied economics, law and philosophy. She took up social work and quickly acquired a reputation as an imaginative and effective professional. She realised the creativity of the group process, and the potential it offered for truly democratic government – which people themselves would have to create.

She advocated replacing bureaucratic institutions by networks in which people themselves analysed their problems and implemented their solutions. True democracy depended on tapping the potential of all members of society by enabling individuals to take part in groups organised to solve particular problems and accepting personal responsibility for the result. Such ideas are finding renewed relevance today in the work of institutions such as community action and tenants' groups.

Key ideas   **Mary Parker Follett on groups**

Follett saw the group as an intermediate institution between the solitary individual and the abstract society, and argued that it was through the institution of the group that people organised co-operative action. In 1926 she wrote:

> Early psychology was based on the study of the individual; early sociology was based on the study of society. But there is no such thing as the 'individual', there is no such thing as 'society'; there is only the group and the group-unit – the social individual. Social psychology must begin with an intensive study of the group, of the selective processes which go on within it, the differentiated reactions, the likenesses and the unlikenesses, and the spiritual energy which unites them.

Source: Graham (1995), p. 230.

In the 1920s, Follett became involved in the business world, when managers invited her to investigate business problems. She again advocated the self-governing principle that would facilitate the growth of individuals and the groups to which they belonged. Conflict was inevitable if people brought valuable differences of view to a problem: the group must then resolve the conflict to create what she called an integrative unity among the members.

She acknowledged that organisations had to optimise production, but did not accept that the strict division of labour was the right way to achieve this (Follett, 1920), as it devalued human creativity. The human side should not be separated from the mechanical side, as the two are bound together. She believed that people, whether managers or workers, behave as they do because of the reciprocal responses in their relationship. If managers tell people to behave as if they are extensions of a machine, they will do so. She implied that effective managers would not manipulate their subordinates, but train them to use power responsibly:

managers should give workers a chance to grow capacity or power for themselves.

Graham (1995) provides an excellent review of Follett's work.

Elton Mayo

Elton Mayo (1880–1949) was an Australian who taught logic, psychology and ethics at the University of Queensland. In 1922 he moved to the US, and in 1926 became Professor of Industrial Research at Harvard Business School, applying psychological methods to industrial conflict. He was an accomplished speaker, and his ideas were arousing wide interest in the academic and business communities (Smith, 1998).

In 1924 managers of the Western Electric Company initiated a series of experiments at their Hawthorne plant in Chicago to discover the effect on output of changing defined factors in the physical environment. The first experiments studied the effect of lighting. The researchers established a control and an experimental group, varied the level of illumination and measured the output. As light rose, so did output. More surprisingly, as light fell, output continued to rise: it also rose in the control group, where conditions had not changed. The team concluded that physical conditions had little effect and so set up a more comprehensive experiment to identify other factors.

They assembled a small number of workers in a separate room and altered variables in turn, including working hours, length of breaks and providing refreshments. The experienced workers were assembling small components to make telephone equipment. A supervisor was in charge and there was also an observer to record how workers reacted to the experiments. Great care was taken to prevent external factors disrupting the effects of the variables under investigation. The researchers were careful to explain what was happening and to ensure that the workers understood what they were expected to do. They also listened to employees' views of working conditions.

The researchers varied conditions every two or three weeks, while the supervisor measured output regularly. This showed a gradual, if erratic, increase – even when the researchers returned conditions to those prevailing at an earlier stage, as Figure 2.3 shows.

> ### Activity 2.6   Explaining the trend
>
> Describe the pattern shown in Figure 2.3. Compare in particular the output in periods 7, 10 and 13. Before reading on, how would you explain this?

In 1928 senior managers invited Mayo to present the research to a wider audience (Smith, 1998; Roethlisberger and Dickson, 1939; Mayo, 1949). They concluded from the relay-assembly test room experiments that the increase in output was not related to the physical changes, but to the change in the social situation of the group:

the major experimental change was introduced when those in charge sought to hold the situation humanly steady (in the interests of critical changes to be introduced) by getting

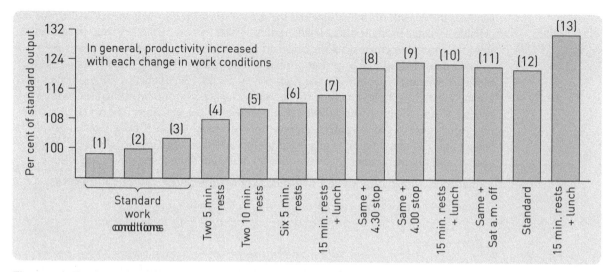

Figure 2.3 The relay assembly test room – average hourly output per week (as percentage of standard) in successive experimental periods

Source: After GREENBERG, JERALD; BARON, ROBERT A., *BEHAVIOR IN ORGANIZATIONS*, 6th Edition © 1997, p. 13. Reprinted by permission of Pearson Education, Inc., Upper Saddle River, NJ.

> the co-operation of the workers. What actually happened was that 6 individuals became a team and the team gave itself wholeheartedly and spontaneously to co-operation in the environment. (Mayo, 1949, p. 64)

The group felt special: managers asked for their views, were involved with them, paid attention to them and they had the chance to influence some aspects of the work.

The research team also observed another part of the factory, the bank wiring room, which revealed a different aspect of group working. Workers here were paid according to a piece-rate system, in which management pays workers a set amount for each item, or piece, that they produce. Such schemes reflect the assumption that financial incentives will encourage staff to work. The researchers observed that employees regularly produced less than they could have done. They had developed a sense of a normal rate of output, and ensured that all adhered to this rate, believing that if they produced, and earned, too much, management would reduce the piece-rate. Group members exercised informal sanctions against colleagues who worked too hard (or too slowly), until they came into line. Members who did too much were known as 'rate-busters', while those who did too little were 'chisellers'. Anyone who told the supervisor about this was a 'squealer'. Sanctions included being 'binged' – tapped on the shoulder to let them know that what they were doing was wrong. Managers had little or no control over these groups, who appointed their leader.

Finally, the research team conducted an extensive interview programme. They began by asking employees about the working environment and how they felt about their job, and then some questions about their life in general. The responses showed that there were often close links between work and domestic life. Work affected people's wider life much more than had been expected, and domestic circumstances affected their feelings about work. This implied that supervisors needed to think of a subordinate as a complete person, not just as a worker.

Activity 2.7   A comparison with Taylor

Compare this evidence with Frederick Taylor's belief that piece-rates would be an incentive to individuals to raise their performance. What may explain the difference?

Mayo's reflections on the Hawthorne studies drew attention to aspects of human behaviour that practitioners of scientific management had neglected. He introduced the idea of 'social man', in contrast to the 'economic man' who was at the centre of earlier theories. While financial rewards would influence the latter, group relationships and loyalties would influence the former, and may outweigh management pressure.

On financial incentives, Mayo wrote:

> Man's desire to be continuously associated in work with his fellows is a strong, if not the strongest, human characteristic. Any disregard of it by management or any ill-advised attempt to defeat this human impulse leads instantly to some form of defeat for management itself. In [a study] the efficiency experts had assumed the primacy of financial incentive; in this they were wrong; not until the conditions of working group formation were satisfied did the financial incentives come into operation. (Mayo, 1949, p. 99)

People had social needs that they sought to satisfy – and how they did so may support management interests or oppose them.

Later analysis of the experimental data by Greenwood *et al.* (1983) suggested that the team had underestimated the influence of financial incentives. Becoming a member of the experimental group in itself increased the worker's income. Despite possible inaccurate interpretations, the findings stimulated interest in social factors in the workplace. Scientific management stressed the technical aspects of work. The Hawthorne studies implied that management should give at least as much attention to human factors, leading to the **human relations approach**. This advocates that employees will work more effectively if management shows some interest in their well-being, such as by having more humane supervision.

Human relations approach is a school of management which emphasises the importance of social processes at work.

Key ideas   **Peters and Waterman – *In Search of Excellence***

In 1982 Peters and Waterman published their best-selling book *In Search of Excellence*. As management consultants with McKinsey & Co., they wanted to understand the success of what they regarded as 43 excellently managed US companies. One conclusion was that they had a distinctive set of philosophies about human nature and the way that people interact in organisations. They did not see people as rational beings, motivated by fear and willing to accept a low-involvement employment relationship. Instead, the excellent companies regarded people as emotional, intuitive and creative social beings who like to celebrate victories and value self-control – but who also need the security and meaning of achieving goals through organisations. From this, Peters and Waterman deduced some general rules for treating workers with dignity and respect, to ensure that people did quality work in an increasingly uncertain environment.

Peters and Waterman had a significant influence on management thinking: they believed that management had relied too much on analytical techniques of the rational goal models, at the expense of more intuitive and human perspectives. They developed the ideas associated with the human relations models and introduced the idea of company culture – discussed in the next chapter.

Source: Peters and Waterman (1982).

Case questions 2.4

- Which of the practices that Robert Owen used took account of workers' social needs?
- Evaluate the extent to which he anticipated the conclusions of the Hawthorne experiments.

Current status

The Hawthorne studies have been controversial, and the interpretations questioned. Also, the idea of social man is itself now seen as an incomplete picture of people at work. Providing good supervision and decent working environments may increase satisfaction but not necessarily productivity. The influences on performance are certainly more complex than Taylor assumed – and also more complex than the additional factors that Mayo identified.

Other writers have followed and developed Mayo's emphasis on human factors. McGregor (1960), Maslow (1970) and Alderfer (1972) have suggested ways of integrating human needs with those of the organisation as expressed by management. Some of this reflected a human relations concern for employees' well-being. A much stronger influence was the changing external environments of organisations, which have become less predictable since the time of Taylor and Mayo. These changes encouraged scholars to develop open systems models.

2.7   Open systems models

The open systems approach builds on earlier work in general systems theory, and has been widely used to help understand management and organisational issues. The basic idea is to think of the organisation not as a **system**, but as an **open system**.

The open systems approach draws attention to the links between the internal parts of a system, and to the links between the whole system and the outside world. The system is separated from its environment by the **system boundary**. An open system imports resources such as energy and materials, which enter it from the environment across this boundary, undergo some transformation process within the system, and leave the system as goods and services. The central theme of the open systems view of management is that organisations depend on the wider environment for inputs if they are to survive and prosper. Figure 2.4 (based on Figure 1.1) is a simple model of the organisation as an open system.

The figure shows input and output processes, conversion processes and feedback loops. The organisation must satisfy those in the wider environment well enough to ensure that they continue to provide resources. The management task is to sustain those links if the organisation is to thrive. **Feedback** refers to information about the performance of the system. It may be deliberate, through customer surveys, or unplanned, such as the loss of business to a competitor. Feedback enables those managing the system to take remedial action.

> A **system** is a set of interrelated parts designed to achieve a purpose.
>
> An **open system** is one that interacts with its environment.
>
> A **system boundary** separates the system from its environment.
>
> **Feedback** (in systems theory) refers to the provision of information about the effects of an activity.

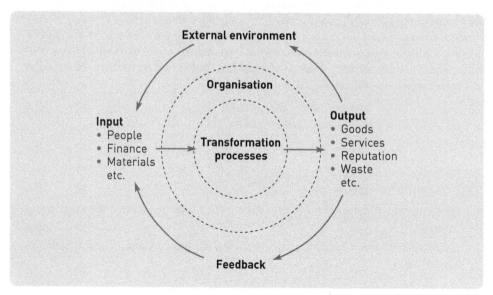

Figure 2.4
The systems model

Subsystems are the separate but related parts that make up the total system.

Another idea is that of **subsystems**. A course is a subsystem within a department or faculty, the faculty is a subsystem of a university, the university is a subsystem of the higher education system. This in turn is part of the whole education system. A course itself will consist of several systems – one for quality assurance, one for enrolling students, one for teaching, another for assessment and so on. In terms of Figure 2.1, each of the organisational elements is itself a subsystem – there is a technical subsystem, a people subsystem, a finance subsystem and so on, as Figure 2.5 shows.

These subsystems interact with each other, and how well people manage these links affects the functioning of the whole system: when a university significantly increases the number of students admitted to a popular course, this affects many parts of the system – such as accommodation (*technology*), teaching resources (*people*) and examinations (*business processes*).

A systems approach emphasises the links between systems, and reminds managers that a change in one will have consequences for others. For example, Danny Potter, Managing Director of Inamo (**www.inamo-restaurant.com**) a new London restaurant where customers place their order directly to the kitchen from an interactive ordering system on their table explains:

> I think the greatest challenge that we faced is communicating our ideas down through the business about what we're trying to achieve. There is a big overlap between essentially the computer software side and the actual restaurant side, to unite those in a way that people [new staff, suppliers, etc.] understand has proven rather tricky.

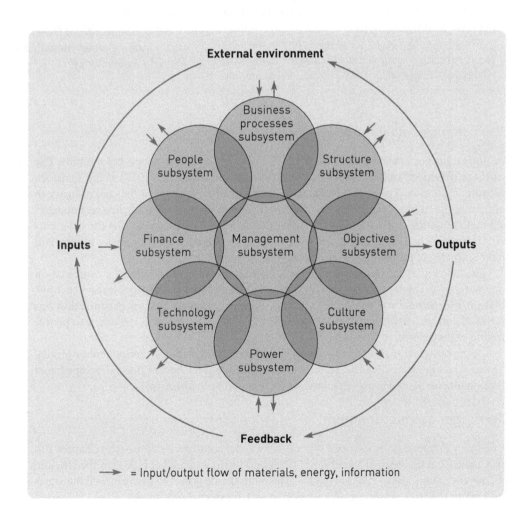

Figure 2.5
Interacting subsystems in organisations

Case study
Robert Owen – the case continues www.newlanark.org.uk

Owen actively managed the links between his business and the wider world. On buying the mills he quickly became part of the Glasgow business establishment, and was closely involved in the activities of the Chamber of Commerce. He took a prominent role in the social and political life of the city. He used these links in particular to argue the case for reforms in the educational and economic systems, and was critical of the effect that industrialisation was having upon working-class life.

Owen believed that education in useful skills would help to release working-class children from poverty. He provided a nursery for workers' children over one-year old, allowing both parents to continue working, and promoted the case for wider educational provision. He also developed several experiments in co-operation and community building, believing that the basis of his successful capitalist enterprise at New Lanark (education, good working conditions and a harmonious community) could be applied to society as a whole.

These attempts to establish new communities (at New Harmony in Indiana, the US, and at Harmony in Hampshire, England) cost him a great deal of money, but soon failed (Royle, 1998), because of difficulties over admission, finance and management processes.

More broadly, he sought new ways of organising the economy to raise wages and protect jobs, at a time of severe business fluctuations. In 1815 he persuaded allies in Parliament to propose a bill making it illegal for children under the age of 10 to work in mills. It would also have limited their working hours to 10 a day. The measure met strong opposition from mill owners and a much weaker measure became law in 1819.

Sources: Butt (1971); Royle (1998).

Case questions 2.5

- Draw a systems diagram detailing the main inputs, transformation and outputs of Robert Owen's mill.
- What assumptions did Owen make about the difference between running a business and running a community?

Socio-technical systems

An important variant of systems theory is the idea of the **socio-technical system**. The approach developed from the work of Eric Trist and Ken Bamforth (1951) at the Tavistock Institute in London. Their most prominent study was of an attempt in the coal industry to mechanise the mining system. Introducing what were in essence assembly line technologies and methods at the coalface had severe consequences for the social system that the older pattern of working had encouraged. The technological system destroyed the social system, and the solution lay in reconciling the needs of both.

> A socio-technical system is one in which outcomes depend on the interaction of both the technical and social subsystems.

This and similar studies showed the benefits of seeing a work system as a combination of a material technology (tools, machinery, techniques) and a social organisation (people, relationships, constitutional arrangements). Figure 2.6 shows that an organisation has technical and social systems: it is a socio-technical system. Each affects the other, so people need to manage both.

A socio-technical analysis aims to integrate the social and technical components: optimising one while ignoring the other is likely to be unproductive. Cherns (1987) developed a set of principles for re-designing organisations on socio-technical principles.

Contingency management

A further development of the open systems view is the contingency approach (Chapter 10). This arose from the work of Woodward (1958) and Burns and Stalker (1961) in the UK, and of Lawrence and Lorsch (1967) in the US. The main theme is that to perform well managers must adapt the structure of the organisation to match external conditions.

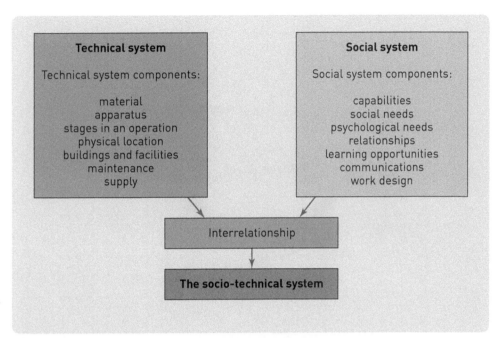

Figure 2.6
The organisation as
a socio-technical
system

The contingency approach implies that managers consciously look out for aspects of their environment which they need to take into account in shaping their organisation – see the Management in Practice feature.

Management in practice   **Hong Kong firms adapt to the environment in China**

Child *et al.* (2003) studied the experience of Hong Kong companies managing affiliated companies in China, predicting that successful firms would be those that adapted their management practices to suit those conditions. Because the business environment at the time was uncertain and difficult for foreign companies, they proposed that a key aspect of management practice in these circumstances would be the extent to which affiliated companies are controlled by, and integrated with, the parent company.

Their results supported this – in this transitional economy successful firms kept their mainland affiliates under close supervision, maintained frequent contact and allowed them little power to make decisions.

Source: Child *et al.* (2003).

As the environment becomes more complex, managers can use contingency perspectives to examine what structure best meets the needs of the business. Contingency theorists emphasise creating organisations that can cope with uncertainty and change, using the values of the open systems model: they also recognise that some functions need work in a stable and predictable way, using the values of the internal process model.

Complexity theory

A popular theme in management thinking is that of managing complexity, which arises from feedback between the parts of linked systems. People in organisations, both as individuals and as members of a web of working relationships, react to an event or an attempt to influence them. That reaction leads to a further response – setting off a complex feedback process. Figure 2.7 illustrates this for three individuals, X, Y and Z.

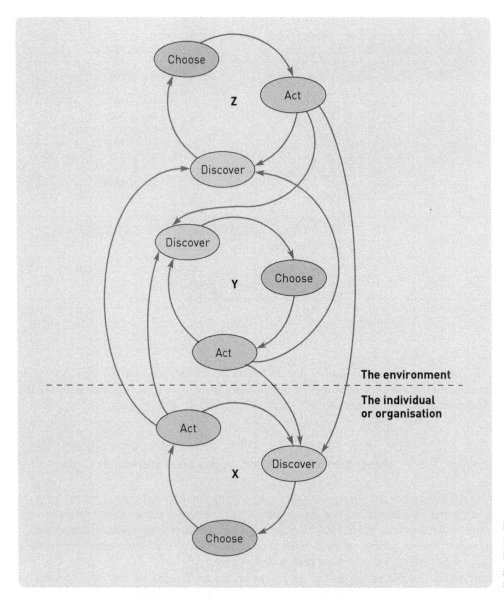

Figure 2.7
Feedback in non-
linear systems
Source: Parker and
Stacey (1994)

If we look at the situation in Figure 2.7 from the perspective of X, then X is in an environment made up from Y and Z. X discovers what Y and Z are doing, chooses how to respond and then acts. That action has consequences for Y and Z, which they discover. This leads them to choose a response, which has consequences that X then discovers and acts on. This continues indefinitely. Every act by X feeds back to have an impact on the next acts of Y and Z – and the same is true of Y and Z. Successive interactions create a feedback system – and the sequence shown for the individuals in the figure also occurs between organisations. These then make up complex systems:

> In contrast to simple systems, such as the pendulum, which have a small number of well-understood components, or complicated systems, such as a Boeing jet, which have many components that interact through predefined coordination rules . . . complex systems typically have many components that can autonomously interact through emergent rules. (Amaral and Uzzi, 2007, p. 1033)

In management, complex systems arise whenever agents (people, organisations or communities) act on the (limited) information available to them without knowing how these actions may affect other (possibly distant) agents, nor how the action of those agents may affect them. There is no central control system to co-ordinate their actions, so the separate agents organise themselves spontaneously, creating new structures and new behaviours as they respond to themselves and their environment: in other words, they change themselves. **Complexity theory** tries to understand how these complex, changing (dynamic) systems learn and adapt from their internal experiences and from their interactions with similar systems.

Complexity theory is concerned with complex dynamic systems that have the capacity to organise themselves spontaneously.

These ideas on self-organising systems have implications for management, especially for how they cope with change and innovation (see Chapter 13). An example would be when senior managers in, say, a pharmaceutical firm such as GlaxoSmithKline or a technology company such as Apple create teams to work with a high degree of autonomy (to encourage creativity) on discrete parts of a larger project. The team members will work creatively within a network of informal contacts and exchanges relevant to their part of the task. These webs of human interactions lead to stable or unstable behaviour, and the skill is to balance these extremes. If an organisation is too stable it will stifle innovation, but if it is too unstable it will disintegrate:

> Successful organisations work between these two conditions. [In changing environments], rather than seeking to control their organisations to maintain equilibrium . . . [managers] need to embrace more flexible and adaptive models of change and innovation. (McMillan and Carlisle, 2007, p. 577)

Table 2.3 contrasts approaches to change suggested by traditional and complexity perspectives.

Non-linear systems are those in which small changes are amplified through many interactions with other variables so that the eventual effect is unpredictable.

This way of thinking about organisations sometimes uses the terms 'linear' and **'non-linear' systems**. 'Linear' describes a system in which an action leads to a predictable reaction. If you light a fire in a room, the thermostat will turn the central heating down. Non-linear systems are those in which outcomes are less predictable. If managers reduce prices they will be surprised if sales match the forecast – they cannot predict the reactions of competitors, changes in taste, or new products. Circumstances in the outside world change in ways that management cannot anticipate, so while short term consequences of an act are clear, long run ones are not.

Current status

Although theories of management develop at particular times in response to current problems, this does not mean that newer is better. While new concerns bring out new theories, old concerns usually remain. While recently developed ideas seek to encourage flexibility and change, some businesses, and some parts of highly flexible businesses, still require control. Rather than thinking of theoretical development as a linear process, see it as circular or iterative

Table 2.3 Traditional and complexity inspired approaches to change

Management practice	Traditional	Complexity inspired
Who initiates change?	Devised at the top	Emerges lower down
Who forms teams to plan and implement change?	Managers appoint members to formal teams	Teams form spontaneously, perhaps after call for volunteers
Who allocates roles?	Managers say who does what	Team members decide
Who sets out authority to act?	Managers empower members	Team empowers individuals
Who controls activities?	Managers either control directly or steer indirectly	Team acts within boundaries, influenced by management

Source: Based on McMillan and Carlisle (2007), p. 577.

Table 2.4 Summary of the models within the competing values framework

Features/model	Rational goal	Internal process	Human relations	Open systems
Main exponents	Taylor Frank and Lillian Gilbreth	Fayol Weber	Mayo Follett Barnard Peters and Waterman	Trist and Bamforth Woodward Burns and Stalker Lawrence and Lorsch Stacey and Parker
Criteria of effectiveness	Productivity, profit	Stability, continuity	Commitment, morale, cohesion	Adaptability, external support
Means/ends theory	Clear direction leads to productive outcomes	Routinisation leads to stability	Involvement leads to commitment	Continual innovation secures external support
Emphasis	Rational analysis, measurement	Defining responsibility, documentation	Participation, consensus building	Creative problem solving, innovation
Role of manager	Director and planner	Monitor and coordinator	Mentor and facilitator	Innovator and broker

in which familiar themes recur as new concerns arise. The competing values approach captures the main theoretical developments in one framework and shows the relationships between them – see Table 2.4.

The emerging management challenges come from many sources. One is the widely accepted need to develop a more sustainable economic system. Another is the need to balance innovation and creativity with closer governance and control, especially in financial services. Deregulation of many areas of activity is allowing new competitors to enter previously protected markets (airlines, financial services). Still another is the closer integration between many previously separate areas of business (telecommunications, consumer electronics and entertainment). There is also the growing internationalisation of business. Managers today look for radical solutions – just as Robert Owen did in the early days of the industrial revolution.

Case study Robert Owen – the case continues www.newlanark.org.uk

The mills at New Lanark continued to operate after Owen's departure in 1825. Competition from new sources of supply meant that the mills eventually became unprofitable and they closed in 1968, threatening the survival of the village community. There had been little new building since Owen left, so the site (with its high mills and rows of workers' cottages) represented a time capsule of industrial and social history. The New Lanark Conservation Trust was created to restore it as a living community, and as a lasting monument to Owen and his philosophies.

Visitors can see the mills and examples of the machinery they contained, visit many of the communal buildings Owen created (such as the store which was the inspiration for the worldwide co-operative movement), and some of the workers housing. New Lanark is not just a tourist destination – it is a living community with most of the houses occupied by people who work elsewhere in the area.

Sources: Published sources and www.newlanark.org.uk

2.8   Integrating themes

Sustainable performance

Current attention to sustainability is an example of the values associated with the open systems model – a recognition, in this case, that human and natural systems interact with each other in complex and often unpredictable ways. Senge *et al.* (2008) present a valuable explanation of the idea that not only do businesses have a duty to society to act sustainably, but that it is in their business interest to do so. Reducing a company's carbon footprint not only reduces environmental damage but also reduces costs and makes the business more efficient. Renewable energy is not just better for the planet than fossil fuels – it may often be cheaper.

In 2002 General Electric began making alternative energy technologies (such as desalination systems) when oil was $25 a barrel. As oil prices have risen to several times that amount, the company is reaping large profits as demand for non-oil energy systems has risen sharply. Customers too played a role – the authors quote the GE chief executive:

> When society changes its mind, you better be in front of it and not behind it, and this is an issue on which society has changed its mind. As CEO, my job is to get out in front of it, or you're going to get ploughed under.

Governments and other institutions are developing policies to try to limit the damage that almost all scientists believe human activities are causing. This work tends to reflect values of order, regulation and control – values associated with the internal process model. Distinct sets of people are working on the same problem, sustainability, from two distinct perspectives: how they reconcile these two approaches will have significant effects on progress towards a more sustainable economy.

Governance and control

Theories of corporate governance, like those of management, continue to evolve in response to evidence that current arrangements are no longer suitable for the job. Much corporate governance focuses on protecting shareholders from potential fraud or dishonesty by senior managers, and that aspect is unlikely to diminish.

An additional theme is to consider whether those responsible for governance and control of an organisation could usefully be more forthright in challenging managers over the quality of their decisions. Pfeffer and Sutton (2006) present the case for basing management actions on substantiated theories and relevant evidence. They acknowledge the difficulties of putting that into practice, given that the demands for decisions are relentless and that information is incomplete. They also acknowledge that evidence-based management depends on being willing to put aside conventional ways of working.

Nevertheless they identify practices which could help those conducting corporate governance responsibilities to foster an evidence-based approach:

> If you ask for evidence of efficacy every time a change is proposed, people will sit up and take notice. If you take the time to parse the logic behind that evidence, people will become more disciplined in their own thinking. If you treat the organization like an unfinished prototype and encourage trial programs, pilot studies, and experimentation – and reward learning from these activities, even when something new fails – your organization will begin to develop its own evidence base. And if you keep learning while acting on the best knowledge you have and expect your people to do the same – if you have what has been called 'the attitude of wisdom' – then your company can profit from evidence-based management. (p. 70)

Pfeffer and Sutton's advice to demand evidence, examine logic, be willing to experiment and to embrace the attitude of wisdom would bring substantial change to the way in which many organisations operate.

Internationalisation

The theories outlined here were developed when most business was conducted within national boundaries, although of course with substantial foreign trade in certain products and services. They take little direct account of the explosion in global trade, and the way in which many organisations are reorganising themselves as international or global businesses. However, the competing values framework provides a useful starting point, by highlighting the importance of underlying assumptions behind a theory, and how this relates to particular contexts. The fact that a theory based on, say, open systems values works well in some economies, does not necessarily mean that it will be suitable in others. As Chapters 3 and 4 show, cultural factors affect performance, yet it is still unclear how multiple national cultures interact with the corporate culture of an international business.

Summary

1 **Explain the value of models of management, and compare unitary, pluralist and critical perspectives**

- Models represent more complex realities, help to understand complexity and offer a range of perspectives on the topic. Their predictive effect is limited by the fact that people interpret information subjectively in deciding how to act.
- A unitary perspective emphasises the common purpose of organisational members, while the pluralist draws attention to competing interest groups. Those who take a critical perspective believe that organisations reflect deep divisions in society, and that attempts to integrate different interests through negotiation ignore persistent differences in the distribution of power.

2 **State the structure of the competing values framework and evaluate its contribution to our understanding of management**

- A way of integrating the otherwise confusing range of theories of management. Organisations experience tensions between control and flexibility, and between an external and internal focus. Placing these on two axes allows theories to be allocated to one of four types – rational goal, internal process, human relations and open systems.

3 **Summarise the rational goal, internal process, human relations and open systems models and evaluate what each can contribute to a managers understanding of their role**

- Rational goal (Taylor, the Gilbreths and operational research):
  - clear direction leads to productive outcomes, with an emphasis on rational analysis and measurement.
- Internal process (Weber, Fayol):
  - routinisation leads to stability, so an emphasis on defining responsibility and on comprehensive documentation and administrative processes.
- Human relations (Follett, Mayo):
  - people are motivated by social needs, and managers who recognise these will secure commitment. Practices include considerate supervision, participation and seeking consensus.
- Open systems (socio-technical, contingency and complexity):
  - Continual innovation secures external support, achieved by creative problem solving.

These theories have contributed to the management agendas in these ways:

- Rational goal – through techniques such as time and motion study, work measurement and a variety of techniques for planning operations; also the narrow specification of duties, and the separation of management and non-management work.

- Internal process – clear targets and measurement systems, and the creation of clear management and reporting structures. Making decisions objectively on the basis of rules and procedures, rather than on favouritism or family connections.
- Human relations – considerate supervision, consultation and participation in decisions affecting people.
- Open systems – understanding external factors and being able and willing to respond to them through individual and organisational flexibility especially in uncertain, complex conditions characterised by the idea of non-linear systems. While a linear system is one in which a relatively stable environment makes some planning feasible, a non-linear system is strongly influenced by other systems. This means that actions lead to unexpected consequences.

4 **Use the model to classify the dominant form in two or more business units, and to gather evidence about the way this affects the roles of managing in those units**

- You can achieve this objective by asking people (perhaps others on your course) to identify which of the four cultural types in the Competing Values Framework most closely correspond to the unit in which they work. Ask them to note ways in which that cultural type affects their way of working. Compare the answers in a systematic way and review the results.

5 **Show how ideas from the chapter add to your understanding of the integrating themes**

- Increased attention to sustainability is an example of the values associated with the open systems model, while attempts to regulate and control activities are perhaps associated with internal process values.
- Pfeffer and Sutton's ideas on evidence-based management offer a model which those seeking more effective governance and control could use – challenging managers to back-up ideas with more rigorous evidence and analysis to reduce risk.
- The alternative models at the heart of the competing values framework is a reminder that values that shape management practice in one country do not necessarily have the same influence in others.

Review questions

1 Name three ways in which theoretical models help the study of management.

2 What are the different assumptions of the unitary, pluralist and critical perspectives on organisations?

3 Name at least four of Morgan's organisational images and give an original example of each.

4 Draw the two axes of the competing values framework, and then place the theories outlined in this chapter in the most appropriate sector.

5 List Taylor's five principles of scientific management and evaluate their use in examples of your choice.

6 What was the particular contribution that Lillian Gilbreth made concerning how workers' mental capacities should be treated?

7 What did Follett consider to be the value of groups in community as well as business?

8 Compare Taylor's assumptions about people with those of Mayo. Evaluate the accuracy of these views by reference to an organisation of your choice.

9 Compare the conclusions reached by the Hawthorne experimenters in the relay assembly test room with those in the bank wiring room.

10 Is an open system harder to manage than a closed system and, if so, why?

11 How does uncertainty affect organisations and how do non-linear perspectives help to understand this?

12 Summarise an idea from the chapter that adds to your understanding of the integrating themes.

Concluding critical reflection

Think about the way your company, or one with which you are familiar, approaches the task of management, and the theories that seem to lie behind the way people manage themselves and others. Review the material in the chapter, and perhaps visit some of the websites identified. Then make notes on the following questions:

- What examples of the issues discussed in this chapter are currently relevant to your company?

- In responding to these issues, what **assumptions** about the nature of management appear to guide what people do? Do they reflect rational goal, internal process, human relations or open systems perspectives? Or a combination of several? Do these assumptions reflect a unitary or pluralist perspective and, if so, why?

- What factors such as the history or current **context** of the company appear to have influenced the prevailing view? Does the approach appear to be right for the company, its employees and other stakeholders?

- Have people put forward **alternative** ways of managing the business, or even a small part of it, based on evidence about other companies? Does the competing values model suggest other approaches to managing, in addition to the current pattern? How might others react to such alternatives?

- What **limitations** can you see in the theories and evidence presented in the chapter? For example, how valid might the human relations models be in a manufacturing firm in a country with abundant supplies of cheap labour, competing to attract overseas investment? Will open systems models be useful to those managing a public bureaucracy?

Further reading

Drucker, P. (1954), *The Practice of Management*, Harper, New York.

Still the classic introduction to general management.

Fayol, H. (1949), *General and Industrial Management*, Pitman, London.

Taylor, F.W. (1917), *The Principles of Scientific Management*, Harper, New York.

The original works of these writers are short and lucid. Taylor (1917) contains illuminating detail that brings the ideas to life, and Fayol's (1949) surviving ideas came from only two short chapters, which again are worth reading in the original.

Biggs, L. (1996), *The Rational Factory*, The Johns Hopkins University Press, Baltimore, MD.

A short and clear overview of the development of production systems from the eighteenth to the early twentieth centuries in a range of industries, including much detail on Ford's Highland Park plant.

Gamble, J., Morris, J. and Wilkinson, B. (2004), 'Mass production is alive and well: the future of work and organization in east Asia', *International Journal of Human Resource Management*, vol. 15, no. 2, pp. 397–409.

Graham, P. (1995), *Mary Parker Follett: Prophet of management*, Harvard Business School Press, Boston, MA.

The contribution of Mary Parker Follett has been rather ignored, perhaps overshadowed by Mayo's Hawthorne studies – or perhaps it was because she was a woman. This book gives a full appreciation of her work.

McMillan, E. and Carlisle, Y. (2007), 'Strategy as Order Emerging from Chaos: A Public Sector Experience', *Long Range Planning*, vol. 40, no. 6, pp. 574–593.

Shows how complexity theory was used to generate a major change at The Open University.

Mumford, E. (2006), 'The story of socio-technical design: reflections on its successes, failures and potential', *Information Systems Journal*, vol. 16, no. 4, pp. 317–342.

A review of socio-technical design from one of its leading practitioners.

Smith, J.H. (1998), 'The Enduring Legacy of Elton Mayo', *Human Relations*, vol. 51, no. 3, pp. 221–249.

Walton, E.J. (2005), 'The Persistence of Bureaucracy: A Meta-analysis of Weber's Model of Bureaucratic Control', *Organization Studies*, vol. 26, no. 4, pp. 569–600.

Two papers which show the continued application in successful business of early theories of management.

Weblinks

These websites have appeared in the chapter:

> www.newlanark.org.uk
> www.imiplc.com
> www.pret.com
> www.tcl.com
> www.inamo-restaurant.com

Visit two of the business sites in the list, or those of other organisations in which you are interested, and navigate to the pages dealing with recent news, press or investor relations.

- What are the main issues which the organisation appears to be facing?
- Compare and contrast the issues you identify on the two sites.
- What challenges may they imply for those working in, and managing, these organisations?

 For video case studies, audio summaries, flashcards, exercises and annotated weblinks related to this chapter, visit **www.pearsoned.co.uk/mymanagementlab**

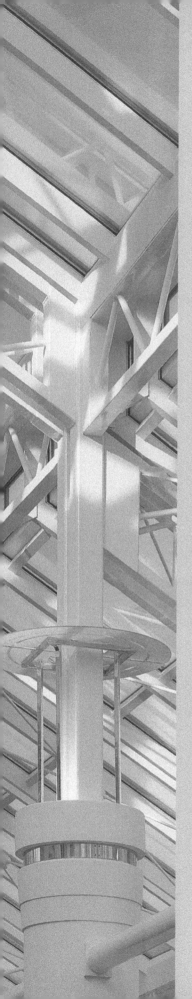

CHAPTER 3
ORGANISATION CULTURES AND CONTEXTS

Aim

To identify the cultures and contexts within which managers work, and to outline some analytical tools.

Objectives

By the end of your work on this chapter you should be able to outline the concepts below in your own terms and:

1 Compare the cultures of two organisational units, using Quinn's or Handy's typologies
2 Use Porter's five forces model to analyse an organisation's competitive environment
3 Collect evidence to make a comparative PESTEL analysis for two organisations
4 Compare environments in terms of their complexity and rate of change
5 Give examples of stakeholder expectations
6 Explain the meaning and purposes of corporate governance
7 Show how ideas from the chapter add to your understanding of the integrating themes

Key terms

This chapter introduces the following ideas:

competitive environment	task culture
general environment	person culture
external environment (or context)	five forces analysis
culture	PESTEL analysis
power culture	corporate governance
role culture	

Each is a term defined within the text, as well as in the Glossary at the end of the book.

Case study   Nokia   www.nokia.com

Nokia is the world's leading manufacturer of mobile phones. With an almost 40 per cent share of the market, it sold twice as many handsets in 2009 as second-placed Motorola and many times the number of other rivals such as Samsung and Ericsson. A Finnish company, founded in 1895 as a paper manufacturer, Nokia grew into a conglomerate with interests including electronics, cable manufacture, rubber, chemicals, electricity generation and, by the 1960s, telephone equipment. In the early 1990s senior managers decided to focus on the new mobile phone industry.

Two factors favoured this move. First, the Finnish government had taken a lead in telecoms deregulation and Nokia was already competing vigorously with other manufacturers supplying equipment to the national phone company. Second, the European Union (EU) adopted a single standard – the Global System for Mobile Telephony (GSM) – for Europe's second generation (digital) phones. Two-thirds of the world's mobile phone subscribers use this standard. Finland's links with its Nordic neighbours also helped, as people in these sparsely populated countries adopted mobile phones enthusiastically.

Nokia has strong design skills, but above all managers were quick to recognise that mobile phones are not a commodity but a fashion accessory. By offering smart designs, different ring tones and coloured covers Nokia became the 'cool' mobile brand for fashion-conscious people. Nokia has also mastered the logistics of getting millions of phones to customers around the world.

While many competitors subcontract the manufacture of handsets, Nokia assembles most of its own, with factories in many countries across the world. Managers believe this gives them a better understanding of the market and the manufacturing process. Nokia buys about 80 billion components a year, and has close relationships with its most important suppliers.

While all of these factors helped Nokia, managers believe there was a further reason. Although competitors such as Motorola and Ericsson already had advantages of scale, experience and distribution networks, the arrival of the new digital technology

Courtesy of Nokia

changed the rules of the game, forcing all players to start from scratch. Managers acknowledge that some external factors helped Nokia, but comment that 'good luck favours the prepared mind'.

The company's leading position in the industry owes much to Jorma Ollila, who became chief executive in 1992. He helped to shape the mobile phone industry by pursuing his vision of a mass market for voice communication while on the move. As he prepared to hand over to a new chief executive (Olli-Pekka Kallasvuo) in 2006, he observed that the next challenge would be to enable users to access the internet, videos, music, games and emails through a new generation of 'smart' phones and hand-held devices.

Source: Based on *The Economist*, 16 June 2001; *Financial Times*, 29 June 2001 and 10 October 2005.

Case questions 3.1

- How has the environment favoured the development of Nokia?
- How could the same factors turn to the disadvantage of the company?
- Visit Nokia's website and read its most recent trading statement (under investor relations). What have been the main developments in the last year?

3.1   Introduction

Nokia's success depends on the ability of its managers to spot and interpret signals from consumers in the mobile phone market, and to ensure that the organisation responds more effectively than competitors. It also depends on identifying ideas emerging within the organisation (such as from the research laboratories) that have commercial potential – and working to ensure that consumers are aware of and receptive to the idea when it is incorporated into the next generation of products. The early success of the company was helped by recognising that many users see a mobile as a fashion item, and by using its design skills to meet that need. It also gained when the EU established common standards for mobile telephony, which the Finnish government supported.

All managers work within a context which both constrains and supports them. How well they understand, interpret and interact with that context affects their performance. Finkelstein (2003) (especially pp. 63–68) shows how Motorola, an early market leader in mobile communications, failed to take account of changes in consumer preferences (for digital rather than the older analogue mobile phones). By the time managers realised the new environment, Nokia had a commanding lead in the market. Each business is unique, so the forces with which they interact differ: those who are able to identify and shape them (Nokia) will perform better than those who are not (Motorola).

Figure 3.1 shows four environmental forces. The inner circle represents the organisation's **internal environment (or context)** – which Chapter 1 introduced. That includes its culture,

The internal environment (or context) consists of elements within the organisation such as its technology, structure or business processes.

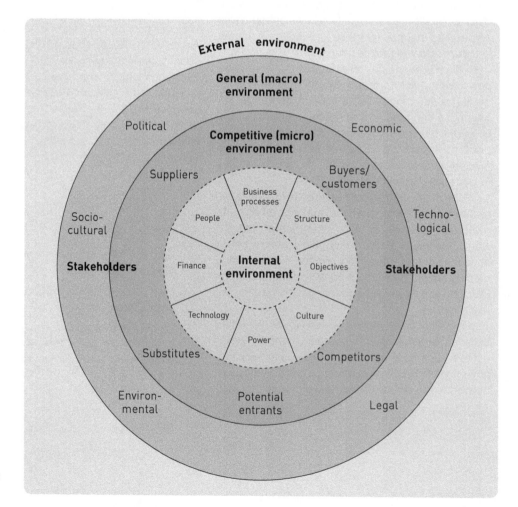

Figure 3.1
Environmental influences on the organisation

which many now regard as a major contextual feature. Beyond that is the immediate **competitive environment (or context),** sometimes known as the micro-environment. This is the industry-specific environment of customers, suppliers, competitors and potential substitute products. The outer circle shows the **general environment (or context)**, sometimes known as the macro-environment – political, economic, social, technological, (natural) environmental and legal factors that affect all organisations. Forces in the internal and competitive environments usually have more impact on, and are more open to influence by, the organisation than those in the general environment.

Together these make up an organisation's **external environment (or context)** – a constantly changing source of threats and opportunities: how well people cope with these affects performance.

Forces in the external environment do not affect practice of their own accord. They become part of the agenda only when internal or external stakeholders act to place them on the management agenda. In terms of Figure 3.1, they are a fourth force. Managers (who are themselves stakeholders) balance conflicting interpretations of their context. They work within an internal context, and look outside for actual and potential changes that may affect the centre of Figure 3.1. The figure implies a constant interaction between an organisation's culture and its external environment.

Managers do not passively accept their business environment, but try to shape it by actively persuading governments and other agencies to act in their favour (known as 'lobbying'). Car makers and airlines, for example, regularly seek subsidies, cheap loans or new regulations to help their businesses, while most industry bodies (such as the European Automobile Manufacturers' Association – **www.acea.be**) lobby international bodies such as the European Commission – often employing a professional lobbying business to support their case.

The next section presents ideas on organisational culture, which is an immediate aspect of a manager's context. Beyond that managers need to interact intelligently with their competitive and general environments. The chapter contrasts stable and dynamic environments, outlines stakeholder expectations and introduces ideas on governance and control.

A competitive environment (or context) is the industry-specific environment comprising the organisation's customers, suppliers and competitors.

The general environment (or context) (sometimes known as the macro-environment) includes political, economic, social technological, (natural) environmental and legal factors that affect all organisations.

The external environment (or context) consists of elements beyond the organisation – it combines the competitive and general environments.

| **Activity 3.1** | **Which elements of the business environment matter?** |

- Write a few notes summarising aspects of the business environment of which you are aware. You may find it helpful to think of a manager you have worked with, or when you have been managing an activity.
- Identify two instances when they (or you) were discussing aspects of the wider context of the job – such as the culture of the organisation or the world outside.
- How did this aspect of the context affect the job of managing?
- How did the way people dealt with the issue affect performance?

3.2 Cultures and their components

Developing cultures

Interest in organisation **culture** has grown as academics and managers have come to believe that it influences behaviour. Several claim that a strong and distinct culture helps to integrate individuals into the team or organisation (Deal and Kennedy, 1982; Peters and Waterman, 1982). Deal and Kennedy (1982) refer to culture as 'the way we do things around here' and Hofstede (1991) sees it as the 'collective programming of the mind', distinguishing one

Culture is a pattern of shared basic assumptions that was learned by a group as it solved its problems of external adaptation and internal integration, and that has worked well enough to be considered valid and transmitted to new members (Schein, 2004, p. 17).

group from another. They claim that having the right culture explains the success of high-performing organisations.

Someone entering a department or organisation for the first time can usually sense and observe the surface elements of the culture. Some buzz with life and activity, others seem asleep; some welcome and look after visitors, others seem inward looking; some work by the rules, while others are entrepreneurial and risk taking; some have regular social occasions while in others staff rarely meet except at work.

Management in practice   A culture of complaint in a bank

John Weeks (2004) spent six years working in a UK bank (believed to be NatWest, which the Royal Bank of Scotland acquired in 2000) as part of his doctoral research. He observed and recorded the bank's distinctive culture – which he described as one of 'complaint'.

No-one liked the culture – from the most senior managers to the most junior counter staff – people spent much of their time complaining about it. Weeks realised that this was a ritual, a form of solidarity among the staff: complaining about the culture *was* the culture. He noticed that most complaints were directed at other parts of the bank – not at the unit in which the complainer worked. He noted:

> Local sub-cultures are sometimes described positively – usually to contrast them with the mainstream – but I never heard anyone [describe the bank's culture in positive terms]. It is described as too bureaucratic, too rules driven, not customer-focused enough, not entrepreneurial enough, too inflexible, too prone to navel gazing, too centralized. (p. 53)

His detailed narrative shows, with many examples, how people in the bank made sense of their culture – using it to achieve their goals, while others did the same to them.

Source: Weeks (2004).

Figure 3.2 illustrates how a distinctive culture develops; as people develop and share common values they use these to establish beliefs and norms which guide their behaviour towards each other and to outsiders. Positive outcomes reinforce their belief in the values underlying their behaviour, which then become a stronger influence on how people should work and relate to each other: should people have job titles? How should they dress? Should meetings be confrontational or supportive?

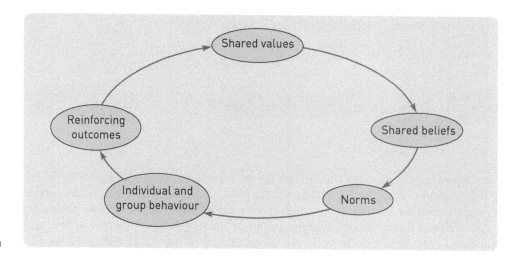

Figure 3.2
The stages of
cultural formation

A shared culture provides members with guidelines about how they can best contribute. The more they work on these issues to develop a common understanding, the better they will perform.

Components of cultures

Schein (2004) identifies three levels of a culture, 'level' referring to the degree to which the observer can see its components.

- **Artifacts** represent the visible level – elements such as the language or etiquette which someone coming into contact with a culture can observe:
  - architecture (open-plan offices without doors or private space)
  - technology and equipment
  - style (clothing, manner of address, emotional displays)
  - rituals and ceremonies (leaving events, awards ceremonies and away-days)
  - courses (to induct employees in the culture as well as the content).

  While it is easy to observe artifacts, it is difficult for outsiders to decipher what they mean to the group, or what underlying assumptions they reflect. That requires an analysis of beliefs and values.
- **Espoused beliefs and values** are the accumulated beliefs that members hold about their work. As a group develops, members refine their ideas about what works in this business: how people make decisions, how teams work together, and how they solve problems. Practices that work become the accepted way to behave:
  - 'Quality pays.'
  - 'We should stick to our core business.'
  - 'Cultivate a sense of personal responsibility.'
  - 'We depend on close team work.'
  - 'Everyone is expected to challenge a proposal – whoever made it.'

  Some companies codify and publish their beliefs and values, to help induct new members and to reinforce them among existing staff. Such beliefs and values shape the visible artifacts, though companies vary in the degree to which employees internalise them. The extent to which they do so depends on how clearly they derive from shared basic underlying assumptions.
- **Basic underlying assumptions** are deeply held by members of the group as being the way to work together. As they act in accordance with their values and beliefs, those that work become embedded as basic underlying assumptions. When the group strongly holds these, members will act in accordance with them, and reject actions based on others:
  - 'We need to satisfy customers to survive as a business.'
  - 'Our business is to help people with X problem live better with X problem.'
  - 'People can make mistakes, as long as they learn from them.'
  - 'We employ highly motivated and competent adults.'
  - 'Financial markets worry about the short term: we are here for the long term.'

Difficulties arise when people with assumptions developed in one group work with people from another. Mergers sometimes experience difficulty when staff who have to work together realise they are from different cultures.

Management in practice   A strong culture at Bosch   www.bosch.com

Franz Fehrenbach is chief executive of Bosch, Germany's largest privately owned engineering group, and the world's largest supplier of car parts. In 2009 he said:

> The company culture, especially our high credibility, is one of our greatest assets. Our competitors cannot match us on that because it takes decades to build up.

▶

The cultural traditions include a rigid control on costs, an emphasis on team thinking, employees taking responsibility for their errors, cautious financial policies, and long-term thinking. For example, to cope with the recession in 2009 Mr Fehrenbach explained that:

We have to cut costs in all areas. We will reduce spending in the ongoing business, but we will not cut back on research and development for important future projects.

Source: Based on an article by Daniel Schaefer, *Financial Times*, 2 March 2009, p. 16.

Activity 3.2   Culture spotting

- Identify as many components of culture (artifacts, beliefs and values, underlying assumptions) in an organisation or unit as you can.
- What may the artifacts suggest about the deeper beliefs and values, or underlying assumptions?
- Gather evidence (preferably by asking people) about how the culture affects behaviour, and whether they think it helps or hinders performance.
- Analyse your results and decide which of the four types in the competing values framework most closely reflects that organisation's culture.

3.3   Types of culture

This section outlines three ways of describing and comparing cultures.

Competing values framework

The competing values model developed by Quinn *et al.* (2003) reflects inherent tensions between flexibility or control and between an internal or an external focus. Figure 3.3 (based on Figure 2.2) shows four cultural types.

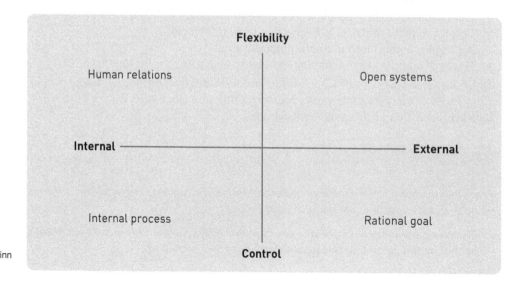

Figure 3.3 Types of organisational culture

Source: Based on Quinn *et al.* (2003).

Open systems

This represents an open systems view, in which people recognise that the external environment plays a significant role, and is a vital source of ideas, energy and resources. It also sees the environment as complex and turbulent, requiring entrepreneurial, visionary leadership and flexible, responsive behaviour. Key motivating factors are growth, stimulation, creativity and variety. Examples are start-up firms and new business units – organic, flexible operations.

Rational goal

Members see the organisation as a rational, efficiency-seeking unit. They define effectiveness in terms of production or economic goals that satisfy external requirements. Managers create structures to deal with the outside world. Leadership tends to be directive, goal-oriented and functional. Key motivating factors include competition and the achievement of goals. Examples are large, established businesses – mechanistic.

Internal process

Here members focus on internal matters. Their goal is to make the unit efficient, stable and controlled. Tasks are repetitive and methods stress specialisation, rules and procedures. Leaders tend to be cautious and spend time on technical issues. Motivating factors include security, stability and order. Examples include utilities and public authorities – suspicious of change.

Human relations

People emphasise the value of informal interpersonal relations rather than formal structures. They try to maintain the organisation and nurture its members, defining effectiveness in terms of their well-being and commitment. Leaders tend to be participative, considerate and supportive. Motivating factors include attachment, cohesiveness and membership. Examples include voluntary groups, professional service firms and some internal support functions.

Charles Handy's cultural types

Charles Handy (1993) distinguished four cultures – **power, role, task** and **person**.

Power

A dominant central figure holds power: others follow the centre's policy and interpret new situations in the way the leader would. Many entrepreneurial firms operate in this way, with few rules but with well-understood, implicit codes on how to behave and work. The firm relies on the individual rather than on seeking consensus through discussion.

Role

Typical characteristics of this culture are the job description or the procedure. Managers define what they expect in clear, detailed job descriptions. They select people for a job if they meet the specified requirements. Procedures guide how people and departments interact. If all follow the rules, co-ordination is straightforward. People's position in the hierarchy determines their power.

Task

People focus on completing the task or project rather than their formal role. They value each other for what they can contribute and expect everyone to help as needed. The emphasis is on getting the resources and people for the job and then relying on their commitment and enthusiasm. People will typically work in teams, to combine diverse skills into a common purpose.

A power culture is one in which people's activities are strongly influenced by a dominant central figure.

A role culture is one in which people's activities are strongly influenced by clear and detailed job descriptions and other formal signals as to what is expected from them.

A task culture is one in which the focus of activity is towards completing a task or project using whatever means are appropriate.

A person culture is one in which activity is strongly influenced by the wishes of the individuals who are part of the organisation.

Person

The individual is at the centre and any structure or system is there to serve them. The form is unusual – small professional and artistic organisations are probably closest to it, and perhaps experiments in communal living. They exist to meet the needs of the professionals or the members, rather than some larger organisational goal.

Activity 3.3   Cultural examples

For each of Handy's four cultural types, identify an example from within this text that seems to correspond most closely to that form.

- What clues about the company have you used to decide that allocation?
- Why do you think that culture is suitable for that organisation?
- What evidence would you seek to decide if that culture was suitable?
- Compare the similarities and differences in the competing values and Handy models.

Multiple cultures

Martin (2002) proposed that organisations have not one, but several cultures: observers take one of three perspectives towards a culture:

- **Integration** – a focus on identifying consistencies in the data, and using those common patterns to explain events.
- **Differentiation** – a focus on conflict, identifying different and possibly conflicting views of members towards events.
- **Fragmentation** – a focus on the fluid nature of organisations, and on the interplay and change of views about events.

Ogbonna and Harris (1998, 2002) provided empirical support for this view, based on interviews with staff in a retail company. They found that a person's position in the hierarchy determined his/her perspective on the culture (see Table 3.1). As consensus on culture was unlikely, they advised managers to recognise the range of sub-cultures within their oganisation, and

Table 3.1 Hierarchical position and cultural perspectives

Position in hierarchy	Cultural perspective	Description	Example
Head office managers	Integration	Cultural values should be shared across the organisation. Unified culture both desirable and attainable	'If we can get every . . . part of the company doing what they should be doing, we'll beat everybody'
Store managers	Differentiation	Reconciling conflicting views of head office and shop floor. See cultural pluralism as inevitable	'People up at head office are all pushing us in different directions. Jill in Marketing wants customer focus, June in Finance wants lower costs'
Store employees	Fragmented	Confused by contradictory nature of the espoused values. See organisation as complex and unpredictable	'One minute it's this, the next it's that. You can't keep up with the flavour of the month'

Source: Based on Ogbonna and Harris (1998).

only seek to reconcile those differences that were essential to policy. They also observed that culture remains a highly subjective idea, largely in the eye of the beholder

and is radically different according to an individual's position in the hierarchy. (Ogbonna and Harris, 1998, p. 45)

Culture and performance

Peters and Waterman (1982) believed that an organisation's culture affected performance, and implied that managers should try to change their culture towards a more productive one. Others are more skeptical about the effects on performance and question whether, even if a suitable culture has a positive effect, managers can consciously change it. Kotter and Heskett (1992) studied 207 companies to assess the link between culture and economic performance. Although they were positively correlated, the relationship was much weaker than advocates of culture as a factor in performance had predicted.

Thompson and McHugh (2002), while also critical of much writing on the topic, observe the potential benefits which a suitable culture can bring to not-for-profit organisations:

Creating a culture resonant with the overall goals is relevant to any organisation, whether it be a trade union, voluntary group or producer co-operative. Indeed, it is more important in such consensual groupings. Co-operatives, for example, can degenerate organisationally because they fail to develop adequate mechanisms for transmitting the original ideals from founders to new members and sustaining them through shared experiences. (pp. 208–209)

Case study   Nokia – the case continues   www.nokia.com

In March 2010 Nokia estimated that it had maintained its market share at 34 per cent of total device sales of 1.14 billion units. It is continuing to add value to its devices, by integrating them with innovative services providing music, maps, apps and email. It also believes that its wide range of handsets means it will be able to meet demand if customers begin to prefer cheaper handsets. It also saw growth opportunities in areas of the world, such as the US and Korea, where it had little or no market share, and in smartphones where the company's products had been weak.

The company had also been reducing its reliance on selling handsets, by diversifying into new growth areas. In 2006 it reached a deal with Siemens to merge their network businesses, creating the world's third largest network equipment supplier. In 2008 it concluded that success depended not just on good quality handsets, but also on the quality of the services and applications. It therefore grouped all handset products into a Device Unit, while applications and services became part of a new Mobile Services and Software unit. Both were supported by a Marketing unit which provided sales, marketing and operational support.

One factor in the company's sustained success appears to have been a culture which encourages co-operation within teams, and across internal and external boundaries. Jorma Ollila, CEO until 2006, believed that Nokia's innovative capacity springs from multi-functional teams working together to bring new insights to products and services. Staff in the four divisions work in teams which may remain constant for many years – but sometimes combine with other teams to work on a common task.

Informal mentoring begins as soon as someone steps into a new job. Within a few days, the employee's manager lists the people in the organisation whom it would be useful for the employee to meet. He/she also reviews what topics the newcomer should discuss with the suggested contact, and why establishing a relationship with each one is important. The gift of time – in the form of hours spent on coaching and building networks – is a crucial part of the collaborative culture.

Nokia also encourages a culture of communication by creating small groups from around the company to work on a strategic issue for four months. This helps them to build ties with many parts of the company – some of which continue during later work. The induction process for new employees also encourages team-building and co-operation: the newcomer's manager must introduce him/her to at least 15 people within and outside the team.

Sources: Grattan and Erickson (2007); Doz and Kosonen (2008); company website.

As managers work within an organisational culture, they also work within an external context – whose members will have expectations from the organisation. They need some tools with which to analyse that external world.

3.4   The competitive environment – Porter's five forces

Five forces analysis is a technique for identifying and listing those aspects of the five forces most relevant to the profitability of an organisation at that time.

Managers are most directly affected by forces in their immediate competitive environment. According to Porter (1980a, 1985), the ability of a firm to earn an acceptable return depends on five forces – the ability of new competitors to enter the industry, the threat of substitute products, the bargaining power of buyers, the bargaining power of suppliers and the rivalry among existing competitors. Figure 3.4 shows Porter's **five forces analysis**.

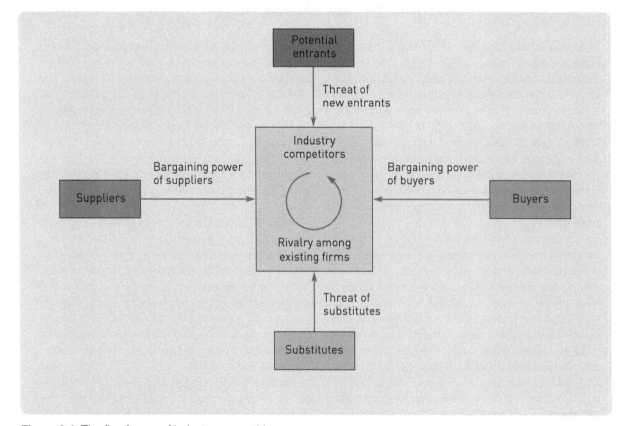

Figure 3.4 The five forces of industry competition

Porter believes that the *collective* strength of the five forces determines industry profitability, through their effects on prices, costs and investment requirements. Buyer power influences the prices a firm can charge, as does the threat of substitutes. The bargaining power of suppliers determines the cost of raw materials and other inputs. The greater the collective strength of the forces, the less profitable the industry: the weaker they are, the more profitable they are. Managers can use their knowledge of these forces to shape strategy.

Threat of new entrants

The extent of this threat depends on how easily new entrants can overcome barriers such as:

- the need for economies of scale (to compete on cost), which are difficult to achieve quickly;
- high capital investment required;
- lack of distribution channels;
- subsidies which benefit existing firms at the expense of potential new entrants;
- cost advantages of existing firms, such as access to raw materials or know-how;
- strong customer loyalty to incumbent companies.

Nokia faces competition from new entrants to the mobile phone industry especially Apple and Research in Motion (BlackBerry) at the top end of the market. The Chinese ZTE Corporation is supplying cheap mobiles to consumers in emerging markets.

Intensity of rivalry among competitors

Strong competitive rivalry lowers profitability, and occurs when:

- there are many firms in an industry;
- there is slow market growth, so companies fight for market share;
- fixed costs are high, so firms use capacity and overproduce;
- exit costs are high; specialised assets (hard to sell) or management loyalty (in old family firms) deter firms from leaving the industry, which prolongs excess capacity and low profitability;
- products are similar, so customers can easily switch to other suppliers.

A highly competitive market will also be one in which the threat of new entrants is high. While Nokia still dominated the mobile phone industry in 2010, it continued to face pressure from established competitors Motorola, Siemens and Ericsson, and from new entrants in Asia.

Management in practice	Competition amongst Chinese brewers

SABMiller and Anheuser-Busch both sought to enter the Chinese market by buying an existing major player, Harbin (with Anheuser-Busch quickly winning the contest). They were attracted by the fact that China is the world's largest market for beer, growing at 6–8 per cent a year. However, it is also fiercely competitive as there are over 400 brewers competing for sales: this keeps prices down, and profits are on average less than 0.5 per cent of sales.

Source: *The Economist*, 15 May 2004.

Power of buyers (customers)

Buyers (customers) seek lower prices or higher quality at constant prices, thus forcing down prices and profitability. Buyer power is high when:

- the buyer purchases a large part of a supplier's output;
- there are many substitute products, allowing easy switching;

- the product is a large part of the buyers' costs, encouraging them to seek lower prices;
- buyers can plausibly threaten to supply their needs internally.

Management in practice   **Wal-Mart's power as a buyer**   www.walmart.com

Wal-Mart (which owns Asda in the UK) is the world's largest company, being three times the size of the second largest retailer, the French company Carrefour. Growth has enabled it to become the largest purchaser in America, controlling much of the business done by almost every major consumer-products company. It accounts for 30 per cent of hair care products sold, 26 per cent of toothpaste, 20 per cent of pet food, and 20 per cent of all sales of CDs, videos and DVDs. This gives it great power over companies in these industries, since their dependence on Wal-Mart reduces their bargaining power.

Source: *Business Week*, 6 October 2003, pp. 48–53; and other sources.

Bargaining power of suppliers

Conditions that increase the bargaining power of suppliers are the opposite of those applying to buyers. The power of suppliers relative to customers is high when:

- there are few suppliers;
- the product is distinctive, so that customers are reluctant to switch;
- the cost of switching is high (e.g. if a company has invested in a supplier's software);
- suppliers can plausibly threaten to extend their business to compete with the customer;
- the customer is a small or irregular purchaser.

Threat of substitutes

In Porter's model, substitutes refer to products in other industries that can perform the same function, e.g. using cans instead of bottles. Close substitutes constrain the ability of firms to raise prices, and the threat is high when buyers are able and willing to change their habits. Technological change and the risk of obsolescence pose a further threat: online news services (such as that freely available from the BBC) and recruitment sites threaten print newspapers.

Analysing the forces in the competitive environment enables managers to seize opportunities, counter threats and generally improve their position relative to competitors. They can consider how to alter the strength of the forces to improve their position by, for example, building barriers to entry or increasing their power over suppliers or buyers. Chapter 8 (Strategy) examines how managers can position their organisation within the competitive environment.

Activity 3.4   **Critical reflection on the five forces**

Conduct a five forces analysis for an organisation with which you are familiar. Discuss with a manager of the organisation how useful he/she finds the technique.

- Evaluate whether it captures the main competitive variables in his/her industry?
- Compare your analysis with one done for Nokia, and present a summary of similarities and differences in the forces affecting the companies.

| **3.5** | ### The general environment – PESTEL |

Forces in the wider world also shape management policies, and a **PESTEL analysis** (short for political, economic, socio-cultural, technological, environmental and legal) helps to identify these – which Figure 3.5 summarises. When these forces combine their effect is more pronounced – pharmaceutical companies face problems located in slower progress in transferring scientific knowledge into commercial products, more risk-averse regulators who require longer and more costly trials, challenges from companies making cheap generic alternatives to patented drugs, and governments trying to reduce the costs of drugs supplied to citizens.

PESTEL analysis is a technique for identifying and listing the political, economic, social, technological, environmental and legal factors in the general environment most relevant to an organisation.

Political factors

Political systems vary between countries and often shape what managers can and cannot do. Governments often regulate industries such as power supply, telecommunications, postal services and transport by specifying, among other things, who can offer services, the conditions they must meet and what they can charge. Regulations differ between countries and are a major factor in managers' decisions.

When the UK and most European governments altered the law on financial services, non-financial companies such as Virgin and Sainsbury's quickly began to offer banking services. Deregulating air transport stimulated the growth of low-cost airlines, especially in the US

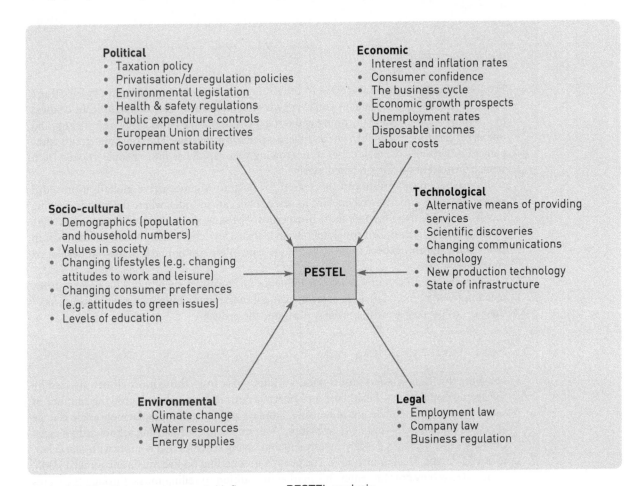

Figure 3.5 Identifying environmental influences – PESTEL analysis

(e.g. Southwest Airlines), Europe (easyJet), Australia (Virgin Blue) and parts of Asia (Air Asia), although as the Ryanair case in Chapter 1 shows, these companies still work in a political environment. The EU is developing regulations to try to manage the environmentally friendly disposal of the millions of personal computers and mobile phones that consumers scrap each year.

Managers aim to influence these political decisions by employing professional lobbyists, especially at international institutions. The European Commission (which performs the detailed analysis behind EU policy) relies on contributions from interested parties to inform its decisions, and lobbying firms provide this. They focus on those people who have decision-making power, often members of the European parliament.

Management in practice   **VT Group depends on government** www.vtplc.com

The UK government is the biggest customer of VT Group, the defence, education and engineering outsourcer. Current contracts include broadcasting the BBC's World Service and managing the Metropolitan Police's vehicle fleet. Contracts with the UK public sector represented 67 per cent of VT's revenues in 2008, and the US public sector made up much of the rest. The company sees both danger and opportunity in this. While shifts in demand for an existing service are usually gradual and predictable, future government policy is often unknown – especially before elections. Paul Lester, who in 2009 was chief executive of the group, maintains close contact with government ministers and leading members of the main opposition party.

Source: *Financial Times*, 29 June 2009.

Economic factors

Economic factors such as wage levels, inflation and interest rates affect an organisation's costs. During the 2009 recession Unilever (**www.unilever.com**) detected significant changes in shopping habits, with many doing without expensive bubble baths, body moisturisers and upmarket cleaning products in favour of less expensive purchases. The consumer goods company said that sales of stock cubes were growing very rapidly as more people 'cooked from scratch' instead of buying prepared meals.

Increasing competition and the search for cost advantages drive globalisation. Ford (**www.ford.com**) has invested in plant to make small cars in India, where demand is growing rapidly as people there become more prosperous. The same economic trend encouraged Tata (**www.tata.com**), the Indian conglomerate, to launch a low-cost car, the Nano: Renault/Nissan (**www.renault.com**) expect to be selling more cars in emerging markets than in developed countries by 2015.

The state of the economy is a major influence on consumer spending, which affects firms meeting those needs. Managers planning capital investments follow economic forecasts: if these suggest slower growth, they may postpone the project.

Socio-cultural factors

Demographic change affects most organisations, apart from those most clearly affected by the ageing population – healthcare and pharmaceuticals businesses. A growing number of single people affects the design of housing, holidays and life assurance. Demographic change affects an organisation's publicity to ensure, for example, that advertising acknowledges racial diversity. Leading banks develop investment and saving schemes that comply with *sharia* law, to attract devout Muslim investors. The growth in spending on live music encouraged HMV Group (**www.hmv.com**) to enter this market in addition to selling music through the stores (see Chapter 8 Case).

Consumer tastes and preferences change. Commenting on a decision to increase the number of healthier products, the chief executive of Nestlé said:

> I think this shows you where the future direction of the company is. This emphasis on (healthier products) is a strategic decision, reflecting changing economic and demographic conditions.

Technological factors

Companies pay close attention to the physical infrastructure – such as the adequacy of power supplies and transport systems. Even more, they monitor advances in information technology, which are dramatically changing the business environment of many companies. Advances in technology do not only affect data systems. Computers traditionally handled data, while other systems handled voice (telephones) and pictures (film and video). These components of the information revolution are familiar as separate devices, but their use of common digital technology greatly increases their ability to exchange information. Digitisation – the packaging of images and sounds into digital form – has profound implications for many industries, as Table 3.2 illustrates.

Table 3.2 Examples of digital technologies affecting established businesses

Technology	Application	Businesses affected
Digital Versatile Discs (DVDs)	Store sound and visual images	Sales of stereophonic sound systems decline sharply
IPOD, MP3 and smartphones	Digital downloads of talking books	New markets created for talking books, with titles to suit new audience
Broadband services delivering online content	Enables advertisers to use online media rather than print or television	Media companies (some of whom have now moved online – NewsCorp acquired MySpace)
Voice over Internet Protocol (VoIP)	Enables telephone calls over the internet at very low cost	Threat to revenues of traditional phone companies
Digital photography	Enables people to store pictures electronically and order prints online	Photographic retailers such as Jessops lose significant part of business

Bernoff and Li (2008) show how social networking (Facebook) and user-generated content sites (YouTube) change the technological context – to which companies are in turn responding: see Chapter 12.

Case study   Nokia – the case continues   www.nokia.com

While Nokia, like all mobile phone companies, regularly introduces more technically sophisticated devices, these account for a small proportion of the units which the industry sells each year. However, the 'smartphone' segment of the market is growing rapidly, with almost 55 million units sold in the first quarter of 2010 – a 57 per cent increase on the same quarter of 2009. Observers expected that, as prices for phones and services continue to drop, demand for more basic devices will continue to grow rapidly in the large markets of China, India, Brazil and Russia.

Nokia has been particularly successful in meeting this demand, making great efforts to secure first-time buyers and then build lifelong loyalty to the brand. Moreover, status-conscious buyers in the third world disdain unknown brands:

> **Brazilians want brand names and are willing to pay a bit more for Nokia or Motorola** (Quoted in *Business Week*, 7 November 2005, p. 21)

More than any other handset maker, the Finnish company has connected with consumers in China and India. Greater China (the mainland, Hong Kong and Taiwan) is the company's biggest market: in 2005 it supplied 31 per cent of all sets sold there, well ahead of the 10 per cent from second-place Motorola. It has about 60 per cent of the market in India, which it expects will be the company's biggest market by 2010. It owes its strong position in both countries in part to a decentralised organisation which can spot local sales trend very quickly, together with an ability to produce sets tailored to local tastes and languages.

It also competes at the top end of the market: in October 2008 it launched a new service – Comes With Music (CWM) as a rival to Apple's iPhone. The CWM devices consist of a mobile handset which also includes a year's free unlimited subscription to Nokia's music catalogue. The company pays music publishers and artists a share of handset sales, depending on the amount of music downloaded.

Chief executive Olli-Pekka Kallasvuo set a target of 300 million users of its mobile services by the end of 2011. This is part of the company's wider strategy to offer mobile services, investing large sums in buying companies to support that – such as Navteq, a digital maps company. Such a move would help it gain higher margins from the sales of these more expensive handsets.

Sources: *Business Week*, 27 March 2006; *Financial Times*, 17 July 2009; International Data Corporation, 7 May 2010.

Case questions 3.3

Gather some information about current developments in the mobile phone industry. Also collect information on Nokia.

- Use Porter's five forces model to outline the competitive environment of the industry.
- Which of these factors may have contributed to Nokia's success?
- Which PESTEL factors are most affecting the development of the industry?

Environmental factors

The natural resources available in an economy – including minerals, agricultural land and the prevailing climate – affect the kind of businesses that managers create: the mills at New Lanark (Chapter 2 case) were built beside a source of water power.

Many senior managers know that climate change will have major implications for their organisations, and are working out how best to respond. It will put most businesses at risk, with the probability of more droughts, floods, storms and heat waves – less rainfall in some places, more in others. For some it represents a threat – insurance companies, house builders and water companies are only the most visible examples of companies that are being affected. For others, sustainability brings opportunities – alternative energy suppliers, emission control businesses and waste management companies are all seeing more interest in their products and services.

Legal factors

Governments create the legal framework within which companies operate, most obviously in areas such as health and safety, employment, consumer protection and pollution control. They also create the legal basis for business – such as when the UK parliament passed the Joint Stock Companies Act in 1862. Previously people were discouraged from putting their money into a business as they were personally liable for the whole of a company's debts if it failed. The Act of 1862 limited their liability to the value of the shares they held in the company – they could lose their investment, but not the rest of their wealth. This stimulated company formation and other countries soon passed similar legislation, paving the way for the countless 'limited liability' companies that exist today (Micklethwait and Wooldridge, 2003).

The PESTEL analysis is just as relevant to public and voluntary sector organisations. Many public service organisations are in business to do things that the market does not, so a PESTEL analysis can identify emerging issues that need attention. An example is the age structure of the population: a country with growing numbers of elderly people has to finance changes in community care services, social services and hospitals. Public sector organisations are often unable to expand their operations where new problems or needs are identified, but the results can be used to lobby for increased funding or to target their existing budgets.

The PESTEL framework is a useful starting point for analysis if managers use it to identify factors that are relevant to their business and how they are changing.

Activity 3.5 **Critical reflection on a PESTEL analysis**

Conduct a PESTEL analysis for your organisation, or one with which you are familiar.

- Which of the external forces you have identified has the most implications for the business?
- Evaluate the extent to which the organisation's policy has taken account of these forces.
- Compare your analysis with that which you did for Nokia, and present a summary of similarities and differences in the forces affecting the companies.

3.6   Types of environment and stakeholders

Perceptions of environments

The axes in Figure 3.6 show two variables (Duncan, 1972) which affect how people see their environment – the degree of complexity and the degree of dynamism. Complexity refers to the number and similarity of factors which people take into consideration when making a decision – the more of these, and the more different they are, the more complex the situation. Dynamism refers to the degree to which these factors remain the same or change.

To consider only the most contrasting cells in Figure 3.6, those who perceive themselves to be in a *simple-static* environment will experience little uncertainty. Competitors offer similar products, newcomers rarely enter the market and there are few technological breakthroughs. Examples could include routine legal work such as house sales and wills, or trades such as joinery. The information required for a decision is likely to be available, so people can assess

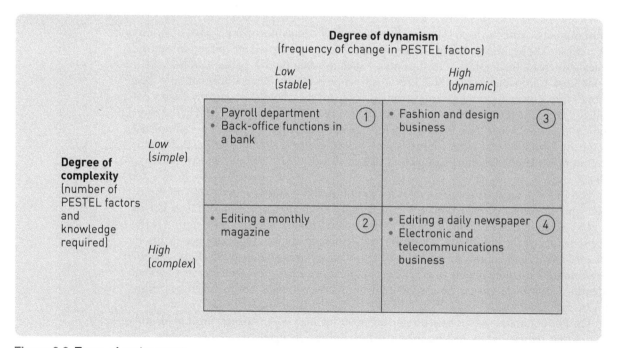

Figure 3.6 Types of environment

the outcome of a decision quickly and accurately. They can use past trends to predict the future with a reasonable degree of confidence. Some aspects of health and education, where demand is driven largely by demographic change, may also fit this pattern: the capacity needed in primary and secondary schools is easy to predict several years ahead.

Key ideas   **Donald Sull – active waiting in unpredictable markets**

Donald Sull (2005) has studied more than 20 pairs of comparable companies in unpredictable industries such as airlines, telecommunications and software development. By comparing similar companies he was able to show how they responded differently to unforeseen threats and opportunities. Successful companies regularly responded more effectively to unexpected shifts in regulation, technology, competitive or macro-environments. They did this by what he termed 'actively waiting', using techniques which included:

- Keeping priorities clear to avoid dissipating energy and resources.
- Conducting reconnaissance to identify gaps in the market.
- Keeping a reserve of cash to fund major opportunities when they emerge.
- Using lulls to push through operational improvements.
- Declare that an opportunity is the company's main effort to seize it faster than rivals.

Source: Based on Sull (2005).

At the other extreme, those working in complex-dynamic environments face great uncertainty. They have to monitor many diverse and changing factors. Companies in the mobile phone or entertainment industries are like this. Multinationals such as Shell and BP experience great complexity, operating across diverse political, legal and cultural systems. Eric Schmidt (Chief Executive of Google) has said that in many high tech and other industries:

> the environment is changing so fast that it requires improvisation in terms of strategy, products and even day-to-day operations. Just when you think you understand the technology landscape, you see a major disruption.

Activity 3.6   **Critical reflection on type of environment**

Use Figure 3.6 to analyse the environment in which your unit of the organisation works. Then try to do the same analysis for one or two other units of the organisation.

- Compare the nature of these environments.
- What are the implications of that for managing these departments, and for the organisation?

Most managers claim to work in dynamic and complex situations. This implies that they face great uncertainty over how the future will unfold. In these circumstances historical analysis is likely to be a less useful guide to the future and managers need to develop different ways of anticipating what may lie ahead.

Case question 3.4

- How would you classify the environment in which Nokia operates? Which factors contributed to your answer?

Stakeholders

All managers need to deal with stakeholders – individuals, groups or other organisations with an interest in, or who are affected by, what the enterprise does (Freeman, 1984). Organisations depend on their micro and macro environments (see Figure 3.1) for the resources they need. Stakeholders in these environments make resources available or withhold them, depending on their view of the organisation. Managers in any sector need to pay attention to stakeholder expectations, and meet these to an acceptable degree to ensure a positive view.

Stakeholders may be internal (employees, managers, different departments or professional groups, owners, shareholders) or external (customers, competitors, bankers, local communities, members of the public, pressure groups and government). The challenge is that:

> Different stakeholders do not generally share the same definition of an organization's 'problems', and hence, they do not in general share the same 'solutions.' As a result, the typical approaches to organizational problem solving, which generally pre-suppose prior consensus or agreement among parties, cannot be used; they break down. Instead a method is needed that builds off a starting point of disagreement . . . (Mitroff, 1983, p. 5)

Stakeholders have expectations of organisations and managers choose whether or not to take account of these. Nutt (2002) shows the dangers of ignoring them: he studied 400 strategic decisions and found that half of them 'failed' – in the sense that they were not implemented or produced poor results – largely because managers failed to attend to stakeholders.

Faced with evidence of excessive risk-taking in banks, shareholders have begun to become more active in criticising directors over the pay and bonus systems through which they reward senior managers in their companies. This has led to changes in corporate governance arrangements.

Figure 3.7 indicates what stakeholders may expect.

Case study · Nokia – the case continues · www.nokia.com

The manufacture of components for mobile phones is being moved rapidly out of the Nordic country to low-cost locations. Early in 2006 three of its subcontractors announced that they were cutting more than 1,100 jobs in Finland, underlining the dramatic shift in the global telecoms business, in which a rapidly growing share of revenue comes from cost-conscious emerging markets.

This is leading the Finns to reassess their high dependence on the industry. An economist at the Bank of Finland slated:

> Nokia's profits, and the tax revenues they have generated for Finland, have exceeded our wildest dreams in the past ten years. But it is disappointing that the production has not provided the highly-paid, large-scale source of employment we hoped for.

The company is also collaborating on long-term technical projects with Intel, whose microprocessors run about 80 per sent of the world's computers. They plan to create a type of mobile computing device beyond today's smartphones and netbooks. Kai Oistamo, Nokia's vice-president in charge of devices said:

> The mobile and computing industries are coming together, and we as leaders in our respective industries, are taking the responsibility to really be the enablers to create this brave new world.

Source: *Financial Times*, 13 March 2006 and 24 June 2009.

Case questions 3.5

- Who are the main stakeholders in Nokia?
- What are their interests in the success of the company?
- How can management ensure it maintains the support of the most important stakeholders?

Shareholders
- Growth in dividend payments
- Growth in share price
- Growth in asset value

Suppliers
- Timely payment of debt
- Adequate liquidity
- Integrity of directors
- Trustworthy purchasing manager

Government
- Adhering to the country's laws
- Paying taxes
- Providing employment
- Value for money in using public funds

Customers
- Competitive price
- Quality product or service
- Guarantee provisions

Employees
- Good pay and benefits
- Job security
- Sense of purpose in the job
- Opportunities for personal development

Lenders
- Financial strength of the company
- Quality of management
- Quality of assets available for security
- Ability to repay interest and capital

Figure 3.7
Examples of possible stakeholder expectations

| 3.7 | Corporate governance |

Why have governance systems?

Scandals and failures in prominent organisations lead people to question the adequacy of their systems of **corporate governance**. They show that senior managers cannot always be trusted to act in the best interests of the company and the shareholders. To reduce this risk, owners have developed rules and processes which are intended to guide and control those responsible for managing public and private organisations, ensuring that they act in the interests of influential stakeholders. Governance systems are based on the principle that those managing an organisation are accountable for their actions, and create mechanisms to do that.

In capitalist economies, ownership typically becomes separated from control. The founder provides the initial capital but growth requires further finance – which investors provide in exchange for an income. They cannot supervise management decisions, but need to be confident that the business is secure before they provide further funds.

Berle and Means (1932) highlighted the dilemma facing owners who become separated from the managers they appoint to run the business:

> The corporation is a means by which the wealth of innumerable individuals has been concentrated into huge aggregates and whereby control over this wealth has been surrendered to a unified direction . . . The direction of industry other than by persons who have ventured their wealth has raised the question . . . of the distribution of the returns from business enterprise. (p. 4)

Their observations led others to develop what is now termed 'agency theory', which seeks to explain what happens when one party (the principal) delegates work to another party (the agent). In this case the shareholders (principals) have financed, and own, the business, but they delegate the work of running it to managers (agents). The principals then face the risk that managers may not act in their (the principals') best interests: they may take excessive investment risks, or withhold information so that the state of the business appears to be better than it is. The principal is then at a disadvantage to the agent, who may use this to personal advantage. Failures at major financial institutions, caused in part by lending money to risky borrowers in the hope of high returns, show that the separation of ownership from management, of principal from agent, is as relevant as ever.

Corporate governance refers to the rules and processes intended to control those responsible for managing an organisation.

The interests of managers and shareholders

While senior managers often claim to be trying to align their interests with those of shareholders, the two often conflict. Mergers often appear to benefit senior managers and their professional advisers rather than shareholders. Acquiring companies often pay too much for the target, but executives inside the enlarged company receive higher pay. Professional advisers (investment bankers) make money on both the merger and the break-up.

Using company money to buy the company's shares in the market uses money that can't be spent on dividends. From the vantage point of many CEOs, paying dividends is about the last thing they would want to do with corporate earnings. In theory, a CEO is carrying out shareholder wishes. In practice, as the spate of recent scandals has shown, the interests of chief executives and their shareholders can widely diverge.

Source: Based on extracts from an article by Robert Kuttner, *Business Week,* 9 September 2002.

Similar issues arise in the public sector, where elected members are nominally in charge of local authorities, health boards and other agencies – and who appoint professional managers to run the organisation on behalf of the citizens. Elected members face the risk that the people they have appointed act in their narrow professional or personal interests, rather than of those of the electorate. Hartley *et al.* (2008) point out:

> a new awareness of the social, economic and cultural contribution of government, public organizations and public services has resulted in a significant period of reform and ex-perimentation. At the heart of these initiatives is the idea that improvements to the way public services can be governed, managed and delivered will produce improved out-comes for citizens. (p. 3)

Stakeholder theory is also relevant, as it tries to explain the evolving relationship between an organisation and its stakeholders. Many believe that governance systems should take account of the interests of this wider group, as well as those of shareholders with only a financial interest.

The substance of corporate governance

Mallin (2007) suggests that to provide an adequate oversight of managers, governance systems should have:

- an adequate system of internal controls which safeguards assets;
- mechanisms to prevent any one person having too much influence;
- processes to manage relationships between managers, directors, shareholders and other stakeholders;
- the aim of managing the company in the interests of shareholders and other stakeholders; and
- the aim of encouraging transparency and accountability, which investors and many external stakeholders expect.

Proposals to deal with these issues affect the context in which managers work, and this book will examine the topic as an integrating theme at the end of each chapter.

3.8 Integrating themes

Sustainable performance

Nicholas Stern advises the UK government on climate change, and his latest book (Stern, 2009) calls for urgent action to mitigate the effects. The paragraphs below summarise some of his points.

Climate change is not a theory struggling to maintain itself in the face of problematic evidence. The opposite is true: as new information comes in, it reinforces our understanding across a whole spectrum of indicators. The subject is full of uncertainty, but there is no serious doubt that emissions are growing as a result of human activity and that more greenhouse gases will lead to further warming.

The last 20 years have seen special and focused attention from the Intergovernmental Panel on Climate Change (IPCC) (**www.ipcc.ch**), which has now published four assessments, the most recent in 2007. With each new report, the evidence on the strength and source of the effects, and the magnitude of the implications and risks, has become stronger. The basic scientific conclusions on climate change are very robust and for good reason. The greenhouse effect is simple science: greenhouse gases trap heat, and humans are emitting ever more greenhouse gases. There will be oscillations, there will be uncertainties. But the logic of the greenhouse effect is rock-solid and the long-term trends associated with the effects of human emissions are clear in the data.

In 2010 a report by the UK Meteorological Office (Stott, 2010) confirmed these conclusions, saying that the evidence was stronger now than when the IPCC carried out its last assessment in 2007. The analysis assessed 110 research papers on the subject, concluding that the earth is changing rapidly, probably because of greenhouse gases. The study found that changes in Arctic sea ice, atmospheric moisture, saltiness of parts of the Atlantic Ocean and temperature changes in the Antarctic are consistent with human influence on our climate.

Governance and control

This chapter has examined the culture of organisations and their external contexts: governance links the two. There are high-profile examples of organisations whose culture has encouraged managers and staff to act in their interests, rather than in the interests of those they were expected to serve. This has focused attention on corporate governance arrangements, which are part of the context within which managers of all organisations work: most of the time these will be far in the background, but they become visible at times of difficulty.

The Cadbury Report (1992) has influenced the development of corporate governance systems around the world, including the UK. Set up following a series of UK financial scandals it made recommendations about the operation of the main board, the establishment and operation of board committees, the roles of non-executive directors, and on reporting and control mechanisms. These recommendations have been combined with the outcomes of related reports into what is known as the Combined Code – the latest version of which was published in 2006 (Financial Reporting Council, 2006). This is a voluntary Code of Best Practice, with which the boards of all companies listed on the London Stock Exchange are expected to comply – or to explain why they have not done so. It includes guidance on matters such as:

The Board. Every company should be headed by an effective board, which is collectively responsible for the success of the company;

Chairman and chief executive. There should be a clear division of responsibilities . . . between the running of the board and the executive responsible [for running the business]. No one individual should have unfettered powers of decision.

Board balance. The board should include a balance of executive and [independent] non-executive directors so that no individual or small group can dominate the board's decision taking

Board appointments. There should be a formal, rigorous and transparent procedure for appointing new directors to the board.

Internationalisation

Models of national culture (see Chapter 4) are highly generalised summaries of diverse populations. Their value is to give some clues about broad differences between the places in which those managing internationally will be working. They encourage people to be ready to adapt the way they work to local circumstances. Others take a more robust view of cultural differences and try to eliminate their influence within the organisation. Steve Chang founded Trend Micro, an anti-virus software company operating in many countries:

> The curse is that national cultures are very different. We have to figure out how to convert everybody to one business culture – no matter where they're from. (*Business Week*, 22 September 2003)

The following Management in Practice feature shows how Iris, a rapidly growing advertising agency with a very strong and distinctive company culture AND many global clients, seeks to gain the benefits of the diversity of its international staff and combine this to add more value for the client.

Management in practice   **Gaining from cultural differences** www.irisnation.com

Iris was founded in 1999 and has established a distinctive position as an independent media and advertising agency, with a growing international business. An innovative technique which is very popular with global clients is 'Project 72'. Steve Bell, chief executive of Iris London, and one of the founding partners, explains:

> Project 72 is a very simple concept, and probably the purest way of bringing different agencies in the group together as one with a common goal and a common vision. [Suppose] Iris Miami is working on a brief for a client: they say 'right, let's engage a Project 72 on this one'. So the brief will go to the other agencies around the world, it will be handed to London, for example, we will work on it for 12 hours, we will then [hand the baton] to Sydney, they will work on it for 12 hours, baton change to Singapore, so you can see how within 72 hours we've got the best freshest brains working on a brief to the common goal of developing the best creative work that we possibly can do. It's been fantastic . . .
>
> Project 72 benefits hugely from the cultural differences, and when I say cultural differences I don't mean within the agency but the societal cultural differences that happen within different areas around the world. So tapping into the fact that Singapore has a certain view around mobile telecomms enables us to look at things in a slightly different way, so it just allows fresh thinking, fresh outlooks, fresh cultures to inject some pace and some innovation around a particular brief at a given time.

Source: Interview with Steve Bell.

Summary

1 **Identify the main elements of the environments in which organisations work**
   - They include the immediate competitive environment, the wider general (or macro) environment and the organisation's stakeholders.

2 **Compare the cultures of two organisational units, using Quinn's or Handy's typologies**
   - Quinn *et al.* (2003) – open systems, rational goal, internal process and human relations.
   - Handy (1993) – power, role, task and person.

3 **Use Porter's five forces model to analyse the competitive environment of an organisation**
   - This identifies the degree of competitive rivalry, customers, competitors, suppliers and potential substitute goods and services.

4 **Collect evidence to make a comparative PESTEL analysis for two organisations**
   - The PESTEL model of the wider external environment identifies political, economic, social, technological, environmental and legal forces.

5 Compare perceptions of environments, and give examples of stakeholder expectations

● Environments can be evaluated in terms of their rate of change (stable/dynamic) and complexity (low/high).

● These are shown in Figure 3.7

6 Explain the meaning and purpose of corporate governance

● Corporate governance frameworks are intended to monitor and control the performance of managers to ensure they act in the interests of organisational stakeholders, and not just of the managers themselves.

7 Show how ideas from the chapter add to your understanding of the integrating themes

● A major feature of the natural environment relevant to managers is the accumulating evidence that climate change is due to human activities, leading to pressure for organisations and people to work and live more sustainably.

● Some organisational cultures encouraged staff to take excessive risks, gravely damaging companies and economies: this is leading stakeholders to press for tighter governance and control mechanisms to reduce the chances of similar events happening again.

● While culture has a powerful effect on what people do in an organisation, when they operate internationally it provides an opportunity to benefit from diverse perspectives.

Review questions

1 Describe an educational or commercial organisation that you know in terms of the competing values model of cultures.

2 What is the significance of the idea of 'fragmented cultures' for those who wish to change a culture to support performance?

3 Identify the relative influence of Porter's five forces on an organisation of your choice and compare your results with a colleague's. What can you learn from that comparison?

4 How should managers decide which of the many factors easily identified in a PESTEL analysis they should attend to? If they have to be selective, what is the value of the PESTEL method?

5 Since people interpret the nature of environmental forces from unique perspectives, what meaning can people attach to statements about external pressures?

6 Illustrate the stakeholder idea with an example of your own, showing their expectations of an organisation.

7 Explain at least two of the mechanisms which Mallin (2007) recommends should be part of a corporate governance system.

8 Summarise an idea from the chapter that adds to your understanding of the integrating themes.

Concluding critical reflection

Think about the culture which seems to be dominant in your company, and how managers deal with the business environment and with stakeholders. Alternatively take another company with which you are familiar, and find what you can about its culture, and how it monitors and assesses the external environment. Review the material in the chapter and make notes on the following questions:

● Which of the issues discussed in this chapter are most relevant to the way you and your colleagues manage? What **assumptions** appear to guide the culture, and the factors in the external environment which managers believe have most effect on the business? Do you all attach the same significance to them or do views vary? Why is that? How do these views affect your tasks as managers and, indeed, the nature of your organisation?

- What factors in the **context** appear to have shaped the prevailing view about which changes in the environment will most affect the business? Why do they think that? Do people have different interpretations?
- Can you compare your business environment with that of colleagues on your course, especially those in similar industries? Does this show up any **alternative** ways of seeing the context, and of dealing with stakeholders?
- What are the **limitations** of the ideas on culture and stakeholders which the chapter has presented. For example, are the cultural types transferable across nations, or how may they need to be adapted to represent different ways of managing?

Further reading

Hawken, P., Lovins, A.B. and Lovins. L.H. (1999), *Natural Capitalism: The next industrial revolution*, Earthscan, London.

> Generally positive account of the environmental challenges facing us all, and what organisations are doing about it.

Johns, G. (2006), 'The essential impact of context on organizational behavior', *Academy of Management Review*, vol. 31, no. 2, pp. 386–408.

> An overview of the many ways in which writers have expressed the idea of 'context', and how it affects organisational behaviour and research. It proposes two ways of thinking about context; one grounded in journalistic practice and the other in classic social psychology.

Frooman, J. (1999), 'Stakeholder influence strategies', *Academy of Management Review*, vol. 24, no. 2, pp. 191–205.

Pajunen, K. (2006), 'Stakeholder influences on organizational survival', *Journal of Management Studies*, vol. 43, no. 6, pp. 1261–1288.

> These two articles provided a comprehensive theoretical background to case studies of stakeholder management.

Steinbock, D. (2001), *The Nokia Revolution*, American Management Association, New York.

> This is an authoritative account of the development of the company, and its interaction with the external environment.

Tapscott, E. and Williams, A.D. (2006), *Wikinomics: How Mass Collaboration Changes Everything*, Viking Penguin, New York.

> Best-selling account of the radical changes which convergent technologies bring to society, especially the relationship between producers and consumers.

Weblinks

These websites have appeared in the chapter:

> www.nokia.com
> www.acea.be
> www.walmart.com

www.bosch.com
www.vtplc.com
www.unilever.com
www.ford.com
www.tata.com
www.renault.com
www.hmv.com
www.ipcc.ch
www.irisnation.com

Visit some of these, or any other companies which interest you, and navigate to the pages dealing with recent news, press or investor relations.

- What can you find about their culture?
- What are the main forces in the external environment which the organisation appears to be facing?
- What assessment would you make of the nature of that environment?
- Compare and contrast the issues you identify on the two sites.
- What challenges may they imply for those working in, and managing, these organisations?

 For video case studies, audio summaries, flashcards, exercises and annotated weblinks related to this chapter, visit **www.pearsoned.co.uk/mymanagementlab**

CHAPTER 6
PLANNING

Aim

To describe the purposes of planning in organisations, and illustrate the iterative tasks in the planning cycle

Objectives

By the end of your work on this chapter you should be able to outline the concepts below in your own terms and:

1 Explain the purposes of planning and the content of different types of plan

2 Compare alternative planning processes, and evaluate when each may be most suitable

3 Outline the seven iterative steps in planning, and describe techniques used in each

4 Use theory to evaluate the motivational effect of the goals stated in a plan

5 Use a framework to evaluate whether a plan is sufficiently comprehensive

6 Evaluate the context that will affect the ability of managers to implement a plan

7 Show how ideas from the chapter can add to your understanding of the integrating themes

Key terms

This chapter introduces the following ideas:

planning
goal (or objective)
business plan
strategic plan
strategic business unit
operational plans
enterprise resource planning
planning system
SWOT analysis

critical success factors
optimism bias
strategic misrepresentation bias
sensitivity analysis
scenario planning
stated goals
real goals
organisational readiness

Each is a term defined within the text, as well as in the Glossary at the end of the book.

Case study   Crossrail www.crossrail.co.uk

Crossrail is a new railway for London and the south-east of England which will connect the City, Canary Wharf, the West End and Heathrow Airport to commuter areas east and west of the capital. It aims to be a world-class, affordable railway, with high-frequency, convenient and accessible services across the capital. The plans are intended to:

- relieve congestion on many Underground and rail lines;
- provide new connections and new services;
- bring modern trains;
- provide eight new stations in central London.

It will add 10 per cent to London's overall transport capacity and provide 40 per cent of the extra rail capacity London needs. Main construction of the railway will begin in 2010, with services commencing in 2017. Crossrail will make travelling in the area easier and quicker, and reduce crowding on London's transport network. It will operate with main-line-size trains, each carrying more than 1,500 passengers.

It is the largest civil engineering project in the UK and the largest single addition to the London transport network for over 50 years. It will run 118 km from Maidenhead and Heathrow in the west, through new twin-bore 21 km tunnels under Central London out to Shenfield and Abbey Wood in the east, joining the Great Western and Great Eastern railway networks.

The project has a long history – it was first proposed in 1990, but amidst considerable opposition from other players it was cancelled in 1996. Pressure continued to build the line as a contribution to solving London's transport problems, and the company claims wide support for Crossrail among UK businesses and business organisations such as the CBI, London First and the London Chamber of Commerce and Industry.

Political conditions changed again, and Royal Assent was given to the Crossrail Act in July 2008 giving authority for the railway to be built. In December 2008 the government and the Mayor of London signed the key funding agreements for Crossrail.

By March 2010 the overall plan was turning into reality as many of the smaller elements were implemented. For example, the company announced the

By kind permission, Crossrail

award of contracts for what it calls enabling work such as various pieces of complex demolition work at several stations and their surrounding area. The company also announced that the Learning & Skills Council had agreed to provide £5 million towards the cost of a new tunnelling and underground construction academy. A senior manager said:

> This is great news for the programme and great news for the tunnelling and underground construction industry. This decision means we can now progress our plans to build this fantastic training facility, which the industry so urgently needs.

Construction would commence soon and the facility is expected to be fully operational by the end of 2010.

Source: Company website and other published sources.

Case questions 6.1

Visit the Crossrail website (see above).

- What are the main items of recent news about the progress of the project?
- From what you read, what are the main challenges the managers face in planning the project?
- What kind of environment do you think the company is operating in (Chapter 3, Section 3.6)?

6.1   Introduction

Crossrail is an example of a major project which managers can only achieve by a substantial investment in planning. From the early political processes to secure support from many interested parties (Glaister and Travers, 2001) – some in favour of the project, some against – through raising capital and securing public consent, managers have engaged in a continual planning process. That now continues, as it turns to the very detailed planning required to drive a new railway through a crowded capital city. The case will illustrate how Crossrail's managers deal with these challenges, some of which are still unforeseen.

Brews and Purahit (2007) show empirically that, as business conditions become more unstable, companies do more planning. Change creates uncertainty, and planning helps people adapt to this by clarifying objectives, specifying how to achieve them, and monitoring progress. Plans include both ends (what to do) and means (how to do it).

Informal plans (not written down, nor widely shared) work perfectly well in many situations, but as the number of people involved in an activity increases they need something more to guide them. That is the focus here – on more formal plans – which put into writing the goals of a business or unit, and who will do what to achieve them. When senior managers at Hiscox, a small but rapidly growing insurance company, decided to add an online service to its traditional way of doing business through insurance brokers, it needed not only a plan for the website, but also a plan to reassure the brokers that they would still have a role. When two entrepreneurs decided to create the City Inn hotel chain they planned in detail the kind of hotels they would be: contemporary, city centre, newly built, 'active and open' atmosphere, and a consistent room design across the group. Plans like this can then be communicated to relevant players, to ensure they act consistently.

Figure 6.1 provides an overview of the themes. At the centre are seven generic tasks in planning – but people vary the order, and how much attention they give to each. The chapter outlines the benefits of planning and distinguishes the content of plans. Later sections examine the process of planning, and its seven generic steps – stressing throughout that these take place iteratively, and that their form depends on circumstances.

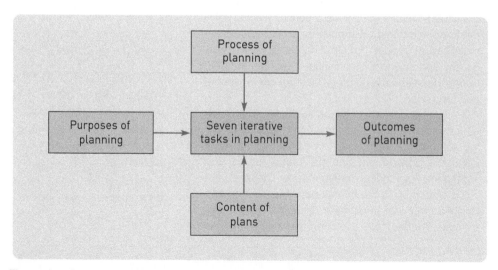

Figure 6.1 An overview of the chapter

6.2 | Purposes of planning

A planner is an individual who contemplates future actions: the activity of **planning** involves establishing the **goals** (or **objectives**) for the task, specifying how to achieve them, implementing the plan and evaluating the results. Goals are the desired future state of an activity or organisational unit, and planning to meet them typically includes allocating resources and specifying what people need to do to meet the goals.

Planning, if done well:

- clarifies direction;
- motivates people;
- uses resources efficiently; and
- increases control, by enabling people to measure progress against targets.

The act of planning may in itself add value, by ensuring that people base decisions on a wider range of evidence than if there was no planning system. Giraudeau (2008) shows how the planning process in one of Renault's divisions enhanced debate among managers, and stimulated their strategic imagination. Closely observing the company's planners as they developed their plan to build a plant in Brazil, the author shows how providing detailed draft plans to other managers (many of whom were unfamiliar with that country) led them to visualise opportunities they had not considered. If done badly, planning has the opposite effect, leading to confusion and waste.

Good plans give direction to the people whose work contributes to their achievement. If everyone knows the purpose of a larger activity and how their task contributes, they can work more effectively. They adjust their work to the plan (or vice versa), and co-operate and co-ordinate with others. It helps them to cope with uncertainty: if they know the end result they can respond to unexpected changes, without waiting to be told. People like to know how their task fits the bigger picture, as it adds interest and enables them to take more responsibility.

> Planning is the iterative task of setting goals, specifying how to achieve them, implementing the plan and evaluating the results.
>
> A goal (or objective) is a desired future state for an activity or organisational unit.

Management in practice   Maersk – planning key to strategy www.maersk.com

Maersk is the world's largest container operator, and depends on planning. Mark Cornwall, Operations Manager, explains:

Maersk operates 470 container ships with 1.9 million individual containers that are all travelling around the world, and our job is to build efficiencies into the system – moving the cargo to the customer on time.

Part of our strategy is to deliver unmatched reliability, and operations is key to that. From the top of the company right down to the clerks on the desk, everybody's focused on meeting deadlines and the requirements of the customer every step of the way. So whether it's a ship arriving in a port on time, or a container loading on a ship on time, or a truck delivery to a warehouse, everybody's focused all the way through the chain on making sure that everything happens against the deadline as planned.

Efficiency's all about making the best use of your assets, so whether it's putting as many containers as possible on a ship, or maximising your utilisation of a particular train, or getting as many miles out of a truck as you can during a shift, it's all about planning your assets to get the biggest use out of them during that period.

Source: Interview with Mark Cornwall.

Planning reduces overlap and at the same time ensures that someone is responsible for each activity. A plan helps people co-ordinate their separate tasks, so saving time and resources; without a plan they may work at cross-purposes. If people are clear on the goal they can spot inefficiencies or unnecessary delays and act to fix them.

Key ideas   **Does planning help entrepreneurial behaviour and new ventures?**

Delmar and Shane (2003) studied whether planning helps new ventures, by gathering data from over 200 new firms in Sweden. They hypothesised that planning would support new ventures by:

- enabling quicker decisions;
- providing a tool for managing resources to minimise bottlenecks;
- identifying actions to achieve broader goals in a timely manner.

They gathered extensive data from the firms at their start-up in 1998, and then at regular intervals for three years. The results supported each of their hypotheses, leading them to conclude that planning did indeed support the creation of successful new ventures.

Source: Delmar and Shane (2003).

Setting final and interim goals lets people know how well they are progressing, and when they have finished. Comparing actual progress against the intended progress enables people to adjust the goal or change the way they are using resources.

Preparing a plan may also perform a ceremonial function. Kirsch *et al.* (2009) in a study of entrepreneurs seeking funding from venture capitalists found that:

> neither the presence of business planning documents nor their content serve a communicative role for venture capitalists [in the sense of conveying information that influences the funding decision]. With some qualifications, we find that business planning documents may serve a limited ceremonial role [in the sense of showing that the presenter understands how the target expects them to behave].

The content of a plan is the subject – *what* aspect of business it deals with: strategic, business unit, operational, tactical or special purpose. The next section deals with those topics, and the one which follows focuses on *how* – the planning process.

Activity 6.1   **Reflection on the purpose of plans**

Find an example of a plan that someone has prepared in an organisation – preferably for one of the types listed in the next section.

- Ask someone what its purpose is, and whether it achieves that.
- Ask whether the plan is too detailed, or not detailed enough.
- What do they regard as the strengths and weaknesses of the planning process?
- Refer to your notes as you work on this chapter.

6.3   **The content of plans**

A business plan is a document that sets out the markets the business intends to serve, how it will do so and what finance is required.

People starting a new business or expanding an existing one prepare a **business plan** – a document that sets out the markets the business intends to serve, how it will do so and what finance is required (Sahlman, 1997; Blackwell, 2004). It does so in considerable detail (see Part 3

Skills Development), as it needs to convince potential investors to lend money. Managers seeking capital investment or other corporate resources need to convince senior managers to allocate them – which they do by presenting a convincing plan. People in the public sector do the same: a director of roads, for example, needs to present a plan to convince the chief executive or elected members that planned expenditure on roads will be a better use of resources than competing proposals from (say) the director of social work. Service managers inevitably compete with each other for limited resources, and develop business plans to support their case.

Strategic plans apply to the whole organisation. They set out the overall direction and cover major activities: markets and revenues, together with plans for marketing, human resources and production. Strategy is concerned with deciding what business an organisation should be in, where it wants to be and how it is going to get there. These decisions involve major resource commitments and usually require a series of consequential operational decisions.

> A strategic plan sets out the overall direction for the business, is broad in scope and covers all the major activities.

In a large business there will be divisional plans for each major unit. If subsidiaries operate as autonomous **strategic business units** (SBUs) they develop their plans with limited inputs from the rest of the company, as they manage distinct products or markets.

> A strategic business unit consists of a number of closely related products for which it is meaningful to formulate a separate strategy.

Strategic plans usually set out a direction for several years, although in businesses with long lead times (energy production or aircraft manufacture) they look perhaps 15 years ahead. Ryanair plans to grow capacity to meet demand, and makes a plan showing the financial and other implications of enlarging the fleet, recruiting staff and opening new routes. Such plans are not fixed: managers regularly update them to take account of new conditions, so they are sometimes called 'rolling plans'.

Management in practice   **British Airways plans survival** www.ba.com

In 2009 British Airways reported that it expected to lose money for the second successive year, and said it was planning more cost reductions to help it survive an expected two-year recession. It was shrinking operations at Gatwick Airport reducing the aircraft fleet based there from 32 to 24.

Other plans included:

- cutting thousands of jobs across the business;
- negotiating a merger with Spain's Iberia to create Europe's third-largest aviation group;
- reducing absenteeism among staff;
- negotiating more efficient working practices for cabin staff;
- reducing capacity at London City Airport by a further 17 per cent from an earlier plan.

Source: *Financial Times*, 6 March 2009.

Operational plans detail how managers expect to achieve the strategic objectives. They are narrower in scope, indicating what departments or functions should do to support the strategy. So there may be a family of related plans forming a hierarchy: a strategic plan for the organisation and main divisions, and several operational plans for departments or teams. An example is when Sainsbury announced an aggressive expansion plan in 2009, with the aim of opening 50 new supermarkets and extending another 50, over the next two years. Justin King, chief executive, said that it would concentrate the expansion in areas where it was weak, such as the west of England, Wales and Scotland. Such plans will contain linked objectives and will become more specific as they move down the organisation – eventually dealing with small activities that need to be dealt with for each new store – but aiming to be consistent with the wider expansion strategy. Table 6.1 shows this hierarchical arrangement, and how the character of plans changes at each level.

> Operational plans detail how the overall objectives are to be achieved, by specifying what senior management expects from specific departments or functions.

Table 6.1 A planning hierarchy

Type of plan	Strategic	Operational	Activity
Level	Organisation or business unit	Division, department, function or market	Work unit or team
Focus	Direction and strategy for whole organisation	Functional changes or market activities to support strategic plans	Actions needed to deliver current products or services
Nature	Broad, general direction	Detail on required changes	Specific detail on immediate goals and tasks
Timescale	Long term (2–3 years?)	Medium (up to 18 months?)	Very short term (hours to weeks?)

Case study   Crossrail – the case continues www.crossrail.co.uk

The company has published its outline plans for the station and tunnelling work to be done – making it clear that as detailed design and development of the scheme progresses there will be increasing certainty over the exact times that works will start and finish at each location. The information below gives the assumed timings (early 2010) for main construction works at key locations.

At some locations enabling works (such as the diversion of utilities like gas mains, and demolition of existing buildings) will need to take place before main works. The sites may also be required after main works, for example to support fitting out of stations and tunnels.

Stations

The following table of station start and completion dates reflects the start of construction (main civil contract works) and when enabling works begin. Note that only the first four station sites are shown here.

Location	Enabling works start	Construction starts	Works complete
Canary Wharf	December 2008	May 2009	2016
Tottenham Court Road	January 2009	Early 2010	2016
Farringdon	July 2009	August 2010	2017
Custom House	Early 2012	Late 2012	2014

Tunnelling works

The completion dates shown in the following table refer to the completion of the tunnel. Fit out will take place beyond these dates. Note that only the first three tunnels to be bored are shown here.

Location of tunnel drive	Boring begins	Tunnel drive complete
Royal Oak to Framlington (X)	October 2011	March 2013
Limmo to Farringdon (Y)	April 2012	April 2014
Plumstead to North Woolwich (H)	September 2012	October 2014

On network works

Work on stations and tracks on the existing surface, railway which will be served by Crossrail, will be carried out by Network Rail. These are expected to start in mid 2010. The exact start and duration will vary by location and more detail on the programme will be published when it is available.

Source: Company website.

Case questions 6.2

● How are the strategic plans for the project being turned into operational plans?

● Visit the company website and look for information about developments which may affect these plans.

Most organisations prepare annual plans that focus on finance and set budgets for the coming year – these necessarily include sales, marketing, production or technology plans as well. Activity plans are short-term plans which deal with immediate production or service delivery – a sheet scheduling which orders to deliver next week, or who is on duty tomorrow. Standing plans specify how to deal with routine, recurring issues such as recruitment or customer complaints. Some use a method called **enterprise resource planning (ERP)** to integrate the day-to-day work of complex production systems – Chapter 12 describes this technique in Section 12.6.

Figure 6.2 contrasts specific and directional plans. Specific plans have clear, quantified objectives with little discretion in how to achieve them. When Tesco opens a new store, staff follow defined procedures detailing all the tasks required to ensure that it opens on time and within the budget. Where there is uncertainty about what needs to be done to meet the objective, managers will use a directional plan, setting the objective but leaving staff to decide how they achieve it. Hamm (2007) describes how in the early days of Wipro (a successful Indian information technology company) the founder, Azim Premji, held weekly telephone conversations with his regional managers, in which he set their targets for the following week – but they decided how to meet them. They were accountable for meeting the target, not for how they did so, provided they met his high ethical standards.

Enterprise resource planning (ERP) is a computer-based planning system which links separate databases to plan the use of all resources within the enterprise.

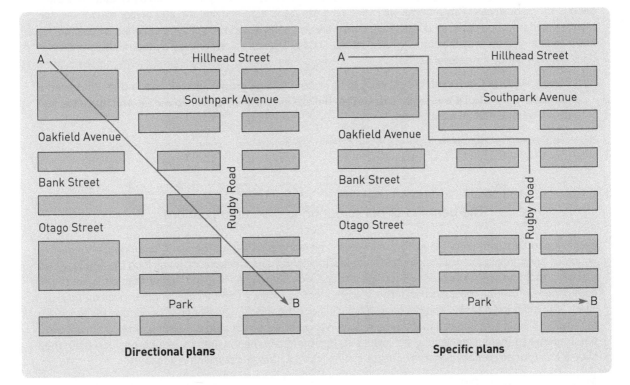

Figure 6.2 Specific and directional plans

Managers also prepare special purpose plans. They may have plans for disaster recovery (after, say, a major computer failure or terrorist action), and project plans to organise and implement specific changes, such as introducing a new computer system or launching a new product. When The Royal Bank of Scotland (RBS) took over NatWest Bank, managers quickly developed over 160 interlocking plans to incorporate NatWest operations into those of RBS (Kennedy *et al.*, 2006).

6.4   The process of planning

The process of planning refers to the way plans are produced – are they developed from the top of the organisation or from the bottom up? How frequently are they revised? Who creates them? A **planning system** organises and co-ordinates the activities of those involved: the process shapes the quality and value of a plan. Designing and maintaining a suitable planning system is part of the planning task.

A planning system refers to the processes by which the members of an organisation produce plans, including their frequency and who takes part in the process.

Participation is one issue – who is involved in making the plan? One approach is to appoint a group of staff specialists to be responsible for producing plans, with or without consultation with the line managers or staff concerned. Others believe the quality of the plan, and especially the ease of implementing it, will be increased if staff familiar with local conditions help to create the plan.

Management in practice   **A new planning process at Merck** www.merck.com

In the early 1990s, Merck was the world's leading pharmaceutical company, but by 2006 it was ranked only eighth. Dick Clark, the new chief executive, was charged with reviving a company: one of his first actions was to make radical changes in the company's planning process. Teams of employees were asked to present the business cases to senior managers to test possible directions for the company – such as whether to build a generic drugs business. This process was vital, said Mr Clark, as it showed the 200 senior executives that Merck would now operate in an atmosphere where assumptions would be openly questioned by anyone. He has also changed the way the company sets its earnings projections. Formerly set by top managers, projections are now set by lower-level teams.

It wasn't like Dick Clark said 'We're going to have double-digit growth, go out and find it!' We tested it and tweaked it . . . but it was legitimate and we believe in it, so let's go public with it. And that's the first time we'd done that as a company.

Source: From an article by Christopher Bowe, *Financial Times*, 27 March 2006, p. 10.

Key ideas   **The benefits of participation and communication**

Ketokivi and Castañer (2004) studied the strategic planning process in 164 manufacturing plants, in five countries and three industries (automotive supplies, machinery and electronics). It has long been recognised that organisational members tend to focus on the goals of their unit or function, rather than on those of the enterprise – known as 'position-bias'. The study sought to establish empirically whether position bias existed, and, more importantly, whether strategic planning reduced this. The evidence confirmed the tendency to position-bias. It also showed that having employees participate in strategic planning, and communicating the outcome to them, significantly diminishes it. If top management wants to reduce position bias, they should incorporate participation and communication into the strategic planning process.

Source: Ketokivi and Castañer (2004).

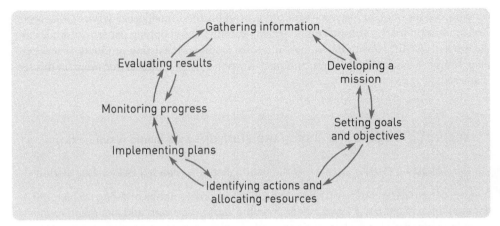

Figure 6.3
Seven iterative tasks in making a plan

A related debate (see Chapter 8, Section 8.7) is between those who advocate a rational approach to planning, and those who favour what are variously called learning or emergent approaches. They argue that when a company is in dynamic context, plans must be essentially temporary and provisional, so that managers can adapt them to suit changing circumstances, drawing on new information from the frequent interaction of a wide range of participants (Fletcher and Harris, 2002; Papke-Shields *et al.*, 2006). Andersen (2000) sought to reconcile these views by studying the use of strategic planning and autonomous action in three industries with different external conditions. He concluded that strategic planning was associated with superior organisational performance in all industrial settings. Whether industries were complex and dynamic or stable and simple, companies that planned performed better than those that did not. In addition, he found that in complex dynamic industries a formal planning process was accompanied by autonomous actions by managers, which further enhanced performance.

Planning and doing may seem like separate activities, and in stable conditions that may be true. In volatile conditions, with markets or technologies changing quickly, people conduct them almost simultaneously. In their study of strategic planning, Whittington *et al.* (2006) conclude that, far from strategising and organising being separate activities

> they become very similar, or even common: in the heat of the moment practitioners may be unable to distinguish the two. (p. 618)

Jennings (2000) shows how companies change their approach to planning as conditions change. A study of the UK electricity generating company PowerGen (now owned by the German company E.on) which was privatised in 1991 traced the evolution since then of the company's corporate planning process. It had retained a formal process with a five-year planning horizon, but it is more devolved. A small central team focuses on overall strategy while business units develop local plans, quickly completing the planning cycle. These changes created a more adaptive style of planning which suited the (new) uncertainty of the business. Grant (2003) also shows how planning systems of large oil companies have changed to deal with uncertainty.

Figure 6.3 shows the seven generic tasks which people can perform when they make a plan. They use them iteratively, often going back to an earlier stage when they find new information that implies, say, that they need to reshape the original goals. And of course they may miss a stage, or spend too little or too much time on them: the figure only indicates a way of analysing the stages of planning.

6.5 Gathering information

Any plan depends on information – including informal, soft information gained from casual encounters with colleagues, as well as formal analyses of economic and market trends.

Chapter 3 outlines the competitive and general environments, and planners usually begin by drawing on information about these. External sources include government economic and demographic statistics, industry surveys and general business intelligence services. Managers also commission market research on, for example, individual shopping patterns, attitudes towards particular firms or brand names, and satisfaction with existing products or services. Many firms use focus groups to test consumer reaction to new products (for more on this see Chapter 9).

Management in practice **Inamo – planning the start-up** www.inamo-restaurant.com

Danny Potter, Managing Director, explained the information they needed before they started:

Well, in terms of market research, we looked into what other interactive ordering restaurants and concepts there might be, a lot of research on the world wide web and just going round London to various restaurants. We also looked at good guides which give you a quick summary. Also meeting people in the industry, going to shows and exhibitions are quick ways of learning a great deal. Also a few brainstorming sessions to get feedback on what people thought of the concept – one piece of feedback from that was that this would not fit a formal French dining environment, for example. We came to the conclusion that Oriental fusion was the appropriate cuisine type.

We spent a great deal of time finding the right location. We went through the government statistics database and built a database of our own, analysing demographics of the whole of London. What we found was that a very small area around central London is really where all the buzz happens, where all of the restaurants want to be. And then focused on finding the right location in this area.

Source: Interview with Danny Potter.

SWOT analysis

A **SWOT analysis** is a way of summarising the organisation's strengths and weaknesses relative to external opportunities and threats.

At a strategic level, planning will usually combine an analysis of external environmental factors with an internal analysis of the organisation's strengths and weaknesses. A **SWOT analysis** does this, bringing together the internal strengths and weaknesses and the external opportunities and threats. Internally, managers would analyse the strengths and weaknesses of the resources within, or available to, the organisation (Grant, 1991), such as a firm's distinctive research capability, or its skill in integrating acquired companies. The external analysis would probably be based on PESTEL and Porter's (1980a) five forces model (see Chapter 3). These tools help to identify the main opportunities and threats that people believe could affect the business.

While the method appears to be a rational way of gathering information, its usefulness depends on recognising that it is a human representation of reality: participants will differ about the significance of factors – a debate which may itself add value to the process (Hodgkinson *et al.,* 2006).

Activity 6.2 **Conducting a SWOT analysis**

Choose one of the companies featured in the text (or any that interests you).

- Gather information from the company's website and other published data to prepare a SWOT analysis.
- Compare your analysis with that of a colleague on your course.
- Identify any differences between you in terms of the factors identified, and the significance given to them. What do those differences tell you about the value of the SWOT method?

Given the diversity and complexity of organisational environments it is easy to have too much information. Managers needs to focus on the few trends and events that are likely to be of greatest significance. De Wit and Meyer (2004) report that planners at Royal Dutch/Shell focus on critical factors such as oil demand (economic), refining capacity (political and economic), the likelihood of government intervention (political) and alternative sources of fuel (technological).

Critical success factors analysis

In considering whether to enter a new market, a widely used planning technique is to assess the **critical success factors** (Leidecker and Bruno, 1984) in that market. These are the things which customers in that particular market most value about a product or service – and they therefore play a key role as people plan whether to move into a line of business. Some value price, others quality, others some curious aspect of the product's features. But in all cases they are things that a company must be able to do well in order to succeed in that market.

> **Critical success factors** are those aspects of a strategy that *must* be achieved to secure competitive advantage.

Forecasting

Forecasts or predictions of the future are often based on an analysis of past trends in factors such as input prices (wages, components, etc.), sales patterns or demographic characteristics. All forecasts are based on assumptions. In relatively simple environments people can reasonably assume that past trends will continue, but in uncertain conditions they need alternative assumptions. A new market might support rapid sales growth, whereas in a saturated market (e.g. basic foods, paid-for newspapers) it might be more realistic to assume a lower or nil growth rate.

> **Optimism bias** refers to a human tendency to judge future events in a more positive light than is warranted by experience.

Forecasting is big business, with companies selling analyses to business and government, using techniques such as time-series analysis, econometric modelling and simulation. However, because forecasts rely heavily on extrapolating past trends, they are of little value as conditions become uncertain. Grant (2003) reports that oil companies have significantly reduced the resources they spend on preparing formal forecasts of oil demand and prices, preferring to rely on broader assumptions about possible trends. Forecasts of cost and demand in major public sector projects are also unreliable (see Key Ideas).

> **Strategic misrepresentation** is where competition for resources leads planners to underestimate costs and overestimate benefits, to increase the likelihood that their project gains approval.

Key ideas   The planning fallacy in large projects

Large public infrastructure projects regularly cost more and deliver less than their promoters promised: Flyvbjerg (2008) quotes research showing that the average cost inaccuracy for rail projects is 44 per cent, for bridges and tunnels 34 per cent, and for roads 20 per cent. He then draws on work by Daniel Kahneman (Lovallo and Kahneman, 2003) which identified a systematic fallacy in planning, whereby people underestimate the costs, completion times and risks of planned actions, whereas they overestimate their benefits. This became known as the 'planning fallacy', which has two sources:

- **optimism bias** – a human tendency to judge future events in a more positive light than is warranted by actual experience; and
- **strategic misrepresentation** – where competition for scarce resources leads forecasters and planners deliberately to underestimate costs and overestimate benefits, to increase the likelihood that their project, not competing ones, gains approval and funding.

Kahneman believes these biases lead planners to take an 'inside view', focusing on the constituents of the plan, rather than an 'outside view' focusing on the outcomes of similar plans that have been completed.

Source: Flyvbjerg (2008).

Sensitivity analysis

A sensitivity analysis tests the effect on a plan of several alternative values of the key variables.

One way to test assumptions is to make a **sensitivity analysis** of key variables in a plan. This may assume that the company will attain a 10 per cent share of a market within a year: what will be the effect on the calculations if they secure 5 per cent or 15 per cent? What if interest rates rise, increasing the cost of financing the projects? Planners can then compare the robustness of the options and assess the relative risks. Johnson *et al.* (2008) give a worked example (pp. 378–379).

Scenario planning

An alternative to forecasting is to consider possible scenarios. Cornelius *et al.* (2005) note:

> scenarios are not projections, predictions or preferences; rather they are coherent and credible stories about the future.

Scenario planning is an attempt to create coherent and credible alternative stories about the future.

Scenario planning typically begin by considering how external forces such as the internet, an ageing population or climate change might affect a company's business over the next five–ten years. Doing so can bring managers new ideas about their environment, enabling them to consider previously unthinkable possibilities. Advocates (Van der Heijden, 1996) claim two benefits. The first is that it discourages reliance on 'single-point forecasting' – a single view of the future; second, it encourages managers to develop alternatives – plans to cope with outcomes that depart from the scenario. Few companies use the technique systematically, as it is time consuming and costly. An exception is at Shell, where:

> Scenario thinking now underpins the established way of thinking at Shell. It has become a part of the culture, such that people throughout the company, dealing with significant decisions, normally will think in terms of multiple, but equally plausible futures to provide a context for decision making. (Van der Heijden, 1996, p. 21)

A combination of PESTEL and five forces analysis should ensure that managers recognise major external factors. Forecasting and scenario planning can help them to consider possible implications for the business.

Management in practice   DSM – business strategy dialogue www.dsm.com

DSM is a Dutch chemical company which has developed a planning process that requires each Business Group to conduct a business strategy dialogue (BSD) every three years. This ensures a consistent method and terminology for the planning process across the company. The reviews have five phases:

- **Characterising the business situation** Collecting information on what business you are in, the competitors, how attractive is the industry (growth, profitability), how do you compare with competitors?
- **Analysing the business system (macro)** Analysing the industry in which the group competes, using Porter's Five Forces model.
- **Analysing the business system (micro)** The internal processes of the business, including its value chain, and strengths and weaknesses.
- **Options and strategic choice** This uses the earlier phases to allow the business managers to choose which strategic option to pursue and what it requires.
- **Action planning and performance measurement** The chosen strategy is then turned into a plan and linked to performance measurement. The team sets performance indicators such as market share, new product development, customer satisfaction and cost per unit of output. These enable managers to monitor implementation.

Source: Based on Bloemhof *et al.*, 2004; company website.

6.6   Setting goals (or objectives)

A clear plan depends on being clear about the ultimate purpose of a task: whether it concerns the organisation or a unit. This seems obvious, but managers favour action above planning (Stewart, 1967) – especially the ambiguities of agreeing on goals (sometimes called objectives). Yet until people clarify goals they make little progress.

Goals (or objectives)

Goals give focus to a task: what will we achieve, by when? Setting goals is difficult as we have to look beyond a (relatively) known present to an unknown future. Bond *et al.* (2008) asked people to set objectives for a personally relevant task (finding a good job) – and they consistently omitted nearly half of the objectives that they later identified as important, when these were drawn to their attention. The researchers secured the same results in a software company.

Goals provide the reference point for other decisions, and the criteria against which to measure performance. At the business level they include quantified financial objectives – earnings per share, return on shareholders' funds and cash flow. At the project level the targets will be expressed in other ways (see Management in Practice).

Management in practice   **Environmental targets at Heathrow Terminal 5**

Building Terminal 5 was an opportunity to embed environmentally sustainable practices into every aspect of the terminal's operation. An environmental assessment group identified several sustainability focus areas, which evolved into the project requirements and then into environmental targets such as:

Aspect	Key performance indicator	Target
Water	Potable water use	70% cut in potable water use (more from other sources)
	Water consumption	25 litres/passenger
Pollution control	Total harmful emissions to water	Capture 25% of surface water runoff for re-use
Waste	Waste recycled/composted	40% by 2010, 80% by 2020
Resource use	Compliance with T5 materials	40% of coarse aggregate in concrete to be re-cycled

Source: Lister (2008).

Activity 6.3   **Developing goals**

- Go to the websites of some companies that interest you and collect examples of planning goals.
- Does the organisation or unit for which you work have stated planning goals? If so, how were they developed?
- Gather examples of goals at either organisational, operational or activity levels. If you can, ask those affected by them about the process by which they were set. Also ask if this has affected their attitudes towards them.

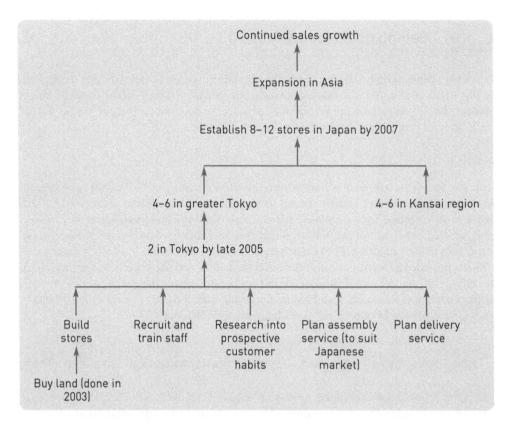

Figure 6.4
Developing a plan
for Ikea (Japan)

A hierarchy of goals

A way of relating goals to each other is to build them into a hierarchy, in which the overall goals are transformed into more specific goals for different parts of the organization, such as marketing, finance, operations and human resources. Managers in those areas develop plans setting out the actions they must undertake in order to meet the overall goal. Figure 6.4 illustrates this by using Ikea's plan to expand in Japan. To meet its planned sales growth, managers decided to open many stores across Asia, of which the first were to be in Japan. That evolved into a plan for their probable location, and then into a precise plan for two near Tokyo. That in turn led managers to develop progressively more detailed plans for the thousands of details that will need to be in good order if the venture is to succeed.

Plans such as this need to be flexible, as they will need to change between design and completion. Managers often stress their firm commitment to the highest-level goals – but leave staff with more discretion about how to achieve lower-level plans.

However convincingly set out, statements of goals only have value if they guide action. Effective goal setting involves balancing multiple goals, considering whether they meet the SMART criteria (see 'Criteria for assessing goals'), and evaluating their likely motivational effects.

Single or multiple goals?

Company statements of goals – whether long or short term – are usually expressed in the plural, since a single measure cannot indicate success or failure. Emphasis on one goal, such as growth, ignores another, such as dividends. Managers balance multiple, possibly conflicting goals: Gerry Murphy, who became chief executive of Kingfisher (a UK DIY retailer), recalled:

> Alan Sheppard, my boss at Grand Metropolitan and one of my mentors, used to say that senior management shouldn't have the luxury of single point objectives. Delivering growth without returns or returns without growth is not something I find attractive or acceptable. Over time we are going to do both. (*Financial Times*, 28 April 2004, p. 23)

As senior managers try to take account of a range of stakeholders, they balance their diverse interests. This can lead to conflict between **stated goals**, as reflected in public announcements, and the **real goals** – those to which people give most attention. The latter reflect senior managers' priorities, expressed through what they say and how they reward and discipline managers.

Stated goals are those which are prominent in company publications and websites.

Real goals are those to which people give most attention.

Criteria for assessing goals

The SMART acronym summarises some criteria for assessing a set of goals. What form of each is effective depends on circumstances (specific goals are not necessarily better than directional ones). The list simply offers some measures against which to evaluate a statement of goals.

- **Specific** Does the goal set specific targets? People who are planning a meeting can set specific goals for what they hope to achieve, such as:

  > By the end of the meeting we will have convinced them to withdraw their current proposal, and to have set a date (within the next two weeks) at which we will start to develop an alternative plan.

  Having a clear statement of what the meeting (or any other activity in a plan) is intended to achieve helps people to focus effort.
- **Measurable** Some goals may be quantified ('increase sales of product X by 5 per cent a year over the next three years') but others, equally important, are more qualitative ('to offer a congenial working environment'). Quantitative goals are not more useful than qualitative ones – what can be measured is not necessarily important. The important point is that goals be defined precisely enough to measure progress towards them.
- **Attainable** Goals should be challenging, but not unreasonably difficult. If people perceive a goal as unrealistic, they will not be committed. Equally, goals should not be too easy, as they too undermine motivation. Goal setting theory (see the following Key Ideas) predicts the motivational consequences of goal setting.
- **Rewarded** People need to see that attaining a goal will bring a reward – this gives meaning and help ensure commitment.
- **Timed** Does the goal specify the time over which it will be achieved, and is that also a reasonable and acceptable standard?

| Key ideas | Practical uses of goal-setting theory |

Goal theory offers some practical implications for those making plans:

- **Goal difficulty**: set goals for work performance at levels that will stretch employees but are just within their ability.
- **Goal specificity**: express goals in clear, precise and, if possible, quantifiable terms, and avoid setting ambiguous or confusing goals.
- **Participation**: where practicable, encourage staff to take part in setting goals to increase their commitment to achieving them.
- **Feedback**: provide information on the results of performance to allow people to adjust their behaviour and perhaps improve their achievement of future plans.

Source: Locke and Latham (2002).

Evaluating a statement of goals

- Choose a significant plan that someone has produced in your organisation within the last year. Is it SMART? Then try to set out how you would amend the goals to meet these criteria more fully. Alternatively, comment on how the criteria set out in the text could be modified, in the light of your experience with these goals.

6.7   Identifying actions and allocating resources

This part of the planning process involves deciding what needs to be done, who will do it and communicating that information. In a small activity such as planning a project in a club this would just mean listing the tasks and dividing them clearly among a few able and willing members. At the other extreme, Ford's plan to build a new car plant in China probably runs to several volumes.

Identifying what needs to be done – and by whom

Figure 1.3 (reproduced here again as Figure 6.5) provides a model to help envisage the implications of a goal, by enabling managers to ask what, if any, changes they need to be make to each element.

If the goal is to launch a new product, the plan could identify which parts of the organisation will be affected (structure), what investment is needed (finance), how production will fit with existing lines (business processes) and so on. New technology projects often fail because planners pay too much attention to the technological aspects, and too little to contextual

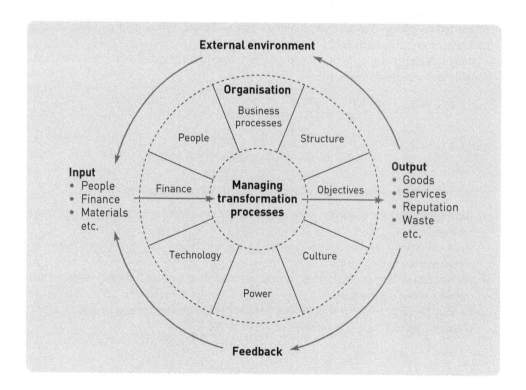

Figure 6.5
Possible action areas in a plan

elements such as structure, culture and people (Boddy *et al.* 2009b). Each main heading will require further actions that people can identify and assign.

Lynch (2003) points out that managers handle this aspect of planning comprehensively, incrementally or selectively.

- **Comprehensive (specific) plan** This happens if managers decide to make a clear-cut change in direction, in response to a reassessment of the market, a financial crisis or a technological development. They assume that success depends on driving the changes rapidly and in a co-ordinated way across the organisation – which implies a comprehensive plan.
- **Incremental (directional) plan** People use this approach in uncertain conditions, such as volatile markets or when direction depends on the outcomes of research and development. Tasks, times and even the objective are likely to change as the outcomes of current and planned activities become known; 'Important strategic areas may be left deliberately unclear until the outcomes of current events have been established' (Lynch, 2003, p. 633).
- **Selective plan** This approach may work when neither of the other methods is the best way forward, such as when managers wish to make a comprehensive change, but are unable to do so because of deep opposition in some area affected by the plan. They may then try to implement the major change in only some areas of the business which, while not their preferred choice, may enable them to make some progress towards the objectives.

Communicating the plan

In a small organisation or where the plan deals with only one area, communication in any formal way is probably unnecessary. Equally, those who have been involved in developing the objectives and plans will be well aware of it. However, in larger enterprises managers will probably invest time and effort in communicating both the objectives and the actions required throughout the areas affected. They do this to:

- ensure that everyone understands the plan;
- allow them to resolve any confusion and ambiguity;
- communicate the judgements and assumptions that underlie the plan;
- ensure that activities around the organisation are co-ordinated in practice as well as on paper.

6.8 Implementing plans and monitoring progress

However good the plan, nothing worthwhile happens until people implement it, acting to make visible, physical changes to the organisation and the way people work within it. Many managers find this the most challenging part of the process – when plans, however well developed, are brought into contact with the processes people expect them to change. Those implementing the plan then come up against a variety of organisational and environmental obstacles – and possibly find that some of the assumptions in the plan are incorrect.

Organisations are slower to change than plans are to prepare, so events may overtake the plan. Miller *et al.* (2004) tracked the long-term outcomes of 150 strategic plans to establish how managers put them into action and how that affected performance. They defined implementation as:

> all the processes and outcomes which accrue to a strategic decision once authorisation has been given to . . . put the decision into practice. (Miller *et al.*, 2004, p. 203)

Their intention was to identify the conditions in which implementation occurs, the managerial activities involved in putting plans into practice, and the extent to which they achieved the objectives. They concluded that success was heavily influenced by:

- managers' experience of the issue, and
- **organisational readiness** for a change.

Organisational
readiness refers to the
extent to which staff are
able to specify
objectives, tasks and
resource requirements of
a plan appropriately,
leading to acceptance.

> Having relevant experience of what has to be done . . . enables managers to assess the objectives [and to] specify the tasks and resource implications appropriately, leading [those affected to accept the process].' (Miller *et al.*, 2004, p. 206)

Readiness means a receptive organisational climate that enables managers to implement the change within a positive environment.

The statistical results were illustrated by cases that showed, for example, how managers in a successful company were able to implement a plan to upgrade their computer systems because they had *experience* of many similar changes. They were able to set targets, detail what needed doing and allocate the resources. That is, they could plan and control the implementation effectively. In another illustration, a regional brewer extending into the London area had no directly relevant experience, and so was not able to set a specific plan. But people in the organisation were very *receptive* to new challenges, and could implement the move with little formal planning.

The authors concluded that the activities of planning do not in themselves lead to success, but are a means for gaining acceptance of what has to be done when it is implemented. Planning helps by inducing confidence in the process, leading to high levels of acceptability:

> Planning is a necessary part of this approach to success, but it is not sufficient in itself. (Miller *et al.*, 2004, p. 210)

The final stage in planning is to set up a system that allows people to monitor progress towards the goals. This happens at all levels of planning – from a project manager monitoring and controlling the progress of a discrete project to a Board committee monitoring the progress of a broad strategic change that affects many parts of the business, such as integrating an acquisition or entering a new line of business. This is sometimes called a programme, and monitoring then focuses on the interdependencies between many smaller specific projects.

Project plans define and display every task and activity, but someone managing a programme of linked projects would soon become swamped with such detail. The programme manager needs to maintain a quick-to-understand snapshot of the programme. This should show progress to date, the main events being planned, interdependencies, issues and expected completion dates. This also helps the programme manager to communicate with senior executives and project managers. One way to do this is to create a single chart with a simplified view of each project on an indicative timeline. Figure 6.6 illustrates this. Details vary but the main features are usually:

- An indicative timeline, along which the individual projects are plotted.
- A simplified representation of the major milestones in each project or change area.
- Descriptions of progress made against that expected for each project.
- Indications of interdependencies between projects.

6.9   Integrating themes

Sustainable performance

Many companies are responding to the challenges posed by climate change, and are developing policies to reduce carbon emissions and other environmentally damaging practices. Such policy statements depend on the quality of the plans that managers develop – unless they make detailed plans, they will be no more than good intentions. In 2007 Marks & Spencer announced 'Plan A' – which by 2009 had delivered significant benefits to the environment (such as having diverted 20,000 tonnes of waste from landfill) and to the company (cost savings of about £50 million).

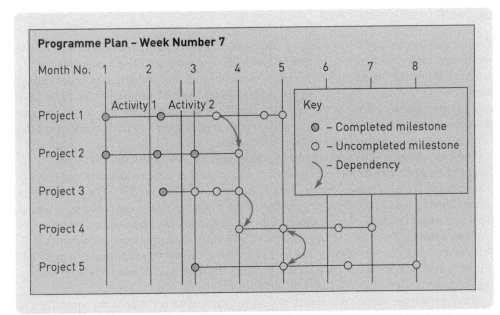

Figure 6.6
A programme
overview chart
Source: Boddy *et al.*
(2009a).

In March 2010 the company launched a programme to become the world's most sustainable retailer by 2015. To achieve this it will extend Plan A to cover all of its 36,000 product lines, so that each carries at least one sustainable or ethical quality, and to fully embed sustainability into the way the company and its suppliers do business. The new Plan A commitments are divided into seven areas:

1 **Customers and Plan A** – to help customers to live more sustainable lives.
2 **Make Plan A part of how we do business** – to accelerate our moves to make Plan A 'how we do business'.
3 **Tackling climate change** – make operations in the UK and Republic of Ireland carbon neutral.
4 **Packaging and waste** – stop sending waste to landfill from stores, offices and warehouses, reduce use of packaging and carrier bags, and find new ways to recycle and reuse the materials.
5 **Being a fair partner** – improve the lives of hundreds of thousands of people in the supply chain and local communities.
6 **Natural resources** – ensure that key raw materials come from the most sustainable source possible, in order to protect the environment and the world's natural resources.
7 **Health and well-being** – helping thousands of customers and employees to choose a healthier lifestyle.

Source: Company website (**www.marksandspencer.com**)

In each of these areas more detailed plans will be required to bring the plan into reality – including ensuring that suppliers also plan changes in the way that they operate.

Activity 6.5	Progress towards the goals of Plan A

- Visit the Marks & Spencer website and navigate to the Plan A pages. These explain the plan fully, and also include current information on progress towards the target.
- Identify a theme that interests you, and find out how Marks & Spencer is implementing the plan, and what progress it has made.

Governance and control

Glaister and Travers (2001) give a graphic account of the range of interests who have invested significant capital or other resources in Crossrail, and who are closely interested in its progress. While the broad project plan has been approved and construction is beginning, managers will face many decisions as the project is implemented, some of which could have serious consequences for one or more parties. They have therefore put in governance arrangements to ensure that, as far as possible, the project team acts in the interests of the Crossrail sponsors – whose interests may well conflict.

The most obvious of these mechanisms is the company structure. Crossrail Limited is the company charged with delivering Crossrail. It was created in 2001 to promote and develop new lines and is a wholly owned subsidiary of Transport for London (TfL). The ten members of the Crossrail Board include representatives of the project sponsors and partners, as well as those appointed for their relevant expertise in, say, finance or law. Sponsors are the Mayor of London (through TfL) and the Department of Transport. Other partners are Network Rail, British Airports Authority (BAA), The City of London, Canary Wharf Group (property developers) and Berkeley Homes (residential property developers). The executive team managing the project report regularly to the Main Board.

Among the issues that they will seek regular reassurance on is the financial control of the project. The Key Ideas feature on page 179 shows that infrastructure projects often cost more than expected. A function of the Main Board will be to monitor how executives manage the project to ensure it stays within budgeted costs, especially as public funds to cover any excess costs will be very hard to secure in the foreseeable financial climate.

Internationalisation

A theme in all international businesses is the extent to which they should plan the business on a global scale, or leave local managers with autonomy to adapt to local conditions. As Chapter 4 points out, the globalisation of markets was observed, and advocated, by Theodore Levitt, who noted the trend in the early 1980s for global brands to displace local products, with identical goods being sold across the globe without modification.

Management in practice   **Coca-Cola finds formula for India** www.cocacola.com

Coca-Cola India totally misjudged rural India, home to two-thirds of the country's 1 billion population, when it re-entered the country in 1993. It paid a high price for the then market leader, Thumbs Up, and then tried to kill it off in the mistaken belief that this would pave the way for Coca-Cola's rise. The approach failed – best illustrated by the fact that India is one of the few markets where Pepsi-Cola leads Coca-Cola. 'We were just not addressing the masses', admitted Sanjeev Gupta, Coca-Cola's operations chief. In 2000, management decided to change their approach, by focusing on the distinctive needs of the Indian rural consumer. This meant using smaller bottles, lower prices, more outlets and an advertising campaign (featuring Bollywood stars) that makes sense to villagers as well as city dwellers.

Source: Extracts from an article by Khozem Merchant, *Financial Times*, 18 June 2003.

This approach began to lose favour, so companies began adapting products to suit local tastes (see the above Management in Practice). The dilemma is how far to plan globally, and how much to leave to local managers. Managers typically identify some features that are important to the overall health of the brand, such as ingredients or design, and are likely to plan these issues at the global level. They leave other matters, such as choice of suppliers or methods of distribution, to local planners. Establishing that balance in planning is likely to affect the value they add.

Summary

1 **Explain the purposes of planning and the content of different types of plan**
   - Effective plans can clarify direction, motivate people, use resources efficiently and allow people to measure progress towards objectives.
   - Plans can be at strategic, tactical and operational levels, and, in new businesses, people prepare business plans to secure capital. Strategic business units also prepare plans relatively independently of the parent. There are also special-purpose or project plans, and standing plans. All can be either specific or directional in nature.

2 **Compare alternative planning processes and evaluate when each may be most suitable**
   - Plans can be formal/rational/top down in nature, or they can be adaptable and flexible (logical incrementalism); accumulating evidence that a combination of approaches most likely to suit firms in volatile conditions.

3 **Outline the seven iterative steps in planning and describe techniques used in each**
   - Recycling through the tasks of gathering information, developing a mission, setting goals, identifying actions and allocating resources, implementing plans, monitoring progress and evaluating results.
   - Planners draw information from the general and competitive environments using tools such as Porter's Five Forces Analysis. They can do this within the framework of a SWOT analysis, and also use forecasting, sensitivity analysis, critical success factors and scenario planning techniques.

4 **Use theory to evaluate the motivational effect of the goals stated in a plan**
   - Goal setting theory predicts that goals can be motivational if people perceive the targets to be difficult but achievable.
   - Goals can also be evaluated in terms of whether they are specific, measurable, attainable, rewarded or timed.

5 **Use a framework to evaluate whether a plan is sufficiently comprehensive**
   - The 'wheel' provides a model for recalling the likely areas in an organisation which a plan should cover, indicating the likely ripple effects of change in one area on others.

6 **Evaluate the context which will affect the ability of managers to implement a plan**
   - The value of a plan depends on people implementing it, but Miller's research shows that that depends on the experience of those implementing it, and the receptivity of the organisation to change.

7 **Show how ideas from the chapter can add to your understanding of the integrating themes**
   - Long-term sustainability depends on organisations making equally long-term plans, which many organisations, such as M&S, are beginning to do.
   - Complex, one-off, projects such as those in construction and information technology, require effective high-level governance and control systems to ensure that the many diverse and possibly conflicting interests work together.
   - Companies operating internationally increasingly try to customise their products for local markets to reflect varying customer preferences. This affects not only the product but also product advice, packaging and distribution methods – and is a significant planning activity in such firms.

Review questions

1 What types of planning do you do in your personal life? Describe them in terms of whether they are (a) strategic or operational, (b) short or long term, and (c) specific or directional.

2 What are four benefits that people in organisations may gain from planning?

3 What are the main sources of information that managers can use in planning? What models can they use to structure this information?

4 What are SMART goals?

5 In what ways can a goal be motivational? What practical things can people do in forming plans that take account of goal-setting theory?

6 What is meant by the term 'hierarchy of goals', and how can that idea help people to build a consistent plan?

7 Explain the term 'organisational readiness', and how people can use the idea in developing a plan that is more likely to work.

8 What are the main ways of monitoring progress on a plan, and why is this so vital a task in planning?

9 Summarise an idea from the chapter that adds to your understanding of the integrating themes.

Concluding critical reflection

Think about the way your company, or one with which you are familiar, makes plans. Review the material in the chapter, and perhaps visit some of the websites identified. Then make notes on the following questions:

- What examples of the themes discussed in this chapter are currently relevant to your company? What types of plans are you most closely involved with? Which of the techniques suggested do you and your colleagues typically use and why? What techniques do you use that are not mentioned here?

- In responding to these issues, what **assumptions** about the nature of planning in business appear to guide your approach? Are the prevailing assumptions closer to the planning or emergent perspectives? Why do you think that is?

- What factors in the **context** of the company appear to shape your approach to planning – what kind of environment are you working in, for example? To what extent does your planning process involve people from other organizations? Why is that?

- Have you compared your planning processes with those in other companies to check if they use **alternative** methods to yours? How do they plan?

- Have you considered the **limitations** of your approach – such as whether you plan too much, or too little? What limitations can you see in some of the ideas presented here – for example the usefulness of scenario planning or SWOT analyses?

Further reading

Grant, R.M. (2003), 'Strategic planning in a turbulent environment: Evidence from the oil majors', *Strategic Management Journal*, vol. 24, no. 6, pp. 491–517.

> Empirical study of the strategic planning systems in major international oil companies, and how these aim to cope with uncertainty in that industry.

Latham, G.P. and Locke, E.A. (2006), 'Enhancing the benefits and overcoming the pitfalls of goal setting', *Organizational Dynamics*, vol. 35, no. 4, pp. 332–340.

Leidecker, J.K. and Bruno, A.V. (1984), 'Identifying and using critical success factors', *Long Range Planning*, vol. 17, no. 1, pp. 23–32.

This useful article identifies eight possible sources for identifying critical success factors, gives examples, and suggests ways of assessing their relative importance.

Sahlman, W.A. (1997), 'How to write a great business plan', *Harvard Business Review*, vol. 75, no. 4, pp. 98–108.

Valuable guidance by an experienced investor, relevant to start-ups and established businesses.

Whittington, R., Molloy, E., Mayer, M. and Smith, A. (2006), 'Practices of strategising/organising: Broadening strategy work and skills', *Long Range Planning*, vol. 39, no. 6, pp. 615–629.

Weblinks

These websites have appeared in the chapter:

www.crossrail.co.uk
www.maersk.com
www.ba.com
www.sabmiller.com
www.merck.com
www.dsm.com
www.marksandspencer.com
www.inamo-restaurant.com
www.cocacola.com

Visit two of the sites in the list, and navigate to the pages dealing with corporate news or investor relations.

- What planning issues can you identify that managers in the company are likely to be dealing with?
- What kind of environment are they likely to be working in, and how will that affect their planning methods and processes?

 For video case studies, audio summaries, flashcards, exercises and annotated weblinks related to this chapter, visit **www.pearsoned.co.uk/mymanagementlab**

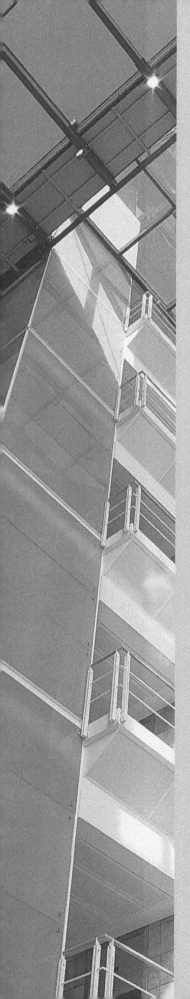

CHAPTER 7
DECISION MAKING

Aims

To identify major aspects of decision making in organisations and to outline alternative ways of making decisions.

Objectives

By the end of your work on this chapter you should be able to outline the concepts below in your own terms and:

1 Outline the (iterative) stages of the decision making process and the tasks required in each

2 Explain, and give examples of, programmed and non-programmed decisions

3 Distinguish decision-making conditions of certainty, risk, uncertainty and ambiguity

4 Contrast rational, administrative, political and garbage-can decision models

5 Give examples of common sources of bias in decisions

6 Explain the contribution of Vroom and Yetton, and of Irving Janis, to our understanding of decision making

7 Show how ideas from the chapter add to your understanding of the integrating themes

Key terms

This chapter introduces the following ideas:

decision
decision making
problem
opportunity
decision criteria
decision tree
programmed decision
procedure
rule
policy
non-programmed decision
certainty
risk
uncertainty
ambiguity

rational model of decision making
administrative model of
   decision making
bounded rationality
satisficing
incremental model
political model
heuristics
prior hypothesis bias
representativeness bias
optimism bias
illusion of control
escalation of commitment
groupthink

Each is a term defined within the text, as well as in the Glossary at the end of the book.

Case study   Ikea   www.ikea.com

In early 2010 there were over 300 Ikea home furnishing stores in 38 countries: the stores had generated sales of over 22 billion euros in 2009. This represented a slower rate of increase than usual, as the recession had affected demand. The company had also decided to slow the rate at which it would open new stores, and to reduce the 130,000 co-workers it employs by about 5,000.

The Ikea Concept is founded on a low-price offer in home furnishings. It aims to offer a wide range of well-designed home furnishing products at prices so low that as many people as possible can afford them. The way Ikea products are designed, manufactured, transported, sold and assembled contributes to transforming the Concept into reality.

The Concept began when Ingvar Kamprad, a Swedish entrepreneur, had the idea of offering well-designed furniture at low prices. He decided to achieve this not by cutting quality but by applying simple cost-cutting solutions to manufacture and distribution. Its first showroom opened in 1953 and until 1963 all the stores were in Sweden. In that year the international expansion began with a store in Norway: it has entered one new country in almost every year since then.

The objective of the parent company, Inter Ikea Systems BV, is to increase availability of Ikea products by the worldwide franchising of the Ikea Concept. It operates very large stores close to major cities. Ikea employs its own designers, although other companies manufacture most of the products. It is renowned for modern innovative design, and for supplying large products in a form that customers must assemble themselves. An example of its innovative approach is 'Children's Ikea', introduced in 1997. The company worked with child psychologists to develop products that would help children develop their motor skills, social development and creativity. Children helped to make the final selection of the range.

The company employs about 130,000 staff – whom it calls co-workers. In 1999 Ingvar Kamprad initiated the Big Thank You Event as a millennium reward for the co-workers. The total value of all sales on that day was divided equally among everyone in the company. For most it was more than a month's pay.

© Inter Ikea Systems BV 2006.

The company vision is to create a better everyday life for many people, and acknowledges that it is the co-workers who make that possible. They aim to give people the possibility to grow both as individuals and in their professional roles 'we are strongly committed to creating a better life for ourselves and our customers'. In its recruitment the company looks for people who share the company's values which include togetherness, cost-consciousness, respect and simplicity. The website explains that, as well as being able to do the job, the company seeks people with many other personal qualities such as a strong desire to learn, the motivation to continually do things better, simplicity and common sense, the ability to lead by example, efficiency and cost-consciousness:

These values are important to us because our way of working is less structured than at many other organisations.

Source: Company website.

Case questions 7.1

- Make a note of the decisions which have appeared in the story so far.
- How have they affected the development of the business?
- Visit the company's website and note examples of recent decisions which have shaped the company.

7.1   Introduction

The case recounts the recent history of one of Europe's biggest and most successful companies, which is now a global player in the home furnishing market. To develop the business from a Swedish general retailer to its present position, senior managers at Ikea needed to decide where to allocate time, effort and other resources. Over the years their decisions paid off and they now face new issues, such as how to attract customers and well-qualified staff against competition from established global companies. They also face critical comments from environmental campaigners about their sources of timber, and need to decide how to respond. How they do so will shape Ikea's future.

The performance of every organisation reflects (as well as luck and good fortune) the decisions that people make, and there are many studies of the activity – Buchanan and O'Connell (2006) provide a historical review. People at all levels of an organisation continually make choices as they see problems that need attention or ideas they may be able to use. Resources are limited, there are many demands and people have different goals. Choices relate to all aspects of the management task: inputs (how to raise capital, who to employ), outputs (what products to make, how to distribute them) and transformations (how to deliver a new service, how to manage the finances). Decisions affect how well the organisation uses resources, and whether it adds sufficient value to ensure survival.

> Like management itself, decision-making is a generic process that is applicable to all forms of organised activity. (Harrison, 1999, p. 8)

Choice brings tension as it makes us worry about 'what if' we had selected the other option (Schwartz, 2004). Speed is sometimes more important than certainty: the chief executive of Eli Lilly (pharmaceuticals) recalled that when he took over he realised the company needed to make decisions more quickly:

> We've had the luxury of moving at our own pace. Sometimes you can think for so long that your competitors pass you by. We need to act with 80 per cent, not 99.5 per cent, of the information.

He gives the example of a biotech company for which a rival company made a take-over offer, triggering a rapid and ultimately successful counter-bid from Lilly.

> We had them on our radar, and we had no premonition the other company would bid. But we were well-prepared and, within a couple of days, we convinced ourselves that we should get into the process. (From an article by John Lechleiter, *Financial Times*, 6 April 2009)

Figure 7.1 illustrates the themes of the chapter, showing that decision making involves:

- identifying the type of decision;
- identifying the conditions surrounding the decision;
- using one or more models to guide the approach;
- selecting a decision-making style;
- working through the process and implementing the decision.

This chapter outlines the iterative steps in any decision process, and explains the difference between decisions that are called 'programmed' and those that are 'non-programmed'. It identifies four 'conditions' surrounding a decision, compares four models of the process, shows how bias affects decisions and finally examines how managers can shape the context of decision making.

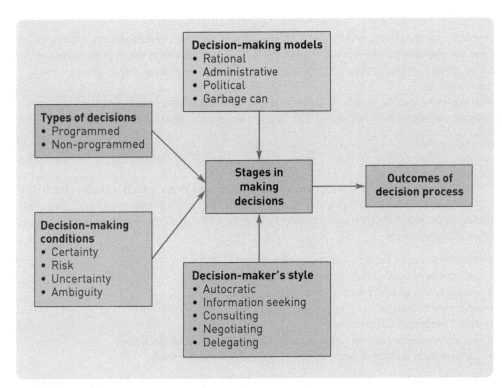

Figure 7.1
Overview of decision
making in
organisations

Activity 7.1 **Questions about a decision**

Identify a management decision of which you are aware. You may find it helpful to discuss this with a manager you know, or use an activity you have managed.

- Note what the decision involved, and what was decided.
- Was it an easy decision to make, or complex and messy? What made it so?
- How did those involved make the decision? Note just two or three main points
- Did you (and they) consider the outcome of the decision satisfactory or not? Why was that?

7.2 **Stages in making decisions**

A **decision** is a specific commitment to action (usually a commitment of resources). People make such choices at all levels: some affecting the business significantly (Barclay's Bank deciding during the 2008 banking crisis to raise capital privately, rather than accept support from the UK government – RBS and HBOS made the opposite decision). Others affect local operations: whether to recruit staff, how much to spend on advertising next week.

A decision is a specific commitment to action (usually a commitment of resources).

Management in practice **Deciding which treatment to provide** www.nice.org.uk

Expenditure on healthcare is limited by competing demands for public funds, while scientific advances bring new treatments to prolong life, and so increase the demand for services from an aging population.

This means that managers at all levels in the health service decide how to ration care; which patients or conditions should receive treatment, and which not. Most of this is done implicitly, by those at the centre, setting budgets for the units delivering care: their managers must then ration care to stay within budget.

Others are made explicitly, by specifying criteria about which patients, or which conditions, are eligible for treatment. In the UK the National Institute for Clinical Excellence (NICE) decides which drugs or technologies are cost effective. It then gives explicit guidance to hospitals on whether, and in what circumstances, they should use them to treat patients.

The committees making these decisions include representatives of medical and patient interests, as well as those of the pharmaceutical industries. They make their (sometimes controversial) decisions public.

Sources: Published information; NICE website.

Decision making is the process of identifying problems and opportunities and then resolving them.

Such choices are part of a wider process of **decision making** – which includes identifying problems, opportunities and possible solutions, and involves effort before and after the actual choice. In deciding whether to select Jean, Bob or Rasul for a job, the manager would, among other things, have to:

- identify the need for a new member of staff;
- perhaps persuade his/her boss to authorise the budget;
- decide where to advertise the post;
- interview candidates;
- select the preferred candidate;
- decide whether or not to agree to his/her request for a better deal; and
- arrange their induction into the job so that they work effectively.

At each of these stages the manager may go back in the process to think again, or to deal with another set of decisions – such as who to include on the selection committee. In Nokia's case the choice of model would follow decisions about the target market and basic design concept, and lead to decisions about production volumes and price. A manager makes small but potentially significant decisions all the time: which of several urgent jobs to deal with next; whose advice to seek; which report to read; which customer to call. These shape the way that people use their time, and the issues which they decide are sufficiently important to place on the agenda.

As we make decisions we attend to the tasks shown in Figure 7.2. The arrows show the iterative nature of the process, as we move back and forwards between the tasks. As we move through an activity we find new information, reconsider what we are doing, go back a stage or two and perhaps decide on a different route. People may miss a stage, or give too much attention to one topic and too little to others. Giving just enough time to each stage is a decision-making skill.

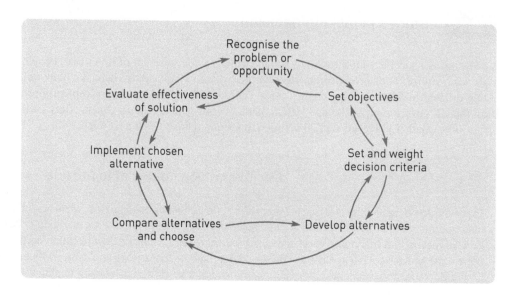

Figure 7.2
Stages in making decisions

Key ideas   Paul Nutt on 'idea discovery' and 'idea imposition'

Paul Nutt studied over 400 decisions involving major commitments of resources. He distinguished between an 'idea discovery process' which usually led to success, and an 'idea imposition process' which usually led to failure. Decision makers select tactics that push their process towards one or other of these types, and Nutt argues that, by being aware of these, managers have a better chance of success than failure.

Those following a discovery process spend time at the start looking beyond the initial claim that 'a problem has arisen that requires a decision': they spend time *understanding the claims* – by talking to stakeholders to judge the strength of their concerns and their views. This leads to a better-informed expression of the 'arena of action' on which to take a decision. They also identify at the outset the forces that may block them from *implementing the preferred idea*, as this helps to understand the interests of stakeholders whose support may be required.

These early actions enable decision makers *to set a direction* – an agreed outcome of the decision. Dealing thoroughly with these three stages makes the remaining stages – *uncovering and evaluating ideas* – comparatively easy, as they help build agreement on what the decision is expected to achieve.

Those following an idea imposition process

skip some stages . . . jump to conclusions and then try to implement the solution they have stumbled upon. This bias for action causes them to limit their search, consider very few ideas, and pay too little attention to people who are affected, despite the fact that decisions fail for just these reasons. (Nutt, 2002, p. 49)

Analysis of more decisions (Nutt, 2008) confirmed that decision makers were as likely to use the failure-prone 'idea imposition process' as they were to use the (usually more successful) 'discovery process'.

Sources: Nutt (2002, 2008).

Recognising a problem or opportunity

People make decisions which commit time and other resources towards an objective. They do so when they become aware of a **problem** – a gap between an existing and a desired state of affairs – or an **opportunity** – the chance to do something not previously expected. An example to illustrate the steps is a manager who needs to decide whether to buy new laptops for the sales team, who say that the machines they have are too slow and waste their time – so they are presenting the manager with a clear problem. Most situations are more ambiguous, and people will have different views about the significance of an event or a piece of information: labelling a problem as significant is a subjective, possibly contentious matter. Before a problem (or opportunity) gets onto the agenda, enough people have to be aware of it and feel sufficient pressure to act. Managers at Microsoft were slow to realise that Linux software was a serious threat to their growth, and this delay lost valuable time.

A **problem** is a gap between an existing and a desired state of affairs.

An **opportunity** is the chance to do something not previously expected.

Management in practice   The opportunity for Iris   www.irisnation.com

Ian Millner explains the decision to start Iris:

We started about ten years ago, and we were essentially a group of friends all working within a really large advertising agency group, and we just decided that we could do it better. And then I guess one thing led to another and before we knew it we were having conversations with one of the clients that we had at the time, which was Eriksson. Once we had that conversation Iris was quite quickly born, and then over a period of months, myself and those friends, we sort of left the building and set Iris up.

I think without doubt the biggest success that we've had is around momentum and being able to keep the momentum high and continue to change as we've gone from being a small company which is just defined by a group of friends, to a large company that is global, expanding really quickly and driving the strategic agenda of a lot of clients all over the world. We've always had a strong entrepreneurial streak, we've always been willing to try things and learn quickly.

Source: Interview with Ian Millner.

Managers become aware of a problem as they compare existing conditions with the state they desire. If things are not as they should be – the sales reps are complaining that their slow laptops prevent them doing their jobs properly – then there is a problem. People are only likely to act if they feel pressure, such as a rep threatening to leave or a customer complaining. Pressure comes from many sources, and people differ in whether they pay attention: some react quickly, others ignore uncomfortable information and postpone a difficult (to them) decision.

Setting and weighting the decision criteria

Decision criteria define the factors that are relevant in making a decision.

To decide between options people need **decision criteria**: the factors that are relevant to the decision. Until people set these, they cannot choose between options: in the laptop case, criteria could include usefulness of features, price, delivery, warranty, compatibility with other systems, ease of use and many more. Some criteria are more important than others and the decision process needs to represent this in some way, perhaps by assigning 100 points between the factors depending on their relative importance. We can measure some of these criteria (price or delivery) quite objectively, while others (features, ease of use) are subjective.

Like problem recognition, setting criteria is subjective: people vary in the factors they wish to include, and the weights they give them. They may also have private and unexpressed criteria, such as 'will cause least trouble', 'will do what the boss wants' or 'will help my career'. Changing the criteria or their relative weights will change the decision: so the manager in the laptop case has to decide whether to set and weight the criteria him/herself, or to invite the views of the reps.

Developing alternatives

Another task is to identify solutions: in the laptop case this is just a list of available brands. In more complex problems the alternatives need to be developed but how many and at what cost? Too few will limit choice, but too many will be costly. Schwartz (2004) found that giving people more choices beyond a certain point is counter-productive as it leads to stress, frustration and anxiety about making the wrong decision (see Key Ideas).

Key ideas   **Too many jams to choose**

Iyengar and Lepper (2000) demonstrated that consumers protect themselves from the stress of too much choice by refusing to purchase. In an experiment conducted in a food store, they set up a tasting booth offering different types of jam. When 24 types were on display, about 60 per cent of passers-by stopped at the booth, compared with just 40 per cent when only six jams were shown. But when it came to choosing a pot of jam to buy, the proportions changed. Just 3 per cent of the visits to the 24-jam booth resulted in a purchase, while 30 per cent of those who visited the smaller display made a purchase. The limited selection was the most effective in converting interest into sales.

Source: Iyengar and Lepper (2000).

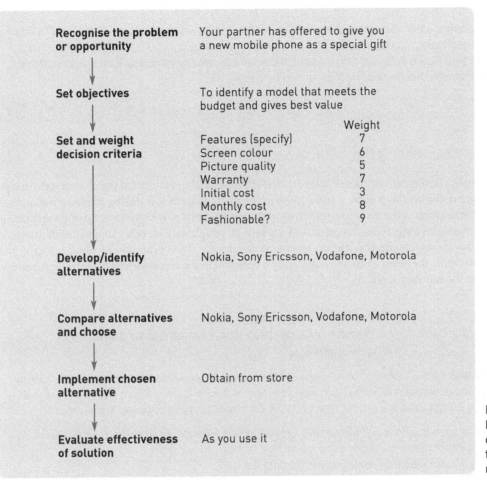

Recognise the problem or opportunity	Your partner has offered to give you a new mobile phone as a special gift	
Set objectives	To identify a model that meets the budget and gives best value	
Set and weight decision criteria		Weight
	Features (specify)	7
	Screen colour	6
	Picture quality	5
	Warranty	7
	Initial cost	3
	Monthly cost	8
	Fashionable?	9
Develop/identify alternatives	Nokia, Sony Ericsson, Vodafone, Motorola	
Compare alternatives and choose	Nokia, Sony Ericsson, Vodafone, Motorola	
Implement chosen alternative	Obtain from store	
Evaluate effectiveness of solution	As you use it	

Figure 7.3
Illustrating the decision-making tasks – a new mobile phone

Comparing alternatives and making a choice

As in daily life, management decisions need a system for comparing and choosing. Since criteria and weights are subjective, several people making a choice can easily end in argument.

Figure 7.3 illustrates the tasks in making a decision through a simple personal example. Although superficially simple, people find it difficult to set criteria, which are often subjective and so open to different interpretations – especially if several people take part.

Another way to structure a situation in which there are several alternative actions is to draw a **decision tree**. This helps to assess the relative suitability of the options by assessing them against identified criteria: successively eliminating the options as each relevant factor is introduced. Figure 7.8 is an example of a decision tree – it shows how a manager can decide the most suitable method of solving a problem by asking a succession of questions about the situation, leading to the most likely solution for those circumstances. The main challenge in using the technique is to identify the logical sequence of intermediate decisions and how they relate to each other.

A decision tree helps someone to make a choice by progressively eliminating options as additional criteria or events are added to the tree.

| Key ideas | Mintzberg's study of major decisions |

Henry Mintzberg and his colleagues studied 25 major, unstructured decisions in 25 organisations, finding that rational techniques could not cope with the complexity of strategic decisions. They concluded that:

- whether people recognised the need for a decision depended on the strength of the stimuli, the reputation of the source, and the availability of a potential solution;

- most decisions depended on designing a custom-made solution (a new organisation structure, a new product or a new technology); and
- the choice phase (see Figure 7.2), was less significant than the development phase: it was essentially ratifying a solution that was determined implicitly during development.

Source: Mintzberg *et al.* (1976).

Implementing the choice

In the laptop case this is a simple matter if the manager has conducted the process well. In bigger decisions this will be a much more problematic stage as it is during implementation that the decision commits scarce resources, and perhaps meets new objections. So implementation often takes longer than expected, and depends on people making other supportive decisions. It also shows the effects of the decision-making process: if the promoter involved others in the decision, they may be more willing to co-operate with the consequential changes, for example in the way they work.

| Management in practice | Decide quickly, and don't be afraid to switch |

www.wipro.com

Wipro is a very successful Indian information services company, competing around the world. It faces rapidly changing technical and business conditions, so needs to make decisions quickly. Wipro has evolved a management rhythm that is organised around the type of decisions managers have to make. There are:

- weekly meetings in each business unit about spotting and fixing problems, or exploiting opportunities;
- monthly IT management meetings to introduce and adjust tactics;
- quarterly strategy council meetings to decide longer-term issues.

In each of these meetings, the spirit of experimentation is pervasive. Managers are inclined to try things and get them going fast – essentially pilot projects. They track the projects closely, so if something doesn't work, they spot it quickly and make adjustments, or even pull the plug. (Hamm, 2007, p. 286)

Source: Hamm (2007).

Evaluating the decision

The final stage is evaluation: looking back to see if the decision has resolved the problem, and what can be learned. It is a form of control, which people are often reluctant to do formally, preferring to turn their attention to future tasks, rather than reflect on the past. That choice inhibits their ability to learn from experience.

Having given this simplified overview of the process, the following sections outline different types of decisions, and some models that seek to explain how people make them.

| Activity 7.2 | Critical reflection on making a decision |

Work through the steps in Figure 7.3 for a decision you currently face, such as where to go on holiday, which courses to choose next year, or which job to apply for. Then do the same for a decision that involves several other people, such as which assignment to do in your study group or where to go for a night out together.

If you work in an organisation, select two business decisions as the focus of your work.

- How did working through the steps affect the way you reached a decision?
- Did it help you think more widely about the alternatives?
- How did the second decision, involving more people, affect the usefulness of the method?
- Then reflect on the technique itself: did it give insight into the decision process? What other tasks should it include?

7.3	Programmed and non-programmed decisions

Many decisions that managers face are straightforward and need not involve intense discussion, others require unique or novel solutions.

Programmed decisions

Programmed (or structured) decisions (Simon, 1960) deal with problems that are familiar and, where the information required is easy to define and obtain, the situation is well structured. If a store manager notices that a product is selling more than expected there will be a simple, routine procedure for deciding how much extra to order from the supplier. Decisions are structured to the extent that they arise frequently and can be dealt with routinely by following an established **procedure**: a series of related steps, often set out in a manual, to deal with a structured problem. They may also reach a decision by using an established **rule**, which sets out what someone can or cannot do in a given situation. They may also refer to a **policy**: a guideline that establishes some general principles for making a decision.

> A programmed (or structured) decision is a repetitive decision that can be handled by a routine approach.
>
> A procedure is a series of related steps to deal with a structured problem.
>
> A rule sets out what someone can or cannot do in a given situation.
>
> A policy is a guideline that establishes some general principles for making a decision.

People make programmed decisions to resolve recurring problems: to reorder supplies when stocks drop below a defined level, to set the qualifications required for a job, or to decide whether to lend money to a bank customer. Once managers formulate procedures, rules or policies, others can usually make the decisions. Computers handle many decisions of this type, for example the checkout systems in supermarkets calculate the items sold and order new stock.

Non-programmed decisions

Simon (1960) also observed that people make **non-programmed (unstructured) decisions** to deal with situations that are novel or unusual, and so require a unique solution. The issue has not arisen in quite that form, and the information required is unclear, vague or open to several interpretations. Major management decisions are of this type, such as the choice that managers at Marks and Spencer faced in deciding whether to launch their (2010) programme to become the world's most sustainable retailer by 2015. This will bring many benefits to the environment and the company, but will be challenging and time-consuming to introduce as it involves changing the way suppliers work. While the company will have done a lot of research before making the decision, no-one has made this commitment before, and it cannot be sure how customers and competitors will respond. Most issues of strategy are of this type, because they involve great uncertainty and many interests.

> A non-programmed (unstructured) decision is a unique decision that requires a custom-made solution when information is lacking or unclear.

Management in practice   Inamo – choosing a designer   www.inamo-restaurant.com

Inamo is a new London restaurant where customers place their order directly to the kitchen from an interactive ordering system on their table. Selecting the designer for such a novel idea was a big step. Noel Hunwick, Chief Operating Officer said:

An early and crucial decision we had to make was to select our interior design company. The way we've always worked is to make sure that we always [have] options from which to choose, so based on recommendations and on web research, and going to various shows and events, I put together a large portfolio of work . . . to get a rough price per square foot that these companies generally charged.

We then selected eight companies to give us a full design brief, and then cut that down to three – who came out with three entirely different concepts so I think that then allowed us to narrow it down to two and have a final showdown. [Given that our ordering system was so novel] I think that was a crucial decision – we had to make sure it wasn't an overload on the customer, so I think that was a very delicate and difficult business decision. We always want options. Every single decision, whether it's the cleaning company that we use, everything, we want three options at least. I think that's very important.

Source: Interview with Noel Hunwick.

People need to deal with programmed and non-programmed decisions in different ways. The former are amenable to procedures, routines, rules and quantitative analytical techniques such as those associated with operational research (see Chapter 2). They are also suitable for resolution by modern information systems. Non-programmed decisions depend on judgement and intuition.

Figure 7.4 relates the type of decision to the levels of the organisation. Those lower in the organisation typically deal with routine, structured problems, which they can resolve by applying procedures. As people move up the hierarchy they face more unstructured decisions: lower-level staff hand decisions that do not fit the rules to someone above them, while the latter pass routine matters to subordinates.

Case study   Ikea - the case continues www.ikea.com

In mid-2009 the founder of Ikea warned that the Swedish retailer must lose more jobs after the recession squeezed sales of flat-pack furniture. Ingvar Kamprad believes that the 5,000 jobs that the company has already shed will not be enough to deal with the tougher economic climate:

We need to decrease the number of staff further, particularly within manufacturing and logistics. It's about adjusting to sales being a lot less and becoming more efficient.

The Swedish billionaire revealed that sales are running at about 7 per cent below target, adding that the company can no longer match its recent rate of expansion, when up to 20 stores would open every year. Kamprad said:

The forecast is that our margins and profits are decreasing substantially this year. This is proof that we have been too negligent in how we take care of our existing stores. Actually, I have long tried to warn about our excessive focus on expansion, and now the board has decided to hit the brakes,

A spokeswoman confirmed that there may be further job cuts, but insisted that the company was also hiring at its new stores, and was committed to opening between ten and 15 stores a year. It had however suspended its investment in Russia, a major target, blaming the 'unpredictability of administrative processes'.

Source: IKEA's founder warns: we must cut more jobs, *The Guardian*, 07/07/2009 (Graeme Wearden), Copyright Guardian News & Media Ltd 2009.

Case questions 7.2

- Are these decisions programmed or non-programmed?
- What other insights does this part of the case give into decision making processes at Ikea?

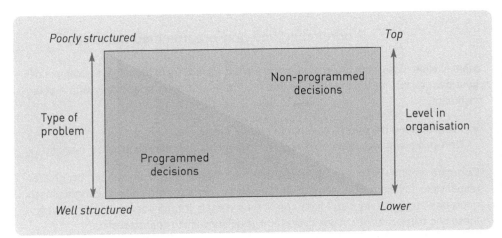

Figure 7.4
Types of decision,
types of problem
and level in the
organisation

Source: ROBBINS,
STEPHEN P.; COULTER,
MARY, *MANAGEMENT*,
8th Edition, © 2005,
p. 144. Reprinted by
permission of Pearson
Education, Inc. Upper
Saddle River, NJ.

Many decisions have elements of each type. Non-programmed decisions probably contain elements that can be handled in a programmed way.

Dependent or independent

Another way to categorise decisions is in terms of their links to other decisions. People make decisions in a historical and social context, and so are influenced by past and possible future decisions and the influence of other parts of the organisation. Legacy computer systems (the result of earlier decisions) frequently constrain how quickly a company can adopt new systems.

Some decisions have few implications beyond their immediate area, but others have significant ripples around the organisation. Changes in technology, for example, usually require consistent, supportive changes in structures and processes if they are to be effective. Although decisions on these areas are harder to make than those affecting the technology. More generally, local units may be limited in their decisions by wider company policies. Figure 7.5 illustrates this.

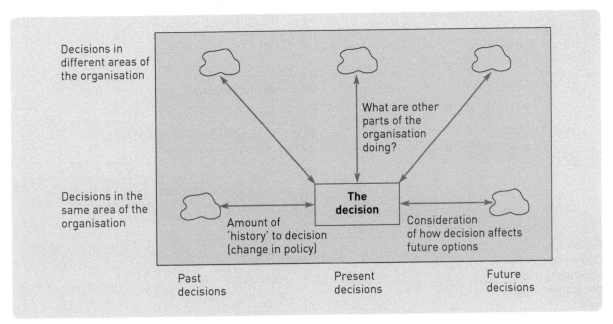

Figure 7.5 Possible relationships between decisions

Source: Cooke and Slack (1991), p. 24.

7.4   Decision-making conditions

Certainty describes the situation when all the information the decision maker needs is available.

Risk refers to situations in which the decision maker is able to estimate the likelihood of the alternative outcomes.

Uncertainty is when people are clear about their goals, but have little information about which course of action is most likely to succeed.

Decisions arise within a wider context, and the conditions in this context, as measured by the degree of **certainty**, **risk**, **uncertainty** and **ambiguity** materially affect the decision process. Figure 7.6 relates the nature of the problem to the type of decision. Whereas people can deal with conditions of certainty by making programmed decisions, many situations are both uncertain and ambiguous. Here people need to be able to use a non-programmed approach.

Certainty

Certainty is when the decision makers have all the information they need; they are fully informed about the costs and benefits of each alternative. A company treasurer wanting to place reserve funds can readily compare rates of interest from several banks, and calculate exactly the return from each. Few decisions are that certain, and most contain risk and/or uncertainty.

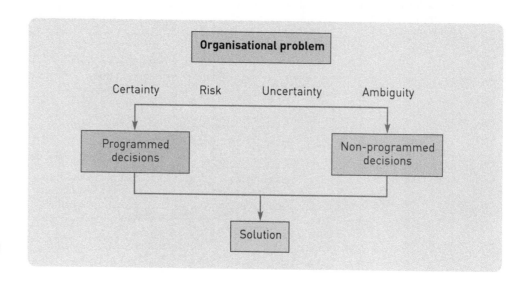

Figure 7.6
Degree of uncertainty and decision-making type

Risk

Risk refers to situations in which the decision maker can estimate the likelihood of the alternative outcomes, possibly using statistical methods. Banks have developed tools to assess credit risk, and so reduce the risk of the borrower not repaying the loan. The questions on an application form for a loan (home ownership, time at this address, employer's name, etc.) enable the bank to assess the risk of lending money to that person.

Uncertainty

Uncertainty means that people know what they wish to achieve, but they do not have enough information about alternatives and future events to estimate the risk confidently. Factors that may affect the outcomes of deciding to launch a new product (future growth in the market, changes in customer interests, competitors' actions) are difficult to predict.

Managers at GSK, the pharmaceutical group, experience great uncertainty in deciding how to allocate research funds. Scientists who wished to develop a new range of vaccines have to persuade the Board to divert resources to their project. Uncertainties include the fact that science is evolving rapidly, other companies are making competing discoveries, and it will be many years before the company receives income from the research results (if any).

Case study   Ikea - the case continues   www.ikea.com

In June 2009 the company announced it was abandoning efforts to set up stores in India, afer failing to persuade the Indian government to ease restrictions on foreign investment. It has tried to do this for over two years, and had believed the change was imminent – but it did not happen. Ikea's Asia-Pacific retail manager said:

> We still face a very high level of uncertainty. It is a very sensitive political issue in India and it may take a new government more time to negotiate with the different parties and agree the changes that are required to open up and develop the retail sector.

More generally, managers in Ikea have placed great emphasis on developing a strong culture within the company, transmitting this to new employees and reinforcing it by events for existing ones. The belief is that if co-workers develop a strong sense of shared meaning of the Ikea concept, they deliver good service wherever in the group they are. As Edvardsson and Enquist (2002) observe,

> The strong culture in Ikea can give Ikea an image as a religion. In this aspect the *Testament of a Furniture Dealer* [written by Kamprad and given to all co-workers] is the holy script. The preface reads:

> Once and for all we have decided to side with the many. What is good for our customers is also good for us in the long run. After the preface the testament is divided into nine points: (1) The Product Range – our identity, (2) The Ikea Spirit: A Strong and Living Reality, (3) Profit Gives us Resources, (4) To Reach Good Results with Small Means, (5) Simplicity is a Virtue, (6) The Different Way, (7) Concentration of Energy – important to our success, (8) To Assume Responsibility – a privilege, (9) Most Things Still Remain to be Done. A Glorious Future! (p. 166)

Source: Edvardsson and Enquist (2002).

Case questions 7.3

- What implications may the Indian episode have for Ikea's next decisions about expansion?
- How may the culture described here affect decision-making processes in Ikea?

Ambiguity

Ambiguity is when people are uncertain about their goals and how best to achieve them.

Ambiguity describes a situation in which the intended goals are unclear, and so the alternative ways of reaching them are equally fluid. Ambiguity is by far the most difficult decision situation. Students would experience ambiguity if their teacher created student groups, told each group to complete a project, but gave them no topic, direction or guidelines. Ambiguous problems are often associated with rapidly changing circumstances, and unclear links between decision elements (see Management in Practice).

Management in practice   Ambiguity at EADS defers a decision   www.eads.com

EADS is the parent company of Airbus, and has experienced long-running conflicts between French and German shareholders. In 2007 the Board was under pressure to approve a cost-cutting plan proposed by the chief executive of Airbus, necessary because of the delays to the A380, which had increased losses at the company. It was also trying to launch a project to build a new fleet of aircraft to compete with Boeing's Dreamliner, but had been unable to agree how to divide the work between operations in France, Germany, Spain and the UK. National political conflicts at the highest level over this long-term issue were delaying the Board's decision on the short-term re-structuring issue.

Source: *Financial Times*, 20 February 2007.

Case questions 7.4

- Reflect on Ikea's decision to invest in Russia, and its attempts to enter India. What risks, uncertainties or ambiguities were probably associated with these situations?
- What dependencies may the moves have involved (use Figure 7.5 to help you structure your answer)?

7.5   Decision-making models

James Thompson (1967) distinguished decisions on two dimensions: agreement or disagreement over goals, and the beliefs that decision makers hold about the relationship between cause and effect. A decision can be mapped on these two dimensions: whether or not there is agreement on goals, and how certain people are about the consequences of their decisions. Figure 7.7 shows these, and an approach to making decisions that seems best suited to each cell.

Computational strategy – rational model

The **rational model of decision making** assumes that people make consistent choices to maximise economic value within specified constraints.

The **rational model of decision making** is based on economic assumptions. Traditional economic models suggested that the role of a manager was to maximise the economic return to the firm, and that they did this by making decisions on economically rational criteria. The assumptions underlying this model are that the decision maker:

- aims for goals that are known and agreed, and that the problem is structured;
- strives for conditions of certainty, gathering complete information and calculating the likely results of each alternative;
- selects the alternative that will maximise economic returns;
- is rational and logical in assigning values, setting preferences and evaluating alternatives.

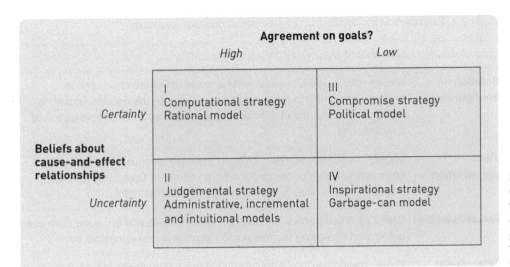

Figure 7.7
Conditions favouring different decision processes
Source: Based on Thompson (1967), p. 134.

The rational model is normative, in that it defines how a decision maker should act. It does not describe how managers make decisions. It aims to help decision makers act more rationally, rather than rely solely on intuition and personal preferences, and is most valuable for programmed decisions where there is little conflict. Where the information required is available and people can agree the criteria for choice, the approach can work well.

Key ideas   **Evidence-based management?**

Pfeffer and Sutton (2006) note that managers frequently make decisions without considering the evidence about what works, and what does not. They often base decisions on:

- experience (which may or may not fit current circumstances);
- solutions with which they are familiar;
- accepting commercially motivated claims about a technique;
- dogmas or beliefs for which there is no reliable evidence.

After enumerating the possible reasons for this, they advocate that evidence-based management could change the way every manager thinks and acts.

> We believe that facing the hard facts and truth about what works and what doesn't, understanding the dangerous half-truths that constitute so much conventional wisdom about management, and rejecting the total nonsense that too often passes for sound advice will help organizations perform better. (p. 74)

Source: Pfeffer and Sutton (2006).

Developments in technology enable computers to take some decisions traditionally made by people. Many early attempts to use what are known as artificial intelligence or decision support systems failed, but Davenport and Harris (2005) report successful modern examples. They work well when decisions require rapid analysis of large quantities of data, with complex relationships, such as in power supply, transport management and banking. Automated decision systems:

> sense online data or conditions, apply codified knowledge or logic and make decisions – all with minimal amounts of human intervention. (Davenport and Harris, 2005, p. 84)

Table 7.1 shows examples.

Table 7.1 Examples of the application of automated decision systems

Type of decision	Example of automated decision application
Solution configuration	Mobile phone operators who offer a range of features and service options: an automated programme can weigh all the options, including information about the customer, and present the most suitable option to the customer
Yield optimisation	Widely used in the airline industry to increase revenue by enabling companies to vary prices depending on demand. Spreading to other transport companies, hotels, retailing and entertainment
Fraud detection	Credit card companies, online gaming companies and tax authorities use automated screening techniques to detect and deter possible fraud
Operational control	Power companies use automated systems to sense changes in the physical environment (power supply, temperature or rainfall), and respond rapidly to changes in demand, by redirecting supplies across the network

Source: Based on Davenport and Harris (2005).

Such applications will continue to spread, supporting companies where many decisions can be handled by using rational, quantitative methods. When decisions are more complex and controversial, the rational approach itself will not be able to resolve a decision. It can play a part but only as one input to a wider set of methods.

Judgemental strategies – administrative, incremental and intuitional

Administrative models

The administrative model of decision making describes how people make decisions in uncertain, ambiguous situations.

Simon's (1960) **administrative model of decision making** aims to describe how managers make decisions in situations which are uncertain and ambiguous. Many management problems are unstructured and not suitable for the precise quantitative analysis implied by the rational model. People rely heavily on their judgement to resolve such issues.

Simon based the model on two concepts: bounded rationality and satisficing. **Bounded rationality** expresses the fact that people have mental limits, or boundaries, on how rational they can be. While organisations and their environments are complex and uncertain, people can process only a limited amount of information. This constrains our ability to operate in the way envisaged by the rational model, which we deal with by **satisficing**: we choose the first solution that is 'good enough'. While searching for other options may eventually produce a better return, identifying and evaluating them costs more than the benefits. Suppose we are in a strange city and need coffee before a meeting. We look for the first acceptable coffee shop that will do the job: we satisfice. In a similar fashion, managers may seek alternatives only until they find one they believe will work.

Bounded rationality is behaviour that is rational within a decision process which is limited (bounded) by an individual's ability to process information.

Satisficing is the acceptance by decision makers of the first solution that is 'good enough'.

Key ideas	A behavioural theory of decision making

Richard Cyert, James March and Herbert Simon (Simon, 1960; Cyert and March, 1963; March, 1988) developed an influential model of decision making. It is sometimes referred to as the behavioural theory of decision making since it treats decision making as an aspect of human behaviour. Also referred to as the administrative model, it recognises that in the real world people are restricted in their decision processes, and therefore have to accept what is probably a less than perfect solution. It introduced the concepts of 'bounded rationality' and 'satisficing' to the study of decision making.

The administrative model focuses on the human and organisational factors that influence decisions. It is more realistic than the rational model for non-programmed, ambiguous decisions. According to the administrative model, managers:

- have goals that are typically vague and conflicting, and are unable to reach a consensus on what to do – as indicated by the EADS example on page 206;
- have different levels of interest in the problems or opportunities facing the business, and interpret information subjectively;
- rarely use rational procedures, or use them in a way that does not reflect the full complexity of the issue;
- limit their search for alternatives;
- usually settle for a satisficing rather than a maximising solution; having both limited information and only vague criteria of what would be 'maximising'.

The administrative model is descriptive, aiming to show how managers make decisions in complex situations rather than stating how they should make them.

Management in practice   **Satisficing in e-health projects**

Boddy *et al.* (2009) studied the implementation of several 'e-health' projects, in which modern information and communication technologies assist clinicians in delivering care. These include applications such as remote diagnostic systems, in which a consultant, assisted by video-conferencing equipment, examines the condition of a patient in a clinic hundreds of miles away. Such methods offer significant savings in patient travel time, and in the better use of scarce consultants' time, especially in remote parts of the country. Despite this, uptake of e-health systems has been slow.

To secure the fullest benefits, managers and staff also need to make significant changes throughout the organisation. The processes for interacting with patients change, as does the work of consultants, nurses and other medical staff. These changes are harder to implement than a decision to buy the technology. Many small pilot projects are producing modest benefits, but nothing like those which could flow from a national programme. A reasonable conclusion is that managers have unconsciously decided to satisfice; they can show they are trying the new methods and producing benefits. To secure the full potential would require more effort than they are willing to give.

Source: Boddy *et al.* (2009b).

Incremental models

Charles Lindblom (1959) developed what he termed an **incremental model**, which he observed people used when they were uncertain about the consequences of their choice. In the rational model these are known, but people face many decisions in which they cannot know what the effects will be. Lindblom built on Simon's idea of bounded rationality to show that if people made only a limited search for options their chosen solution would differ only slightly from what already existed. Current choices would be heavily influenced by past choices – and would not move far from them.

On this view, policy unfolds not from a single event, but from many cumulative small decisions. Small decisions help people to minimise the risk of mistakes, and to reverse the decision

People use an incremental model of decision making when they are uncertain about the consequences. They search for a limited range of options, and policy unfolds from a series of cumulative small decisions.

if necessary. He called this incrementalism, or the 'science of muddling through'. Lindblom contrasted what he called the 'root' method of decision making with the 'branch' method. The root method required a comprehensive evaluation of options in the light of defined objectives. The branch method involved building out, step-by-step and by small degrees, from the current situation. He claimed that the root method is not suitable for complex policy questions, so the practical person must follow the branch approach: the science of muddling through. The incremental model (like the administrative one) recognises human limitations.

Intuitional models

George Klein (1997) studied how effective decision makers work, including those working under extreme time pressure such as surgeons, firefighters and nurses. He found that they rarely used classical decision theory to weigh the options: instead they used pattern recognition to relate the situation to their experience. They acted on intuition – a subconscious process of basing decisions on experience and accumulated judgement – sometimes called 'tacit knowledge'. Klein concluded that effective decision makers use their intuition as much as formal processes – perhaps using both as the situation demands. Experienced managers act quickly on what seems like very little information. Rather than formal analysis, they rely on experience and judgement to make their decisions. Woiceshyn (2009) provides experimental evidence that senior managers use rational and intuitive methods to decide between options, and Hodgkinson *et al.* (2009) quote the co-founder of Sony, Akio Mariata, who was the driving force behind one of the great entertainment innovations of the twentieth century:

> Creativity requires something more than the processing of information. It requires human thought, spontaneous intuition and a lot of courage. (p. 278)

Compromise strategy – political model

The political model is a model of decision making that reflects the view that an organisation consists of groups with different interests, goals and values.

The **political model** examines how people make decisions when managers disagree over goals and how to pursue them (Pfeffer, 1992b; Buchanan and Badham, 1999). It recognises that an organisation is not only a working system but also a political system, which establishes the relative power of people and functions. A decision will enhance the power of some people and limit that of others. People will pursue goals relating to personal and sub-unit interests, as well as those of the organisation as a whole. They will evaluate a decision in terms of its likely effects on those possible conflicting objectives.

They will often try to support their position by building a coalition with those who share their interest. This gives others the opportunity to contribute their ideas and enhance their commitment if the decision is adopted.

The political model assumes that:

- organisations contain groups with diverse interests, goals and values. Managers disagree about problem priorities and may not understand or share the goals and interests of other managers;
- information is ambiguous and incomplete. Rationality is limited by the complexity of many problems as well as personal interests; and
- managers engage in the push and pull of debate to decide goals and discuss alternatives – decisions arise from bargaining and discussion.

Inspirational strategy – garbage-can model

This approach is likely when those concerned are not only unclear about cause-and-effect relationships, but are also uncertain about the outcome they seek. James March observed that in this situation the processes of reaching a decision become separated from the decisions reached. In the other models there is an assumption that the processes which the decision makers pass through lead to a decision. In this situation of extreme uncertainty the elements that constitute the decision problem are independent of each other, coming together in random ways.

March argued that decisions arise when four independent streams of activities meet. When this happens will depend largely on accident or chance. The four streams are:

- **Choice opportunities** Organisations have occasions at which there is an expectation that a decision will be made – budgets must be set, there are regular management meetings, people meet by chance, etc.
- **Participants** A stream of people who have the opportunity to shape decisions.
- **Problems** A stream of problems that represent matters of concern to people: a lost sale, a new opportunity, a vacancy.
- **Solutions** A stream of potential solutions seeking problems – ideas, proposals, information – that people continually generate.

In this view, the choice opportunities (scheduled or unscheduled meetings) act as the container (garbage can) for the mixture of participants, problems and solutions. One combination of the three may be such that enough participants are interested in a solution, which they can match to a problem – and make a decision accordingly. Another group of participants may not have made those connections, or made them in a different way, thus creating a different outcome.

This may at first sight seem an unlikely way to run a business, yet in highly uncertain, volatile environments this approach may work. Creative businesses depend on a rapid interchange of ideas, not only about specified problems but on information about new discoveries, research at other companies, what someone heard at a conference. They depend on people bringing these solutions and problems together – and deliberately foster structures that maximise opportunities for face-to-face contact and rapid decisions. The practical implication is that encouraging frequent informal contact between creative people will improve decisions and performance.

Management in practice   Oticon builds a better garbage can   www.oticon.com

Oticon, a leading maker of sophisticated hearing aids, underwent a massive transformation in the early 1990s, in which the chief executive, Lars Kolind, broke down all barriers to communication. He realised that the key to success in the face of severe competition was to ensure that the talents of staff in the company were applied to any problems that arose. In March's terms, problems were expressed as a project, for which a member of staff (a participant) took responsibility, depending on other staff to suggest or help develop a solution.

> Any and all measures were taken to encourage contact and informal communication between employees. Elevators were made inoperable so that employees would meet each other on the stairs, where they were more likely to engage in conversation. Bars were installed on all three floors where coffee was served and meetings could be organised – standing up. Rooms with circular sofas were provided, complete with small coffee tables, to encourage discussion. (Rivard *et al.*, 2004, p. 170)

> These discussions centred on reaching fast and creative decisions about problems and new product ideas. The arrangement is credited with helping the continuing success of the company.

Source: Rivard *et al.*, (2004); see also Chapter 10 case.

Table 7.2 summarises these four models, which are complementary in that a skilful manager or a well-managed organisation will use all of them, depending on the decision and the immediate context. A new product idea may emerge from a process resembling the garbage-can model, but will then need a rational business investment case to persuade the Board to develop it.

Table 7.2 Four models of decision making

Features	Rational	Administrative/incremental	Political	Garbage can
Clarity of problem and goal	Clear problem and goals	Vague problems and goals	Conflict over goals	Goals and solutions independent
Degree of certainty	High degree of certainty	High degree of uncertainty	Uncertainty and/or conflict	Ambiguity
Available information on costs and benefits	Full information about costs and benefits of alternatives	Little information about costs and benefits of alternatives	Conflicting views about costs and benefits of alternatives	Costs and benefits unconnected at start
Method of choice	Rational choice to maximise benefit	Satisficing choice – good enough	Choice by bargaining among players	Choice by accidental merging of streams

---

Activity 7.4   Identify decision requiring one of these approaches

Here are some decisions which Virgin (see Part case) has faced:

- Whether or not to order further airliners.
- How severely to cut services during the economic downturn.
- Whether to increase their sponsorship of the 2014 Olympics.
- Whether to become involved with Crossrail.

In each case, decide which of the four decision models best describes the situation, and explain why.

Compare your answers with colleagues on your course, and prepare a short report summarising your conclusions from this activity.

7.6   Biases in making decisions

Heuristics – simple rules or mental short cuts that simplify making decisions

Since people are subject to bounded rationality (limited capacity to process information) they tend to use **heuristics** – simple rules or short cuts, that help us to overcome our limited capacity to deal with information and complexity (Kahneman and Tversky, 1974). While these short cuts help us to make decisions, they expose us to the danger of biases: four of which are prior hypothesis, representativeness, illusion of control and escalating commitment (Schwenk, 1984): a fifth is emotional attachment (Finkelstein *et al.*, 2009a, 2009b).

Prior hypothesis bias

Prior hypothesis bias results from a tendency to base decisions on strong prior beliefs, even if the evidence shows that they are wrong.

People who have strong prior beliefs about the relationship between two alternatives base their decisions on those beliefs, even when they receive evidence that the beliefs are wrong. In doing so they fall victim to the **prior hypothesis bias**, which is strengthened by a tendency to use information consistent with their beliefs, and ignore that which is inconsistent. People recall vivid events more readily than others, and these bias their decisions, even if circumstances have changed.

Representativeness bias

This is the tendency to generalise from a small sample or single episode, and to ignore other relevant information. Examples of this **representativeness bias** are:

- predicting the success of a new product on the basis of an earlier success;
- appointing someone with a certain type of experience because a previous successful appointment had a similar background.

Representativeness bias results from a tendency to generalise inappropriately from a small sample or a single vivid event.

Optimism bias

Lovallo and Kahneman (2003) believe that a major reason for poor decisions is the 'planning fallacy' discussed in Chapter 6. This is when people systematically underestimate the costs and overestimate the benefits of a proposal. One source of this fallacy is what they call **optimism bias** – a human tendency to judge future events in a more positive light than is warranted by actual experience. People often exaggerate their talents and their role in success, leading them to make optimistic assessments.

Optimism bias is a human tendency to see the future in a more positive light than is warranted by experience.

Illusion of control

Other errors in making decisions result from the **illusion of control**, which is the human tendency to overestimate our ability to control activities and events. Those in senior positions, especially if they have a record of successes, are prone to this bias which causes them to overestimate the odds of a favourable outcome.

The illusion of control is a source of bias resulting from the tendency to overestimate one's ability to control activities and events.

Escalating commitment

Managers may also be influenced by the phenomenon known as the **escalation of commitment**, which is an increased commitment to a previous decision despite evidence that it may have been wrong (Drummond, 1996). People are reluctant to admit mistakes, and rather than search for a new solution, they increase their commitment to the original decision.

Escalation of commitment is a bias which leads to increased commitment to a previous decision despite evidence that it may have been wrong.

Management in practice   A study of escalation – Taurus at the Stock Exchange

Helga Drummond studied the attempt by management at the London Stock Exchange to implement a computerised system to deal with the settlement of shares traded on the Exchange. The project was announced in May 1986 and was due to be completed by 1989 at a cost of £6 million. After many crises and difficulties, the Stock Exchange finally abandoned the project in March 1993. By that time the Exchange had spent £80 million on developing a non-existent system. Drummond interviewed many key participants to explore the reasons for this disaster – which occurred despite the commitment of the system designers.

She concluded that the project suffered from fundamental structural problems, in that it challenged several powerful vested interests in the financial community, each of whom had their own idea about what should be done. Each new demand, reflecting this continuing power struggle, made the system more complicated. However, while many interests needed to work together, structural barriers throughout the organisation prevented this. There was little upward communication, so that senior managers were largely unaware of staff concerns about the timetable commitments being made.

Senior managers continued to claim that the project was on track until a few days before it was finally, and very publicly, terminated. The lack of proper mechanisms to identify pressing issues lulled those making decisions into a false sense of security about the state of the project.

Source: Drummond (1996).

Guler (2007) found exactly the same phenomenon in the venture capital industry, whose firms lend money to entrepreneurs starting and building a business. Investors provide money in instalments over several years, which allows them to limit their exposure to risk. Guler found that investors became less likely to terminate an investment as they participated in further rounds, despite evidence that returns were declining. This was influenced by three factors: social (losing face among colleagues), political (pressure from other investors) and institutional (damage to reputation if it pulled out of an investment).

Emotional attachment

A final source of bias is emotional attachments to people, ideas or places. Finkelstein *et al.* (2009a, 2009b) note that people are frequently influenced by emotional attachments to:

* family and friends;
* communities and colleagues;
* objects – things and places which have meaning for us.

Finkelstein and his colleagues suggest that these attachments (negative or positive), which bring us meaning and happiness, are bound to influence our decisions. Most of the effects are insignificant, but sometimes a manager's emotional attachments can lead him/her to make bad business decisions. They give examples such as Samsung's disastrous investment in car manufacturing (widely opposed as a poor use of resources, but initiated and supported by a chairman who liked cars); and the chairman who justified the retention of a small and unprofitable design consultancy because:

> I like it! It's exciting. I enjoy it . . . So I'm keeping it! (Finkelstein *et al.*, 2009a, p. 87)

Activity 7.5 Examples of bias

* List the sources of bias on a screen or sheet of paper.
* Try to identify one example of each which you have personally experienced in your everyday discussions with friends, family or colleagues.
* What (be specific) did they (or you) say which led you to label it as being of that type?
* Compare your results, so that, if possible, you have a clear example of each type of decision bias.

7.7 Group decision making

While people often make decisions as individuals, they also do so within the context of a group. This section looks at two ideas: Vroom and Yetton's decision model and Irving Janis' identification of groupthink.

Vroom and Yetton's decision model

The idea behind Vroom and Yetton's (1973) contingency model of decision making is to influence the quality and acceptability of decisions. This depends on the manager choosing how best to involve subordinates in making a decision – and being willing to change his/her style to match the situation. The model defines five leadership styles and seven characteristics of problems. Managers can use these characteristics to diagnose the situation. They can find the recommended way of reaching a decision on that problem by using the decision tree shown in Figure 7.8. The five leadership styles defined are:

- **AI (Autocratic)** You solve the problem or make the decision yourself using information available to you at that time.
- **AII (Information-seeking)** You obtain the necessary information from your subordinate(s), then decide on the solution to the problem yourself. You may or may not tell your subordinates what the problem is when getting the information from them. The role played by your subordinates in making the decision is clearly one of providing the necessary information to you rather than generating or evaluating alternative solutions.
- **CI (Consulting)** You share the problem with relevant subordinates individually, getting their ideas and suggestions without bringing them together as a group. Then *you* make the decision that may or may not reflect your subordinates' influence.

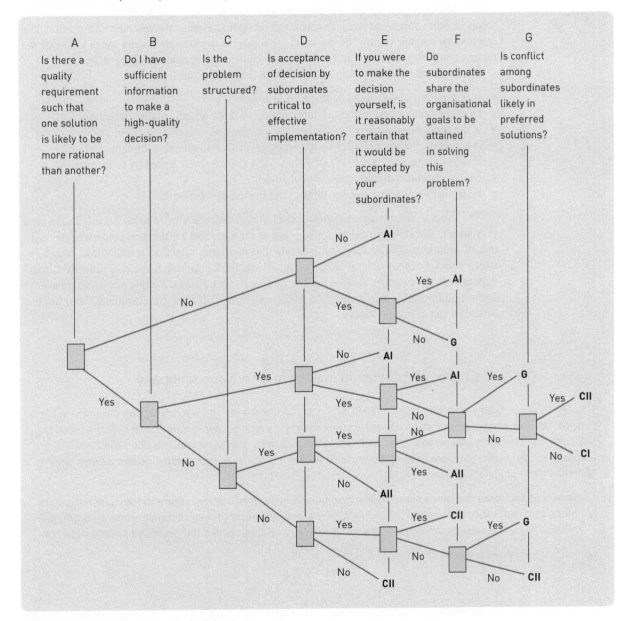

Figure 7.8 Vroom and Yetton's decision tree

Source: Figure 9.1 Decision-Process Flow Chart from *Leadership and Decision-Making*, and the taxonomy used in the figure is from Table 2.1 Decision Method for Group and Individual Problems from *Leadership and Decision-Making*, by Victor H. Vroom and Philip W. Yetton, © 1973. Reprinted by permission of the University of Pittsburgh Press.

- CII (**Negotiating**) You share the problem with your subordinates as a group, obtaining their collective ideas and suggestions. Then you make the decision that may or may not reflect your subordinates' influence.
- G (**Group**) You share the problem with your subordinates as a group. Together you generate and evaluate alternatives and attempt to reach agreement (consensus) on a solution. Your role is much like that of a chairperson. You do not try to influence the group to adopt 'your' solution, and you are willing to accept and implement any solution that has the support of the entire group.

The idea behind the model is that no style is in itself better than another. Some believe that consultative or delegating styles are inherently preferable to autocratic approaches, as being more in keeping with democratic principles. Vroom and Yetton argue otherwise. In some situations (such as when time is short or the manager has all the information needed for a minor decision) going through the process of consultation will waste time and add little value. In other situations, such as where the subordinates have the relevant information, it is essential to consult them. The point of the model is to make managers more aware of the range of factors to take into account in using a particular decision-making style.

The problem criteria are expressed in seven diagnostic questions:

- Is one solution likely to be better than another?
- Does the manager have enough information to make a high-quality decision?
- Is the problem structured?
- Is acceptance of the decision by subordinates critical to effective implementation?
- If the manager makes the decision alone, is it likely to be accepted by subordinates?
- Do subordinates share organisational goals?
- Is conflict likely among subordinates over preferred solutions?

The Vroom–Yetton decision model implies that managers need to be flexible in the style they adopt. The style should be appropriate to the situation rather than consistent throughout all situations. The problem with this is that managers may find it difficult to switch between styles, perhaps several times a day. Although the approach appears objective, it still depends on the manager answering the questions. Requiring a simple yes or no answer to complex questions is too simple, and managers often want to say 'it all depends' on other historical or contextual factors.

Management in practice   Decision making in a software company

This Swedish company was founded in 1998, and now concentrates on developing software for mobile phones, such as an application which sends text messages from a computer to a mobile. It sells the products mainly to the operating companies who use them to add value to their services. The business depends on teams of highly skilled software developers, able to produce innovative, competitive products very rapidly. The chief technology officer commented:

As well as technical decisions we regularly face business decisions about where to focus development effort, or which customers to target. In this highly industrialised technocratic environment I am highly influenced by the experts in the team, and routinely consult them about the preferred course of action.

Source: Private communication from the chief technology officer.

Nevertheless the model is used in management training to alert managers to the style they prefer to use and to the range of options available. It also prompts managers to consider systematically whether that preferred style is always appropriate. They may then handle situations more deliberately than if they relied only on their preferred style or intuition.

Irving Janis and groupthink

Groupthink is a pattern of biased decision making that occurs in groups that become too co-hesive. Members strive for agreement among themselves at the expense of accurately and dis-passionately assessing relevant, and especially disturbing information. An influential analysis of how it occurs was put forward by the social psychologist Irving Janis. His research (Janis, 1972) began by studying major and highly publicised failures of decision making, looking for some common theme that might explain why apparently able and intelligent people were able to make such bad decisions, such as President Kennedy's decision to have US forces in-vade Cuba in 1961. One common thread he observed was the inability of the groups involved to consider a range of alternatives rationally, or to see the likely consequences of the choice they made. Members were also keen to be seen as team players, and not to say things that might end their membership of the group. Janis termed this phenomenon 'groupthink', and defined it as:

> . . . a mode of thinking that people engage in when they are deeply involved in a cohesive in-group, when the members' striving for unanimity overrides their motivation to realis-tically appraise alternative courses of action. (Janis, 1972, p. 9)

He identified eight symptoms of groupthink, shown in the Key Ideas.

Groupthink is 'a mode of thinking that people engage in when they are deeply involved in a cohesive in-group, when the members' striving for unanimity overrides their motivation to realistically appraise alternative courses of action' (Janis, 1972).

Key ideas   **Irving Janis on the symptoms of groupthink**

Janis (1977) identified eight symptoms that give early warning of groupthink developing. The more of them that are present, the more likely it is that the 'disease' will strike. The symptoms are:

- **Illusion of invulnerability** The belief that any decision they make will be successful.
- **Belief in the inherent morality of the group** Justifying a decision by reference to some higher value.
- **Rationalisation** Playing down the negative consequences or risks of a decision.
- **Stereotyping out-groups** Characterising opponents or doubters in unfavourable terms, making it easier to dismiss even valid criticism from that source.
- **Self-censorship** Suppressing legitimate doubts in the interest of group loyalty.
- **Direct pressure** Strong expressions from other members (or the leader) that dissent to their favoured approach will be unwelcome.
- **Mindguards** Keeping uncomfortable facts or opinions out of the discussion.
- **Illusion of unanimity** Playing down any remaining doubts or questions, even if they become stronger or more persistent.

Source: Based on Janis (1977).

Management in practice   **Groupthink in medicine**

An experienced nurse observed three of the symptoms of groupthink in the work of senior doctors:

- **Illusion of invulnerability** A feeling of power and authority leads a group to see themselves as invulner-able. Traditionally the medical profession has been very powerful and this makes it very difficult for non-clinicians to question their actions or plans.
- **Belief in the inherent morality of the group** This happens when clinical staff use the term 'individual clin-ical judgement' as a justification for their actions. An example is when a business manager is trying to re-duce drug costs and one consultant's practice is very different from those of his colleagues. Consultants often reply that they are entitled to use their clinical judgement. This is never challenged by their col-leagues, and it is often impossible to achieve change.

- **Self-censorship** Being a doctor is similar to being in a very exclusive club, and none of the members want to be excluded. Therefore doctors will usually support each other, particularly against management. They are also extremely unlikely to report each other for mistakes or poor performance. A government scheme to encourage 'whistle-blowing' was met with much derision in the ranks.

Source: Private communication.

When groupthink occurs, pressures for agreement and harmony within the group have the unintended effects of discouraging individuals from raising issues that run counter to the majority opinion (Turner and Pratkanis, 1998). An often-quoted example is *Challenger* disaster in 1986, when the space shuttle exploded shortly after take-off. Investigations showed that NASA and the main contractors, Morton Thiokol, were so anxious to keep the Shuttle programme on schedule that they ignored or discounted evidence that would slow the programme down. On a lighter note, Professor Jerry Harvey tells the story of how members of his extended family drove 40 miles into town on a hot day, to no obvious purpose – and everyone was miserable. Discussing the episode with the family later, each person admitted that they had not wanted to go, but went along to please the others. Harvey (1988) coined the term 'Abilene paradox' to describe this tendency to go along with others for the sake of avoiding conflict.

| 7.8 | Integrating themes |

Sustainable performance

As expectations of organisations' sustainability become more demanding and circumstances more volatile, the task of making decisions to promote sustainable performance are correspondingly more challenging. While some members of the management team will wish to promote strategies to enhance sustainable performance, either as strategically valuable or, at the very least, as enlightened self-interest, others may disagree, leading to a contested decision. Nutt (2002) identifies the causes of failure in decision making and point towards practices that he claims increase the chances of a successful outcome. His suggestions include:

- avoid making premature commitments – the hazard of grabbing hold of the first idea that comes up;
- maintaining an exploratory mind-set – keeping an open-mind towards other possibilities;
- letting go of the quick-fix – deferring choice until understanding has been gained;
- pausing to reflect – even if this means resisting demands for a quick fix;
- use resources to evaluate options, not just the preferred solution (or current quick fix);
- pay attention to both the rational and the political aspects of a decision process.

Adopting such practices would undoubtedly add to the quality of decision making: the challenge is whether they will be able to resist the pressures from others to deal with issues in a more risky way, especially if they are susceptible to bias or groupthink.

Governance and control

Several themes in this chapter highlight the traps that await decision makers, but also show how good governance arrangements can help to protect them and the organisation. The top level strategic decisions which shape an organisation's future are inherently unprogrammed, unstructured decisions which no-one has dealt with in quite that form. Senior managers make these decisions in conditions of risk, uncertainty and ambiguity – further placing at risk the assets and resources of the business. They are prone to any and all of the biases the chapter set out: a good example is the failure of the Taurus project at the London Stock Exchange, where those in charge continued to commit additional resources to the project, despite evidence that the project would not be able to deliver a solution acceptable to the main players. This was as much as anything a failure of governance.

More generally, the evidence on groupthink shows the delusions to which powerful senior managers are susceptible, as they come to believe in the soundness of their decisions, and are dismissive of those who question their views. This was evident in the 2008 banking crisis, where not enough, if any, of the non-executive directors were able and willing to provide the necessary challenges to the over-enthusiasm of executives taking too many risky decisions. Put another way, these companies had, on the face of it, put in place the governance procedures recommended in the Combined Code (see Chapter 3, Section 3.9), but those with the power to do so did not exercise those responsibilities.

Internationalisation

The structure of decision-making processes change as companies become international. Decisions will cross the boundaries between managers at global headquarters and those in local business units. Neither of the extreme possibilities is likely to work. If decision making tilts too far in favour of global managers at the centre, local preferences are likely to be overlooked, and local managers are likely to lack commitment to decisions in which they have had no say. Leaving too many decisions to local managers can waste opportunities for economies of scale or opportunities to serve global clients consistently.

A solution may be to identify the major ways in which the company adds value to resources, and align the decision-making processes to make the most of them. For example, if procurement is a critical factor *and* can best be done on a global scale, that would imply that those at the centre should make these decisions. Once supply contracts are agreed, however, responsibility for operating them could pass back to local level. Conversely, they might leave decisions on pricing or advertising expenditure to local managers. The central issue is to spend time on the difficult choices about the location of each set of decisions, to achieve an acceptable balance between global and local expectations.

Summary

1 **Outline the (iterative) stages of the decision making process and the tasks required in each**

   - Decisions are choices about how to act in relation to organisational inputs, outputs and transformation processes. The chapter identifies seven *iterative* steps in the process:
   - Recognise the problem – which depends on seeing and attending to ambiguous signals.
   - Set and weight criteria – the features of the result most likely to meet problem requirements, and that can guide the choice between alternatives.
   - Develop alternatives – identify existing or develop custom-built ways of dealing with the problem.
   - Compare and choose – using the criteria to select the preferred alternative.
   - Implement – the task that turns a decision into an action.
   - Evaluate – check whether the decision resolved the problem.
   - Most decisions affect other interests, whose response will be affected by how the decision process is conducted, in matters such as participation and communication.

2 **Explain, and give examples of, programmed and non-programmed decisions**

- Programmed decisions deal with familiar issues within existing policy – recruitment, minor capital expenditure, small price changes.
- Non-programmed decisions move the business in a new direction – new markets, mergers, a major investment decision.

3 **Distinguish decision-making conditions of certainty, risk, uncertainty and ambiguity**

- Certainty – decision makers have all the information they need, especially the costs and benefits of each alternative action.
- Risk – where the decision maker can estimate the likelihood of the alternative outcomes. These are still subject to chance, but decision makers have enough information to estimate probabilities.
- Uncertainty – when people know what they wish to achieve, but information about alternatives and future events is incomplete. They cannot be clear about alternatives or estimate their risk.
- Ambiguity – when people are unsure about their objectives and about the relation between cause and effect.

4 **Contrast rational, administrative, political and garbage-can decision models**

- Rational models are based on economic assumptions which suggest that the role of a manager is to maximise the economic return to the firm, and that they do this by making decisions on economically rational criteria.
- The administrative model aims to describe how managers actually make decisions in situations of uncertainty and ambiguity. Many management problems are unstructured and not suitable for the precise quantitative analysis implied by the rational model.
- The political model examines how people make decisions when conditions are uncertain, information is limited, and there is disagreement among managers over goals and how to pursue them. It recognises that an organisation is not only a working system, but also a political system, which establishes the relative power of people and functions.
- The garbage-can model identifies four independent streams of activities that enable a decision when they meet. When participants, problems and solutions come together in a relevant forum (a 'garbage can'), then a decision will be made.

5 **Give examples of common sources of bias in decisions**

- Sources of bias stem from the use of heuristics – mental short-cuts which allow us to cope with excessive information. Four biases are:
  - Representativeness bias – basing decisions on unrepresentative samples or single incidents.
  - Prior hypothesis bias – basing decisions on prior beliefs, despite evidence they are wrong.
  - Illusion of control – excessive belief in one's ability to control people and events.
  - Escalating commitment – committing more resources to a project despite evidence of failure.

6 **Explain the contribution of Vroom and Yetton, and of Irving Janis, to our understanding of decision making in groups**

- Vroom and Yetton introduced the idea that decision-making styles in groups should reflect the situation – which of the five ways of involving subordinates in a decision (autocratic, information-seeking, consulting, negotiating and delegating) to use depended on identifiable circumstances, such as whether the manager has the information required.
- Irving Janis observed the phenomenon of groupthink, and set out the symptoms which indicate that it is affecting a group's decision-making processes.

7 **Show how ideas from the chapter add to your understanding of the integrating themes**

- The analysis by Nutt (2002) of successful approaches to decision making, and that by Pfeffer and Sutton (2006) are highly relevant to situations in which managers are dealing with difficult decisions about how to improve the sustainability of their operations.
- The chapter shows the many traps and biases that afflict decision makers – good governance can protect them and their organisations from these by subjecting them to close external scrutiny. Groupthink is likely to have been present in many groups of senior managers as they made bad decisions which damaged their firms and the wider economy.
- Those managing internationally constantly search for the best balance between central and local decision making.

Review questions

1 Explain the difference between risk and ambiguity. How may people make decisions in different ways for each situation?

2 List three decisions you have recently observed or taken part in. Which of them were programmed and which unprogrammed?

3 What are the major differences between the rational and administrative models of decision making?

4 What is meant by satisficing in decision making? Can you illustrate the concept with an example from your experience? Why did those involved not try to achieve an economically superior decision?

5 What did Henry Mintzberg's research on decision making contribute to our understanding of the process?

6 List and explain three common biases in making decisions.

7 The Vroom–Yetton model describes five styles. How should the manager decide which style to use?

8 Recall four of the symptoms of groupthink, and give an example to illustrate each of them.

9 Summarise an idea from the chapter that adds to your understanding of the integrating themes.

Concluding critical reflection

Think about the ways in which your company, or one with which you are familiar, makes decisions. Review the material in the chapter, and perhaps visit some of the websites identified. Then make notes on these questions:

- What examples of the issues discussed in this chapter struck you as being relevant to practice in your company?
- Are people you work with typically dealing mainly with programmed or non-programmed decisions? What **assumptions** about the nature of decision making appear to guide their approach: rational, administrative, political or garbage can? On balance, do their assumptions accurately reflect the reality you see?
- What factors, such as the history or current **context** of the company, appear to influence people who are expected to reach decisions? Does the current approach appear to be right for the company in its context, or would a different view of the context lead to a different approach? (Perhaps refer to some of the Management in Practice features for how different contexts encourage different approaches.)
- Have people put forward **alternative** approaches to decision making, based on evidence companies? If you could find such evidence, how may it affect company practice?
- Can you identify **limitations** in the ideas and theories presented here, for example are you convinced of the garbage-can model of decision making? Can you find evidence that supports or challenges that view?

Further reading

Bazerman, M.H. (2005), *Judgment in Managerial Decision Making* (6th edn), John Wiley, New York.

Comprehensive and interactive account, aimed at developing the skill of judgement among students, and so enabling them to improve how they make decisions.

Buchanan, L. and O'Connell, A. (2006), 'A brief history of decision making', *Harvard Business Review*, vol. 84, no. 1, pp. 32–41.

Informative overview, placing many of the ideas mentioned in the chapter within a historical context. Part of a special issue of the *Harvard Business Review* devoted to decision making.

Finkelstein, S., Whitehead, J. and Campbell, A. (2009), 'How inappropriate attachments can drive good leaders to make bad decisions', *Organizational Dynamics*, vol. 38, no. 2, pp. 83–92.

Revealing insights into this source of bias in decision making.

Harrison, E.F. (1999), *The Managerial Decision-making Process* (5th edn), Houghton Mifflin, Boston, MA.

Comprehensive interdisciplinary approach to the generic process of decision making, with a focus on the strategic level. The author draws on a wide range of scholarly perspectives and presents them in a lucid and well-organised way.

Harvey, J.B. (1988), 'The abilene paradox: The management of agreement', *Organizational Dynamics*, vol. 17, no. 1, pp. 17–43.

First published in the same journal in 1974, this reprint also includes an epilogue by Harvey, and further commentaries on this classic paper by other management writers.

Schwartz, B. (2004), *The Paradox of Choice*, Ecco, New York.

An excellent study of decision making at the individual level. It shows how people in modern society face an ever-widening and increasingly bewildering range of choices, which is a source of increasing tension and stress. Many of the issues the author raises apply equally well to decision making in organisations.

Weblinks

These websites have appeared in the chapter:

www.ikea.com
www.nice.org.uk
www.wipro.com
www.pg.com
www.inamo-restaurant.com
www.eads.com
www.oticon.com

Visit two of the business sites in the list, or any other company that interests you, and navigate to the pages dealing with recent news or investor relations.

- What examples of decisions which the company has recently had to take can you find?
- How would you classify those decisions in terms of the models in this chapter?
- Gather information from the media websites (such as **www.FT.com**) which relate to the companies you have chosen. What stories can you find that indicate something about the decisions the companies have faced, and what the outcomes have been?

For video case studies, audio summaries, flashcards, exercises and annotated weblinks related to this chapter, visit **www.pearsoned.co.uk/mymanagementlab**

CHAPTER 10
ORGANISATION STRUCTURE

Aim

To introduce terms and practices that show the choices managers face in shaping organisational structures.

Objectives

By the end of your work on this chapter you should be able to outline the concepts below in your terms and:

1 Outline the links between strategy, structure and performance

2 Give examples of how managers divide and co-ordinate work, with their likely advantages and disadvantages

3 Compare the features of mechanistic and organic structures

4 Summarise the work of Woodward, Burns and Stalker, Lawrence and Lorsch and John Child, showing how they contributed to this area of management

5 Use the 'contingencies' believed to influence choice of structure to evaluate the structure unit

6 Explain and illustrate the features of a learning organisation

7 Show how ideas from the chapter add to your understanding of the integrating themes

Key terms

This chapter introduces the following ideas:

organisation structure
organisation chart
formal structure
informal structure
vertical specialisation
horizontal specialisation
formal authority
responsibility
delegation
span of control
centralisation
decentralisation
formalisation
functional structure

divisional structure
matrix structure
network structure
mechanistic structure
organic structure
contingencies
technology
differentiation
integration
contingency approaches
determinism
structural choice
learning organisation

Each is a term defined within the text, as well as in the Glossary at the end of the book.

Case study   Oticon www.oticon.com

Oticon is a small Danish company which competes successfully with larger firms – in part because of its unusual organisation structure. It employs about 1,200 staff in Denmark in its research and production facilities, which supply high-tech devices to the rapidly growing number of people with hearing difficulties. Competition intensified during the 1980s and the company began to lose market share to larger rivals such as Siemens. Lars Kolind was appointed chief executive in 1988. In 1990 he concluded that a new approach was needed to counter the threats from larger competitors that were becoming stronger. Oticon's only hope for survival was to be radical in all aspects of the business. Kolind intended the changes to turn Oticon from an *industrial* organisation into a *service* organisation with a physical product.

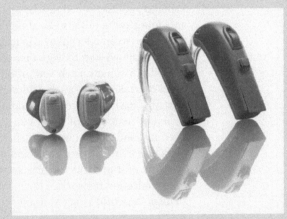

Oticon

He organised product development around projects. The project leader was appointed by the management team and recruited staff from within the firm to do the work: they chose whether or not to join – and could only do so if their current project leader agreed. Previously most people had a single skill; they were now required to be active in at least three specialties – one based on professional qualification and two others unrelated to the first. A chip designer could develop skills in customer support and advertising, for example. These arrangements allowed the company to respond quickly to unexpected events and use skills fully.

Previously Oticon had a conventional hierarchical structure, and a horizontal structure of separate functional departments. The only remnant of the hierarchy is the ten-person management team, each member of which acts as an 'owner' to the many projects through which work is done. Kolind refers to this as 'managed chaos'. The company tries to overcome the dangers of this by developing a strong and clear mission – 'to help people with X problem to live better with X'; and a common set of written values. Examples include: 'an assumption that we only employ adults (who can be expected to act responsibly)', and 'an assumption that staff want to know what and why they are doing it', so all information is available to everyone (with a few legally excepted areas).

There are no titles – people do whatever they think is right at the time. The potential for chaos is averted by building the flexible organisation on a foundation of clearly defined business processes, setting out essential tasks:

The better your processes are defined, the more flexible you can be.

The absence of departments avoids people protecting local interests and makes it easier to cope with fluctuations in workload.

Oticon was one of the earliest companies to redesign the workplace to maximise disturbance. This was most visible in the 'mobile office', in which each workstation was a desk without drawers (nowhere to file paper). There were no installed telephones, although everyone had a mobile. The workstations were equipped with powerful PCs through which people worked (staff had a small personal trolley for personal belongings which they wheeled to wherever they were working that day). Although common today, this arrangement was revolutionary at the time

Sources: Based on Bjorn-Andersen and Turner (1994); Rivard *et al.* (2004): and company website.

Case questions 10.1

- What factors persuaded management to change the structure at Oticon?
- How would you expect staff to react to these changes?

10.1 Introduction

Managers at Oticon had to adapt its structure to survive new competition. This required not only lower costs, but also an ability to respond more quickly to the needs of individual customers and to broader changes in technology and the market. The move to a project-based team approach allows staff to work on a wide range of tasks – which also bring them into close contact with customers. Each new product is designed in conjunction with members of a test-user panel who take part in analysis, design and testing phases of the work. This allows the company to maintain a rapid pace of innovation, and is one of the top three suppliers in the industry.

Senior managers of other companies whose performance has been below expectations often respond by announcing structural changes. Motorola's mobile devices have been losing market share for several years, and in 2009 the Board responded by dividing the company in two: one unit to focus exclusively on the handset market, the other on home and business communication networks. Others follow a policy of frequent small changes. The chairman of L'Oreal, the world's biggest beauty company refers to its

> culture of permanent mini-restructuring. I don't think there has ever been a major restructuring in the whole of L'Oreal's corporate history . . . but there have been hundreds of little ones. What we do is try to live a life of permanent small change to avoid the major disasters. (*Financial Times*, 3 March 2008)

When an owner-manager is running a small business he/she decides what tasks to do and co-ordinates them. If the enterprise grows the entrepreneur usually passes some of the work to newly recruited staff, although the division will probably be flexible and informal. Owner and staff can easily communicate directly with each other, so co-ordination is easy. If the business continues to grow, some find that informality causes problems – so begin to introduce more structure. This often means clarifying tasks to ensure that people know where to focus their effort, and finding ways to ensure they communicate with others.

There are many elements in a structure, and some work better than others in different circumstances. This chapter will outline some of the choices available for dividing and co-ordinating work, and give examples of how managers have used them. It will contrast 'mechanistic' and 'organic' forms, and present a theory which predicts when each is likely to be most suitable. The chapter concludes with some ideas on learning organisations. Figure 10.1 shows these themes.

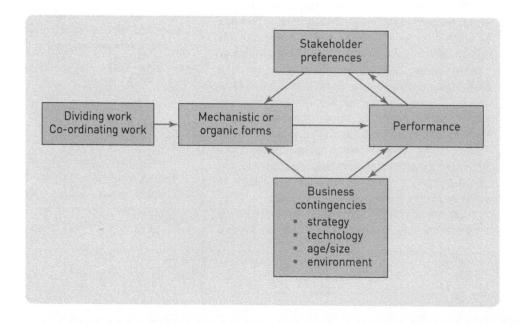

Figure 10.1
Alternative
structures and
performance

10.2 Perspectives on strategy, structure and performance

Alfred Chandler (1962) traced the evolution of America's largest industrial firms, showing how their strategies of growth and diversification placed too many demands on the centralised structures they had created. As the diversity of products and geographies grew, issues arose which those at the (increasingly remote) centre could not handle, as they lacked the knowledge of local circumstances. Chandler's historical analysis of du Pont, General Motors, Standard Oil and Sears, Roebuck shows how they responded by creating decentralised, divisional structures – a significant organisational innovation which many companies use today. It allowed managers at corporate headquarters to provide overall guidance and control, leaving the detailed running of each division to local managers (strategy shaped structure).

Chandler also shows that structure could influence strategy. A new legal requirement to break Standard Oil into small regional companies encouraged one of these – Standard Oil (New Jersey) – to expand into foreign markets as a way of increasing profits (structure shaped strategy). Chandler's aim was to study the interaction of strategy and structure in a changing business environment. In successive cases he traces how strategies to launch new products or enter new regions strained current structures, and how managers responded by gradually, through trial and error, developing new variants of the decentralised divisional form.

That research tradition continues in, for example, Grant's (2003) study of strategy in major oil companies – see Chapter 8. Eli Lilly (**www.lilly.com**), a pharmaceutical company, provides further evidence. The company faced commercial disaster when, quite unexpectedly, it lost patent protection of Prozac: at the time its most profitable drug. Colville and Murphy (2006) show how recovery involved intense debate about a new strategy and a new structure, followed by rapid implementation. This was so successful that the group began launching new drugs at an unprecedented rate, rapidly returning to profit. Whittington *et al.* (2006) also found that managers frequently re-think strategies and structures, and Table 10.1 gives examples of visible, corporate changes.

Table 10.1 Examples of strategic and organisational decisions

Example	Strategic issue	Structural issue
Royal Dutch Shell, 2009. **www.shell.com**	Shell's new CEO decided the present structure was too complex and costly. Aim of change was to cut costs and speed up large projects	Combined two largest divisions into one; some common functions (such as IT) moved from divisions to a central service.
Reed Elsevier, 2008 **www. reed-elsevier.com**	Long-serving CEO accelerates move to profitable online information services, and out of businesses with fluctuating revenue	Sells print-based educational publishing business, and uses funds to buy online risk assessment firm. Integrating this will reduce costs
Multi-show Events (see p. 297)	How to control growing business to ensure continued success.	Divided staff into departments to improve focus and skill; created distinct management roles
Sony Ericsson joint venture 2009 **www. sonyericsson.com**	Had not yet developed a smartphone, and lacked a plan to sell cheap mobiles in emerging markets. Development groups competing	New CEO cut 30 per cent of staff; centralised decision making to end internal rivalry; will use other companies' technology in first smartphone

While senior managers discuss these prominent changes, those at other levels work on fundamentally similar issues within their respective units, such as:

● Should we divide a job into three parts and give each to a separate employee, or have them work as a team with joint responsibility for the whole task?

- Should Team A do this task, or Team B?
- Should that employee report to supervisor A or supervisor B?

Whether the issue is at a multi-national business such as Motorola or a small company such as Multi-show Events, the fundamental structural task is the same – how to enhance performance by clarifying and co-ordinating peoples' roles and responsibilities.

The next section introduces the main tools that people can use to shape the structure of an organisation or of a unit within it.

10.3   Designing a structure

Organisation structure
'The structure of an organisation [is] the sum total of the ways in which it divides its labour into distinct tasks and then achieves co-ordination among them' (Mintzberg, 1979).

Organisation structure describes how managers divide, supervise and co-ordinate work. It gives someone accepting a job a reasonably clear idea of what they should do – the marketing assistant should deal with marketing, not finance. The topic is closely related to culture (Chapter 3) and to human resource management (Chapter 11), since managers intend recruitment, appraisal and reward systems to support the basic structure by encouraging people to act consistently with it.

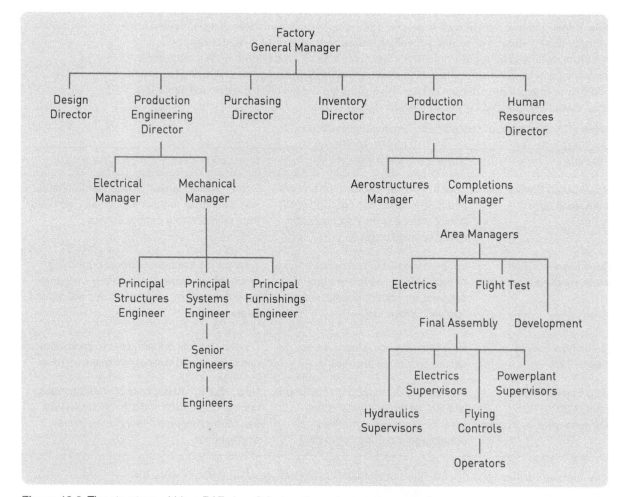

Figure 10.2 The structure within a BAE aircraft factory (**www.baesystems.com**)

The organisation chart

The **organisation chart** shows the main departments and job titles, with lines linking senior executives to the departments or people for whose work they are responsible. It shows who people report to, and clarifies four features of the **formal structure**:

- tasks – the major tasks or activities of the organisation;
- subdivisions – how they are divided;
- levels – the position of each post within the hierarchy;
- lines of authority – these link the boxes to show who people report to.

Organisation charts give a convenient (although transient) summary of tasks and who is responsible for them. Figure 10.2 shows that for an aircraft factory which was then part of BAE Systems, a UK defence contractor. There are six departments; design, production engineering, purchasing, inventory, production and human resources. It also shows the chain of command within the plant and the tasks of the respective departments (only some of which are shown). In this case the chart includes direct staff such as operators and engineers, and shows the lines of authority throughout the factory. It does *not* show the **informal structure** – the many patterns of work and communication that are part of organisational life.

Work specialisation

Within the formal structure managers divide work into smaller tasks, in which people or departments specialise. They become more expert in one task than they could be in several and are more likely to come up with improved ideas or methods. Taken too far it leads to the negative effects on motivation described in Chapter 15.

> **Management in practice   Multi-show Events**
>
> Multi-show Events employs 11 people providing a variety of entertainment and promotional services to large businesses. When Brian Simpson created the business there were two staff – so there was no formal structure. He reflected on the process of growth and structure:
>
> > While the company was small, thinking about a structure never occurred to me. It became a consideration as sales grew and the complexity of what we offered increased. There were also more people around and I believed that I should introduce a structure so that clear divisions of responsibility would be visible. It seemed natural to split sales and marketing from the actual delivery and production of events as these were two distinct areas. I felt that by creating 'specialised' departments we could give a better service to clients as each area of the company could focus more on their own roles. [Figure 10.3 shows the structure.]
> >
> > We had to redesign the office layout and introduce a more formalised communication process to ensure all relevant information is being passed on – and on the whole I think this structure will see us through the next stage of business growth and development.
>
> Source: Private communication.

Figure 10.2 shows specialisation in the BAE factory: at the top it is between design, production, purchasing and so on. It shows a **vertical specialisation** in that people at each level deal with distinct activities, and a **horizontal specialisation**. Within production engineering some specialise in electrical problems and others in mechanical: within the latter, people focus on structures, systems or furnishings. Although Multi-show Events is still a small company, it also has begun to create a structure showing who is responsible for which tasks.

Side notes:

An organisation chart shows the main departments and senior positions in an organisation and the reporting relations between them.

Formal structure consists of guidelines, documents or procedures setting out how the organisation's activities are divided and co-ordinated.

Informal structure is the undocumented relationships between members of the organisation that emerge as people adapt systems to new conditions, and satisfy personal and group needs.

Vertical specialisation refers to the extent to which responsibilities at different levels are defined.

Horizontal specialisation is the degree to which tasks are divided among separate people or departments.

Draw a structure

Select a job you have held (such as in a pub, call centre or shop) and draw a chart showing the structure of your area, such as:

- your position
- the person(s) to whom you reported
- who else reported to them
- the person(s) to whom they reported.

Chain of command

The lines of authority show the links between people – who they report to and who reports to them. It shows who they can ask to do work, who they can ask for help – and who will be expecting results from them. In Figure 10.2 the Production Director can give instructions to the Aerostructures Manager, but not to the Electrical Manager in production engineering. Figure 10.3 shows the lines of authority in Multi-show Events. In both, people have countless informal contacts which make the system live, and help people to cope with unplanned events.

Formal authority is the right that a person in a specified role has to make decisions, allocate resources or give instructions.

In drawing the lines of authority, managers decide where to allocate **formal authority** – giving people the right to make decisions, allocate resources or give instructions. It is based on the position, not the person. The Production Engineering Director at BAE has formal authority over a defined range of matters – and anyone else taking over the job would have the same formal authority.

Subordinates comply with instructions because they accept the person has the formal (sometimes called legitimate) authority to make them. An operator in the hydraulics area of final assembly would accept an instruction from the hydraulics foreman, but probably not from the powerplant foreman (they may help as a personal favour, but that is different from accepting formal authority). If managers give instructions beyond their area of formal authority, they meet resistance.

Responsibility refers to a person's duty to meet the expectations others have of him/her in his/her role.

Responsibility is a person's duty to meet the expectations associated with a task. The Production Director and the Hydraulics Foreman are responsible for the tasks that go with those positions. To fulfil those responsibilities they require formal authority to manage relevant resources.

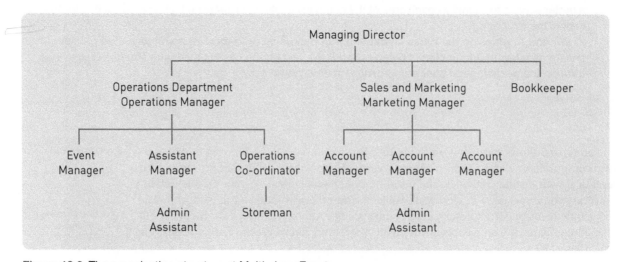

Figure 10.3 The organisation structure at Multi-show Events

Accountability means that people with formal authority over an area are required to report on their work to those above them in the chain of command. The Principal Systems Engineer is accountable to the Mechanical Manager for the way he/she has used resources: have they achieved what was expected as measured by the cost, quantity, quality or timeliness of the work?

Case study   Oticon – the case continues – hierarchy and rank

Before the change, the company had six distinct hierarchical levels, with privileges based on rank:

Not only was there a specific company car assigned to each management level, but other material signs existed . . . prestige and reward were very apparent: in the length of the curtains, the type of carpet . . . the size of people's desks. It all gave status. And that was what people strove for. (Rivard *et al.*, 2004, p. 181)

Horizontal boundaries were also strong, as the two main divisions – Electronics (product development) and International (sales) communicated poorly. Within these divisions work was organised round specific departments and tasks.

People were locked into specific roles and responsibilities and were rewarded only for those – nobody took initiatives (Rivard *et al.*, 2004, p. 180)

Sources: Based on Bjorn-Andersen and Turner (1994); Rivard *et al.* (2004).

Delegation is the process by which people transfer responsibility and authority for part of their work to people below them in the hierarchy. While the Production Director is responsible and accountable for all the work in that area, he/she can only do this by delegating. He/she must account for the results, but pass responsibility and necessary authority to subordinates – and this continues down the hierarchy. If managers delegate to their subordinates this enables quicker decisions and more rapid responses, although some managers are reluctant to delegate in case it reduces their power (Chapter 14).

Delegation occurs when one person gives another the authority to undertake specific activities or decisions.

The span of control

The **span of control** is the number of subordinates reporting to a supervisor. If managers supervise staff closely there is a narrow span of control – as shown in the top half of Figure 10.4. If they allow staff to have more autonomy and responsibility that means less supervision, so more can report to the same manager: the span of control becomes wider, and the structure flatter – the lower half of Figure 10.4.

A span of control is the number of subordinates reporting directly to the person above them in the hierarchy.

Key ideas   Joan Woodward's research

Joan Woodward's study of 100 firms in Essex found great variety between them in the number of subordinates managers supervised (Woodward, 1965). The number of people reporting directly to the chief executive ranged from 2 to 18, with the median span of control being 6. The average span of control of the first line supervisors varied from 10 to 90, with a median of 37. Woodward explained the variation by the technological system used (more in Section 10.7).

Centralisation and decentralisation

As an organisation grows, managers divide work vertically, delegating decisions to those below them – and so begin to create a hierarchy as in Figure 10.4. As the business grows, the

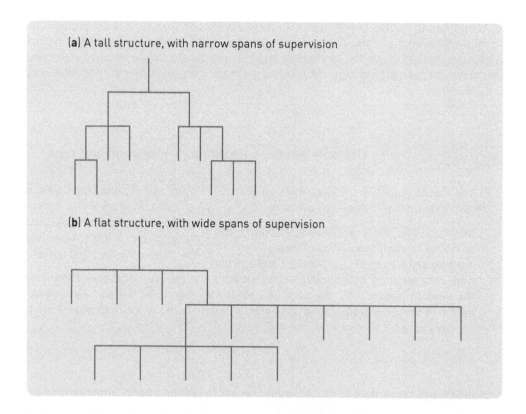

Figure 10.4
Tall and flat
organisation
structures

hierarchy becomes more complex, but it is usually possible to see three levels – corporate, divisional and operating – such as at The Royal Bank of Scotland (RBS) (**www.rbs.com**).

- **Corporate** The most senior group: the Board of RBS has overall responsibility for leading and controlling the company. It approves strategy across the group, monitors performance at major units, and maintains links with significant external institutions such as regulators and political bodies.
- **Divisional** Responsible for implementing policy, and allocating budgets and other resources. RBS is organised partly by customer (UK Personal and UK Corporate); partly by product (RBS Insurance); and partly geographically (Europe and Middle East Retail and Commercial Banking). Division managers are responsible for meeting the targets which the Board sets for them. They also represent the division's interests to the Board and monitor the performance of the division's operating units.
- **Operating** Responsible for the technical work of the organisation – making products, catching thieves, caring for patients or delivering services. Within UK Personal at RBS there are teams responsible for ensuring that, for example, branches and cash machines work smoothly.

The vertical hierarchy establishes what decisions people at each level can make. The theme is especially relevant in large multinational companies, which experience constant tension between calls for global integration and local responsiveness – see Section 10.10 (Internationalisation).

Centralisation is when those at the top make most decisions, with managers at divisional level ensuring those at operating level follow the policy.

Decentralisation is when a relatively large number of decisions are taken in the divisions or operating units. Branch managers in ATMays, a chain of retail travel agents (now part of Going Places) had considerable freedom over pricing and promotional activities, but were required to follow very tight financial reporting routines.

Centralisation is when a relatively large number of decisions are taken by management at the top of the organisation.

Decentralisation is when a relatively large number of decisions are taken lower down the organisation in the operating units.

Roche, based in Switzerland, is one of the world's most successful and profitable pharmaceutical companies. The board appointed a new chief executive in 2010 – Severin Schwan (a graduate in business and law) who, at the age of 40, has spent his career in the company. The group has a decentralised structure and a hands-off relationship with subsidiaries which analysts believe has been a major factor in its success. The federal structure fosters focused research, with each company concentrating on specific diseases, but supple enough to collaborate on marketing. Mr Schwan says teamwork is essential in this knowledge-based business:

> When I toured our labs, I grasped the potential and the enthusiasm of our people. We have to capitalise on that. If you tell your people all the time what to do, don't be surprised if they don't come up with new ideas. Innovative people need air to breathe. Our culture of working together at Roche is based on mutual trust and teamwork. An informal friendly manner supports this: at the same time this must not lead to negligence or shoddy compromises – goals must be achieved and, at times, tough decisions have to be implemented.

Source: *Financial Times*, 4 August 2008.

Many organisations display a mix of both. Network Rail (responsible for all the railway track and signals) has highly standardised processes and highly centralised control systems, but local managers have high autonomy in deciding how to organise their resources. They can co-ordinate track improvements and engineering schedules to meet the needs of local train operating companies (*Financial Times*, 23 July 2007).

This tension between centralising and decentralising is common, with the balance at any time reflecting managers' relative power and their views on the advantages of one direction or the other (see Table 10.2).

Table 10.2 Advantages and disadvantages of centralisation

Factor	Advantages	Disadvantages
Response to change	Thorough debate of issues	Slower response to local conditions
Use of expertise	Concentration of expertise at the centre makes it easier to develop new services and promote best practice methods	Less likely to take account of local knowledge or innovative people
Cost	Economies of scale in purchasing Efficient administration by using common systems	Local suppliers may be better value than corporate suppliers
Policy implications	Less risk of local managers breaching legal requirements	More risk of local managers breaching legal requirements
Staff commitment	Backing of centre ensures wide support	Staff motivated by greater local responsibility
Consistency	Provides consistent image to the public – less variation in service standards	Local staff discouraged from taking responsibility – can blame centre

Formalisation

Formalisation is the practice of using written or electronic documents to direct and control employees.

Formalisation is when managers use written or electronic documents to direct and control employees. These include rule books, procedures, instruction manuals, job descriptions – anything that shows what people must do. Operators in most call centres use scripts to guide their conversation with a customer: managers create these to bring consistency and pre-dictability to the work.

There is always tension between formality and informality. If people want to respond to individual needs or local conditions, they favour informal arrangements with few rules, as this seems the best way to meet those needs. Industry regulators or consumer legislation may specify detailed procedures that companies must follow: these are meant to protect customers against unsuitable selling methods, or to protect staff against unfounded complaints. This leads to more formal systems and recording procedures.

Activity 10.2   Critical reflection on structures

Select an organisation with which you are familiar, or which you can find out about. Gather information about aspects of the structure, such as:

- Does the organisation chart look tall or flat?
- What evidence is there of high or low levels of formality?
- Which decisions are centralised and which are decentralised?
- Share your information with colleagues on your course, to increase your awareness of the range of ways in which people have designed structures.

10.4   Grouping jobs into functions and divisions

While work specialisation divides tasks into smaller jobs for individuals, an opposite process groups them together in functional, divisional or matrix forms. Two other forms use teams and networks as the basis of structure. Figure 10.5 shows these alternatives.

Specialisation by function

A functional structure is when tasks are grouped into departments based on similar skills and expertise.

In a **functional structure**, managers group staff according to their profession or function, such as production or finance. The BAE chart shows design, production engineering, pur-chasing, inventory, production and human resources functions. Figure 10.6 shows a hospital chart, with a functional structure at senior level.

The functional approach can be efficient as people with common expertise work together to provide a service, and follow a professional career path. It can lead to conflict if functions have different perceptions of organisational goals (Nauta and Sanders, 2001) or priorities. Le Meunier-FitzHugh and Piercy (2008) show how staff in sales and marketing experience this – the former stressing immediate sales, the latter long-term customer relations. Func-tional staff face conflicts when product managers compete for access to functional resources such as information technology.

Specialisation by divisions

A divisional structure is when tasks are grouped in relation to their outputs, such as products or the needs of different types of customer.

Managers create a **divisional structure** when they arrange the organisation around products, services or customers, giving those in charge of each unit the authority to design, produce and deliver the product or service. Functions within the division are likely to co-operate as they depend on satisfying the same set of customers.

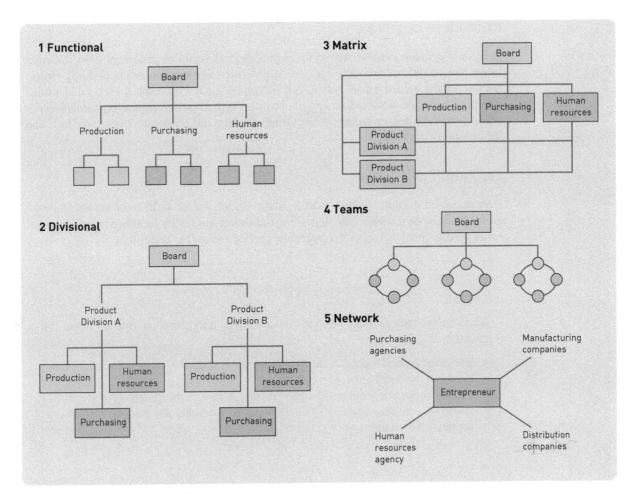

Figure 10.5 Five types of structure

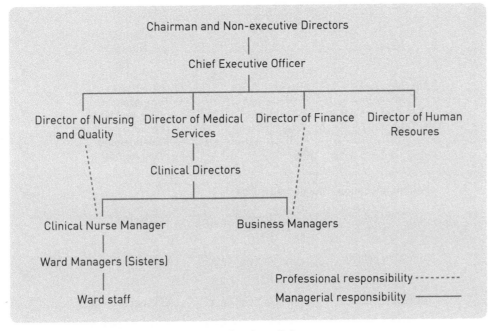

Figure 10.6 Partial organisation structure in a hospital

Product or customer

Divisional structures enable staff to focus on a distinct group of customers – HMV Group (**www.hmv.co.uk**) has two divisions – the HMV stores, and Waterstone's bookshops. Hospitals can use the 'named-nurse' system, in which one nurse is responsible for several identified patients. That nurse is the patient's point of contact with the system, managing the delivery of services to the patient from other (functional) departments. Figure 10.7 contrasts 'task' and 'named-nurse' approaches.

Geographic divisions

Here managers in companies with many service outlets – such as Tesco or Wetherspoon's – group them by geography. This allows front-line staff to identify local needs, and makes it easier for divisional managers to control local performance (see Table 10.3).

Activity 10.3   **Choosing between approaches**

Go to the website of a company that interests you and gather information about the structure of the company.

- Decide whether it has a functional or a divisional structure – and, if the latter, is that based on products or geography?
- If it has international operations, how are they shown in the structure?
- Compare your research with colleagues on your course, and prepare a short presentation summarising your conclusions

---

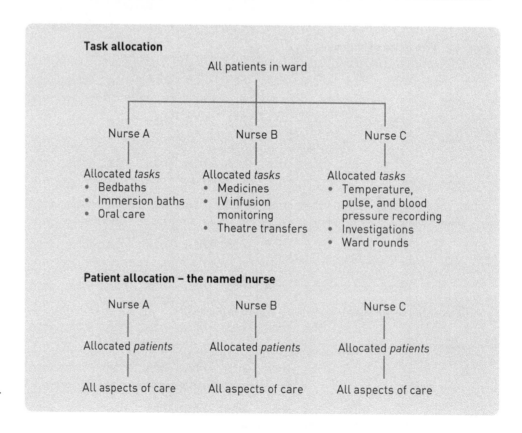

Figure 10.7
Task and named-nurse structures

Table 10.3 Advantages and disadvantages of functional and divisional structures

Structure	Advantages	Disadvantages
Functional	Clear career paths and professional development	Isolation from wider interests damages promotion prospects
	Specialisation leads to high standards and efficiency	Conflict over priorities
	Common professional interests support good internal relations	Lack of wider awareness damages external relations
Divisional	Functional staff focus on product and customer needs	Isolation from wider professional and technical developments
	Dedicated facilities meet customer needs quickly	Costs of duplicate resources
	Common customer focus enables good internal relations	Potential conflict with other divisions over priorities
		Focus on local, not corporate, needs

10.5   Grouping jobs in matrices, teams and networks

Matrix structure

A matrix structure combines functional and divisional structures: function on one axis of the matrix and products or projects on the other. Functional staff work on one or more projects, moving between them as required. They report to two bosses – a functional head and the head of the current project.

A matrix structure is when those doing a task report both to a functional and a project or divisional boss.

Teams

In their search for more flexibility, lower costs and faster response some companies organise work into teams – especially those that depend on a steady flow of new products, such as Nokia or EMI Music. Management delegates significant responsibility and authority to an identifiable team, which is then accountable for results (Chapter 17).

Management in practice   **Team launches new albums at EMI**   www.emi.com

New music albums often fail when managers are unable to manage the launch effectively. There is often tension between marketing staff who have a short-term outlook, being expected to satisfy current consumers by exploiting existing resources, and creative staff who take a medium-term view. The latter do so as they are expected to find new artists to change the repertoire – and who therefore need longer to become credible.

Ordanini *et al.* (2008) show how EMI Music adopted a team approach to launching new albums. They appointed a single team to be responsible for all aspects of the launch of an album by an unknown and possibly controversial artist. The team included marketing and creative staff, and enabled them to work together in this way for the first time. In this case the launch was successful on several dimensions, and appeared to vindicate the choice of a team approach.

Source: Ordanini *et al.* (2008).

Networks

A network structure is when tasks required by one company are performed by other companies with expertise in those areas.

Network structures refer to situations in which organisations remain independent but agree to work together to deliver products or services. Sometimes this happens when managers arrange for other companies to undertake certain non-core activities on their behalf. The remaining organisation concentrates on setting strategy direction and managing the core units. Electronic companies often do this: Dell's products are made under contract by companies that specialise in such work. The arrangement is becoming common in personal services – such as when Care UK runs schools for disturbed children for local government, and in Community Health Partnerships (see the following Management in Practice).

Management in practice
Community Health Partnerships (CHP)
www.communityhealthpartnerships.co.uk

Many social and health problems are caused by a range of conditions which have traditionally been the responsibility of distinct public bodies – health, social work, education, housing and police. Many practitioners believe that effective solutions depend on these independent agencies working together to offer a more comprehensive service than any agency could do alone.

A prominent example is Community Health Partnerships (CHP), an independent company, wholly owned by the UK Department of Health. It aims to deliver innovative ways to improve health and local authority services through the Local Improvement Finance Trust (LIFT) Initiative which provides modern premises for health and local authority services in England.

It has established 48 LIFT partnerships, covering two-thirds of England's population, and is responsible for more than 250 buildings that are either open or under construction. More recently, CHP has developed new models of public–private partnership, such as Community Ventures and Social Enterprises, to improve health and social care.

The different backgrounds, priorities and cultures of the organisations taking part make such ventures challenging to manage.

Sources: Company website; other published sources.

Mixed forms

Large organisations typically combine functional, product and geographical structures within the same company – see for example BP (Part 2 Case) or RBS (Part 4 Case).

The counterpart of dividing work is to co-ordinate it, or there will be confusion and poor performance.

Activity 10.4   Comparing structures

Think of an organisation you have worked in or about which you can gather information.

- Which of the five structural forms did it correspond to most closely?
- What were the benefits and disadvantages of that approach?
- Compare your conclusions with colleagues on your course, and use your experience to prepare a list of the advantages and disadvantages of each type of structure.

10.6   Co-ordinating work

There are five common ways to co-ordinate work.

Direct supervision

This is where a manager ensures co-ordination by directly supervising his/her staff to ensure they work as expected. The number of people whom a manager can effectively supervise directly reflects the idea of the span of control – that beyond some (variable) point direct supervision is no longer sufficient.

Hierarchy

If disputes or problems arise between staff or departments, they can put the arguments to their common boss in the hierarchy, making it the boss's responsibility to reach a solution. At BAE (Figure 10.2), if the engineer responsible for structures has a disagreement with the Systems Engineer, they can ask the Mechanical Manager to adjudicate. If that fails they can escalate the problem to the Production Engineering Director – but this takes time. In rapidly changing circumstances the hierarchy cannot cope with the many issues requiring attention and so delays decisions.

Standardising inputs and outputs

If the buyer of a component specifies exactly what is required, and the supplier meets that specification, co-ordination between any users will be easy. If staff meet the specifications, that helps them to co-ordinate with the next stage. If they receive the same training they will need less direct supervision, as their manager can be confident they will work consistently. All new staff at Pret A Manger must complete a very precise training course before they begin work, which is then constantly reinforced once they are in a post.

Rules and procedures

Another method is to prepare rules or procedures, like those in the following Management in Practice. As another example, organisations have procedures for approving capital expenditure. To compare proposals accurately they set strict guidelines on the questions a bid should answer, how people should prepare a case and to whom they should submit it. Software developers face the challenge of co-ordinating the work of the designers working on different parts of a project, so they use strict change control procedures to ensure that the sub-projects fit together.

Management in practice   **Safety procedures in a power station**

The following instructions govern the steps that staff must follow when they inspect control equipment in a nuclear power station:

1 Before commencing work you must read and understand the relevant Permit-to-Work and/or other safety documents as appropriate.
2 Obtain keys for relevant cubicles.
3 Visually inspect the interior of each bay for dirt, water and evidence of condensation.
4 Visually inspect the cabling, glands, terminal blocks and components for damage.
5 Visually check for loose connections at all terminals.
6 Lock all cubicles and return the keys.
7 Clear the safety document and return it to the Supervisor/Senior Authorised person.

Information systems

Information systems help to ensure that people who need to work in a consistent way have common information, so that they can co-ordinate their activities. Computer systems and internet applications enable different parts of an organisation, as well as suppliers and customers, to work from common information, making co-ordination much easier (see Chapter 12).

Key ideas   **Co-ordinating sales and marketing**

Large organisations typically create separate sales and marketing departments, which must then co-ordinate their work to ensure co-operation, customer satisfaction and profitability. Homberg *et al.* (2008) concluded (from a survey of German firms in financial services, consumer goods and chemicals) that the best performance was in firms where managers had:

- developed strong structural links between the two functions, especially by using teams, and requiring staff to plan projects jointly; and
- ensured that staff in both functions had high market knowledge, by rotating them between other functions in the firm to develop knowledge about customers and competitors, which then helped the two functions to work effectively together.

Source: Homburg *et al.* (2008).

Most companies purchase goods and services electronically, ensuring that orders and payments to suppliers flow automatically to match current demand. This co-ordinates a laborious task where mistakes were common.

Direct personal contact

The most human form of co-ordination is when people talk to each other. Mintzberg (1979) found that people use this method in both the simplest and the most complex situations. There is so much uncertainty in the latter that information systems cannot cope – only direct contact can do this, by enabling people to making personal commitments across business units (Sull and Spinosa, 2005) (see the above Key Ideas and the following Management in Practice).

Management in practice   **Co-ordination in a social service**

The organisation cares for the elderly in a large city. Someone who had worked there for several years reflected on co-ordination:

Within the centre there was a manager, two deputies, an assistant manager, five senior care officers (SCOs) and 30 officers. Each SCO is responsible for six care officers, allowing daily contact between the supervisor and the subordinates. While this defines job roles quite tightly, it allows a good communication structure to exist. Feedback is common as there are frequent meetings of the separate groups, and individual appraisals of the care officers by the SCOs. Staff value this opportunity for praise and comments on how they are doing.

Contact at all levels is common between supervisor and care officers during meetings to assess the needs of clients, for whom the care officers have direct responsibility. Frequent social gatherings and functions within the department also enhance relations and satisfy social needs. Controls placed on the behaviour of the care officers come from senior management, often derived from legislation such as the Social Work Acts or the Health and Safety Executive.

Source: Private communication.

Activity 10.5   Comparing co-ordination

Think of an organisation you have worked in or about which you can gather information

- Which forms of co-ordination did it use?
- What were the benefits and disadvantages of that approach?
- Compare your conclusions with colleagues on your course, and use your experience to prepare a list of the advantages and disadvantages of each method of co-ordination.

Managers make a succession of decisions on any or all of these ways to divide and co-ordinate work: as they do so they build a structure which in varying degrees correspond to a mechanistic or organic form.

10.7   Mechanistic and organic structures

The purpose of structure is to encourage people to act in a way that supports strategy. Some structures emphasise the vertical hierarchy by defining responsibilities clearly, taking decisions at the centre, delegating tightly defined tasks and requiring frequent reports. This enables those at the centre to know what is happening and whether staff are working correctly. The organisation presents a uniform image and ensures that customers receive consistent treatment. Communication is mainly vertical, as the centre passes instructions down and staff pass queries up. Burns and Stalker (1961) called this a **mechanistic structure**.

Others develop a structure with broadly defined, flexible tasks, many cross-functional teams, and base authority on expertise rather than position. Management accepts that the centre depend on those nearest the action to find the best solution. Communication is mainly horizontal among those familiar with the task. There may not be an organisation chart, as the division of work is so fluid. Burns and Stalker (1961) called this an **organic structure**. Table 10.4 compares mechanistic and organic forms.

> A **mechanistic structure** means there is a high degree of task specialisation, people's responsibility and authority are closely defined and decision making is centralised.

> An **organic structure** is one where people are expected to work together and use their initiative to solve problems; job descriptions and rules are few and imprecise.

Management in practice   An organic structure at Pixar   www.pixar.com

The company's string of successful movies depends not only on the creative people that it employs, but on how it manages that talent. Ed Catmull (co-founder of Pixar and president of Pixar and Disney Animation Studios) has written about what he calls the 'collective creativity' of the process, and how the senior team fosters this. Something that he believes sets Pixar apart from other studios is the way that people at all levels support each other. An example of how they do this is the process of daily reviews. He writes:

> The practice of working together as peers is core to our culture, and it's not limited to our directors and producers. One example is our daily reviews, or 'dailies' a process for giving and getting constant feedback in a positive way . . . People show work in an incomplete state to the whole animation crew, and although the director makes decisions, everyone is encouraged to comment. There are several benefits. First, once people get over the embarrassment of showing work still in progress, they become more creative. Second, director or creative leads . . . can communicate important points to the entire crew at the same time. Third, people learn from and inspire each other: a highly creative piece of animation will spark others to raise their game. Finally, there are no surprises at the end: when you're done, you're done. People's overwhelming desire to make sure their work is 'good' before they show it to others increases the possibility that their finished version won't be what the director wants. The dailies process avoids such wasted efforts.

Source: Catmull (2008), p. 70.

Table 10.4 Characteristics of mechanistic and organic systems

Mechanistic	Organic
Specialised tasks	Contribute experience to common tasks
Hierarchical structure of control	Network structure of contacts
Knowledge located at top of hierarchy	Knowledge widely spread
Vertical communication	Horizontal communication
Loyalty and obedience stressed	Commitment to goals more important

Source: Based on Burns and Stalker (1961).

Within a large organisation some units will correspond to a mechanistic form and others to an organic. A company may have a centralised information system and tightly controlled policies on capital expenditure – while also allowing business units autonomy on research or advertising budgets.

> **Case questions 10.2**
>
> - What was the role of strategy and technology in encouraging the change at Oticon?
> - What features of the present form correspond to the organic model?
> - How does management hope that the new structure will support their strategy?

Contingencies are factors such as uncertainty, interdependence and size that reflect the situation of the organisation.

Why do managers favour one form of structure rather than another? One (though disputed) view is that it depends on how they interpret **contingencies**:

the essence of the contingency paradigm is that organizational effectiveness results from fitting characteristics of the organization, such as its structure, to contingencies that reflect the situation of the organization. (Donaldson, 2001, p. 1)

Successful organisations appear to be those in which managers maintain a good fit between contingent factors and the structure within which people work. Figure 10.1 illustrates four contingent factors – strategy, technology, age/size and environment.

Strategy

Chapter 8 outlines Porter's view that firms adopt one of three generic strategies: cost leadership, differentiation or focus. With a cost leadership strategy managers try to increase efficiency to keep costs low. A mechanistic structure is likely to support this strategy, with closely defined tasks in an efficient functional structure. A hierarchical chain of command ensures that people work to plan and vertical communication keeps the centre informed. Powergen, an electricity utility, initially had a cost-leadership strategy, supporting this with a functional structure with detailed rules and performance measures.

A differentiation strategy focuses on innovation – developing new products rapidly and imaginatively. An organic structure is most likely to support this, by enabling ideas to flow easily between people able to contribute, regardless of their function. Hill and Pickering (1986) showed that companies which allowed business units more decision-making authority were more successful than those which limited this. The Part 5 Case shows how, like Pixar in animation, W.L. Gore uses an organic form in its high-tech businesses. Oticon adopted a team-based structure, as has Monsanto (see the following Management in Practice).

Although many see Monsanto as a predatory chemical company pressing genetically modified seeds on the world, its chief executive (Mr Grant) sees it as a vibrant biotechnology company with all the dynamism of a Silicon Valley start-up:

> In some companies the scientists are in the back room, separate from the business people. The culture here is much closer to a software company, where there are developers that invent cool stuff and there is a very intimate link between the scientists and the business people.

This is reflected, Mr Grant says, in the company's day-to-day operations.

> If we're making decisions, there's usually five or six people at the table. That makes for a culture that is extraordinarily team-based – not in the sense of group hugs and the fluff factor, but because most decisions we make are multi-disciplinary and if you want to make a decision once, you had better have those people at the table.
>
> It's an environment where people need to have an equal voice . . . Quite often you will have a business person, a regulatory person, a breeding person, a production person and a couple of others. That has created a culture where people come together, form teams, make decisions, break up and move on to the next thing. It's more amorphous than the hierarchical corporate structure, and that makes it feel more like a modern company than an old world company.

Source: *Financial Times*, 15 June 2009.

Figure 10.8 expresses the idea that different strategies require different structures. The more the strategy corresponds to cost leadership, the more likely it is that managers will support it with a functional structure. If the balance is towards differentiation, the more likely there will be a divisional, team or network structure.

Technology

Technology refers to the knowledge, tools and techniques used to transform inputs into outputs. It includes buildings, machines, computer systems, and the knowledge and procedures associated with them.

Joan Woodward (1965) gathered information from 100 British firms to establish whether structural features such as the span of control or the number of levels in the hierarchy varied between them, and whether this affected performance. The researchers saw no pattern until they analysed companies by their manufacturing process, grouping these into three types according to their technical complexity. This showed a relationship between technical complexity and company structure.

Technology is the knowledge, equipment and activities used to transform inputs into outputs.

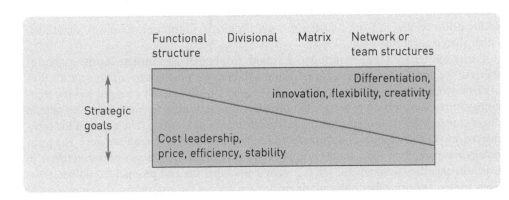

Figure 10.8
Relationship between strategies and structural types

- **Unit and small batch production** Firms make unique goods to a customer's order. It is similar to craft work, as people and their skills are deeply involved in the process – custom-built cycles, designer furniture, luxury yachts.
- **Large batch and mass production** Large quantities of standard products move along an assembly line, with people complementing the machinery – mobile phones, Ford cars or Electrolux washing machines.
- **Continuous process** Material flows through complex technology which makes the product as operators monitor it, fixing faults and generally overseeing the process – a Guinness Brewery, BP refinery or Mittal steel plant.

Woodward concluded that the different technologies impose different demands on people. Unit production requires close supervision to ensure each staff meet each customer's unique requirements. Supervisors can communicate directly with those working on different parts of the task and so manage the uncertainties involved in producing 'one-off' items. On an assembly line the work is routine and predictable, so a supervisor can monitor more staff: there is a wide span of control. Commercially successful firms were those where managers had created a structure providing the right support to staff using the technology.

Technology also delivers services, and managers create structures to shape the way staff interact with customers. Bank staff used to handle many cash transactions, and sat behind secure glass screens which made them remote. Technology means that bank branches now handle very little cash, so banks re-designed them to bring staff and customers closer together. The Part 4 Case – The Royal Bank of Scotland – traces structural changes in that service business, including the centralised Manufacturing Division which has a mechanistic structure. When Steve Jobs was at Pixar, like Lars Kolind at Oticon, he designed the building:

> to maximize inadvertent encounters. At the centre is a large atrium which contains the cafeteria, meeting rooms, bathrooms, and mailboxes. As a result, everyone has strong reasons to go there repeatedly during the course of the workday. It's hard to describe just how valuable the resulting chance encounters are. (Catmull, 2008, p. 71)

Environment

Chapter 3 shows how environments vary in terms of their complexity and dynamism: does this mean that firms need a structure that suits the nature of their environment? Burns and Stalker (1961) compared the structure of a long-established rayon plant in Manchester with the structures of several new electronics companies then being created in the east of Scotland. Both types of organisation were successful – but they had different structures.

The rayon plant had clearly set-out rules, tight job descriptions, clear procedures and co-ordination was primarily through the hierarchy. There was a high degree of specialisation, with tasks divided into small parts. Managers had defined responsibilities clearly and discouraged people from acting outside of their remit. They had centralised decisions, with information flowing up the hierarchy and instructions flowing down.

The small companies in the newly created electronics industry had few job descriptions, while procedures were ambiguous and imprecise. Staff were expected to use their initiative to decide priorities and to work together to solve problems. Communication was horizontal, rather than vertical (see Table 10.4).

Burns and Stalker (1961) concluded that both forms were appropriate for their circumstances. The rayon plant had a stable environment, as its purpose was to supply a steady flow of rayon to the company's spinning factories. Delivery schedules rarely changed and the technology of rayon manufacture was well known. In contrast, the electronics companies were in direct contact with their customers, mainly the Ministry of Defence. The demand for commercial and military products was volatile, with frequent changes in requirements. The technology was new, often applying the results of recent research. Contracts were often taken, in which neither the customer nor the company knew what the end product would be: it was likely to change during the course of the work.

Case study   ## Oticon – the case continues – communication and technology

Lars Kolind knew that the dramatic change in structure he proposed would not be achieved without pain: he was attacking the established culture, privileges tied to seniority and titles, and wasteful work processes. In moving to an organisation in which there would be only project members, project leaders and project owners, many would not easily accept losing the power they derived from controlling information. He used his power to drive the change, announcing:

> I am 100 per cent sure that we will try this. There's enough time so that you can make a choice – whether you are going to try it with us or whether . . . you find another job. (Quoted in Rivard *et al.*, 2004, p. 174)

While the company used advanced IS for many functions, Kolind believed that dialogue is better than email, and designed the building to support face-to-face dialogue between staff. The problem owner will usually use email or personal contact to bring two or three people together and have a stand-up meeting. Decisions are noted on the computer (accessible by everyone).

By 1994 the company had halved product development time and more than doubled sales. It employed half as many administrative staff as in 1990, but double the number on product development. Financial performance improved dramatically in the years following the change.

> Hardware companies have organisations that look like machines: a company that produces knowledge needs an organisation that looks like a brain, i.e. which looks chaotic and is unhierarchical. (Lars Kolind)

Sources: Based on Bjorn-Andersen and Turner (1994); Rivard *et al.* (2004).

Case questions 10.3

- Oticon has had both mechanistic and organic structures: what prompted the change?
- Why has the new structure improved business performance?

Burns and Stalker (1961) concluded that stable, predictable environments were likely to encourage a mechanistic structure. Volatile, unpredictable environments were likely to encourage an organic structure. This recognition that environmental conditions place different demands upon organisations was a major step in understanding why companies adopt contrasting structures – an idea which Figure 10.9 illustrates.

		Structure	
		Mechanistic	*Organic*
Environment	*Uncertain (unstable)*	**Incorrect fit:** Mechanistic structure in uncertain environment Structure too tight	**Correct fit:** Organic structure in uncertain environment
	Certain (stable)	**Correct fit:** Mechanistic structure in certain environment	**Incorrect fit:** Organic structure in certain environment Structure too loose

Figure 10.9 Relationship between environment and structure

> ### Activity 10.6 Comparing mechanistic and organic forms
>
> Think of a department you have worked in or about which you can gather information.
>
> - Was it broadly mechanistic or organic?
> - Why has that form evolved and is it suitable?
> - How does it compare with other departments in the organisation?

> ### Management in practice Organic problem solving in a mechanistic structure
>
> The organisation I work for has just come through a short-term cash-flow crisis. The problem arose because, while expenditures on contracts are relatively predictable and even the income flow was disrupted by a series of contractual disputes.
>
> The role culture permeates the head office, and at first the problem was pushed ever upwards. But faced with this crisis all departments were asked for ideas on how to improve performance. Some have been turned into new methods of working, and others are still being considered by the 'ideas team', drawn from all grades of personnel and departments. This was a totally new perspective, of a task culture operating within a role culture – that is, we developed an organic approach. What could be more simple than asking people who do the job how they could be more efficient?
>
> To maintain the change in the long run is difficult, and some parts have now started to drift back to the role culture.
>
> Source: Private communication.

Differentiation The state of segmentation of the organisation into subsystems, each of which tends to develop particular attributes in response to the particular demands posed by its relevant external environment.

Integration is the process of achieving unity of effort among the various subsystems in the accomplishment of the organisation's task.

Organisations do not face a single environment. People in each department try to meet the expectations of players in the wider environment, and gradually develop structures which help them to do that. A payroll section has to meet legal requirements on, among other things, salary entitlements, taxation and pensions records. Staff must follow strict rules, with little scope to use their initiative: they work in a mechanistic structure. Staff in product development face different requirements – and will expect to work in a structure that encourages creativity and innovation: they expect to work in an organic structure.

An implication of this is that co-ordination between such departments will be difficult, as they will work in different ways. Paul Lawrence and Jay Lorsch explored this issue, and their contribution is in the following Key Ideas.

> ### Key ideas Lawrence and Lorsch: differentiation and integration
>
> Two American scholars, Paul Lawrence and Jay Lorsch, developed Burns and Stalker's work. They observed that departments doing different tasks face a separate segment of the environment – some relatively stable, others unstable. Lawrence and Lorsch predicted that to cope with these varying conditions departments will develop different structures and ways of working. Those in stable environments would move towards mechanistic forms, those in unstable environments would move towards organic.
>
> Empirical research in six organisations enabled Lawrence and Lorsch to show that departments did indeed differ from each other, and in ways they had predicted. Those facing unstable environments (research

and development) had less formal structures than those facing stable ones (production). The greater the **differentiation** between departments the more effort was needed to integrate their work. Successful firms achieved more **integration** between units by using a variety of integrating devices such as task forces and project managers with the required interpersonal skills. The less effective companies in the uncertain environment used rules and procedures.

Source: Lawrence and Lorsch (1967).

Age and size

Small organisations tend to be informal – people work on several tasks and co-ordinate with each other by face-to-face contact or direct supervision. Weber (1947) noted that larger organisations had formal, bureaucratic structures: research by Blau (1970) and Pugh and Hickson (1976) confirmed that as organisations grow they develop formal structures, hierarchies and specialised units. Like the head of Multi-show Events, as managers divide a growing business into separate units they need more controls such as job descriptions and reporting relationships.

Management in practice — Growth and structure in a housing association

A manager in a housing association, which was created to provide affordable housing for those on low incomes, describes how its structure changed as it grew.

> Housing associations have to give tenants and their representatives the opportunity to influence policy. In the early days it had few staff, no clear division of labour and few rules and procedures. It was successful in providing housing, which attracted more government funds, and the association grew. Managing more houses required a more formal structure to support the work. The association no longer served a single community, but several geographical areas. Staff numbers grew significantly and worked in specialised departments. The changes led to concerns among both staff and committee that the organisation was no longer responsive to community needs and that it had become distant and bureaucratic.

Source: Private communication from the manager.

This implies that organisations go through stages in their lifecycle, with structures adapting to suit. The entrepreneur creates the business alone, or with a few partners or employees. They operate informally with little division of labour – tasks overlap (for a discussion of the unique structural issues facing entrepreneurs in high technology industries, see Alvarez and Barney (2005)). There are few rules or systems for planning and co-ordination. The owner makes the decisions, so they have a centralised structure. If the business succeeds it will need to raise more capital to finance growth. The owner no longer has sole control, but shares decisions with members of the growing management team. Tasks become divided by function or product, creating separate departments and more formal controls to ensure co-ordination. Many small companies fail when they expand rapidly, but fail to impose controls and systems for managing risks – as an executive of a publishing company which got into difficulties recalled:

> We were editors and designers running a large show, and we were completely overstretched. Our systems were simply not up to speed with our creative ambitions.

This observation is consistent with a study by Sine *et al.* (2006), which shows how successful internet companies were those which balanced their essential creativity with a degree of formalisation, specialisation and administrative intensity. They survived, while those which lacked even the most rudimentary structures failed.

If a business continues to grow, it becomes more bureaucratic with more division of responsibilities, and more rules and systems to ensure co-ordination. Mature, established firms tend to become mechanistic, with a strong vertical system and well-developed controls. More decisions are made at the centre – bringing the danger of slower responses to change and, in some industries, a less competitive position than newer rivals. The managing director of Iris, an advertising agency, said:

> Iris London is our oldest and our most mature office – about 300 people. When an agency grows to that sort of size there are things about it that start to become dysfunctional. You start to have to invent admin systems, processes, bureaucracy, and that's countercultural and it stops you being any good, it stops you getting closer to clients and being creative. So in London we've reorganised around clients [with five groups] of between 30 and 60 people: the creative, the planning, the commercial guys are all sat together, all around dedicated clusters of client type. And that we think will make us more efficient, more effective, more instinctive as an agency.

Case study — Oticon – the case continues – limiting risks

While the changes at Oticon had spurred creativity, the Board of the firm also became concerned about profitability in the early years, as the new structure was creating so many initiatives and new products that it was difficult to manage them all effectively. They therefore appointed Neils Jacobsen as co-chief executive in 1992, to place more emphasis on financial discipline and performance. Jacobsen took over from Kolind as chief executive in 1998.

In 1996 more controls were introduced, to balance some of the risks of the new form. A Competence Centre was established which took over some of the rights previously held by project managers. It alone now had the right to initiate projects and appoint project managers – thus restraining the earlier principle that anyone could start a project. It also took over the task of negotiating salaries which had initially been delegated to project managers.

These changes were intended to overcome some of the costs associated with the radical structure. When there was no limit to the number of projects, nor to the number of projects on which a person could work, it had become hard to ensure completion: the most capable staff were spread over too many projects. There was also some concern that staff and teams were not always sharing knowledge as fully as expected. Despite these adjustments, the company remains a radically different form of organisation.

Source: Based on Foss (2003).

Contingencies or managerial choice?

Contingency approaches *propose that the performance of an organisation depends on having a structure that is appropriate to its environment.*

Determinism *is the view that the business environment determines an organisation's structure.*

Contingency approaches propose that the most effective structure will depend (be contingent) upon the situation in which the organisation is operating:

> The organization is seen as existing in an environment that shapes its strategy, technology, size and innovation rate. These contingent factors in turn determine the required structure; that is, the structure that the organization needs to adopt if it is to operate effectively. (Donaldson, 1996, p. 2)

Effective management involves formulating an appropriate strategy and developing a structure which supports that strategy by encouraging appropriate behaviour. The emphasis is **determinist** (the form is determined by the environment) and functionalist (the form is intended to serve organisational effectiveness) (Donaldson, 1995). Management's role is to make suitable adjustments to the structure to improve performance as conditions change – such as by increasing formality as the company grows.

John Child (1972, 1984) disagrees, suggesting that contingency theorists ignore the degree of **structural choice** that managers have. The process of organisational design is not a solely rational matter but one also shaped by political processes. The values and interests of powerful groups are able to influence the structure that emerges even if this reduces performance to some degree. The standards used to assess performance are in any case not always rigorous, and people may tolerate some under-performance caused by an inappropriate structure. There is other evidence that managers have choice over the structure they design without necessarily damaging performance (see the following Management in Practice).

> **Structural choice** emphasises the scope which management has to decide the form of structure, irrespective of environmental conditions.

Management in practice   Retailers' response to the internet

The internet enables online grocery shopping, initially allowing customers to order online and receive home delivery. Sainsbury's responded by creating a new division to handle this business, with a separate management structure, warehouses and distribution system. Tesco chose to integrate the online business with existing stores – staff pick the customer's order from the shelves of a conventional store. Other chains offer the choice of doing the whole transaction in-store, ordering online and collecting from the store, or ordering online for home delivery. The underlying internet technology is the same for all, but managers have chosen to use it in different ways.

Activity 10.7   Critical reflection – contingency or choice?

- Recall some significant changes in the structure of your organisation. Try to establish the reasons for them, and whether they had the intended effects. Do those reasons tend to support the contingency or management choice perspectives?

Case questions 10.3

- Does the Oticon example support contingency or management choice approaches?
- Does the role of management in the company support either of these approaches?

Another consideration is that the direction of causality is not necessarily from strategy to structure. It is also possible that an organisation with a given structure finds that that makes it easier to embark on a particular strategy.

10.8   Learning organisations

Innovation is the main reason why many advocate the development of 'learning organisations', since organisations which operate in complex and dynamic environments can only be successful innovators if they develop the capacity learn and respond quickly to changing circumstances. The term **learning organisation** is used to describe an organisation that has developed the capacity to continuously learn, adapt and change. In a learning organisation the focus is on acquiring, sharing and using knowledge to encourage innovation.

> **A learning organisation** is one that has developed the capacity to continuously learn, adapt and change.

According to Nonaka and Takeuchi (1995) the ability to create knowledge and solve problems has become a core competence in many businesses. In their view, everyone is a knowledge worker – someone dealing with customers, for example, quickly finds out about their likes and dislikes, and their view of the service. Because they are typically in low-paid jobs far from corporate headquarters, this valuable intelligence is often overlooked.

Table 10.5 (based on Pedler *et al.*, 1997) presents a view of the features of an ideal learning organisation – features to which managers can aspire. These features cluster under five headings as shown in Figure 10.10

In a learning organisation members share information and collaborate on work activities wherever required – including across functional and hierarchical boundaries. Boundaries between units are either eliminated (as at Oticon) or are made as porous as possible to ensure that they do not block the flow of ideas and information. Learning organisations tend to emphasise team working, and employees operate with a high degree of autonomy to work as they think will best enhance performance. Rather than directing and controlling, managers act as facilitators, supporters and advocates – enabling their staff to work and learn to the greatest degree possible.

Learning depends on information, so there is an emphasis on sharing information among employees in a timely and open manner. This too depends on managers creating a structure which encourages people to pass information in this way. Leadership is also important in the

Table 10.5 Features of a learning organisation

Feature	Explanation
A learning approach to strategy	The use of trials and experiments to improve understanding and generate improvements, and to modify strategic direction
Participative policy making	All members are involved in strategy formation, influencing decisions and values and addressing conflict
Informative	Information technology is used to make information available to everyone and to enable front-line staff to use their initiative
Formative accounting and control	Accounting, budgeting and reporting systems are designed to help people understand the operations of organisational finance
Internal exchange	Sections and departments think of themselves as customers and suppliers in an internal 'supply chain', learning from each other
Reward flexibility	A flexible and creative reward policy, with financial and non-financial rewards to meet individual needs and performance
Enabling structures	Organisation charts, structures and procedures are seen as temporary, and can be changed to meet task requirements
Boundary workers as environmental scanners	Everyone who has contact with customers, suppliers, clients and business partners is treated as a valuable information source
Inter-company learning	The organisation learns from other organisations through joint ventures, alliances and other information exchanges
A learning climate	The manager's primary task is to facilitate experimentation and learning in others, through questioning, feedback and support
Self-development opportunities for all	People are expected to take responsibility for their own learning, and facilities are made available, especially to 'front-line' staff

Source: Based on Pedler *et al.* (1997).

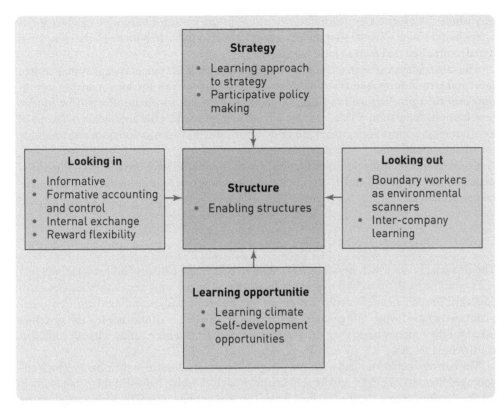

Figure 10.10
Clusters of learning organisation features.
Source: Pedler *et al.* (1997).

sense that one of their primary roles is to facilitate the creation of a shared vision for the business, and ensuring employees are enabled to work continually towards that. Finally, the culture is one in which all agree on a shared vision and understands how all aspects of the organisation – its processes, activities and environment – are related to each other. There is a strong sense of community and mutual trust. People feel free to share ideas and communicate, share and experiment – able to learn without fear of criticism or punishment.

Argyris (1999) distinguished between single-loop and double-loop learning. The classic example of single-loop learning is the domestic thermostat which, by detecting temperature variations, takes action to correct deviations from a predetermined level. In single-loop learning, the system maintains performance at the set level, but is unable to learn that the temperature is set too high or too low. Learning how to learn involves double-loop learning – challenging assumptions, beliefs and norms, rather than accepting them and working within their limitations. In single-loop learning, the question is 'how can we better achieve that standard of performance?' In double-loop learning the question becomes: 'is that an appropriate target in the first place?' In the context of developing the skills to cope more effectively with change, the aim is to enhance the ability of members to engage in double-loop learning.

10.9 Integrating themes

Sustainable performance

Changes in the business environment are encouraging managers to experiment with new forms of organisation, many favouring decentralisation which allows local business units greater autonomy over many decisions. They believe this encourages flexibility and innovation.

The dilemma is that decentralised structures expose the organisation to the risk that decisions by managers in the autonomous units may damage the reputation of the business as a whole. BP (Part 2 Case) suffered when staff at the US subsidiary were careless about safety, as did Union Carbide after the disaster at Bhopal in India. In both cases, the companies had decentralised decisions to local managers.

The same dangers arise in relation to sustainability: while the parent company may seek to meet and exceed international standards on emissions, a policy to give local managers autonomy over their practices, and those of suppliers, may impede corporate efforts. That in turn may harm its reputation. Critics are unlikely to be impressed by the arguments in favour of local autonomy, and will claim that this does not absolve the organisation from responsibility for what happens in their subsidiaries or suppliers.

Conversely decentralising authority over sustainability may have better results, since local managers are more familiar with the operations, and how best to improve their environmental performance.

Governance and control

The financial crises which began in 2008 showed that many bankers had been taking great risks with the bank funds by investing in loans that were not only very risky, but were also packaged in such a complex way that others had difficulty understanding them. Few complaints were raised when things appeared to be going well but, as confidence fell and investors asked for their money back, the extent to which managers had been acting without sufficient control became clear.

The bankers' behaviour had been encouraged in part by a culture in their banks which encouraged them to take risks, and by an incentive structure which rewarded them handsomely for their profits, even if these were short lived. This was not intentional fraud, but a sign of the negligence which failed to pay enough attention to banks' systems of accounting and risk management, and of their governance structures.

The Combined Code (2006) gives clear guidance to companies on how to structure their Boards to ensure adequate governance and control. This is a voluntary Code of Best Practice, with which the Boards of all companies listed on the London Stock Exchange are expected to comply – or to explain why they have not done so. It includes guidance on matters such as:

- **The Board** Every company should be headed by an effective Board, which is collectively responsible for the success of the company.
- **Chairman and chief executive** There should be a clear division of responsibilities . . . between the running of the board and the executive responsible [for running the business]. No one individual should have unfettered powers of decision.
- **Board balance** The Board should include a balance of executive and [independent] non-executive directors so that no individual or small group can dominate the Board's decision taking.
- **Board appointments** There should be a formal, rigorous and transparent procedure for appointing new directors to the Board.

Paradoxically, while this Code is widely seen as a valuable aid to corporate governance, it did not prevent the financial crisis: all the banks which had to be rescued by the government had complied with the Code.

Internationalisation

The growth of multinationals – based in one country but with significant production and sales in many others – continues as managers see new opportunities beyond their home territory. At the same time they have to defend their position against new entrants from other countries. A perennial topic in multinationals is the balance between global integration and local responsiveness. Bartlett and Ghoshal (2002) show how managers at some firms – such as the Japanese Kao and Matsushita – sought to integrate worldwide operations to achieve global efficiency through economies of scale. Others, including Philips and Unilever, were more sensitive to local differences, permitting national subsidiaries high levels of autonomy to respond to local conditions.

They go on to suggest that as global pressures increase, companies needed to develop a more complex range of capabilities:

> To compete effectively, a company had to develop global competitiveness, multinational flexibility, and worldwide learning capability simultaneously. Building these [capabilities] was primarily an organizational challenge, which required organizations to break away from their traditional management modes and adopt a new organizational model. This model we call the transnational. (Bartlett and Ghoshal, 2002, p. 18)

They also observe that successful transnational companies have:

> recognized that formal structure is a powerful but blunt weapon for effecting strategic change . . . a company must go beyond structure . . . and re-shape the core decision-making systems, and in doing so, the management processes of the company – the administrative systems, communication channels and interpersonal relationships, often provided tools for managing such change that were more subtle but also more effective than formal structure. (p. 37)

Bartlett and Ghoshal go on to elaborate the evidence and research on the organisational challenges that companies face if they wish to perform effectively in the international economy.

Summary

1 **Outline the links between strategy, structure and performance**

- The structure signals what people are expected to do within the organisation, and is intended to support actions that are in line with strategy, and so enhance performance. Equally, a structure may enable a new strategy to emerge which a different structure would have hindered.

2 **Give examples of management choices about dividing and co-ordinating work, with their likely advantages and disadvantages**

- Managers divide work to enable individuals and groups to specialise on a limited aspect of the whole, and then combine the work into related areas of activity. Task division needs to be accompanied by suitable methods of co-ordination.
- Centralisation brings consistency and efficiency, but also the danger of being slow and out of touch with local conditions. People in decentralised units can respond quickly to local conditions but risk acting inconsistently.
- Functional forms allow people to specialise and develop expertise and are efficient, but they may be inward looking and prone to conflicting demands.
- Divisional forms allow focus on particular markets of customer groups, but can duplicate facilities thus adding to cost.
- Matrix forms try to balance the benefits of functional and divisional forms, but can again lead to conflicting priorities over resources.
- Networks of organisations enable companies to draw upon a wide range of expertise, but may involve additional management and co-ordination costs.

3 **Compare the features of mechanistic and organic structures**

- Mechanistic – people perform specialised tasks, hierarchical structure of control, knowledge located at top of hierarchy, vertical communication, loyalty and obedience valued.

- Organic – people contribute experience to common tasks, network structure of contacts, knowledge widely spread, horizontal communication, commitment to task goals more important than to superiors.

4 **Summarise the work of Woodward, Burns and Stalker, Lawrence and Lorsch, and John Child, showing how they contributed to this area of management**

- Woodward: appropriate structure depends on the type of production system ('technology') – unit, small batch, process.
- Burns and Stalker: appropriate structure depends on uncertainty of the organisation's environment – mechanistic in stable, organic in unstable.
- Lawrence and Lorsch: units within an organisation face different environmental demands, which implies that there will be both mechanistic and organic forms within the same organisation, raising new problems of co-ordination.
- John Child: contingency theory implies too great a degree of determinism – managers have a greater degree of choice over structure than contingency theories implied.

5 **Use the 'contingencies' believed to influence choice of structure to evaluate the suitability of a form for a given unit**

- Strategy, environment, technology, age/size and political contingencies (Child) are believed to indicate the most suitable form, and the manager's role is to interpret these in relation to their circumstances.

6 **Explain and illustrate the features of a learning organisation**

- Learning organisations are those which have developed the capacity to continuously learn, adapt and change. This depends, according to Pedler *et al*. (1997), on evolving learning-friendly processes for looking in, looking out, learning opportunities, strategy and structure.

7 **Show how ideas from the chapter add to your understanding of the integrating**

- The drive for sustainable is another example of the dilemma between central and local control. Decentralisation may harm the company if local managers ignore corporate policy, or may lead to more sustainable performance if local managers use their knowledge to find better solutions.
- The financial crisis led many to call for tighter systems of governance and control – but many troubled banks already appeared to have such systems in place, which were not used.
- Bartlett and Ghoshal (2002) trace the many dilemmas companies face in creating a structure for their international operations.

Review questions

1 What did Chandler conclude about the relationship between strategy, structure and performance?

2   Draw the organisation chart of a company or department that you know. Compare it with the structures shown in Figure 10.5, writing down points of similarity and difference.

3 List the advantages and disadvantages of centralising organisational functions?

4 Several forms of co-ordination are described. Select two that you have seen in operation and describe in detail how they work – and how well they work.

5 Explain the difference between a mechanistic and an organic form of organisation.

6 Explain the term 'contingency approach' and give an example of each of the factors that influence the choice between mechanistic and organic structures.

7 If contingency approaches stress the influence of external factors on organisational structures, what is the role of management in designing organisational structures?

8 What is the main criticism of the contingency approaches to organisation structure?

9 What examples can you find of organisational activities that correspond to some of the features of a learning organisation identified by Pedler *et al.* (1997)?

10 Summarise an idea from the chapter that adds to your understanding of the integrating themes.

Concluding critical reflection

Think about the structure and culture of your company or one with which you are familiar. Review the material in the chapter, and perhaps visit some of the websites identified. Then make notes on the following questions:

- What examples of the themes discussed in this chapter are currently relevant to your company? What type of structure do you have – centralised or decentralised; functional or divisional, etc? Which of the methods of co-ordination identified do you typically use? Which form of culture best describes the one in which you work? What structural or cultural issues arise that are not mentioned here?

- In responding to issues of structure, what **assumptions** about the nature of organisations appear to guide your approach? If the business seems too centralised or too formal, why do managers take that approach? What are their assumptions, and are they correct?

- What factors in the **context** of the company appear to shape your approach to organising – what kind of environment are you working in, for example? To what extent does your structure involve networking with people from other organisations, and why is that?

- Have you seriously considered whether the present structure is right for the business? Do you regularly compare your structure with that in other companies to look for **alternatives**? How do you do it?

- What **limitations** can you identify in any of the ideas and theories presented here? For example, how helpful is contingency theory to someone deciding whether to make the organisation more or less mechanistic?

Further reading

Burns, T. and Stalker, G.M. (1961), *The Management of Innovation*, Tavistock, London.

Lawrence, P. and Lorsch, J.W. (1967), *Organization and Environment*, Harvard Business School Press, Boston, MA.

Woodward, J. (1965), *Industrial Organization: Theory and practice*, Oxford University Press, Oxford. Second edition 1980.

These influential books give accessible accounts of the research process, and it would add to your understanding to read at least one of them in the original. The second edition of Woodward's book (1980) is even more useful, as it includes a commentary on her work by two later scholars.

Bartlett, C.A. and Ghoshal, S. (2002), *Managing Across Borders: The transnational solution* (2nd edn) Harvard Business School Press, Boston, MA.

Applies ideas on organisations and their structure to international management.

Catmull, E. (2008), 'How Pixar fosters collective creativity', *Harvard Business Review*, vol. 86, no. 9, pp. 64–72.

The cofounder explains how it works.

Homburg, C., Jensen, O. and Krohmer, H. (2008), 'Configurations of marketing and sales: A taxonomy', *Journal of Marketing,* vol. 72, no. 2, pp. 133–154.

An account of research into one of the continuing questions in organisation structure, of particular interest to students with an interest in marketing.

Ordanini, A., Rubera, G. and Sala, M. (2008), 'Integrating functional knowledge and embedding learning in new product launches: How project forms helped EMI Music', *Long Range Planning*, vol. 41, no. 1, pp. 17–32.

How a team approach helped to launch an unknown artist.

Weblinks

These websites have appeared in the chapter:

www.oticon.com
www.lilly.com
www.shell.com
www.reed-elsevier.com
www.sonyericsson.com
www.baesystems.com
www.rbs.com
www.roche.com
www.hmv.com
www.emi.com
www.communityhealthpartnerships.co.uk
www.pixar.com
www.monsanto.com

Visit two of the business sites in the list, and navigate to the pages dealing with corporate news, investor relations or 'our company'.

- What organisational structure issues can you identify that managers in the company are likely to be dealing with? Can you find any information about their likely culture from the website?
- What kind of environment are they likely to be working in, and how may that affect their structure and culture?

 For video case studies, audio summaries, flashcards, exercises and annotated weblinks related to this chapter, visit **www.pearsoned.co.uk/mymanagementlab**

CHAPTER 12

INFORMATION SYSTEMS AND E-BUSINESS

Aim

To show how converging information systems can transform organisations if people manage them intelligently.

Objectives

By the end of your work on this chapter you should be able to outline the concepts below in your own terms and:

1 Explain how converging technologies change the ways in which people add value to resources

2 Recognise that, to use these opportunities, managers change both technology and organisation

3 Distinguish between operations information systems and management information systems

4 Illustrate how organisations use the internet to add value by using three types of information system (IS) – enterprise, knowledge management and customer relations

5 Understand the relationship between IS, organisation and strategy

6 Show how ideas from the chapter add to your understanding of the integrating themes

Key terms

This chapter introduces the following ideas:

internet
intranet
extranet
blogs
social networking sites
user generated content (UGC)
wikinomics
co-creation
Metcalfe's law
information systems management
data
information
transaction processing system (TPS)

process control system
office automation system
management information system
decision support systems
executive information system
e-commerce
e-business
disintermediation
reintermediation
enterprise resource planning (ERP)
knowledge
knowledge management (KM)

Each is a term defined within the text, as well as in the Glossary at the end of the book.

Case study   Google www.google.com

Sergey Brin and Larry Page founded Google in 1999 and by 2010 it was the world's largest search engine, with the mission: 'to organise the world's information and make it universally accessible and useful'. The need for search services arose as the world wide web expanded, making it progressively more difficult for users to find relevant information. The company's initial success was built on the founders' new approach to online searching: their PageRank algorithm (with 500 million variables and 3 billion terms) identifies material relevant to a search by favouring pages that have been linked to other pages. These links were called 'votes', because they signalled that another page's webmaster had decided that the focal page deserved attention. The importance of the focal page is determined by counting the number of votes it has received.

As a business Google generates revenue by providing advertisers with the opportunity to deliver online advertising that is relevant to the search results on a page. The advertisements are displayed as sponsored links, with the message appearing alongside search results for appropriate keywords. They are priced on a cost-per-impression basis, whereby advertisers pay a fixed amount each time their ad is viewed. The charge depends on what the advertiser has bid for the keywords, and the more they bid the nearer the top of the page their advertisement will be.

A feature of Google is the speed with which it returns search results – usually within a second. From the start its focus has been on developing 'the perfect search engine', defined by Larry Page as something that 'understands what you mean and gives you back what you want'. Rather than use a small number of large servers that tend to run slowly at peak times, Google invested in thousands of linked PCs that quickly find the answer to each query.

The software behind the search technology conducts a series of simultaneous equations in a fraction of a second. It uses PageRank to determine which web pages are most important, and then analyses their content to decide which are relevant to the

Photo courtesy Google UK

current search. By combining overall importance and query-specific relevance, Google claims to be able to put the most relevant results first. That enhances its value to advertisers who have bid for the relevant keywords. One estimate is that in October 2008 it took 30 per cent of US online advertising revenue.

When the company offered shares to the public in 2004, Page warned potential investors that Google was not a conventional company and did not intend to become one. In the interests of long-term stability the share ownership structure was such that the founders owned roughly one-third of the shares, but controlled over 80 per cent of the votes. The company had also, in its short existence, developed a distinctive culture.

Sources: Based on Harvard Business School case 9-806-105, *Google Inc.*, prepared by Thomas R. Eisenmann and Kerry Herman; company website.

Case questions 12.1

- What are the inputs and the outputs of the Google business?
- What are the distinctive features of the Google story set out here?
- How would you expect it to have organised the business to secure such a rapid and profitable growth?

12.1 Introduction

Google is an organisation founded on data – it gathers, processes and disseminates it from and to millions of people in a way that gives them valuable information. All have different requirements and work in different ways, yet Google has developed a search engine that works at astonishing speed to meet their needs. Since the search is free, Google survives on income from advertisements – which depends on the quality of the search systems.

Google (like eBay, Facebook or YouTube) is an example of a company created to use the internet – it is a pure 'e-business' company, whose managers built it around computer-based information systems (IS). In that sense it differs from companies founded long before the internet but which now depend on it to support the business. Their managers began by implementing relatively simple information systems which they progressively built, through trial and error, into the complex ones used today. Traditional businesses such as British Airways, Ford or Sainsbury's depend on information about each stage of the value-adding process:

- inputs – cost and availability of materials, staff and equipment;
- transformation – delivery schedules, capacity utilisation, efficiency, quality and costs;
- outputs – prices, market share and customer satisfaction.

Their information systems gather data about inputs, transformation processes and outputs, and feed the information to those working at different levels of the organisation. Figure 12.1 shows how information systems support these fundamental management processes.

Computer-based information systems can make operations more efficient, change the way people work together, and offer new strategic possibilities and threats. Used well, they help managers to add value to resources. Used badly, they destroy wealth – such as when managers decide to implement an expensive IS project which does not deliver what they expected, and is abandoned or replaced. The UK National Health Service Programme for Information Technology (NPfIT) (**www.connectingforhealth.nhs.uk**) contains examples of both – some parts (the Picture Archiving and Communication System) work well; while many observers (in early 2010) see the Electronic Patient Record System as a controversial failure.

Progressively more managers face this kind of responsibility, as information systems move rapidly from background activities (such as accounting and stock control) into foreground activities (online banking or sponsored websites) which directly involve customers, and then into activities which members of the public manage themselves (social networks or music downloads). No organisation is immune: if dissatisfied customers use a popular social networking

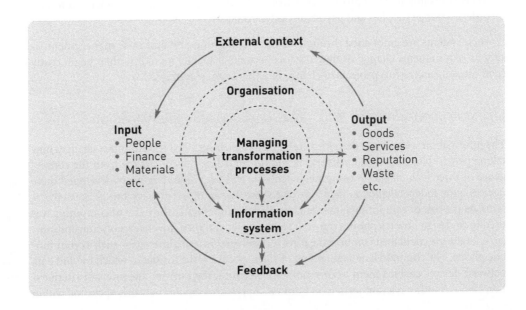

Figure 12.1
The role of information systems in organisations

Source: Boddy *et al.* (2005)

site to spread bad news about a business, managers need to respond – even if they have never heard of the site.

This chapter will show you how IS can transform organisations. It shows how traditional businesses progressively widened the role of computer-based systems in managing data about their operations, and how technical developments have led to the convergence of data, voice and vision systems. This led to the new phenomenon of co-creation of value, in which users not only view content on a site but also create it. In either case, adding value depends on managing both technological and organisational issues – which the chapter will illustrate with accounts of three widely used systems.

Activity 12.1   Applying the open systems model

Apply the open systems model in Figure 12.1 to an organisation that you know.

- What are the inputs and outputs?
- Describe the transformation process.
- List examples of information systems that provide information about inputs, outputs and transformations.

12.2   Converging technologies bring new ways to add value

Using IS to add value to data

Since the 1950s, organisations that make and deliver products or services have progressively extended the tasks which computer-based information systems (IS) undertake, beginning with routine accounting and stock control systems, extending to manufacturing and transport, and now covering almost every aspect of the organisation:

- Allied Bakeries use engineering maintenance systems to monitor equipment and plan maintenance to reduce lost production time.
- The UK Vehicle Licensing Agency encourages drivers to pay their road tax online.
- BP maintains all human resource information on a single database, allowing staff to access their records and company policies online, so that all work to common information.
- Many firms link internal processes electronically with suppliers and customers, to receive orders, arrange supplies and pay invoices electronically.

Such systems are embedded throughout the organisation and still raise management issues as requirements change or new systems become available: managers then begin costly (and often unsuccessful) projects to change or enhance their systems.

Using convergence to add value to data, sound and vision

The information systems just described are all computer-based. The revolutionary changes now taking place – blogging, social networking and downloading music – follow from the convergence of three technologies – computer, telephone and television. Engineers developed these devices quite independently, so they have always worked in different ways and as isolated systems. As the cost of computing power fell, the digital technology at the heart of computing was used to re-design how telephones transmit voice signals, and then how television transmits images. Engineers could then combine the three technologies in a single device – such as your mobile phone. The common language and set of rules specifying the format in which to send data between devices enabled them to communicate electronically, creating the **internet** (Berners-Lee, 1999). Another relevant term is an **intranet**, a private computer network operating within

The **internet** is a web of hundreds of thousands of computer networks linked together by telephone lines and satellite links through which data can be carried.

An **intranet** is a version of the internet that only specified people within an organisation can use.

An **extranet** is a version of the internet that is restricted to specified people in specified companies – usually customers or suppliers.

an organisation by using internet standards and protocols. The opposite is an **extranet**, a network that uses the internet to link organisations with specified suppliers, customers or trading partners, who gain access to it through a password system.

Linking mobile phones to the internet led to the explosive growth of the 'wireless internet', which liberates the computer from the desktop, enabling people to send and/or receive text, voice and visual data wherever they are.

Countless organisations in all sectors of the economy use these technical advances to change traditional enterprises and to create new ones. Many now only accept orders online, and use the internet to manage all aspects of their businesses; established media companies offer online as well as paper copies of their publications; national and local governments increasingly expect to interact with their citizens online. The BBC claims that the iPlayer is changing the way people watch television, with over a million programmes being viewed over the online video site each day (**www.bbc.co.uk**). But the most dramatic shift currently observable is that of co-creation.

Producers and consumers co-create value

A **blog** is a weblog that allows individuals to post opinions and ideas.

Social networking sites use internet technologies which enable people to interact within an online community to share information and ideas.

Individuals using blogs and social network sites are now driving the growth of internet traffic. Convergence enables people to communicate over the internet in many ways – using blogs and social networking sites to send emails, share music files, and search websites for social and business information. **Blogs** attract individuals with an interest in the topic to ask questions or express their views in a discussion group. **Social networking sites** developed from blogs, by providing a communication channel for people who want to share their interests with other members of the online community.

Management in practice   **SelectMinds – social networks for professionals**
www.selectminds.com

The company helps organisations to build connections between groups of employees, former employees, and other constituencies to increase knowledge sharing and productivity. It offers secure, online social networking solutions that organisations use to recruit and retain scarce knowledge workers, and increase the speed of information and knowledge flow.

It pioneered an early form of corporate social networking in 2000 when it began delivering online networks to connect former employees of organisations with each other and their former employer. Employees of professional services firms often leave to work for customers, so are able to refer business to their former employer. Seeding this population with information about their previous company (new services, client successes) helps them to become better brand ambassadors, speaking knowledgeably about it. The site enables companies to benefit from customer and employee relationships as well as to build new relationships based on continued personal connections among current and ex-employees.

Products now include systems to link organisations with customers, retirees, potential new staff and among current employees.

Source: Company website.

User generated content (UGC) is text, visual or audio material which users create and place on a site for others to view.

Wikinomics describes a business culture in which customers are no longer only consumers but also co-creators and co-producers of the service.

This digital culture erodes boundaries between producers and consumers. Wikipedia, written by volunteers, quickly became the world's largest encyclopaedia. YouTube claims to hold the world's largest collection of videos, including a large collection of professional work. Amazon encourages visitors to the site to review books, which others can read before they buy. Media groups encourage readers to write stories for publication. All are examples of **user generated content (UGC)** – content which users create and place on a site for other to view.

Tapscott and Williams (2006) refer to this as **wikinomics,** a business culture that sees customers not as consumers but as co-creators and co-producers. Amazon and Google encourage **co-creation.** Amazon uses customer reviews to exchange information among readers and

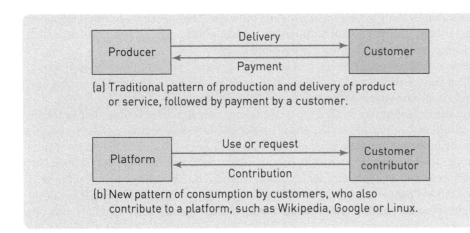

Figure 12.2
Traditional delivery and customer participation

uses buying patterns of customers to suggest books to others with similar interests. Google analyses search requests to develop profiles and make advertisements available to searchers with certain profiles. In both cases, customers create the content, and the more people view the content, the more valuable the network becomes.

This follows from **Metcalfe's law** 'the value of a network increases with the square of the number of users connected to the network'. In other words, the more people who have phones, the more valuable a phone becomes to the next adopter. This 'network effect' encourages more people to use an existing website, and creates barriers for new entrants who at first have few users to attract others.

In a traditional economic system producers create products which consumers order, receive and pay for (Figure 12.2a). The alternative is when companies such as Google, Facebook and many more provide a platform that customers use to offer and view information. They add value to the platform as they provide more information and so enhance the perceived quality of the platform. Consumption does not reduce value but increases it (Figure 12.2b) (see Management in Practice).

Co-creation is product or service development that makes intensive use of the contributions of customers.

Metcalfe's law states that the value of a network increases with the square of the number of users connected to the network.

Management in practice   **An online forum in healthcare**

A physician dealing with fertility treatment at the University Hospital Nijmegen, the Netherlands, spent a lot of time informing couples on the pros and cons of the treatments, and in providing emotional support. As an experiment he started an online forum in which his clients (exclusively) share information and anxieties. It also provides relevant medical information. From time to time the doctor and other staff join the sessions. The 'electronic fertility platform' saves a lot of the time the doctor used to spend advising and supporting clients. Clients contribute anonymously to the platform and so help each other.

Source: Boddy *et al.* (2009a), p. 62.

Activity 12.2   **Reflect on your use of social networking sites**

Have you used a social network or similar site to interact with, or make comments about, an organisation?

- What were the circumstances?
- Did it change your view of the company?
- What evidence was there of staff from the company being aware of the site?
- What could management have done to benefit from the exchanges?

12.3 | Managing the new opportunities to add value

Adding value in traditional delivery systems

The internet is evidently challenging established ways of doing business. Combined with political changes, this is creating a wider, often global, market for many goods and services. The challenge for managers is to make profitable use of these possibilities. This includes looking beyond technology – which receives most attention – to the wider organisation. A manager who played a major role in guiding internet-based changes at his company commented:

> The internet is not a technology challenge. It's a people challenge – all about getting structures, attitudes and skills aligned.

The significance of the internet for everyone who works in organisations cannot be overstated. It affects all aspects of organisational activity, enabling new forms of organisation and new ways of doing business. Established organisations typically go through successive stages in the way they use the internet, which Figure 12.3 illustrates.

The simplest internet applications provide information, enabling customers to view product or other information on a company website; conversely suppliers use their website to show customers what they can offer. The next stage is to use the internet for interaction. Customers enter information and questions about, for example, offers and prices. The system then uses the customer information, such as preferred dates and times of travel, to show availability and costs. Conversely, a supplier who sees a purchasing requirement from a business (perhaps expressed as a purchase order on the website) can agree electronically to meet the order. A third use is for transactions, when customers buy goods and services through a supplier's website. The whole transaction, from accessing information through ordering, delivery and payment, can take place electronically.

A company achieves integration when it links its internal system to the website, so that when a customer orders a product online, it automatically passes to the internal operating systems. These then begin all the processes (including the links with suppliers' systems) required to manufacture and/or deliver the product. Transformation refers to the situation where it is not only linking internal–external systems, but where it is within the participation culture, in which customers are actively involved in the design and consumption of the products, and where the company is actively engaging with online communities of customers and others.

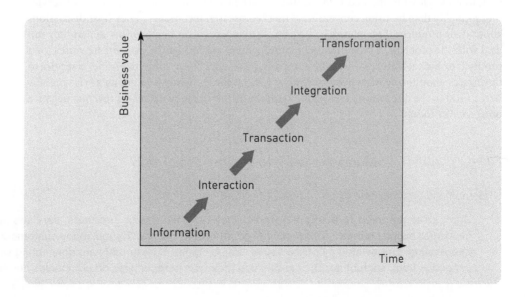

Figure 12.3
Stages in using
the internet

Google – the case continues: customers and product development
www.google.com

Beyond its core search and advertising capabilities, the company has embarked on ventures involving online productivity, blogging, radio and television advertising, online payments, social networks, mobile phone operating systems, and many more information domains. What information management tools the company hasn't developed it has acquired: Picasa for photo management; YouTube for online videos; DoubleClick for web ads; Keyhole for satellite photos (now Google Earth); Urchin for web analytics (now Google Analytics).

Google engineers prototype new applications on the platform; if any of these begin to get users' attention, developers can launch beta [test] versions to see whether the company's vast captive customer base responds enthusiastically. If one of the applications becomes a hit, Google's enormous 'cloud' of computing capability can make room for it. In the development process, Google simultaneously tests and markets them to the user community. In fact, testing and marketing are virtually indistinguishable from one another. This creates a unique relationship with consumers, who become an essential part of the development team as new products take shape and grow. Google does more than just alpha and beta test applications – it can host them on its infrastructure. Google's customers then transition seamlessly from testing to using products as they would any other commercial offering.

The company allows independent developers to share access and create new applications that incorporate elements of the Google system. They can easily test and launch applications and have them hosted in the Google world, where there is an enormous target audience – 132 million customers globally – and a practically unlimited capacity for customer interactions.

Source: Iyer and Davenport (2008).

Case questions 12.2

- What benefits do you expect Google will gain from this close involvement with developers?
- What do the developers gain?
- What may be the risks to either Google or the developers?

Adding value through co-creation

Many managers are working out how to use social networking sites to their advantage, for instance by creating their own customer platforms or by contributing actively to others. While people use these applications to interact socially with friends or with people who share a common interest, the trend gives managers a potentially useful opportunity. While initially uneasy, many now actively encourage the practice. Some create and host customer communities, to move closer to their customers, and to learn how best to improve a product or service more quickly than by using conventional market research techniques. They host discussions about their products: if people are being critical, managers want to know this so that they can deal with the problem. A blog discussion among users might identify possible new uses for a product, or hint at features which the company could add. Some companies offer a service to businesses, monitoring what people are saying about the company, and giving advice on how best to add to the discussion in ways that build a positive image, or at least prevent a negative one (see Key Ideas).

Managers learn to use the social web

Bernoff and Li (2008) note that:

Companies are used to being in control. They typically design products, services and marketing messages based on their . . . view of what people want . . . Now, though, many customers are no longer cooperating. Empowered by online social technologies . . . customers are connecting with, and drawing power from, each other. They're defining their own perspectives on companies and brands, a view that's often at odds with the image a company wants to project. This groundswell of people using technologies to get the things they need from one another, rather than from companies, is now tilting the balance of power from company to customer. (p. 36)

The authors then advise managers how they can best respond to these changing conditions, by 'working with the groundswell' – developing a clear view of how they can put social applications on an equal footing with other business projects to achieve their business goals. Among their examples:

- **'Listening'** A software development company uses an application that allows customers to suggest new product features and then vote on them: this gives valuable information when the company has to decide which of the (thousands of) suggestions to develop.
- **'Talking'** A car company wanted to increase students' awareness of a new model. They created a stunt in which students lived in the car for a week: from there they wrote blogs, posted YouTube videos and contacted thousands of friends through Facebook and MySpace, greatly increasing awareness of the brand, at a fraction of the cost of traditional publicity methods.
- **'Energising'** An old and respected company wanted to build enthusiasm among current and new customers for the brand. It hired four enthusiastic customers to act as 'lead ambassadors', whose job was to build an online community of users to exchange ideas and experiences with the product. The size of this community quickly exceeded expectations, and has generated a substantial increase in sales.

Source: Bernoff and Li (2008).

Whether a business is in a traditional delivery or co-creation mode, it will only add value if managers look beyond the technology, however sophisticated, to see that they also need to manage some organisational issues.

Adding value depends on managing technology AND organisation

Whether the company is an internet-based start-up or a century-old business, it requires deliberate management action to create the IS infrastructure to engage with the internet. Building and maintaining Google's network of an estimated 1 million PCs requires a vast management effort – with established businesses also requiring to devote significant resources to their information systems. **Information systems management** is the term used to describe the activities of planning, acquiring, developing and using IS such as this (the following Management in Practice gives the views of one IS manager).

Information systems management is the planning, acquisition, development and use of these systems.

Management in practice   Jean-Pierre Corniou – Renault's CIO www.renault.com

Frankly my job (as Chief Information Officer) consists of being a bilingual guy: I speak both the language of business and the language of technology. Renault, like other companies, started investing in information technology (IT) in the middle 1960s. It was pioneering work – there were just a few people in IT, working on large systems of great complexity. People inside still have that pioneering attitude, of an era when IT was seen as secret, and complex . . . but we need to open up, to build transparency, to build the confidence and trust of all stakeholders in the company.

We have invested a lot of money in [advanced applications] and websites, and when we analysed the level of utilization of these products and tools, we were very surprised to see how much money had been spent on products that people were not using.

I spend a lot of time in plants, in discussions with foremen in the field, trying to understand how they use technology to increase their efficiency. I spend lots of time in commercial departments too, to understand the key business processes. Bringing IT to the business community means the CIO has to be embedded in the day to day life of the organization, and of course to have a seat on the board. I consider myself more a business guy than an IT guy.

Source: *Financial Times*, 17 September 2003.

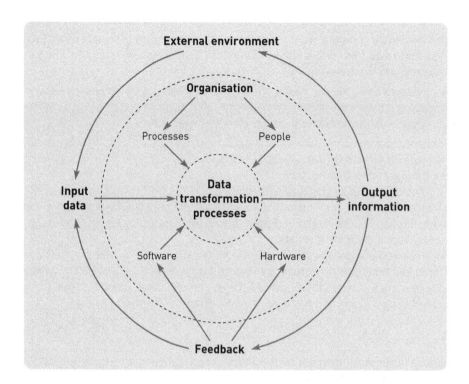

Figure 12.4
The elements of a
computer-based IS
Source: Boddy *et al.*
(2009a)

As M. Corniou's comments clearly show, any information system (internet-based or otherwise) includes people and processes as well as hardware and software, as shown in Figure 12.4.

A computer-based student record system illustrates this. The hardware consists of computers and peripherals such as printers, monitors and keyboards. This runs the record system, using software to manipulate the data and to either print the results for each student or send them electronically – which they see as information. The system also requires people (course administrators) to enter data (name and other information about students and their results) following certain processes – such as that one person reads from a list of grades while another keys the data into the right field on the student's record. Managers of a department might use the output to compare the pass rate of each course, so the record system is now part of the university's management information. Staff will use their knowledge (based on learning and experience) to interpret trends and evaluate their significance.

Figure 12.4 also shows that the hardware and software is part of a wider organisational context, which includes people, working processes, structures and cultures. An information system includes identifiable elements of this context, which affect the outcomes of an IS project, for better or worse, just as much as the design of the technological elements of hardware and software.

Activity 12.3   **Using the model**

Use Figure 12.4 to analyse an IS that you know or about which you can gather information.

- Who promoted the system and what were their objectives?
- Describe the system they implemented, especially the hardware and software.
- What changes did the system lead to for people and procedures?
- What changes for other aspects of the organisation such as its culture and structure?
- What were the outcomes and how did they compare with the objectives?
- What can you learn from the evidence of this case?

Management levels	Generic Categories of Information system	Specific types of information system
Top managers – managing the business	Management information system	Executive information
Middle managers – managing managers		Decision support
		Information reporting
Line managers – managing direct operators	Operations information system	Office automation
		Process control
Operating staff – doing the direct work		Transaction processing

Figure 12.5
Types of
information system

12.4   Types of information systems

Figure 12.5 illustrates two broad types of information system that are very widely used. Operational information systems support the needs of the day-to-day business operations, and how front-line staff and their supervisors work. Management information systems typically guide the decisions of middle and senior managers.

Data and information

Data are raw, unanalysed facts, figures and events.

Information comes from data that have been processed so that they have meaning for the person receiving it.

Both types of system turn 'data' into 'information'. **Data** refers to recorded descriptions of things, events, activities and transactions – their size, colour, cost, weight, date and so on. It may be a number, a piece of text, a drawing or photograph, or a sound. In itself it may or may not convey information to a person. **Information** is a subset of data that means something to the people receiving them, which they judge to be useful, significant or urgent. It comes from data that have been processed (by people or with the aid of technology) so that it has meaning and value, by linking it to other pieces of data to show a comparison, sequence of events or trend. The output is subjective since what one person sees as valuable information, another may see as insignificant data – their interpretation reflects diverse backgrounds and interests.

Operations information systems

A transaction processing system (TPS) records and processes data from routine transactions such as payroll, sales or purchases.

A process control system monitors and controls variables describing the state of a physical process.

An office automation system uses several systems to create, process, store and distribute information.

Operations systems support the information processing needs to keep current work moving efficiently. They include technologies that help people perform standalone tasks more efficiently, such as word processors and spreadsheets. Most professional people use these technologies routinely – for instance, research and development (R&D) engineers can use a computer-aided design (CAD) program to improve the way they work, as the system includes software that performs routine tasks automatically, so that the engineer can focus on design issues.

Transaction processing systems (TPS) record and process data from customer and supplier transactions, salary and other systems affecting employees, as well as those with banks and tax authorities. A TPS collects data as transactions occur and stores this in a central database, which is then the source of other reports such as customer statements or supplier payments. Such systems help managers to keep track of recent transactions, especially their financial implications.

They also need systems to monitor and control physical processes. So breweries, bakeries, refineries and similar operations use **process control systems** to monitor defined variables such as temperature, pressure or flow, compare them with the required state, and adjust as necessary. Staff monitor the systems to check if they need to take further action.

Office automation systems bring together email, word processing, spreadsheet and many other systems to create, process, store and distribute information. They can also link to TPS or process control systems to make structured decisions. Banks analyse the pattern of a customer's transactions to decide whether to grant a request for credit. Office automation systems stream-line the administrative processes of a business, and can provide an input into other systems.

Management information systems (MIS)

A **management information system (MIS)** is a computer-based system that provides managers with the information they need for effective decision making. The MIS is supported by the oper-ations information systems, as well as other sources of internal and external information. It typi-cally includes systems for information reporting, decision support and executive information, each of which is described below. An important management choice is how many people throughout the organisation can access and use information from these systems, with many advo-cating their widespread use as a way of supporting decentralised and responsive decision making.

> A **management information system** provides information and support for managerial decision making.

Managers in charge of production or service facilities constantly face choices about, for ex-ample, whether to engage more or fewer staff, arrange schedules or accept a reservation. To increase the chances that their decisions add value, they need information about, for ex-ample, existing capacity, current orders or available materials. Good information increases their confidence, and information reporting systems help to achieve this, by providing accu-rate and up-to-date information on the current operation.

Decision support systems (DSS), sometimes called expert or knowledge systems, help managers to calculate the likely consequences of alternative actions. A DSS incorporates a model of the process or situation, and will often draw data from operational systems. Some examples include:

> **Decision support systems** help people to calculate the consequences of alternatives before they decide which to choose.

- businesses use DSS to calculate the financial consequences of investments;
- banks use knowledge systems to analyse proposed loans. These incorporate years of lend-ing experience and enable less experienced staff to make decisions;
- NHS Direct in the UK uses an expert system to enable nurses in a call centre to deal with calls from patients who would otherwise visit their doctor. The system proposes the questions to ask, interprets the answers and recommends the advice the nurse should give to the caller.

Executive information systems are essentially management information systems aimed at the most senior people in the business. Rather than great detail, they aim to provide easy access to data that have been derived from many sources, and processed in a way that meets top management requirements.

> An **executive information system** provides those at the top of the organisation with easy access to timely and relevant information.

Activity 12.4   Collecting examples of applications

Collect new examples of one operational and one management information system, from someone working in an organisation.

- What information do they deal with?
- How do they help people who use them in their work?
- What issues about the design of these systems should managers be considering, in view of the growth of social networking and similar technologies?
- Have they begun to think about these in the organisations you have studied?

12.5   The internet and e-business

> **e-commerce** refers to the activity of selling goods or service over the internet.

> **e-business** refers to the integration, through the internet, of all an organisation's processes from its suppliers through to its customers.

The internet is clearly transforming the way many organisations work, and creating new re-lationships between them and their customers, suppliers and business partners. Two com-monly used terms are **e-commerce** and **e-business**.

e-commerce and e-business

Many businesses use the internet to support their distribution, by offering goods and services through a website – which is defined here as e-commerce. A more radical way to use the internet is for what is here called e-business, when companies use a website to manage information about sales, capacity, inventory, payment and so on – and exchange that information with their suppliers or business customers. This enables them to use the internet to connect all the links in their supply chain, so creating an integrated process to meet customer needs (see the following Management in Practice).

Management in practice   **Using the internet at Siemens**   www.siemens.com

Siemens' plans to do much of their business over the internet includes:

1 Knowledge management – using a company-wide system to capture and share knowledge about scientific and technical developments throughout the business.
2 Online purchasing (or e-procurement). Large savings are expected from pooling the demands of buying departments through a company-wide system called click2procure.
3 Online sales. Most of Siemens' customers are other companies who can click on 'buy from Siemens' on the website and place orders for most Siemens products.
4 Internal administrative processes – such as by handling 30,000 job applications a year online, or expecting employees to book their business travel arrangements over the internet.

The chief executive at the time said:

If you want to transform a company to an e-business company, the problem is not so much e-procurement and the face to the customer. All this can be done rather fast. What is truly difficult is to reorganise all the internal processes. That is what we see as our main task and where the main positive results will come from.

Sources: Boddy *et al.* (2009a); company website.

Disintermediation
Removing intermediaries such as distributors or brokers that formerly linked a company to its customers.

The relationship between a company and its channel partners can be changed by the internet because electronic networks can bypass channel partners, also called **disintermediation**. Figure 12.6 shows how a manufacturer and a wholesaler can bypass other partners and reach customers directly.

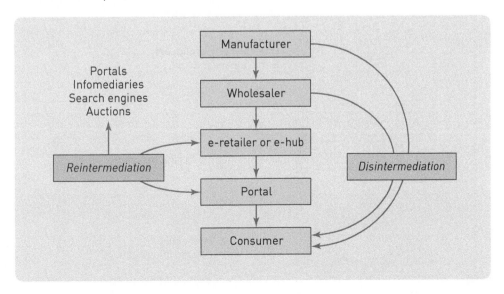

Figure 12.6
Reinventing the supply chain

The benefits of disintermediation are that transaction costs are reduced and that it enables direct contact with customers. This also makes it possible to increase the reach of companies, e.g. from a local presence to a national or international presence. **Reintermediation** is the creation of new intermediaries between customers and suppliers by providing (new) service such as supplier search and product evaluation. Examples are portals such as **www.Yahoo.com**, **www.amazon.com** and **www.moneyfacts.co.uk** which help customers to compare offers and link them to suppliers.

A major concern of companies moving towards e-commerce or e-business has been to ensure that they can handle the associated physical processes. These include handling orders, arranging shipment, receiving payment and dealing with after-sales service. This gives an advantage to traditional retailers who can support their website with existing fulfilment processes.

Kanter (2001) found that the move to e-business for established companies involves a deep change. She found that top management absence, shortsighted marketing staff and other internal barriers were common obstacles. Based on interviews with more than 80 companies on their move to e-business, her research provides 'deadly mistakes' as well as some lessons, including:

- create experiments and act simply and quickly to convert the sceptics;
- create dedicated teams, and give them resources and autonomy;
- recognise that e-business requires systemic changes in many ways of working.

Three widely used internet applications are known as customer relationship management, enterprise resource planning and knowledge management systems.

Reintermediation Creating intermediaries between customers and suppliers, providing services such as supplier search and product evaluation.

Customer relationship management (CRM)

Chapter 9 (Section 9.5) introduces the idea of customer relationship management, a process by which companies aim to build long-term, profitable relationships with their customers. This involves many changes in the way the organisation works, and information systems play a major role in supporting this. CRM software tries to align business processes with customer strategies to recruit, satisfy and retain profitable customers (Ryals, 2005; Kumar *et al.*, 2006). Figure 12.7 shows three approaches. The first treats all customers in the same way by sending impersonal messages in one direction. The second sends one-sided, but different messages to customers, depending on their profile. The third personalises the messages which may lead to real interaction, in the hope of increasing customer loyalty.

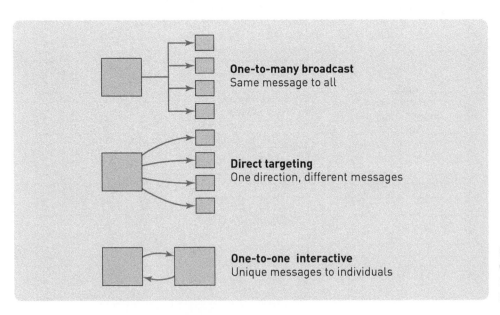

Figure 12.7 Communications methods and message

In many businesses the key to increasing profitability is to focus on recruiting and retaining high lifetime value customers. So the promise of CRM is to:

- gather customer data swiftly;
- identify and capture valuable customers while discouraging less valuable ones;
- increase customer loyalty and retention by providing customised products;
- reduce costs of serving customers;
- make it easier to acquire similar customers.

Some CRM systems consolidate customer data from many sources to answer questions such as:

- Who are our most loyal customers?
- Who are our most profitable customers?
- What do these profitable customers want to buy?

The Tesco Clubcard described in the Part 6 Case (**www.tesco.com**) is an excellent example of this, which has played a major role in the success of the company: the system processes the information about what each customer purchases, and uses this to identify promotional vouchers that are most likely to be useful to that customer. Suitable vouchers encourage them to return to the store to make further purchases. Ahearne *et al.* (2008) analysed the effectiveness of a CRM system designed to automate the collection, processing and distribution of customer data to sales staff. The company hoped this would enable them to share market intelligence more widely, help staff manage customer contacts, make better presentations and deal more efficiently with post-visit reports. Studying the impact of the system in a pharmaceutical company showed that it did indeed improve sales-force performance, mainly through enabling them to provide better customer service, and through being more adaptable to customer needs (see also Management in Practice).

Management in practice   Iris and 'The Source'   www.irisnation.com

Iris is a rapidly growing advertising agency, with close relationships with international customers. As an example of the services it offers, Ian Millner, Managing Director describes 'The Source':

A key part of our global relationship with Sony Ericsson is a digital asset management system, that has now been branded The Source. The role of that system is to collect all marketing assets of value, most of which will have been originated by Iris, have it all in one place so that if you're Sony Ericsson in Brazil or in Indonesia or in China, instantly you're able to access marketing materials that have value and relevance for you to use really, really quickly in your marketplace.

So this idea of real time sharing is a key part of working with clients in dynamic and competitive markets, and I think the other bit that comes with that is not only value but also speed to market. It's so important now to be able to do things quickly, so that is a massive asset in our sort of overall strategic relationship with that client but also our anticipation is that there'll be more and more clients now who want that type of agency partner globally.

Source: Interview with Ian Millner.

Massey *et al.* (2001) shows how implementing successful CRM depends more on strategy than on technology, and that even when a customer strategy is established, other dimensions such as business processes, (other) systems, structure and people need to change to support it. If a company wants to develop better relationships with its customers it needs first to rethink the key business processes that relate to customers, from customer service to order fulfilment. If consumers have a choice of channels – such as email, web or telephone – marketing, sales and service can no longer be treated separately. A customer may place an order by phone, use the web page to check the status of the order and send a complaint by mail. Multi-channel interactions pose considerable challenge if the company is to maintain a single comprehensive and up-to-date view of each customer.

For companies focused on products or services, this means realigning around the customer – which can be a radical change in a company's culture. All employees, but especially those in marketing, sales, service and any other customer contact functions, have to think in a customer oriented way. Much time and financial resource of CRM projects has to be spent on organisational issues. Successful CRM depends on co-ordinated actions by all departments within a company rather than being driven by a single department (Boulding *et al.*, 2005).

Enterprise resource planning (ERP) systems

Fulfilling a customer order requires that people in sales, accounting, production, purchasing and so on co-operate with each other to exchange information. However the IS on which they depend were often designed to meet the needs of a single function. They were built independently and cannot automatically exchange information. Manufacturing will not automatically know the number and types of product to make because their systems are not linked to the systems that process orders. A common solution is to use **enterprise resource planning (ERP)** systems, which aim to co-ordinate activities and decisions across many functions by creating an integrated platform which integrates them into company-wide business processes. Information flows between the functions and levels, as shown in Figure 12.8.

At the heart of an enterprise system is a central database that draws data from and feeds data into a series of applications throughout the company. Using a single database streamlines the flow of information. Table 12.1 shows examples of business processes and functions

> Enterprise resource planning (ERP) An integrated process of planning and managing all resources and their use in the enterprise. It includes contacts with business partners.

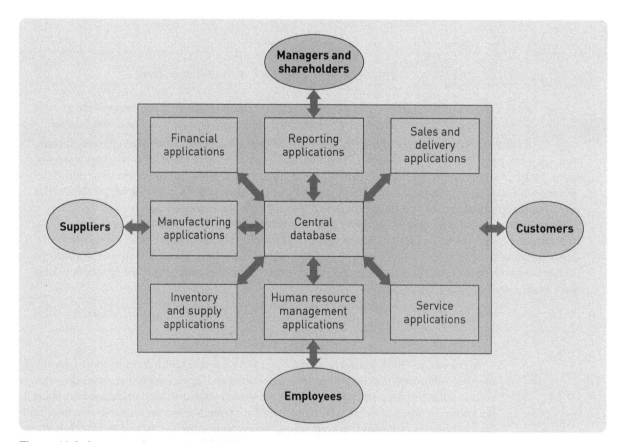

Figure 12.8 Anatomy of an enterprise system.

Table 12.1 Examples of business processes supported by enterprise systems

Financial	Accounts receivable and payable, cash management and forecasting, management information, cost accounting, profitability analysis, profit-centre accounting, financial reporting
Human resources	Payroll, personnel planning, travel expenses, benefits accounting, applicant tracking
Operations and logistics	Inventory management, maintenance, production planning, purchasing, quality management, vendor evaluation, shipping
Sales and marketing	Order management, pricing, sales management, sales planning, billing

which enterprise systems support. These 'modules' can be implemented separately, but promise much greater benefits when they are linked to exchange information continuously through the central database.

ERP systems give management direct access to current operating information and so enable companies to, among other things:

- integrate customer and financial information;
- standardise manufacturing processes and reduce inventory;
- improve information for management decisions across sites;
- enable online connections with systems of suppliers and customers with the internal information processing.

There is controversy about whether adopting an ERP system gives a competitive advantage (McKeen and Smith, 2003). ERP systems promote centralised co-ordination and decision making, which may not suit a particular firm, and some companies do not need the level of integration they provide:

> Enterprise systems are basically generic solutions. The design reflects a series of assumptions about the way companies operate in general. Vendors of ES try to structure the systems to reflect best practices, but it is the vendor that is defining what 'best' means. Of course, some degree of ES customisation is possible, but major modifications are very expensive and impracticable. As a result, most companies installing ES will have to adapt or rework their processes to reach a fit with the system. (Davenport, 1998, p. 125)

Some believe that ERP systems lock companies into rigid processes which make it difficult to adapt to market changes (Hagel and Brown, 2001). This may help explain the results of a study by Wieder *et al.* (2006) which found no significant differences in performance between adopters and non-adopters of ERP systems. Bozarth (2006) illustrates the complexities of implementing such systems and contrasts alternative approaches. The following Management in Practice illustrates these issues from the experience of Nestlé.

Management in practice   **Nestlé struggles with enterprise systems** www.nestle.com

Nestlé is a food and pharmaceuticals company that operates all over the world. Traditionally it allowed local units to operate as they saw fit, taking into account local conditions and business cultures. The company had many purchasing systems and no information on how much business they did with each supplier: each factory made independent arrangements. Nestlé's management concluded that these local differences were inefficient and costly. They wanted to integrate the systems to act as a single entity, using its worldwide buying power to lower prices.

Managers therefore started a program to standardise and co-ordinate its processes and information systems. The project team decided to install SAP's financial, purchasing, sales and distribution modules throughout every Nestlé USA division. The new system would standardise and co-ordinate the company's information systems and processes.

A year after the project started, a stock market analyst in London doubted its success: 'it touches the corporate culture, which is decentralised and tries to centralise it. That's risky. It's always a risk when you touch the corporate culture'. Jeri Dunn from Nestlé later agreed: at an American plant most of the key stakeholders failed to realise how much the project would change their business processes. Dunn said: 'they still thought it was just software'. A rebellion had taken place when the plant moved to install the manufacturing modules. The lower-level workers did not understand how to use the new system and did not understand the changes. Their only hope was to call the project help desk, which received 300 calls a day. Turnover increased and no one seemed motivated to learn and use the system.

The project team stopped the project and removed the project leader. This person had put too much pressure on the project and the technology. By doing so the team had lost sight of the bigger picture.

Sources: Laudon and Laudon (2004); 'Nestlé's ERP Odyssey', *CIO-magazine*, 15 May; Konicki (2000), 'Nestlé Taps SAP for e-business', *Information Week*, 26 June 2000.

Knowledge management (KM) systems

'**Knowledge** builds on information that is extracted from data' (Boisot, 1998, p. 12). While data are a property of things (size, price, etc.) knowledge is a property of people, which predisposes them to act in a particular way. It embodies prior understanding, experience and learning, and is either confirmed or modified as people receive new information. The significance of the distinction is that knowledge enables people to add more value to resources, since they can react more intelligently to information and data than those without that experience and learning. Someone with good knowledge of a market will use it to interpret information about current sales. They can identify significant patterns or trends, and so attach a different meaning to the information than someone without that knowledge.

> **Knowledge** builds on information and embodies a person's prior understanding, experience and learning.

Managers (especially those employing many skilled professionals) have long wanted to make better use of their employees' knowledge, believing it to be vital to innovation and the primary source of wealth in modern economies. People in large organisations often believe that the knowledge they need to improve performance is available within the business – but that they cannot find it. **Knowledge management (KM)** refers to attempts to improve the way organisations create, acquire, capture, store, share and use knowledge. This will usually relate to customers, markets, products, services and internal processes, but may also refer to knowledge about relevant external developments.

> **Knowledge management systems** are a type of IS intended to support people as they create, store, transfer and apply knowledge.

Managing knowledge is not new – the Industrial Revolution occurred when people applied new knowledge to manufacturing processes. What is new is the degree to which developments in IS make it easier for people to share data, information and knowledge irrespective of physical distance. This growing technological capacity has encouraged many to believe that implementing KM or similar systems to make better use of knowledge assets will enhance performance – and some studies, such as that by Feng *et al.* (2004), support that view. Three common purposes of KM systems are to:

- code and share best practices;
- create corporate knowledge directories;
- create knowledge networks.

Echikson (2001) outlined how the oil company BP uses advanced information systems to enable staff in the huge global business (including those in recently acquired companies) to share and use information and knowledge. These include a web-based employee directory (an intranet) called 'Connect', which contains a home page for almost every BP employee. Clicking on someone's name brings up a picture, contact details, interests (useful for breaking the ice between people who have not met) and areas of expertise. When a manager in a BP business needed to translate his safety video into French, he used Connect to identify French-speaking employees who could do the work, rather than an external translation service. At the core of the business, decisions on where to drill are now informed by an internet system which brings geological data to one of several high-tech facilities. Engineers view the images and make decisions in hours, which used to take weeks – and help reduce the danger of expensive drilling mistakes.

Management in practice   **Buckman Labs – successful KM**   www.buckman.com

Buckman Labs is a science-based company, operating around the world. The founder realised that the company needed to become more effective in managing the knowledge of its 1,300 scientific staff. The company has steadily developed systems which connect codified databases around the world – containing information on current global best-practice methods, ideas and problems. This enables scientists throughout the company to keep in touch with each other and to share knowledge electronically among themselves and with customers. 'This single knowledge network aims to encompass all of the company's knowledge and experience, empowering Buckman representatives to focus all of their company's capabilities on customer challenges' (Pan, 1999, p. 77).

A notable feature of the company's approach has been the extent to which it has supported technological innovation with organisational change. Initial attempts at knowledge sharing were unsuccessful, with little activity on the system. Managers then instituted a series of changes to encourage greater use. These included producing weekly statistics showing which staff had used the system. Non-users were penalised, frequent contributors rewarded. Processes were also changed to ensure the immediate capture of information during projects.

Source: Pan (1999).

Recall the distinction between data, information and knowledge. Many systems that people refer to as 'knowledge' management systems appear on closer examination to deal with data and information, rather than knowledge. While computer-based systems are effective at dealing with (structured) data and information, they are much less effective at dealing with (unstructured) knowledge. As Hinds and Pfeffer (2003) observe:

> systems (to facilitate the sharing of expertise) generally capture *information or data*, rather than *knowledge or expertise*. Information and information systems are extremely useful but do not replace expertise or the learning that takes place through interpersonal contact. (p. 21)

This point was developed by Scarbrough and Swan (1999) who propose that while technological systems deal well with explicit data and information, they are much less use when dealing with tacit knowledge, which develops among people as they learn to work together. Tacit knowledge reflects the shared understanding and meaning that is unique to a situation. While a 'cognitive' model of KM is an appropriate way to deal with explicit knowledge, a 'community' model is more suitable for tacit knowledge. Table 12.2 contrasts these views.

Presenting the community model alongside the cognitive model helps to identify the issues in the success or failure of knowledge management projects:

> whilst it might be relatively easy to share knowledge across a group that is homogenous, it is extremely difficult to share knowledge where the group is heterogeneous. Yet it is precisely the sharing of knowledge across functional or organisational boundaries . . . that is seen as the key to the effective exploitation of knowledge. (Scarbrough and Swan, 1999, p. 11)

Systems with a technical, cognitive perspective do not take account of structures and cultures, which represent peoples' beliefs and values about what to do and how to reward it. These contexts may inhibit people from sharing knowledge in the way intended.

Table 12.2 Two views of the knowledge management process

Cognitive model	Community model
Knowledge is objectively defined concepts and facts	Knowledge is socially constructed and based on experience
Knowledge is transferred through text, and information systems have a crucial role	Knowledge is transferred through participation in social networks including occupational groups and teams
Gains from KM include recycling knowledge and standardising systems	Gains from KM include greater awareness of internal and external sources of knowledge
The primary function of KM is to codify and capture knowledge	The primary function of KM is to encourage individuals and groups to share knowledge
The dominant metaphor is human memory	The dominant metaphor is human community
The critical success factor is technology	The critical success factor is trust

Source: *Case studies in knowledge management*, CIPD (Scarborough, H. and Swan, J. 1999) with the permission of the publisher, the Chartered Institute of Personnel and Development, London (www.cipd.co.uk).

Case study — **Google – the case continues: a culture built to build**
www.google.com

Google has a technocratic culture, in that individuals prosper based on the quality of their ideas and their technological acumen. Engineers are expected to spend 20 per cent of their time working on their own creative projects. The company provides plenty of intellectual stimulation which, for a company founded on technology, can be the opportunity to learn from the best and brightest technologists.

There are regular talks by distinguished researchers from around the world. Google's founders and executives have thought-through many aspects of the knowledge work environment, including the design and occupancy of offices (jam-packed for better communication); the frequency of all-hands meetings (every Friday); and the approach to interviewing and hiring new employees (rigorous, with many interviews). None of these principles is rocket science, but in combination they suggest an unusually high level of recognition for the human dimensions of innovation. Brin and Page have taken ideas from other organisations – such as the software firm SAS Institute – that are celebrated for how they treat their knowledge workers.

Source: Iyer and Davenport (2008).

Case questions 12.3

- What are the likely advantages to Google, and to its staff, of these practices?

- Read the cases studies of Oticon (Chapter 10 Case), W.L. Gore (Part 5 Case) and Pixar (pages 309 and 403), and note any similarities and differences between their practices and those of Google.

Emerging technical possibilities provide an infrastructure that enables global access to data, information and knowledge. KM tools can exploit explicit knowledge about previous projects, technical discoveries or useful techniques. But re-using existing knowledge may do less for business performance than using it to create new knowledge that suits the situation. This creative process depends more on human interaction than on technology. Since most managers receive too much information it does not follow that pushing more information across such boundaries will improve performance. That depends not only on knowledge, but also on insight and judgement. Gupta and Govindarajan (2000) observed:

> effective knowledge management depends not merely on information-technology platforms but . . . on the social ecology of an organisation – the social system in which people operate [made up of] culture, structure, information systems, reward systems, processes, people and leadership. (p. 72)

People are more likely to use a KM system if the culture recognises and rewards knowledge sharing – lively communities of practice will be more effective than technology (Thompson and Walsham, 2004).

Activity 12.5   What knowledge do you need for a task?

- Identify for an employee (perhaps yourself) what knowledge he/she creates, acquires, captures, shares and uses while doing a specified task.
- Identify examples of explicit and tacit knowledge in this example.
- Discuss to what extent could a computerised knowledge system be useful in managing that knowledge.
- Also discuss whether such a system would be in your interests or those of the organisation?

12.6   IS, strategy and organisation – the big picture

Computer-based IS can contribute to an organisation's strategy, in the same way as any other capability – human resources, finance or marketing. They are all resources which managers can incorporate into their strategic planning. Equally, to use these resources to add value to them, managers need to ensure that they align with each other, so that they complement each other, rather than pull in opposite directions. The following sections illustrate this by showing how managers can take a strategic perspective on IS, and on the major organisational changes this requires.

Case study   Google – the case continues   www.google.com

The company has rapidly extended the range of services it offers, while remaining rigorously focused on search. Although the headquarters are in California, their mission is to facilitate access to information across the world – more than half of their searches are delivered to users living outside the US, in more than 35 languages. The company offers volunteers the opportunity to help in translating the site into additional languages.

While a principle within the company has been that it did not interfere with the results of a search (not favouring one advertiser over another, once they had bid for keywords) it faced criticism when it agreed to place certain restrictions on the site in China.

The company acquired YouTube, the video-sharing site, in 2006, as a further extension of its services. In 2007 Viacom, a major entertainment producer, sued YouTube and Google, contending that 160,000 unauthorised clips of Viacom programmes were available on YouTube, and that this infringed the company's copyrights over the material.

Such acquisitions can be seen as a way of growing the business in a way that stays focused on Google's distinctive competence, (developing superior search solutions) and earning revenue from these through targeted advertising. One alternative direction would be to aggregate the content into thematic channels, similar to Yahoo! Another could be to extend its service beyond the search process (which helps buyers to identify suitable sellers) and into the transaction process – by developing systems (such as eBay) that would facilitate the actual transactions.

Sources: Company website; other published sources.

Case questions 12.4

- Referring to Chapter 8, what kind of strategy is Google following?
- What 'strategic direction' (Section 8.6) does the purchase of YouTube represent?
- Visit the website to identify recent strategic developments, and consider what they reveal about the company's strategy for growth.

IS and strategy

Chapter 8 shows that strategy sets the overall direction of the business, and suggests that a Porter's five forces model is a useful tool for identifying the competitive forces affecting a business. Figure 12.9 shows that IS can become a source of competitive advantage that can use technology to strengthen one or more of the forces, and Table 12.3 gives some examples.

This helps managers to identify ways of using their IS as a source of competitive advantage (or to identify potential threats from others).

Managers also use IS to support their chosen strategy, such as a differentiation or cost leadership. They can use IS to achieve a cost leadership strategy by, for example, using:

- computer-aided manufacturing (CAM) to replace manual labour;
- stock control systems to cut expensive inventory; or
- online order entry to cut order processing costs.

They can support a differentiation strategy by using:

- computer-aided manufacturing to offer flexible delivery;

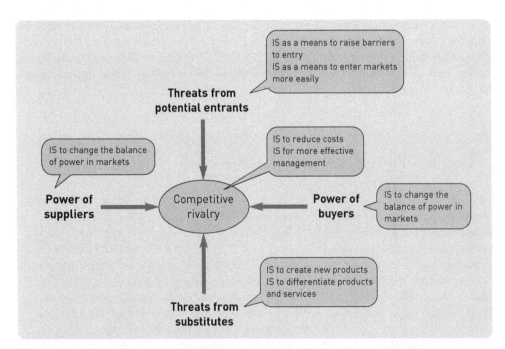

Figure 12.9 How information systems can change competitive forces: Porter's model

Source: Adapted and reprinted by permission of Harvard Business Review. Exhibit adapted from Strategy and the Internet, *Harvard Business Review*, vol. 79, no. 3, pp. 63–78 by M. E. Porter, Copyright © 2001 by Harvard Business School Publishing Corporation; all rights reserved.

Table 12.3 Using information systems to affect the five forces

Porter's five forces		Examples of information systems support
Threat of potential entrants	Raise entry barriers	Electronic links with customers make it more costly for them to move to competitors. Supermarkets use electronic links to banks and suppliers, and so gain a cost advantage over small retailers
	Entering markets more easily	Bertelsmann, a German media group, entered book retailing by setting up an online store. Virgin offers financial services by using online systems
Threat of substitutes	Creating new products	Online banking has only been possible with modern information systems
	Differentiating their products	Using database technology and CRM systems to identify precise customer needs and then create unique offers and incentives
Bargaining power of suppliers	Increasing power of suppliers	Airlines use yield management systems to track actual reservations against capacity on each flight, and then adjust prices for the remaining seats to maximise revenue
	Decreasing power of suppliers	Online recruitment through a website reduces the need to advertise vacancies in newspapers, reducing their power to earn advertising revenue
Bargaining power of buyers		Buyers can use the internet to access more suppliers and compare prices for standard commodities
Intensity of rivalry	Using IS to reduce costs	Enterprise resource planning systems make it possible to make radical changes in manufacturing systems, leading to greater consistency in planning and lower costs
	More effective management	Information systems provide more detailed information on trading patterns, enabling management to make more informed decisions

- stock control systems to extend the range of goods on offer at any time; or
- using online systems to remember customer preferences, and suggest purchases.

They can support a focus strategy by using:

- computer-aided manufacturing to meet unique, non-standard requirements;
- online ordering to allow customers to create a unique product by selecting its features.

IS, strategy and organisation

Managers who wish to use one or more of these applications of IS to support their strategy also need to ensure that their organisation structure supports the strategy, as there is abundant evidence that having a structure and culture that complements, or is aligned with, the strategy will produce better results than one that is not (Sabherwal *et al.*, 2001; Boddy and Paton, 2005). Whittington *et al.* (2006) showed that in a world of accelerating change strategising and organising are best conducted as tightly linked practical activities.

One aspect of organisation that illustrates this is that of how the IS function is organised – especially whether it is centralised or decentralised. In a centralised arrangement, a corporate IS unit is responsible for all computing activities. When a user department requires a new or enhanced system, it applies for it through the IS department. The IS department sets priorities using guidelines agreed with senior management, and then delivers and supports the services. This approach can be very efficient, allowing tight integration of all systems, and the benefits of expertise being concentrated in one unit. A disadvantage is that the dominant, centralised department can be inflexible and remote from the business and may appear technologically arrogant to users. Departments have different information needs, so a system that gives a common service to all will find it hard to satisfy everyone. The centralised model fits best with organisations that make other decisions centrally, that work in a stable environment and where there is little communication between units.

The opposite approach is to decentralise IS delivery, so that managers of each major unit are responsible for their own system – including development, acquisition, operations and maintenance. This is only possible when the units are independent, with little communication between them. Kahay *et al.* (2003) discussed with more than 100 IS executives their plans to decentralise IS. The researchers concluded that while most believed that IS should be decentralised in the interests of responsiveness, they also advocated that a central unit should be responsible for security, standards and IS governance. If managers see the advantages of decentralisation but also the disadvantages of full independence, they may choose a mixed model, in which business units decide their requirements and manage their systems, but the centre retains control over tasks such as data standards and hardware compatibility. A centralised department can determine information strategy for the organisation and administer the corporate system and database. The decentralised departments can develop and manage local IS within those corporate guidelines. This model fits best in organisations with a high interdependence, a high need to share data and a turbulent environment.

The theme, however, is to ensure that managers are conscious of the benefits of maintaining alignment between strategy, organisation and information systems.

12.7   Integrating themes

Sustainable performance

Developments in information technology have had, and will continue to have, both negative and positive effects on sustainability. The electronics industry itself adds massively to the emission of greenhouse gases by:

- Manufacturing and distribution – the products themselves are produced in worldwide manufacturing supply chains, usually linked by air-freight; frequent updates mean that many machines are discarded after a few years, most of which are still dumped in landfill sites.
- Use – the energy consumption of millions of users, together with the energy used by websites. Greenpeace has called on technology giants such as Apple, Microsoft and Google to power their data centres with renewable energy sources. At present their electricity comes from utility companies which generate power from burning coal, leading to a growing carbon footprint. The launch of portable online devices such as smartphones, netbooks and the iPad means more data are stored remotely so that it can be accessed from wherever the user has an internet connection. So firms are building massive data centres to cope with the demand (*BBC News*, 30 March 2010).

Conversely (Hawken *et al.*, 1999) show that the clever use of IT can significantly reduce the use of energy and raw materials by applications such as:

- online meeting facilities such as video-conferencing or social networking sites, which can reduce the need for people to travel to meetings;
- energy management systems to monitor and control energy use in buildings and other physical facilities;
- manufacturing planning systems which enhance the design and manufacture of products to minimise the use of energy and raw materials;
- transport systems which monitor and control engine efficiency to save fuel.

Governance and control

Advances in information systems technology offer senior managers the promise of greatly improved performance: but many IS projects fail to deliver, and destroy a great deal of wealth. Weill and Ross (2005) believe that the waste of resources this represents could be avoided by better IS governance systems, since:

> without them individual managers resolve isolated issues as they arise, and those individual actions may be at odds with each other. Our study of almost 300 companies around the world suggests that IT governance is a mystery to key decision makers in most companies . . . [yet] when senior managers take time to design, implement and communicate IT governance processes, companies get more value from IT. (p. 26)

They believe that the key issue for managers is to be clear about how they are going to control decisions about investments in IS. This is a multi-stage process in which players at various levels and in many functional areas exercise their power to influence IS decisions. To ensure that these decisions align information systems' wider organisational objectives, IS governance is the practice of allocating decision rights, and establishing an accountability framework for IS decisions. These decisions arise in five domains:

- principles – high level choices about the strategic role of IS in the organisation;
- architecture – an integrated set of technical choices to satisfy business needs;
- infrastructure – the shared resources that are the foundation of the enterprise's IS capability;
- business applications – what the business needs from IS; and
- investment priorities – how much and where to invest.

Each of these areas can be addressed at corporate, business unit or functional levels, or a combination of them all. So, they suggest, the first step in designing IS governance is to decide who should make, and be held accountable for, each decision area, and whether this should be a centralised or decentralised approach, or something in between.

Finally they suggest that senior managers design a set of governance mechanisms that clarify:

- decision-making structures – the organisational committees and roles that specify and locate decision making responsibilities;
- alignment processes – management techniques for securing wide involvement in governance decisions and their implementation according, for example to the degree of centralisation;
- formal communications – ensuring that all players are aware of, and understand, the governance processes through which IS decisions are made.

Internationalisation

New technologies are enabling the processes of international business, since firms can disperse their operations around the globe, and manage them economically from a distance. The technology enables managers to keep in close touch with dispersed operations and to transfer knowledge between them. Paik and Choi (2005) showed the difficulties in applying technology across national boundaries, in their study of one of the leading global management consultancies, with over 75,000 consultants in over 40 countries. Like most such firms, it considers the knowledge of its staff to be a core capability for achieving competitive advantage. To ensure that this knowledge is widely shared, it has spent large sums on KM systems, especially knowledge exchange (KX) – a repository of internally generated knowledge about clients, topics, best practices and so on – to which consultants were expected to contribute ideas as they completed projects for clients.

However, the authors found that few East Asian consultants contributed to the database and identified three reasons:

- a perception among East Asian consultants that others did not appreciate their regional knowledge;

- a requirement to provide ideas in English; East Asian consultants were conversant in English, but found it difficult and time-consuming to translate documents into English before submitting them;
- cultural differences; in some countries staff were not motivated to contribute if there was no direct personal incentive – which the global reward system did not take into account.

They conclude that their study shows that global companies seeking a common approach to knowledge management need to make allowances for local cultural differences, as shown in Chapter 4.

Summary

1 **Explain how converging technologies change the way people add value to resources**
   - Continuing advances in information systems for processing data have been enhanced by the convergence of systems so that they now integrate data, sound and visual systems.
   - The radical result is that this enables producers and customers to co-create value.

2 **Recognise that, to use these opportunities, managers change both technology and orginisation**
   - Established organisations use IS to make radical changes in the services they offer and how they work.
   - They also, as do new internet-based organisations, find ways to benefit from the possibilities of co-creation with customers.
   - Both depend on managing both technical and organisational issues.

3 **Distinguish between operations information systems and management information systems**
   - Operations information systems – such as transaction processing and office automation systems – support processes that keep current work running smoothly.
   - Management information systems – for information reporting, decision support and executive systems provide managers with information to support decision making.

4 **Illustrate how organisations use the internet to add value by using three types of information system – customer relations, enterprise and knowledge**
   - Internet-based (e-business) are systems which operate across organisational boundaries, enabling new relations with business partners and customers.
   - Enterprise systems use a central database to integrate data about many aspects of the business as an aid to planning.
   - Knowledge management systems attempt to improve the ability of an organisation to use the information which it possesses.
   - Customer relations systems aim to capture and process information about each customer, so that products and services can be tailored more closely to individual needs.

5 **Understand the relation between IS, strategy and organisation**
   - Computer-based IS can support strategy: each of Porter's five forces are potentially affected by IS, leading to either threats or opportunities.
   - Similarly managers can use IS to support a low cost, differentiation or niche strategy.
   - Whatever strategy they follow it will be more successful if they ensure that complementary organisational changes – such as ensuring the alignment of strategy and structure, and the appropriate governance structures for the IS function – to ensure, for example, the right balance between central and local provision.

6 **Show how ideas from the chapter add to your understanding of the integrating themes**
- The rapid spread in the use of information systems is both one cause of the unsustainable use of resources, and also part of the solution, by enabling managers to re-design and monitor their processes to minimise resource use.
- Organisations waste huge amounts of money on information systems projects that fail to deliver what was expected, partly because senior managers have not paid sufficient attention to their systems for the governance and control of the IS function.
- While information systems enable managers to monitor and control international operations, to be effective they need to take account of national cultural differences (see Chapter 4), and of how people in different countries interpret and use information.

Review questions

1 Explain the significance of information systems to the management of organisations? How do they relate to the core task of managing?
2 Give some original examples of companies using information systems to add value.
3 Identify examples of co-creation or 'wikinomics', and explain the benefits to company and customer.
4 For what purposes are commercial companies using social networking sites?
5 Draw a sketch to illustrate why computer-based information systems require more than the management of technology.
6 Give examples of how an information system can affect at least two of the forces in Porter's model and so affect the competitiveness of a business.
7 Outline the stages through which organisations go in using the internet, giving an original example of each.
8 Use the Nestlé case (Management in Practice feature) to identify some possible difficulties in using ERP systems.
9 What is the difference between a cognitive and a communal view of knowledge?
10 Describe how the five forces model can show the likely effects of information systems on strategy.
11 Summarise an idea from the chapter that adds to your understanding of the integrating themes.

Concluding critical reflection

Think about the main computer-based information systems that you use in your company, or that feature in one with which you are familiar. Review the material in the chapter and perhaps visit some of the websites identified. Then make notes on these questions:

- What examples of the themes discussed in this chapter are currently relevant to your company? How have information systems helped or hindered managers' performance? How well have the social as well as the technological aspects of new systems been managed? How, if at all, have they altered the tasks and roles of managers, staff or professionals? What stage have you reached in using the internet?
- If the business seems to pay too much attention to the technical aspects of IS projects, and not enough to the social and organisational aspects, why is that? What **assumptions** appear to have shaped the managers' approach?
- How have changes in the business **context** shaped the applications being implemented? Do they seem well-suited to their organisational (structural, cultural, etc. factors) and external contexts? Have managers considered any **alternatives** to the way IS projects are managed differently to improve their return on investment, for example by greater user involvement in the projects?
- Do they regularly and systematically review IS projects after implementation to identify any **limitations** in their approaches? Do the presentations on ERP and CRM systems match experience in your organisation with such systems?

Further reading

Bernoff, J. and Li, C. (2008), 'Harnessing the power of the oh-so-social web', *MIT Sloan Management Review*, vol. 49, no. 3, pp. 36–42.

Boulding, W., Staelin, R. and Ehret, M. (2005), 'A customer relationship management roadmap: What is known, potential pitfalls, and where to go', *Journal of Marketing*, vol. 69, no. 4, pp. 155–166.

Bozarth, C. (2006), 'ERP implementation efforts at three firms', *International Journal of Operations & Production Management*, vol. 26, no. 11, pp. 1223–1239.

Three recent empirical studies of the organisational aspects of managing information systems.

Iyer, B. and Davenport, T. H. (2008), 'Reverse engineering Google's innovation machine', *Harvard Business Review*, vol. 86, no. 4, pp. 58–68.

Many insights into the company.

Laudon, K.C. and Laudon, J.P. (2004), *Management Information Systems: Organization and technology in the networked enterprise*, Prentice Hall, Harlow.

This text, written from a management perspective, focuses on the opportunities and pitfalls of information systems.

Phillips, P. (2003), *E-Business Strategy: Text and cases*, McGraw-Hill, Maidenhead.

A comprehensive European perspective on internet developments relevant to business and strategy.

Tapscott, E. and Williams, A.D. (2006), *Wikinomics: How mass collaboration changes everything*, Viking Penguin, New York.

Best-selling account of the rise of co-creation.

Weblinks

These websites are those that have appeared in the chapter:

www.google.com
www.connectingforhealth.nhs.uk
www.bbc.co.uk
www.selectminds.com
www.renault.com
www.siemens.com
www.Yahoo.com
www.amazon.com
www.moneyfacts.com
www.tesco.com
www.irisnation.com
www.nestle.com
www.buckman.com

Visit two of the business sites in the list, or any others that interest you, and answer the following questions:

- If you were a potential employee, how well does it present information about the company and the career opportunities available? Could you apply for a job online?

- Evaluate the sites on these criteria, which are based on those used in an annual survey of corporate websites:

  - Does it give the current share price on the front page?

  - How many languages is it available in?

  - Is it possible to email key people or functions from the site?

  - Does it give a diagram of the main structural units in the business?

  - Does it set out the main mission or business idea of the company?

  - Are there any other positive or negative features?

For video case studies, audio summaries, flashcards, exercises and annotated weblinks related to this chapter, visit **www.pearsoned.co.uk/mymanagementlab**

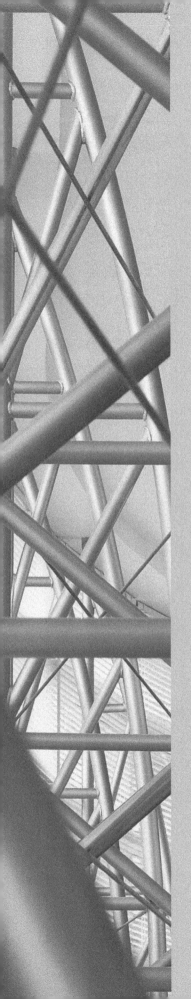

CHAPTER 13
MANAGING CHANGE AND INNOVATION

Aim

To outline theories of change and innovation, and show how these can guide practice.

Objectives

By the end of your work on this chapter you should be able to outline the concepts below in your own terms and:

1 Explain the meaning of organisational change and give examples
2 Explain what the links between change and context imply for those managing a change
3 Compare lifecycle, emergent, participative and political theories of change
4 Evaluate systematically the possible sources of resistance to change
5 Explain how innovations benefit organisations
6 Illustrate the organisational factors believed to support innovation
7 Show how ideas from the chapter add to your understanding of the integrating themes.

Key terms

This chapter introduces the following ideas:

perceived performance gap
performance imperatives
organisational change
interaction model
receptive contexts
non-receptive contexts
lifecycle

emergent models
participative model
political model
creativity
incremental innovations
radical innovations

Each is a term defined within the text, as well as in the Glossary at the end of the book.

Case study
Vodafone/Ericsson   www.vodafone.com
www.ericsson.com

In 2010 Vodafone offered mobile services to sub-scribers in 31 countries and was the world's largest mobile network operator, with about one-quarter of the market. Ericsson was the world's largest supplier of mobile network infrastructure, and Vodafone its largest customer. Vodafone has achieved its strong market position partly by internal growth and by ac-quiring other operators, such as AirTouch (USA) in 1998 and Mannesmann (Germany) in 2000. Many of these acquisitions also had shareholdings in other mobile operators, meaning that in some countries Vodafone operates through partially rather than wholly owned subsidiaries.

As demand for mobile services grew, Vodafone extended the network on a country-by-country basis, with local management teams running the business. It usually ordered network equipment from Ericsson, negotiating terms with Ericsson staff in their country. Although Vodafone's in-country man-agers communicated with their counterparts in other countries, Vodafone did not attempt to co-ordinate the way they operated. Ericsson operated in a more centralised fashion, although with some scope for local managers to establish terms of business that reflected their market or competitive environment. This had the following consequences:

- Terms and conditions for purchasing network equipment varied between countries.
- Communication between the two companies in each country was direct, through meetings, tele-phones, letters, fax and email.
- Communication about Ericsson products be-tween Vodafone operators in different countries was *ad hoc*.
- Sharing of product information between Ericsson and Vodafone was in-country, mainly through written documents.
- Ordering and order tracking was done by local systems in each country.
- Configuration of network equipment varied be-tween countries, as did service and support arrangements.

Before the merger with AirTouch, Vodafone man-agement had begun to assess what synergies it could gain from the merger, especially in the supply of network equipment. The company expected to make big savings if it could aggregate its worldwide

© Vodafone 2007

requirements for network equipment, and source this from common global suppliers. The acquisition of Mannesmann increased the scope for synergy – and claims about the potential savings in this area were made to shareholders and the financial markets.

Vodafone therefore began a project with Ericsson to develop new ways of managing the relationship. The intention was to find ways of aggregating Vodafone's global requirements so that the com-panies would manage their relationship in a unified way. They realised that managing a change of this scale would raise difficult issues about the:

- degree of planning to undertake;
- scale and value of the synergies from a new global relationship;
- attitudes of those managing Vodafone operations in the various countries;
- resources that would be needed to manage the change.

Source: Based on Ibbott and O'Keefe (2004).

Case questions 13.1
- How may the structure of Vodafone's in-country operations affect the project?
- Will a new global relationship mean a more centralised or a more decentralised company?
- Should the two companies put significant re-sources into planning the change in advance?

13.1   Introduction

The manager whom Vodafone appointed to lead this change faces a familiar problem that is familiar to many managers. The chief executive has put him in charge of implementing a major change that will affect many people, some of whom will be uneasy about how it will affect them. Changing from a country to a global structure will have implications for the way they run the business in their country, and change their relationship with their main equipment supplier.

Managers initiate or experience change so regularly that in many organisations change is the normal state of affairs, interrupted by occasional periods of relative stability. In the most innovative areas of the economy senior managers see their primary task as being to challenge current practices, fostering a climate of exploration and innovation. They want people to see change as the norm: one intervention in a continuing flow, rather than as something from which stability will follow. At BP, for example, the challenge to successive senior managers has been to continue transforming the business from a relatively small (for that industry), diversified business into one of the world's largest oil companies. Mergers, such as that between Chrysler (USA) and Daimler (Germany), are usually followed by internal changes as the companies integrate.

The external environment described in Chapter 3 is the main source of change. The evolving PESTEL factors change what people expect of a business: which may encourage managers to alter their strategy or operations. Anecdotal evidence is that while most managers accept the need for change, many are critical of the way their organisations introduce it. Managers still experience great difficulty in implementing major organisational changes.

This chapter presents theories about the nature of change in organisations. It begins by explaining current external pressures for change, and how these prompt internal change to one or more elements of the organisation. The chapter then outlines a model that shows how change depends on the interaction between the external and internal environments of the organisation. It then presents four complementary perspectives on how people try to manage that interaction. It finishes by investigating how innovation can be managed to bring change to organisations, products and markets.

Activity 13.1   Recording a major change

From discussion with colleagues or managers, identify a major attempt at change in an organisation. Make notes on the following questions and use them as a point of reference throughout the chapter.

- What was the change?
- Why did management introduce it?
- What were the objectives?
- How did management plan and implement it?
- How well did it meet the objectives?
- What lessons have those involved taken from the experience?

13.2   Initiating change

Chapter 1 introduced the idea that managers work within a context that shapes what they do, which they may also change. This chapter explains the interactive nature of that process, and Figure 13.1 illustrates the themes it will cover. A particular episode of change begins when enough people perceive a gap between desired and actual performance – usually because the internal context of the organisation is unable to meet the external demands upon it. Using

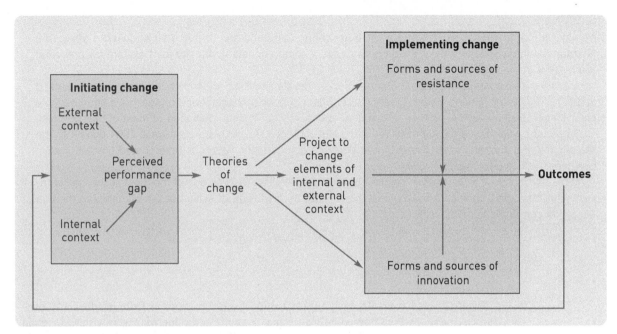

Figure 13.1 A model of the change process

their implicit or explicit theory of change, they initiate a project to change one or more aspects of the internal context in the hope of closing the performance gap. The outcomes of the change effort will be affected by practical issues of design and implementation – but whatever the outcomes they will in turn affect the subsequent shape of the external and internal contexts, providing the starting point for future changes.

The external context

Chapter 3 describes the external environment (or context) of business, and successive chapters have illustrated the changes taking place, such as internationalisation, information technology and expectations about sustainable performance. Together with deregulation and the privatisation of former state businesses, these are transforming the competitive landscape and threatening the survival of established players. Managers at British Airways and KLM have had to respond to the pressure of new competition from low-cost airlines such as Ryanair and easyJet. Established banks face competition from new entrants such as retailers (Sainsbury's) or conglomerates (Virgin) offering financial services. The growth of the internet has enabled companies offering high-value/low-weight products to open new distribution channels and invade previously protected markets.

> **Management in practice**   Successful change at GKN www.gknplc.com
>
> GKN is a leading global supplier to automotive, aerospace and off-highway manufacturers, employing 40,000 people in GKN companies and joint ventures. It was created by a series of mergers at the start of the twentieth century, creating Guest, Keen and Nettlefolds – then one of the largest manufacturing businesses in the world. It was involved in iron and coal mining, steel production and finished products such as nuts, bolts and fasteners.
>
> Its present form reflects a small number of successful decisions made in the 1980s. The first was to abandon any thought of re-entering the steel industry (its interests there had been nationalised in the 1960s), and to focus instead on seeking growth in the motor components business. This decision was shaped by a piece

of luck, in that in 1966 it had bought a UK engineering company and in doing so acquired a share in a German business which had worldwide patents for a unique constant velocity joint system for powering front-wheel drive cars.

A second decision was to cut back sharply on non-vehicle activities, into which the group had diversified in the 1970s. At that time unrelated diversification was a popular management strategy, but it soon became clear that unrelated businesses were best run independently: GKN soon disposed of most of that portfolio.

The third decision was to purchase Westland Helicopters – mainly because it gave GKN entry into the rapidly growing business of manufacturing aerospace components, which complemented the automotive business (Westland was sold in 2004).

In his book *Change Without, Pain* Abrahamson (2004) identifies GKN as one of the most successful companies at managing significant strategic changes – not by disposing of skills but by recombining them in ways that create even greater value.

Sources: *Financial Times*, 6 January 2004, 28 February 2007; *Independent*, 15 March 2007; company website.

These forces have collectively meant a shift of economic power from producers to consumers, many of whom now enjoy greater quality, choice and value. Managers wishing to retain customers continually need to seek new ways of adding value to resources if they are to retain their market position. Unless they do so they will experience a widening performance gap.

Perceived performance gap

A perceived performance gap arises when people believe that the actual performance of a unit or business is out of line with the level they desire.

A **perceived performance gap** arises when people believe that the actual performance of a unit or business is out of line with the level they desire. If those responsible for transforming resources into outputs do so in a way that does not meet customer expectations, there is a performance gap. Cumulatively this will lead to other performance gaps emerging – such as revenue from sales being below the level needed to secure further resources. If uncorrected this will eventually cause the business to fail.

In the current business climate, two aspects of performance dominate discussion – what Prastacos *et al.* (2002) call '**performance imperatives**': the need for flexibility and the need for innovation. In a very uncertain business world the scope for long-term planning is seriously limited. Successful businesses are likely to be those that develop a high degree of strategic and organisational flexibility, while also maintaining efficient and stable processes. This apparent paradox reflects the fact that while companies need to respond rapidly they also need to respond efficiently. This usually depends on having developed a degree of stability and predictability in the way they transform resources into goods and services.

Performance imperatives are aspects of performance that are especially important for an organisation to do well, such as flexibility and innovation.

The other imperative identified by Prastacos *et al.* (2002) is innovation:

to generate a variety of successful new products or services (embedding technological innovation), and to continuously innovate in all aspects of the business. (p. 58)

In many areas of business, customers expect a constant flow of new products, embodying the latest scientific and technological developments: companies that fail to meet these expectations will experience a performance gap. Nokia selling an advanced mobile phone profitably depends not only on the quality of the applied research which goes into a better screen display, but also on turning that research into a desirable product *and* delivering the devices at a price that customers will pay. This depends on organisation – the internal context of management.

The internal context

Chapter 1 introduces the internal context (Figure 1.3, repeated here as Figure 13.2) as the set of elements within an organisation that shape behaviour. Change begins to happen when

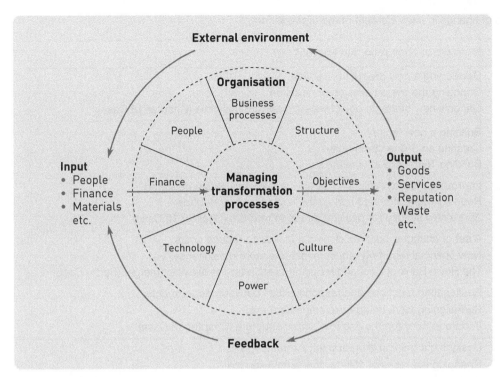

Figure 13.2
Elements of the
internal context of
management

sufficient influential people believe, say, that outdated technology or a confusing structure is causing a performance gap, by inhibiting flexibility or innovation. They notice external or internal events and interpret them as threatening the performance that influential stakeholders expect. This interpretation, and their (implicit) theory of change, encourages them to propose changing one or more aspects of the organisation shown in Figure 13.2.

They then have to persuade enough other people that the matter is serious enough to earn a place on the management agenda. People in some organisations are open to proposals for change, others tend to ignore them – BP faced new competitive pressures throughout the 1980s, but it was only around 1990 that sufficient senior people took the threats seriously enough to initiate a period of rapid change.

People initiate organisational change for reasons other than a conscious awareness of a performance gap – fashion, empire building or a powerful player's personal whim can all play a part. Employees or trade unions can propose changes in the way things are done to improve working conditions. The need for change is subjective – what some see as urgent others will leave until later. People can affect that process by managing external information – magnifying customer complaints to make the case for change, or minimising them if they wish to avoid change.

Whatever the underlying motivations, **organisational change** is an attempt to change one or more of the elements shown in Figure 13.2. Table 13.1 illustrates specific types of change that people initiate under each element, including some that appear elsewhere in this book.

Change in any of these areas will have implications for others – and these interconnections make life difficult. When Tesco introduced its online shopping service alongside its established retail business, the company needed to create a website (technology). Managers also needed to decide issues of structure and people (would it be part of the existing stores or a separate unit with its own premises and staff?) and about business processes (how would an order on the website be converted to a box of groceries delivered to the customer's door?). They had to manage these ripples initiated by the main decision. Managers who ignore these consequential changes achieve less than they expect.

Organisational change is a deliberate attempt to improve organisational performance by changing one or more aspects of the organisation, such as its technology, structure or business processes.

Table 13.1 Examples of change in each element of the organisation

Element	Example of change to this element
Objectives	Developing a new product or service Changing the overall mission or direction Oticon's new strategic objectives as a service business (Chapter 18 Case)
Technology	Building a new factory Creating an online community Building Terminal 5 at Heathrow
Business processes	Improving the way maintenance and repair services are delivered Redesigning systems to handle the flow of cash and funds Zara's new system for passing goods to retailers (Chapter 18 Case)
Financial resources	A set of changes, such as closing a facility, to reduce costs New financial reporting requirements to ensure consistency The Royal Bank of Scotland reducing costs after the NatWest merger (Part 4 Case)
Structure	Reallocating functions and responsibilities between departments Redesigning work to increase empowerment Vodafone/Ericsson moving to a global structure (Chapter 13 Case)
People	Designing a training programme to enhance skills Changing the tasks of staff to offer a new service
Culture	Unifying the culture between two or more merged businesses Encouraging greater emphasis on quality and reliability
Power	An empowerment programme giving greater authority to junior staff Centralising decisions to increase the control of HQ over subsidiaries

Case questions 13.2

Identify the possible ripple effects that may need to be managed in the Vodafone/Ericsson change, using the elements in Figure 13.2 as a guide.

- How may the move to a global relationship affect the structure area?
- What implications may that change have for other elements?
- Which of these are likely to cause most difficulty?

These begin to form the management agenda for this project. If possible compare your answers with others on the course, to see how many alternative possibilities you have identified.

The interaction model is a theory of change that stresses the continuing interaction between the internal and external contexts of an organisation, making the outcomes of change hard to predict.

13.3   The interaction of context and change

How managers implement change depends on their theory about its nature. This section presents an **interaction model**, a theory of how change and context interact. The following section outlines four complementary perspectives on managing that interaction.

People introduce change to alter the context

Management attempts to change elements of its context to encourage behaviours that close the performance gap. Vodafone wanted to change the context within which it worked with Ericsson. By moving from country relationships with Ericsson to a more unified global structure, management hoped to create a structure that enabled people in both companies to reduce the cost of expanding the network. When Tesco introduced online shopping, management needed (at least) to change technology, structure, people and business processes to enable staff to deliver the new service. When people plan and implement a change they are creating new 'rules' (Walsham, 1993) that they hope will guide the behaviour of people involved in the activity.

People do not necessarily accept the new arrangements without question, or without adapting them in some way: in doing so they make further changes to the context. As people begin to work in new circumstances – with a new technology or new structure – they make small adjustments to the original plan. As they use a new information system or website they decide which aspects to ignore, use or adapt.

As people become used to working with the new system their behaviours become routine and taken for granted. They become part of the context that staff have created informally. These new elements add to, or replace, the context that those formally responsible for planning the change created, and may or may not support the original intentions of the project. People and context continue to interact.

The context affects the ability to change

While people managing a project aim to change the context, the context within which they work will itself help or hinder them. All of the elements of Figure 13.2 will be present as the project begins, and some of these will influence how people react. Managers who occupy influential positions will review a proposal from their personal career perspective, as well as that of the organisation. At Tesco the existing technology (stores, distribution systems and information systems) and business processes would influence managers' decisions about how to implement the internet shopping strategy.

The prevailing culture (Chapter 3) – shared values, ideals and beliefs – influences how people view change. Members are likely to welcome a project that they believe fits their culture or subculture, and resist one that threatens it.

Management in practice   **Culture and change at a European bank**

While teaching a course to managers at a European bank, the author invited members to identify which of the four cultural types identified in Chapter 2 best described their unit within the bank. They were then asked to describe the reaction of these units to an internet banking venture that the company was introducing.

Course members observed that colleagues in a unit that had an internal process culture (routine back-office data processing) were hostile to the internet venture. They appeared to be 'stuck with their own systems', which were so large and interlinked that any change was threatening. Staff in new business areas of the company (open systems) were much more positive, seeing the internet as a way towards new business opportunities.

Source: Data collected by the author.

Culture is a powerful influence on the success or failure of innovation (see Jones *et al.*, 2005, for evidence of how it affected the acceptance of a new computer system). Some cultures support change: a manager in Sun Microsystems commented on that fast-moving business:

A very dynamic organisation, it's incredibly fast and the change thing is just a constant that you live with. They really promote flexibility and adaptability in their employees.

Change is just a constant, there's change happening all of the time and people have become very acclimatised to that, it's part of the job. The attitude to change, certainly within the organisation, is very positive at the moment.

At companies such as Google or Facebook the culture encourages change, while elsewhere it encourages caution. Cultural beliefs are hard to change, yet shape how people respond:

Managers learn to be guided by these beliefs because they have worked successfully in the past. (Lorsch, 1986, p. 97)

Key ideas **Receptive and non-receptive contexts**

Pettigrew *et al.* (1992) sought to explain why managers in some organisations were able to introduce change successfully, while others in the same sector (the UK National Health Service) found it very hard to move away from established practices. Their comparative research programme identified the influence of context on ability to change: **receptive contexts** are those where features of the context 'seem to be favourably associated with forward movement. On the other hand, in **non-receptive contexts** there is a configuration of features that may be associated with blocks on change' (p. 268).

Their research identified seven such contextual factors, which provide a linked set of conditions that are likely to provide the energy around change. These are:

1 quality and coherence of policy;
2 availability of key people leading change;
3 long-term environmental pressure – intensity and scale;
4 a supportive organisational culture;
5 effective managerial–clinical relations;
6 co-operative interorganisational networks;
7 the fit between the district's change agenda and its locale.

While some of these factors are specific to the health sector, they can easily be adapted to other settings. Together these factors give a widely applicable model of how the context affects ability to change.

Source: Pettigrew *et al.* (1992).

Receptive contexts are those where features of the organisation (such as culture or technology) appear likely to help change.

Non-receptive contexts are those where the combined effects of features of the organisation (such as culture or technology) appear likely to hinder change.

The distribution of power also affects receptiveness to change. Change threatens the status quo, and is likely to be resisted by stakeholders who benefit from the prevailing arrangements. Innovation depends on those behind the change developing political will and expertise that they can only attempt within the prevailing pattern of power.

The context has a history and several levels

The present context is the result of past decisions and events: Balogun *et al.* (2005) show how internal change agents adapted practice to suit aspects of their context, such as the degree of local autonomy, senior management preferences, rewards systems and financial reporting systems. Management implements change against a background of previous events that shaped the context. The promoter of a major project in a multinational experienced this in his colleagues' attitudes:

They were a little sceptical and wary of whether it was actually going to enhance our processes. Major pan-European redesign work had been attempted in the past and had failed miserably. The solutions had not been appropriate and had not been accepted by the divisions. Europe-wide programmes therefore had a bad name. (Boddy, 2002, p. 38)

Beliefs about the future also affect how people react. Optimists are more open to change than those who feel threatened and vulnerable.

Vodafone conducted business in each country in partnership with other operators, with Vodafone sometimes having a minority shareholding in the company. For example, in the UK it owned 100 per cent of the equity, in Germany 99 per cent and in Australia 91 per cent. In the Netherlands, Portugal and Spain this fell to 70, 50 and 22 per cent respectively.

This meant that considerable political skill and discussion were required to handle the attitudes of the various operating companies with regard to Ericsson's local in-country operations. Some countries had acquired very favourable terms and conditions that would not necessarily be matched by the global agreements, while others had key skills that would now be 'given up' to the global effort.

Source: Ibbott and O'Keefe (2004), p. 226.

The context represented by Figure 13.2 occurs at, say, operating, divisional and corporate levels. People at any of these levels will be acting to change their context – which may help or hinder those managing change elsewhere. A project at one level may depend on decisions at another about resources, as the manager leading an oil refinery project discovered:

> One of the main drawbacks was that commissioning staff could have been supplemented by skilled professionals from within the company, but this was denied to me as project manager. This threw a heavy strain and responsibility on myself and my assistant. It put me in a position of high stress, as I knew that the future of the company rested upon the successful outcome of this project. One disappointment (and, I believe, a significant factor in the project) was that just before commissioning, the manager of the pilot plant development team was transferred to another job. He had been promised to me at the project inception, and I had designed him into the working operation. (Boddy, 2002, pp. 38–39)

Acting to change an element at one level will have effects at this and other levels, and elements may change independently. The manager's job is to create a coherent context that encourages desired behaviour, by using his/her preferred model of change.

Case questions 13.3

- How may the existing context of Vodafone and Ericsson affect how in-country managers react to the proposed change?
- How may that affect the way the project leader manages the change?

13.4   Four models of change

There are four complementary models of change, each with different implications for managers: lifecycle, emergent, participative and political.

Lifecycle

Much advice given to those responsible for managing projects uses the idea of the project **lifecycle**. Projects go through successive stages, and results depend on managing each one in an orderly and controlled way. The labels vary, but common themes are:

1 Define objectives.
2 Allocate responsibilities.
3 Fix deadlines and milestones.

Lifecycle models of change are those that view change as an activity which follows a logical, orderly sequence of activities that can be planned in advance.

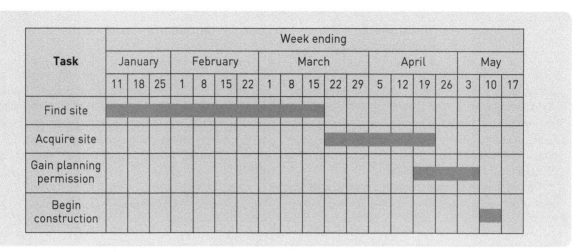

Task	Week ending																	
	January			February				March					April				May	
	11	18	25	1	8	15	22	1	8	15	22	29	5	12	19	26	3	10	17
Find site	██	██	██	██	██	██	██	██	██	██									
Acquire site											██	██	██	██					
Gain planning permission															██	██	██		
Begin construction																		██	

Figure 13.3 A simple bar chart

4 Set budgets.
5 Monitor and control.

This approach (sometimes called a 'rational–linear' approach) reflects the idea that people can identify smaller tasks within a change and plan the (overlapping) order in which to do them. It predicts that people can make reasonably accurate estimates of the time required to complete each task and when it will be feasible to start work on later ones. People can use tools such as bar charts (sometimes called Gantt charts after the American industrial engineer Henry Gantt, who worked with Frederick Taylor), to show all the tasks required for a project, and their likely duration. These help to visualise the work required and to plan the likely sequence of events, which Figure 13.3 illustrates.

In the lifecycle model, successfully managing change depends on specifying these elements at the start and then monitoring them to ensure the project stays on target. Ineffective implementation is due to managers failing to do this. Figure 13.4 shows the stages in the lifecycle of

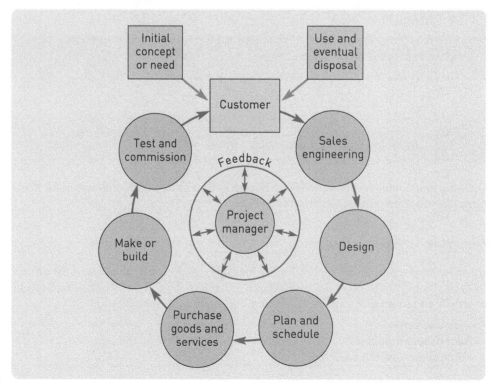

Figure 13.4
A project lifecycle
Source: Lock (2007) p. 8.

a small project (Lock, 2007). It is cyclical because the stages begin and end with the customer. Lock emphasises this is an oversimplification of a complex, iterative reality, but that it helps identify where decisions arise:

> Travelling clockwise round the cycle reveals a number of steps or *phases*, each of which is represented by a circle in the diagram. The boundaries between these phases are usually blurred in practice, because the phases tend to overlap. (Lock, 2007, pp. 8–9)

Many books on project management, such as Lock (2007), present advice on tools for each stage of the lifecycle. Those advising on IS changes usually take a similar approach, recommending a variety of 'system development lifecycle' approaches (Chaffey, 2003). For some changes the lifecycle gives valuable guidance. It is not necessarily sufficient in itself, since people may not be able at the start to specify the end point of the change – or the tasks which will lead to that. In uncertain conditions it may make little sense to plan the outcomes in too much detail. It may be wiser to set the general direction, and adapt the target to suit new conditions that develop during the change. Those managing such change need an additional theory to cope with emergent change.

Activity 13.2 Critical reflection on the project lifecycle

You may be able to gain some insight into the project lifecycle by using it on a practical task. For example:

- If you have a piece of work to do that is connected with your studies, such as an assignment or project, sketch out the steps to be followed by adapting Figure 13.4; alternatively do the same for some domestic, social or management project.
- If you work in an organisation, try to find examples of projects that use this approach, and ask those involved when the method is most useful, and when least useful.
- Make notes summarising how the lifecycle approach helps, and when it is most likely to be useful.

Emergent

In Chapter 8 (Section 8.6) Barthélemy (2006) offers an insight into the strategy process at Ikea (Chapter 7 Case), showing how many of its strategies have emerged from chance events or external conditions, rather than from a formal planning process. Evidence such as this led Quinn (1980) and Mintzberg (1994a, 1994b) to see strategy as an *emergent* or adaptive process. These ideas apply to change projects as much as they do to strategy. Projects are the means through which organisations deliver strategy. They take place in the same volatile, uncertain environment in which the organisation operates. People with different interests and priorities influence the means and ends of a project. So while the planning techniques associated with the lifecycle approach can help, their value will be limited if the change is closer to the **emergent model**.

Emergent models of change emphasise that in uncertain conditions a project will be affected by unknown factors, and that planning has little effect on the outcome.

Case study Vodafone/Ericsson – the case continues www.vodafone.com
www.ericsson.com

The globalisation strategy was developed and implemented through the Global Supply Chain Management (GSCM) forum that first met in 1999. Initially it was attended by representatives from both companies in those countries where Vodafone had a majority shareholding in the local operating company, although membership gradually expanded to include most countries in which Vodafone operated. The initial meeting resolved that all joint activities should be conducted in an open and transparent way: 'It would be a

▶

process of learning through experience; there would be no requirement to produce plans that formed a rigid basis of change control' (Ibbott and O'Keefe, 2004, p. 224).

The members believed that a planned project approach would not have worked, as it was important to be able to cope with rapid change:

> Both the end point and direction were uncertain, and fundamental process changes had to be agreed within and between companies. The acquisition of Mannesmann of Germany, unplanned at the start of the transformation, provided an opportunity for further benefits. (Ibbott and O'Keefe, 2004, p. 229)

The forum also recognised that the two sides would benefit in different ways, but there was no attempt to plan how to share the benefits – either party would retain whatever benefits they secured. Vodafone's equity-based structure in the different countries meant that those leading the project had to sell the concept of the global endeavour to the management teams of each entity. Ericsson's more unified structure of wholly owned subsidiaries gave it less scope for resisting proposals.

GSCM meetings set up several work streams that would move the relationship towards global collaboration. The leadership of each work stream was assigned to one or other of the participating countries. The teams leading them had to secure resources for the project from within their country operations, working as they saw fit. Examples of work streams were:

- creating a global price book for all products bought from Ericsson (UK team);
- agreeing a standard base station design (UK team);
- agreeing a common procedure for software design and testing (Australia);
- developing a computer-based information system linking the parties for information sharing – initially called groupware (the Netherlands).

While the groupware project was at first intended to support communications between the teams working on the globalisation project, it later evolved into a system through which both parties conducted routine transactions – such as ordering products. The simple communication system emerged, without any formal plan, into a system for handling all orders from Vodafone to Ericsson that had a global price.

Source: Ibbott and O'Keefe (2004).

Boddy *et al.* (2000) show how this emergent process occurred when Sun Microsystems began working with a new supplier of the bulky plastic enclosures that contain their products, while the supplier wished to widen its customer base. There were few discussions about a long-term plan. As Sun became more confident in the supplier's ability, it gave them more complex work. Both gained from this emerging relationship. A sales co-ordinator commented:

> It's something we've learnt by being with Sun – we didn't imagine that at the time. Also at the time we wouldn't have imagined we would be dealing with America the way we do now – it was far beyond our thoughts. (Boddy *et al.*, 2000, p. 1010)

Mintzberg's point is that managers should not expect rigid adherence to a plan. Some departure is inevitable as circumstances change, so a wise approach to change recognises that:

> the real world inevitably involves some thinking ahead of time as well as some adaptation en route. (Mintzberg, 1994a, p. 24)

Case questions 13.4

- Were those leading the change taking a lifecycle or an emergent view?
- Which of those views does the evidence of later events seem to support?

Participative

The participative model is the belief that if people are able to take part in planning a change they will be more willing to accept and implement the change.

Those advocating **participative models** stress the benefits of personal involvement in, and contribution to, events and outcomes. The underlying belief is that if people can say 'I helped to build this', they will be more willing to live and work with it, whatever it is. It is also *possible* that since participation allows more people to express their views, the outcome will be better. Ketokivi and Castañer (2004) found that when employees participated in planning strategic change, they were more likely to view the issues from the perspective of the organisation, rather than their own position or function. Participation can be good for the organisation, as well as the individual.

While participation is consistent with democratic values, it takes time and effort, and may raise unrealistic expectations. It may be inappropriate when:

- the scope for change is limited, because of decisions made elsewhere;
- participants know little about the topic;
- decisions must be made quickly;
- management has decided what to do and will do so whatever views people express;
- there are fundamental disagreements and/or inflexible opposition to the proposed change.

Participative approaches assume that a sensitive approach by reasonable people will result in the willing acceptance and implementation of change. Some situations contain conflicts that participation alone cannot solve.

Activity 13.3   Critical reflection on participation

Have you been involved in, or affected by, a change in your work or studies?
If so:

- What evidence was there that those managing the change agreed with the participative approach?
- In what way, if any, were you able to participate?
- How did that affect your reaction to the change?

If not:

- Identify three advantages and three disadvantages for the project manager in adopting a participative approach.
- Suggest how managers should decide when to use the approach.

Political models

Change often involves people from several levels and functions pulling in different directions:

> Strategic processes of change are . . . widely accepted as multi-level activities and not just as the province of a . . . single general manager. Outcomes of decisions are no longer assumed to be a product of rational . . . debates but are also shaped by the interests and commitments of individuals and groups, forces of bureaucratic momentum, and the manipulation of the structural context around decisions and changes. (Whipp *et al.*, 1988, p. 51)

Several analyses of organisational change emphasise a **political model** (Pettigrew, 1985, 1987; Pfeffer, 1992a; Pinto, 1998; Buchanan and Badham, 1999). Pettigrew (1985) was an early advocate of the view that change requires political as well as rational (lifecycle) skills. Successful change managers create a climate in which people accept the change as legitimate – often by manipulating apparently rational information to build support for their ideas.

Political models reflect the view that organisations are made up from groups with separate interests, goals and values, and that these affect how they respond to change.

Key ideas   Tom Burns on politics and language

Tom Burns (1961) observed that political behaviour in the organisation is invariably concealed or made acceptable by subtle shifts in the language that people use:

> Normally, either side in any conflict called political by observers claims to speak in the interests of the corporation as a whole. In fact, the only recognised, indeed feasible, way of advancing political interests

▶

is to present them in terms of improved welfare or efficiency, as contributing to the organisation's capacity to meet its task and to prosper. In managerial and academic, as in other legislatures, both sides to any debate claim to speak in the interests of the community as a whole; this is the only permissible mode of expression. (Burns, 1961, p. 260)

Pfeffer (1992a) also believes that power is essential to get things done, since decisions in themselves change nothing – people only see a difference when someone implements them. He proposes that projects frequently threaten the status quo: people who have done well are likely to resist the change. Innovators need to ensure the project is put onto the senior management agenda, and that influential people support and resource it. Innovators need to develop a political will, and build and use their power. Buchanan and Badham (1999) conclude that the roots of political behaviour:

lie in personal ambition, in organisation structures that create roles and departments which compete with each other, and in major decisions that cannot be resolved by reason and logic alone but which rely on the values and preferences of the key actors. Power politics and change are inextricably linked. Change creates uncertainty and ambiguity. People wonder how their jobs will change, how their work will be affected, how their relationships with colleagues will be damaged or enhanced. (p. 11)

Reasonable people may disagree about means and ends, and fight for the action they prefer. This implies that successful project managers understand that their job requires more than technical competence, and are able and willing to engage in political actions.

Key ideas   Henry Kissinger on politics in politics

In another work Pfeffer (1992b) quotes Henry Kissinger:

Before I served as a consultant to Kennedy, I had believed, like most academics, that the process of decision-making was largely intellectual and all one had to do was to walk into the President's office and convince him of the correctness of one's view. This perspective I soon realised is as dangerously immature as it is widely held. (p. 31)

Source: Pfeffer (1992b).

The political perspective recognises the messy realities of organisational life. Major changes will be technically complex and challenge established interests. These will pull in different directions and pursue personal as well as organisational goals. To manage these tensions managers need political skills as well as those implied by life cycle, emergent and participative perspectives.

Management in practice   Political action in hospital re-engineering

Managers in a hospital responded to a persistent performance gap (especially unacceptably long waiting times) by 're-engineering' the way patients moved through and between the different clinical areas. This included creating multi-functional teams responsible for all aspects of the flow of the patient through a clinic, rather than dealing with narrow functional tasks. The programme was successful, but it was also controversial. One of those leading the change recalled:

I don't like to use the word manipulate, but . . . you do need to manipulate people. It's about playing the game. I remember being accosted by a very cross consultant who had heard something about one of the changes and he really wasn't very happy with it. And it was about how am I going to deal with this now? And it is about being able to think quickly. So I put it over to him in a way that he then accepted, and he was quite happy with. And it wasn't a lie and it wasn't totally the truth. But he was happy with it and it has gone on.

Source: Buchanan (2001), p. 13.

These perspectives (lifecycle, emergent, participative, political) are complementary in that successful large-scale change, such as that at Vodafone/Ericsson, is likely to require elements of each. Table 13.2 illustrates how each perspective links to management practice.

Table 13.2 Perspectives on change and examples of management practice

Perspective	Themes	Example of management practices
Lifecycle	Rational, linear, single agreed aim, technical focus	Measurable objectives; planning and control devices such as Gantt charts and critical path analysis
Emergent	Objectives change as learning occurs during the project and new possibilities appear	Open to new ideas about scope and direction, and willing to add new resources if needed
Participative	Ownership, commitment, shared goals, people focus	Inviting ideas and comments on proposals, ensuring agreement before action, seeking consensus
Political	Oppositional, influence, conflicting goals, power focus	Building allies and coalitions, securing support from powerful players, managing information

13.5 Forms and sources of resistance to change

Most managers are expected to implement change by using their power to influence others to act in a particular way. People at all levels will sometimes resist, either because they see change as a threat to their interests or because they believe it will damage the organisation. Many change programmes fade from view – unless someone is able to make the change stick by creating a favourable context.

Forms of resistance

Overt and public resistance is often unnecessary. There are many other ways in which those opposed to a change can delay it, including:

- making no effort to learn;
- not attending meetings to discuss the project;
- excessive fault finding and criticism;
- saying it has been tried before and did not work then;
- protracted discussion and requests for more information;
- linking the issue with pay or other industrial relations matters;
- not releasing staff for training.

These delaying tactics come from anywhere in the organisation – they are as likely to come from managers who see a change as a threat to their interests as they are to come from more junior staff.

Activity 13.4   Critical reflection on resistance

Discuss with someone who has tried to introduce change in an organisation what evidence there was of resistance. Then consider the following questions:

- Have you ever resisted a proposed change?
- What form did your resistance take?

Sources of resistance

Kotter and Schlesinger (1979) identified that sources of resistance included self-interest, misunderstanding and lack of trust: 'people also resist change when they do not understand its implications and perceive that it might cost them much more than they will gain' (p. 108). Employees assess the situation differently from their managers and may see more costs than benefits for both themselves and the company. Change requires learning and exposure to uncertainty, insecurity and new social interactions, yet communication about the changes is often poor. Additional factors identified as causing resistance are reward systems that do not reward the desired behaviour and a poor fit between the change and the culture.

Key ideas   Lewin's driving and restraining forces

Lewin (1947) observed that any social system is in a state of temporary equilibrium. Driving forces try to change the situation in directions they favour. Restraining forces push the other way to prevent change. This equilibrium 'can be changed either by adding forces in the desired direction, or by diminishing the opposing forces' (p. 26). Figure 13.5 illustrates the idea.

Driving forces encourage change from the present position. They encourage people and groups to give up past practice and to act in ways that support the change. They take many forms, such as a newly available technology or the support of a powerful player. Mr Yun Jong-yon, chief executive of Samsung Electronics, transformed the company into one of the world's best-performing and most respected IT companies. He explained part of his approach:

I'm the chaos-maker. I have tried to encourage a sense of crisis to drive change. We instilled in management a sense that we could go bankrupt any day. (*Financial Times*, 13 March 2003, p. 15)

Restraining forces include the already-installed technology, shortage of finance, or the company culture, or the perceived complexity of implementing the change.

Source: Lewin (1947).

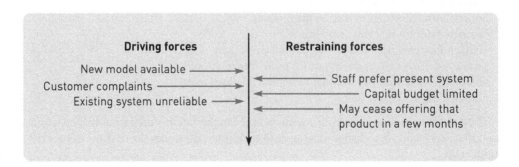

Figure 13.5
Driving and
restraining forces

Table 13.3 Sources of resistance to change

Element	Source of resistance
Objectives	Lack of clarity or understanding of objectives, or disagreement with those proposed
People	Change may threaten important values, preferences, skills, needs and interests
Technology	May be poorly designed, hard to use, incompatible with existing equipment, or require more work than is worthwhile
Business processes	As for technology, and may require unwelcome changes to the way people deal with colleagues and customers
Financial resources	Scepticism about whether the change will be financially worthwhile, or less so than other competing changes; lack of money
Structure	New reporting relationships or means of control may disrupt working relationships and patterns of authority
Culture	People likely to resist a change that challenges core values and beliefs, especially if they have worked well before
Power	If change affects ownership of and access to information, those who see they will lose autonomy will resist

These views can be enlarged by using the elements of the organisation shown in Figure 13.2. People can base their resistance on any of these contextual elements, as shown in Table 13.3.

13.6 Forms and sources of innovation

Creativity and innovation

Creativity refers to the ability to combine ideas in a new way or to make unusual associations between ideas. This helps people and organisations to generate imaginative ideas or ways of working, but that in itself does not ensure added value.

The systems model introduced in Chapter 1 helps to understand how organisations can become more innovative. Figure 13.6 shows that getting the desired outputs (more innovative products or work methods) depends on both the inputs and the transformation of those inputs.

Inputs include having creative people and groups who are able to generate novel ideas and methods, but they only flourish in a favourable context. Managers need to create a context which encourages both creative people and then the application of those creative ideas into goods and services that people want to buy. So in the business context it is useful to think of innovation as the process through which new ideas, objects, behaviours and practices are created, developed and implemented into a product or service.

> **Creativity** is the ability to combine ideas in a unique way or to make unusual associations between ideas.

Degrees of innovation – radical and incremental

Some innovations – such as the aerofoil that allows heavier than air flight and the transistor that is the basis of all modern electronics – have fundamentally changed society. Others such as Velcro or the ball-point pen are useful, but have more modest effects on life as we know it.

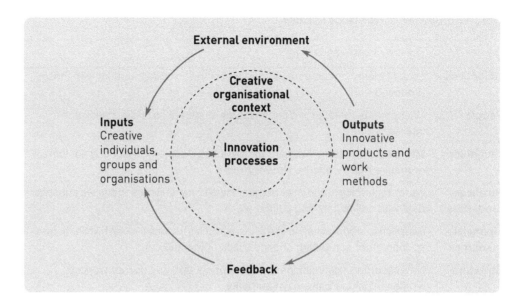

Figure 13.6
Systems view of
innovation

The effects of an innovation depend on how they are used, what they are replacing and who is evaluating them. Using hydrogen-fuelled engines instead of fossil-fuelled ones is a very useful technological innovation, but will have little effect on how people drive cars: so from the driver's perspective it is an **incremental innovation**. However it will have a very large environmental effect – so from the point of view of someone who cares about the environment it will be a **radical innovation**.

Organisational impact of innovations

Managers have to decide whether to invest possibly large sums to develop an innovation – when they cannot know whether it will succeed in the market. They can gain some sense of the likely cost to the organisation of using the innovation by relating it to their resources and competencies (Chapters 1 and 8). An incremental innovation will use existing skills, processes, equipment and infrastructure – such as one that involves resetting machinery or re-arranging a production line. It requires few internal changes, so will be low cost and low risk. A radical innovation requires significant revision to skills, processes and equipment, such as a metal working company developing a product that uses carbon fibre. It requires major internal changes, so will be high cost and high risk.

Most (although by no means all) innovations are incremental. The motor car has evolved from early radical innovations (internal combustion engine, inflatable tyres and plastics technology) to a situation in which new models incorporate incremental improvements to the suspension or electrics. Similarly in services, most innovations involve doing something a little differently and a little better.

Incremental innovations are small changes in a current product or process which brings a minor improvement.

Radical innovations are large game changing developments that alter the competitive landscape.

Activity 13.5   Everyday Innovation

- We are surrounded by so-called innovative products. Consider everyday items such as the iPod or the mobile phone. Try to identify the radical innovations that made the technology possible and the incremental innovations that matured the product to its current level of sophistication.

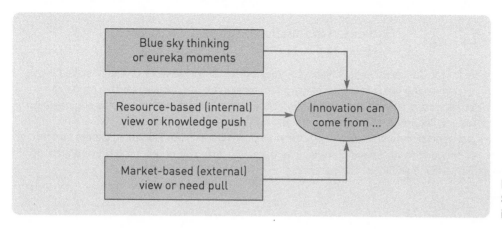

Figure 13.7
Sources of
innovation

The sources of innovation

Figure 13.7 illustrates the main sources of innovation.

Eureka moments

The word 'eureka' is associated with the experience of having an idea. A common example of a 'eureka' moment was when Art Fry used a recently invented 'sticky but not too sticky' adhesive to keep his bookmark in place. This gave him the idea for the Post-it note which, after a process of design and development, became the familiar product range. The Management in Practice describes a recent example.

Management in practice   **Plugging a 'mole' in the market** www.magnamole.co.uk

Sharon Wright had her eureka moment while having a phone-line installed in her home. Under pressure for time, she offered to help the engineer thread the cable through the wall of her house. To Sharon's surprise the engineer produced a makeshift tool made from a wire coat-hanger. As well as being difficult to use, Sharon's experience in health and safety management told her this device was unsuitable and hazardous. Market research showed there were no alternative tools available for cable threading.

Within hours she had sketched the design of the Magnamole tool, a plastic rod with a magnet at one end and an accompanying metallic cap for attaching to the wire to be threaded through the wall. She soon had a prototype, and orders followed from large customers around the world.

What is remarkable about Sharon is that she had little knowledge or experience of this area of business, but that did not stop her from taking advantage of an obvious gap in the market.

Source: Company website.

Knowledge push

Most innovation now comes from the research and development laboratories of large companies – GlaxoSmithKline, DuPont, Apple and many more. They have a strong commitment to innovation, reflected in the systematic organisation of scientific staff, equipment and facilities to solve specific problems. To produce consistent innovation, specialising in one area is critical, as only by developing a depth of expertise will understanding be created.

Need pull

No matter how innovative a new product might be, it will not make money unless there is a market for it. Before investing significant resources in developing a new product, managers need a sense of the likely need. This may not be as straightforward as it seems: before lightweight digital music players and headphones became available, sportsmen and women trained without equipment to combat boredom. However, this technology is now an essential part of a runner's or cyclist's training kit, and versions are now available for swimmers.

Many products, especially in the area of consumer electronics, were inconceivable a few years ago. While it is logical that the typewriter could pave the way for a product such as Microsoft Word it is less conceivable that it would lead to PowerPoint. While the link between the home phone and the mobile phone is clear, the jump from the basic mobile phone to the functionality embodied in the iPhone would have been difficult to envisage. Another way to think of need pull is that it results in more niches being carved in a market as product differentiation becomes more subtle.

It is important to be aware of the driving forces in the external environment that may yield an opportunity. While scanning the market by analysing what competitor products may be useful, there are other more specific external areas that may yield opportunity for an innovative product or service.

Regulation changes

The makers of the Segway encountered regulatory problems in relation to safety and traffic laws, and regulations often hinder innovation. Others trigger it by requiring change – of which those on environmental pollution are a current example, in that they have encouraged the search for renewable sources of energy. On a smaller scale, regulations intended to improve road safety have led to the development of speed cameras and air bags. Potential innovators ensure that they are aware of impending changes in relevant regulations.

Management in practice   **Innovating on health** www.rjrt.com
www.philipmorristobacco.com

Legislative change can also have indirect effects on innovation. Restrictions on advertising and other actions to curb smoking have encouraged tobacco companies to invest heavily in alternatives to tobacco aiming for a new 'safe' cigarette such as the Philip Morris Accord and the RJR Eclipse.

Sources: Company websites.

Accidents and the unexpected

Many innovations have been accidental – from Fleming's discovery of Penicillin to the Post-it note. Indeed, the innovative gyro which makes the Segway possible was developed in BAE Systems' defence laboratories. Terrorist attacks have led to innovations in safety and security products, such as the biometric scanning device. One of the largest service industries in the world – personal insurance – developed from the need to guard against unplanned events, and is highly innovative in the risks against which it will offer cover to those prepared to pay – including Bruce Springsteen's voice for $6 million. Hedge funds are an innovative form of insuring against negative movements in the investment markets.

Users as innovators

Users are sometimes the source of ideas for innovation, three categories being particularly important:

- Lead users – people who not only use the product but also help in its development. Ivor Tiefenbrun, the founder of hi-fi maker Linn Products, developed his model when he became dissatisfied with products then available.
- User communities – groups of users who congregate around a product or product platform, such as early personal computer users, and find new and innovative ways to use the systems.
- Extreme users – push products to their limit, creating a need for improved performance. The bicycle is an example, with the relentless drive for more durable and higher performing machines.

Case study   **Vodafone/Ericsson – the case continues** www.vodafone.com
www.ericsson.com

Today, Vodafone is a global telecommunications company and as such sees innovation in products and services as critical to its strategy. As part of this they have set up the Joint Innovation Lab (JIL) with Verizon Wireless, China Mobile and Softbank Mobile. Together, these operators have access to over 1.1 billion customers around the world.

The four companies will use the JIL as a platform to develop mobile services and drive innovation. The purpose of the JIL is to launch projects based on emerging technologies and market demand and will focus on the rapidly growing areas of mobile internet services.

JIL's first project is to develop a widget (interactive virtual tool) ecosystem that will allow developers to benefit from access to the combined customer base of the four JIL operators. Consumers will get access to the innovation and creativity of a global developer community and operators benefit by providing great content to their customers.

This is an example of a mechanism to help users become part of the innovation process by, in effect, combining technology 'push' and need 'pull'.

Sources: *Vodafone Annual Report 2009*; company website.

13.7   The process of innovation

Organisations which depend on innovation implement deliberate systems to ensure an adequate flow. Figure 13.8 shows a model of the innovation process, portraying it as a filter through which ideas are gathered, channelled and focused before selecting those believed to have most potential. Generating the initial idea is necessarily random – but thereafter firms try to create order from this randomness as quickly as possible. They apply resources and effort to these promising ideas to develop them into something that can be implemented. The steps in this system are sequential but their duration and complexity will vary – some may require a significant research and development, others merely a change in the focus of the sales effort.

The 4 P's of innovation

Innovations become manifest in one or more of four areas; the product itself, the process of delivery or manufacture, positioning in the market and in the overall paradigm of the business.

Product innovations

An innovation here could be a change in the function or feature of a product such as the incorporation of a music player within a mobile phone or, in relation to a service, the incorporation of the facility to carry out personal banking on the internet. These innovations are intended to enhance the utility of the offering to make sales more likely.

Process innovations

An innovation here could be the addition of a self-service checkout at a supermarket where customers can scan their purchases using a barcode reader, or an online banking system to allow customers to manage their finances. Examples in manufacturing would be using robots for assembly to give higher quality and more efficiently produced products.

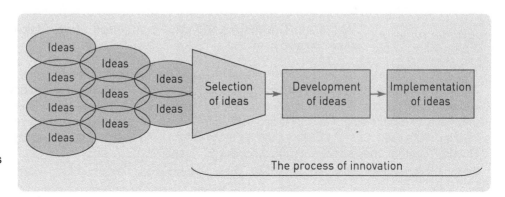

Figure 13.8
A model of the innovation process
Source: Based on Tidd and Bessant (2009).

Position innovations

These are changes in the target market or customers base for a product or service. Lucozade is a familiar example – once aimed at people recovering from illness, it is now for healthy people engaged in sport. Another example is the four-wheel drive: originally used for off-road work, but now sold as a fashionable family car to carry large loads.

Paradigm innovations

These are changes in how companies frame what they do; for example the reframing of a supermarket such as Sainsbury's from a simple seller of food products to a provider of many more of a family's needs such as petrol, clothing and financial products. Here the reframing has provided synergies where shoppers can buy all that they require, and pay for it all with their Sainsbury's bank card.

Organisational factors in managing innovation

One of the most notable innovative companies is Pixar, with a unique record of technological and artistic advances (see the following Management in Practice).

Management in practice   Behind Pixar's magic www.pixar.com

Ed Catmull (co-founder of Pixar, and president of Pixar and Disney Animation Studios) has written about the 'collective creativity' at the company: many of its methods are relevant to other organisations. He emphasises the uncertainty of the innovative process – the idea that starts the process may not work – by definition it is new, and the innovator cannot know at the start if it will lead to a worthwhile result:

at the start of making [Ratatouille] we simply didn't know if [it] would work. However, since we're supposed to offer something that isn't obvious, we bought into somebody's initial vision and took a chance. (p. 66)

'Taking chances' that consistently succeed is not due to luck, but to the principles and practices that Pixar uses to support the people who turn the idea into a useful product. These include:

Getting talented people to work effectively with each other . . . [by constructing] an environment that nurtures trusting relationships and unleashes everyone's creativity. If we get that right, the result is a vibrant community where talented people are loyal to one another and their collective work. (p. 66)

Everyone must be free to communicate with anyone . . . the most efficient way to deal with numerous problems is to trust people to work out the difficulties directly with each other without having to check for permission. (p. 71)

We must stay close to innovations happening in the academic community. We strongly encourage our technical artists to publish their research and participate in industry conferences. Publication may give away ideas . . . but the connection is worth far more than any ideas we may have revealed: it helps us attract exceptional talent and reinforces the belief throughout the company that people are more important than ideas. (p. 71)

[Measure progress]. Because we're a creative organization, people [think that what we do can't be measured]. That's wrong. Most of our processes involve activities and deliverables that can be quantified. We keep track of the rates at which things happen, how often something had to be reworked, whether a piece of work was completely finished or not when it was sent to another department . . . Data can show things in a neutral way, which can stimulate discussion. (p. 72).

See Chapter 10 (p. 309) for more on Pixar.

Source: Catmull (2008).

Organisations that depend on innovation aim to create an environment which encourages all staff (not just those with specific R&D responsibilities) to help create and implement a strong flow of successful new things. Smith *et al.* (2008) developed a prescriptive model of the organisational features shaping the effectiveness of its innovation process – the 4 S's of innovation: strategy, structure, style and support.

- *Strategy* The organisational strategy must communicate a shared vision and goals (Jager *et al.*, 2004), indicating that innovation is central to its competitive advantage.
- *Style* The strategy must be enacted by the management style of the senior team to reinforce the strategic intention. A 'facilitate and empower' style is more likely to foster innovation than a 'command and control' style (Muthusamy *et al.*, 2005). But, in addition, employees are likely to require resources and time for ideas to emerge.
- *Structure* A highly specialised division of tasks is detrimental to innovation, while enriched jobs (Chapter 15) and easy horizontal communication will support it. While lone employees can be innovative, teams of employees working together are more likely to succeed.
- *Support* Technology can facilitate the transfer of knowledge by creating a knowledge repository (Jantunen, 2005), enabling staff to access information easily.

Staff as innovators

Lastly it is worth returning to the people aspects of innovation. Designing an organisational structure that emphasises communication and flexibility supported by an empowering management style and the appropriate information technology is the beginning of this journey and must be supplemented by other mechanisms. Recently much has been made of employee participation. This initially emerged with the 'quality miracle' of the Japanese manufacturers which was enabled by the system of *Kaizen* or 'continuous improvement' (Imai, 1986), where employees were encouraged to question work processes and look for incremental improvements in all that they did, leading to a better production process and therefore better product quality and organisational efficiency.

While suggestion schemes are not new, the more systematic and proactive approach of the Japanese was a key factor in the success of *Kaizen*. It has been joined by other systems such as total quality management (George and Weimerskirch, 1998) and lean manufacturing (Womack and Jones, 1996). While differing slightly in emphasis, the key to them all is in getting employees involved in the thinking behind the product and process, and encouraging them to generate ideas that lead to improvements that ultimately benefits overall revenue and profit.

As a framework it is useful to think of areas where employees can contribute ideas. Tonnessen (2005) has identified places that staff can be encouraged to become involved in innovation. These are within their immediate work area and activity, within the overall process that they are involved in, within their group or department and in relation to the overall company operation and strategy.

13.8   Integrating themes

Sustainable performance

Across the world, governments and international agencies are setting targets with the aim of reducing greenhouse gas emissions: an example is that by the EU to aim for a 20 per cent reduction by 2020. This is a significant opportunity for innovative businesses in developing new technologies that reduce CO_2 emissions. As well as the existing hydro-electric power infrastructure, currently there are 254 operational wind-farms in the UK, generating 5,100 MW, with another 28 under construction. In addition significant investment is now being made in marine forms of generation such as wave, tidal and current.

Innovation opportunities are not limited to the generation of power but also arise in infrastructure and especially transport. Hydrogen fuel cells for use in personal vehicles are maturing as a technology and solar powered vehicles for public transport are being developed. An example is the Solar-shuttle project which is developing solar powered boats for passenger transport on the Thames during the 2012 Olympic Games (**www.solarshuttle.co.uk**).

Governance and control

Thomas Midgely, although unknown to most people, has possibly done more damage to the environment that any other individual. A prolific innovator, among other things he put the lead in petrol and the CFCs in aerosols – doing great damage to the ozone layer. Midgely's is a cautionary tale, showing how lack of governance and control of innovation in product design can have disastrous and unforeseen consequences.

The financial crisis in 2008 is a contemporary example of innovation out of control. Its origins lay in some banks selling mortgages to (sub-prime) customers who could not afford the repayments. The innovation was the way in which the companies making the loans 'packaged' these loans and sold them to other players in the financial supply chain. Innovative bankers converted the original (very dubious) loans into financial products called mortgage-backed securities. These were sold on to hedge funds and investment banks which saw them as high return investments. When borrowers started to default on their loans, the value of the investments fell, leading to huge losses. Investors then became nervous about buying any investment linked to mortgages, no matter how high their quality, so that lenders found it increasingly difficult to borrow money in the capital markets – with the familiar results.

Much of the blame was placed on the lack of governance within the banking industry that allowed innovative ideas to be implemented without regard to the risks they posed or their longer-term consequences. The Management in Practice feature gives an example of a bank with very tight governance and control systems.

> ### Management in practice | Governance and control at Banco Santander
> www.santander.com
>
> In a speech to the first Santander Conference on International Banking, Emilio Botin, the chairman said:
>
> Banks must focus on customers, focus on recurring business based on long-term relationships and be cautious in managing risk. You do not need to be innovative to do this well. You do not need to invent anything. You need to dedicate time and attention at the highest level.
>
> Many are surprised to learn that the Banco Santander board's risk committee meets for half a day twice a week and that the board's 10-person executive committee meets every Monday for at least four hours, devoting a large portion of that time to reviewing risks and approving transactions. Not many banks do this. It consumes a lot of our directors' time. But we find it essential and it is never too much.
>
> Source: *Financial Times*, 16 October 2008.

Internationalisation

The growing internationalisation of business has implications for the way international or global firms manage change and innovation. The issue here reflects one of the central themes within Chapter 4, namely the balance between a unified, global approach seeking to establish a common identity across all operations, or an approach that adapts the way the company operates to local conditions. Managers of local business units will have local priorities, and are likely to be unreceptive to change that the centre, or even another unit, appears to be imposing. This balancing act faces all companies operating internationally.

The same dilemma arises in relation to innovation: companies often want to allow research teams considerable autonomy, yet to do so could lead to expensive duplication of scientific resources and potentially harmful competition between national units. As an example an associate at W.L. Gore (see Part 5 Case) commented:

> One challenge is to retain the team-working ethos while working globally. There is a danger of duplication if the interests of separate teams in different parts of the world evolve in such a way that they are working on similar products. Yet at the same time we don't want to create structures or processes that stifle creativity. We don't want to say that people should focus on specific areas of research. We need to find ways of sharing expertise globally. (Part 5 Case, p. 540)

Summary

1 **Explain the meaning of organisational change and give examples**
   - Organisational change refers to deliberate attempts to change one or more elements of the internal environment, such as technology or structure. Change in one element usually stimulates change in other areas.

2 **Explain what the links between change and context imply for those managing a change**
   - A change programme is an attempt to change one or more aspects of the internal context, which then provides the context of future actions. The prevailing context can itself help or hinder change efforts.

3 **Compare lifecycle, emergent, participative and political theories of change**
   - Lifecycle: change projects can be planned, monitored and controlled towards achieving their objectives.
   - Emergent: reflecting the uncertainties of the environment, change is hard to plan in detail but emerges incrementally from events and actions.
   - Participative: successful change depends on human commitment, which is best obtained by involving participants in planning and implementation.
   - Political: change threatens some of those affected, who will use their power to block progress, or to direct the change in ways that suit local objectives.

4 **Evaluate systematically the possible sources of resistance to change**
   - Reasons can be assessed using the internal context model, as each element (objectives, people, power, etc.) is a potential source of resistance. Analysing these indicates potential ways of overcoming resistance.
   - The force field analysis model allows players to identify the forces driving and restraining a change, and implies that reducing the restraining forces will help change more than increasing the driving forces.

5 **Explain how innovations can be used to benefit companies**
   - Product innovation – changes what the organisation offers for sale.
   - Process innovation – changes how it creates the product.
   - Position innovation – changes how the product is offered or targeted.
   - Paradigm innovation – changes how a company frames what it does.

6 **Illustrate the organisational factors believed to support innovation**
   - Strategy – innovation is explicitly called for in the corporate strategy.
   - Structure – roles and jobs are defined to aid in innovative behaviour.
   - Style – management empowers the workforce to behave innovatively.
   - Support – IT systems are available to support innovative behaviour.

7 **Show how ideas from the chapter add to your understanding of the integrating themes**

- The search for sustainable performance offers significant opportunities to innovators who can find ways of reducing the use of energy throughout the value-adding chain.
- The 2008 financial crisis showed the negative side of innovation, when it is not balanced by effective governance and control systems – such as those at banks like Santander whose managers take risk seriously.
- International companies often wish to encourage local units to be innovative but, as the W.L. Gore case shows, they also need to avoid wasteful duplication if several sites work on similar projects.

Review questions

1 What does the term 'performance gap' mean, and what is its significance for change?
2 What are the implications for management of the systemic nature of major change?
3 Can managers alter the receptiveness of an organisation to change? Would doing so be an example of an interaction approach?
4 Outline the lifecycle perspective on change and explain when it is most likely to be useful.
5 How does it differ from the 'emergent' perspective?
6 What are the distinctive characteristics of a participative approach, and when is it likely to be least successful?
7 What skills are used by those employing a political model?
8 Is resistance to change necessarily something to be overcome? How would you advise someone to resist a change to which he/she was opposed?
9 In a technology product such as the Segway do you think further technological innovation or marketing innovation will be the key to its continued success?
10 Think of products and services that are currently successful, determine the innovations that created that success and categorise them using the 4Ps model.
11 Summarise an idea from the chapter that adds to your understanding of the integrating themes.

Concluding critical reflection

Think about the way people handle major change in your company, or one with which you are familiar. Review the material in the chapter, and perhaps visit some of the websites identified. Then make notes on these questions:

- What examples of the themes discussed in this chapter are currently relevant to your company? What performance imperatives are dominant, and to what extent do people see a performance gap? What perspective do people have on the change process – life cycle, emergent, participative or political?
- In implementing change, what **assumptions** about the nature of change in organisations appear to guide the approach? Is one perspective dominant, or do people typically use several methods in combination?
- What factors in the **context** of the company appear to shape your approach to managing change – is your organisation seen as being receptive or non-receptive to change, for example, and what lies behind that?
- Has there been any serious attempt to find **alternative** ways to manage major change in your organisation – for example by comparing your methods systematically with those of other companies, or with the theories set out here?
- Does the approach typically used generally work? If not, do managers recognise the **limitations** of their approach, and question their assumptions?

Further reading

Balogun, J., Gleadle, P., Hailey, V.H. and Willmott, H. (2005), 'Managing change across boundaries: boundary-shaking practices', *British Journal of Management,* vol. 16, no. 4, pp. 261–278.

An empirical study of the practices that change agents used to introduce major boundary-shaking changes in large companies, and how the context shaped their use.

Catmull, E. (2008), 'How Pixar fosters collective creativity', *Harvard Business Review*, vol. 86, no. 9, pp. 64–72.

The co-founder explains how it works.

Pettigrew, A., Ferlie, E. and McKee, L. (1992), *Shaping Strategic Change*, Sage, London.

Pettigrew, A.M. and Whipp, R. (1991), *Managing Change for Competitive Success*, Blackwell, Oxford.

Both of these books provide detailed, long-term analyses of major changes – the first in four commercial businesses and the second in several units within the UK National Health Service. Although the cases are old, they still provide useful empirical insights into the task of managing change.

Roberto, M.A. and Levesque, L.C. (2005), 'The art of making change initiatives stick', *MIT Sloan Management Review*, vol. 46, no. 4, pp. 53–60.

Another empirical study, this time in a single organisation, of how the context affected the willingness of people to change, and how senior managers needed to create a supportive context.

Tidd, J. and Bessant, J. (2009), *Managing Innovation: Integrating technological, market and organisational change*, Chichester, Wiley.

An easy to read text combining a comprehensive account of innovation theories with many contemporary examples.

Weblinks

These websites have appeared in this chapter:

www.vodafone.com
www.ericsson.com
www.gknplc.com
www.magnamole.co.uk
www.dupont.com
www.audi.com
www.segway.com
www.rjrt.com
www.philipmorristobacco.com
www.pixar.com
www.solarshuttle.co.uk
www.santander.com

Visit two of the business sites in the list, and navigate to the pages dealing with corporate news, investor relations or 'our company'.

- What signs of major changes taking place in the organisation can you find?
- Does the site give you a sense of an organisation that is receptive or non-receptive to change?
- What kind of environment are they likely to be working in, and how may that affect their approach to change?

 For video case studies, audio summaries, flashcards, exercises and annotated weblinks, related to this chapter, visit **www.pearsoned.co.uk/mymanagementlab**

CHAPTER 18
MANAGING OPERATIONS AND QUALITY

Aim

To introduce the organisation as a set of linked operational processes working together to deliver a product that conforms to a predefined quality standard.

Objectives

By the end of your work on this chapter you should be able to outline the concepts below in your own terms and:

1 Define the term operations management
2 Describe the transformation process model of operations management
3 Show how operations management can contribute to the competitiveness of the organisation
4 Identify different forms of operational activity
5 Define the term quality in the operational context
6 Show how ideas from the chapter add to your understanding of the integrating themes

Key terms

This chapter introduces the following ideas:

operations management
transformation process
craft system
factory production
operations strategy

span of processes
break-even analysis
layout planning
total quality management

Each is a term defined within the text, as well as in the Glossary at the end of the book.

Case study   Zara

Amancio Ortega Gaona began working as a delivery boy for a shirt-maker when he was 13 years old. He later managed a tailor's shop where he made night-shirts and pyjamas. In 1963, when still in his 20s, he started 'Confecciones GOA' in La Coruña to manu-facture women's pyjamas (and later lingerie prod-ucts), initially for sale directly to garment wholesalers. In 1975, however, when a German customer can-celled a large order, the firm opened its first Zara retail shop in La Coruña, Spain. The original intent was simply to have an outlet for cancelled orders, but this experience taught Ortega the importance of the 'mar-riage' between the operations of production and retailing. This was a lesson that guided the evolution of the company from then on. As Mr Miguel Diaz, a senior marketing executive reiterated in 2001:

> **It is critical for us to have five fingers touching the factory and the other five touching the customer.**

The company had six stores by 1979 and estab-lished retail operations in all the major Spanish cities during the 1980s. In 1988 the first international Zara store opened in Porto, Portugal, followed shortly by New York City in 1989 and Paris in 1990. But the real 'step-up' in foreign expansion took place during the 1990s when Zara entered Europe, the Americas and Asia.

Zara is now present across the world, with a net-work of over 1,500 stores. Its international presence shows that national frontiers are no impediment to sharing a single fashion culture. Zara claims to move with society, dressing the ideas, trends and tastes that society itself creates. It is claimed that Zara needs only two weeks to develop a product and get it into stores, in comparison with the industry aver-age of nearly six months. Zara has a large design

Copyright © Inditex

team and the design process is closely linked to the public. Information travels from the stores to the de-sign teams, transmitting the demands and concerns of the market. The vertical integration of activities – design, production, logistics and sales in the com-pany's own stores – means that Zara is flexible and fast in adapting to the market. Its model is charac-terised by continuous product renovation. Zara pays special attention to the design of its stores, its shop windows and interior decor, and locates them in the best sites of major shopping districts.

Source: Author's own, based on www.zara.com

Case question 18.1

Good operations management is based on process consistency.

- What do you think are the major managerial challenges in setting up an operations system to serve a fast-moving and fickle market such as fashion?

18.1   Introduction

Zara is a fashion company that relies heavily on good operational systems. It is an integrated business in that it does most of the work itself: it designs, manufactures, distributes and sells the products. It relies on quick turnaround times on most products, which it sells in relatively large quantities. Its garments must be available on time to catch the latest fashion trend and must also be of a consistent quality to ensure that customers will return to buy again.

Two factors are critical to Zara's success: the creative ability to catch the mood of the customer with interesting and exciting designs; and the operational capability to design, manufacture and distribute goods quickly and efficiently. Neither factor can exist alone – it needs both good design AND good operational processes.

Good process and practice has always been important in production and manufacturing areas, but many companies in the service sector now use the methods of operations management. The chapter begins by introducing the basic concepts and language that underpin operations management, which you will be able to use in any sector of the economy. It will then discuss what a 'product' is in services and manufacturing respectively. It then shows what operations managers typically do, and concludes by exploring the meaning of quality and how to manage it.

18.2   What is operations management?

System and process

> The Matrix is a system, Neo. That system is our enemy. But when you're inside, you look around, what do you see? Businessmen, teachers, lawyers, carpenters – the very minds of the people we are trying to save . . . Many of them are so inured, so hopelessly dependent on the system, that they will fight to protect it. Source: Morpheos to Neo, *The Matrix.*

Morpheus is attempting to open the mind of his student Neo to the true nature of life in *The Matrix* and show that reality is a fabrication, a virtual world created to enslave the human race. The challenge Morpheus faces is that Neo, like the rest of humanity, is so familiar with the current situation that he cannot imagine another state of being.

Modern societies are similar in that the state of organisation of our everyday lives is so pervasive that it is difficult for most people to imagine a different way. We live in a world of systems, which shape our personal lives, our transport, our security and our work. Our lives are continually 'managed' within the system that is our society. Such systems bring safety and economy by removing many random events, and allowing better use of time and energy. Organisations also benefit from consistency and predictability. Creating effective systems is the central challenge of operations management.

The operations challenge

Operations management is all of the activities, decisions and responsibilities of managing the production and delivery of products and services.

Slack *et al.* (2007) define **operations management** as the activities, decisions and responsibilities of managing the production and delivery of products and services.

The way to do this is to implement systems and processes that are:

- repeatable – can be done over and over again;
- consistent – produce the same result every time;
- reliable – do not break down randomly.

The standard of performance now required against each criterion is growing because of:

- increased competition in cost and quality as a result of globalisation and the development of new technologies, especially in information and communications;
- more complex activities as more sophisticated customers expect more differentiated products with higher functionality;
- tighter environmental regulation to control pollution; and
- legislation on employment and working conditions.

Process therefore needs also to be:

- efficient – producing most output for least input;
- competitive – at least as good as others who are doing the same types of things;
- compliant with the legislation that governs the industrial environment.

Case question 18.2

- Do you think the current tendency towards globalisation will help or hinder Zara's success?

The transformation process

The first step in achieving an efficient, process-based organisation is to understand the work of the organisation as a **transformation process** which turns inputs (or resources) into the outputs that are the product.

Figure 1.1 (slightly adapted here as Figure 18.1) models the transformation process. It shows inputs entering the operational processes of the organisation which transforms them into an output that is the product or service to be sold. There are two types of input:

- **transforming** resources are the elements that carry out the transformation; and
- **transformable** resources are the elements that the process transforms into the product.

> The transformation process refers to the operational system that takes all of the inputs; raw materials, information, facilities, capital and people and converts them into an output product to be delivered to the market.

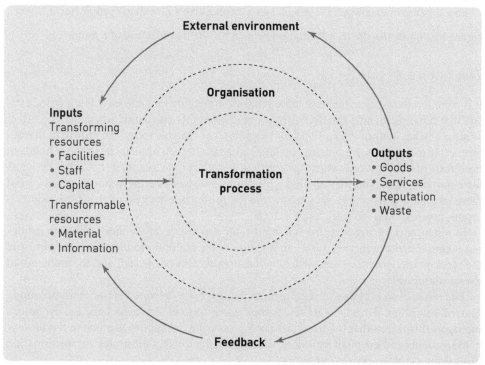

Figure 18.1
The transformation process

Transforming resources are:

- facilities – buildings, equipment/tools and process technology;
- staff – people involved in the transformation process working to complete activities, operate machinery or maintain the equipment;
- capital which is needed to buy materials and pay for the facilities and staff.

Transformable resources are:

- materials such as metal, wood or plastic, which become parts such as nuts and bolts, structures, or printed circuit boards, which can be built into the final product such as cars, buildings or phones. In moving through the transformation process the physical form of input materials will change to create the eventual product;
- information such as design specifications, assembly instructions, scientific concepts or market intelligence. Information is used in two ways. First, it can be used to inform the transformation process, such as design specifications or diagrams. Second, the information itself can become part of the output, such as turning raw financial data into published accounts.

Also included in the transformation process is a feedback system which monitors and captures deviations from the process norms. Feedback is needed to ensure the process performs in a repeatable, reliable and consistent manner. As there are bound to be variations in material quality and in the wear and tear of equipment, monitoring is essential in even the best processes.

There are two broad types of process feedback:

- Feedback that is internal to the transformation process ensures that it results in a consistent product. This feedback is generally quantitative in nature and monitors key aspects of the product or process, e.g. the number of units produced, dimensions such as weight of a chocolate bar or measurements such as the temperature of an oven. Any deviation in the measurements indicates that the process is not performing correctly and requires some remedial action.
- Feedback that is external to the transformation process ensures that the product is accepted by the market and satisfies the customer. This type of feedback can be either qualitative – how the customer enjoyed the product – or quantitative – how many people buy it.

Figure 18.2 illustrates the transformation process for the manufacture of a motor car.

The nature of products

It is common to associate the term 'product' with something tangible such as a physical artifact that can be seen, held and used. Until very recently this association was generally correct as most of what was bought and sold took a physical or tangible form. The growth of the service sector means the term is often applied to intangibles such as financial services, holidays, healthcare or legal advice. A mortgage is no less a product than a car or a watch. It is designed for a purpose, sold, paid for and used. Operations managers see the 'production' process of these intangible products in the same way as the production process of tangible products – inputs, processes and feedback loops.

In restaurants the product that is bought is the experience of the meal. Although eating-out is considered as a service, it is a combination of the physical product that is the meal and the service experience that is provided by the attentiveness of the staff and the ambience of the surroundings.

The distinction between physical product and service delivered is therefore becoming blurred. Few physical products are sold without some form of service package. For operations managers this means that the transformation process model applies as much to restaurants, banks, schools and hospitals as it does to factories. Figure 18.3 illustrates a transformation process for a typical service – education.

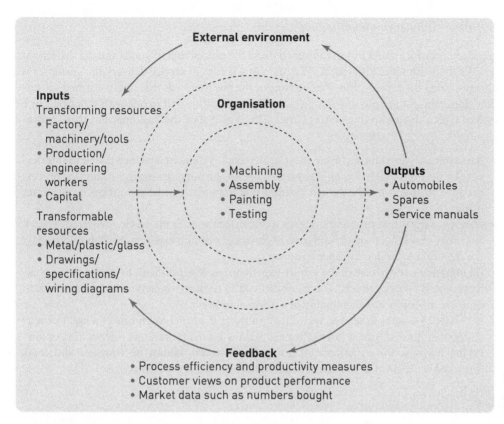

Figure 18.2
A manufacturing transformation

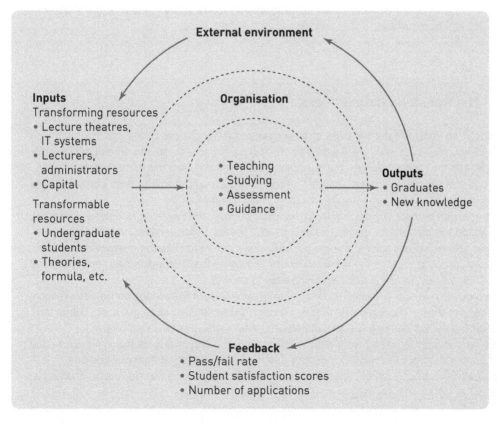

Figure 18.3
An educational transformation

Service delivery and the customer

While the transformation process applies both to the production of goods and the delivery of services there are some differences. The main one is that in service delivery the customer is present during the process, and is indeed one of the raw materials that is transformed – a student from non-graduate to graduate, a customer with untidy hair to one with styled hair or a patient with a disease to one who is cured. The presence of the customer has these consequences for operations managers:

- Randomness – in manufacturing most of the work is done in a factory closed to interference by the eventual customer. The presence of the customer in services means the process needs to be able to handle the randomness that unpredictable behaviour by the customer brings.
- Heterogeneity – that randomness leads to inconsistencies in the service delivered, as each customer may have a slightly different experience: a dining experience will be affected by the atmosphere created by other customers.
- Intangibility – the nature of the service experience makes it difficult to ensure that a quality service is being produced. It is more difficult to measure the service experience than to measure the utility or functionality of a physical product.
- Perishability – services tend to be difficult to store, if a hotel room misses a night's occupation then this revenue is lost as the next night is a different revenue – generating opportunity. Likewise the experience of going to a concert cannot be wrapped and mass produced. The CD of the concert cannot match the actual experience.

Activity 18.1   Service operations

- If you have ever sought legal advice consider, from a customer's perspective, how a lawyer can ensure consistency, reliability and repeatability in the process of delivering legal services.

Key ideas   The transformation process

As operations managers we need to view the work of the organisation, regardless of the industry sector or product, as a set of linked processes that take a set of inputs and reconfigure these into something that the organisation can provide to the market. Despite the apparent differences between the form of tangible products and intangible services the transformation process model is equally applicable to both contexts. This allows operations managers to use similar methods and tools in each sector.

This operational model can therefore be applied to any industry context, the key thing is to determine what the product actually is and this may not be as straightforward as it seems. In some cases, such as consumer goods, the need being fulfilled is easy to see, the product may be a car which fills the customer's need for transport. In service organisations such as the police force or a university the customer's need and therefore the nature of the product required to fulfil that need is less easy to define.

In a university the product is education – the student's need maybe to gain knowledge for no other reason than knowledge possession itself, or it maybe for a more practical purpose such as to get a job. Some students may want the process of education to be an isolated one, others may want a social one.

In relation to policing some citizens may want high visibility, proliferation policing as this will provide the perception of a safe and ordered environment. Others may see this as a violation of their civil liberties.

Understanding exactly what the nature of the product is can affect the way the transformation process is set up.

18.3 | The practice of operations management

The birth of process management

When we walk into a McDonald's we enter a process for queuing, are served by someone who is not a trained waiter, and purchase a meal cooked by someone who is not a skilled chef. It has been designed to particular standards of quality; is the product of a process of manufacture; and will be exactly the same way regardless of where or when it is bought. McDonald's is the ultimate in systemisation.

Process design is often associated with Fredrick Winslow Taylor (who we have met previously in Chapter 2) and his five principles of management. In the late nineteenth and early twentieth centuries the US was experiencing rapid industrialisation. Driven by new technologies, more complex forms of organisation were emerging and many of the world's best known companies were being founded – including ESSO, General Motors and Ford. Skilled workers were scarce, even basic language skills were difficult to find. Taylor and his idea of scientific management solved this problem by making the attributes of the worker mostly irrelevant. Taylor and his supporters believed in 'rationalism' or the view that if one understands something one should be able to state it explicitly and write a rule for it. Taylor's objective in applying rules and procedures to work was to replace uncertainty with predictability. By applying this thinking to the process of manufacture then reliability, consistency and repeatability would result.

The **craft system** refers to a system in which the craft producers do everything. With or without customer involvement, they design, source materials, manufacture, sell and perhaps service. The craft system is based on workers with the embodied knowledge, skill and experience to carry out all necessary activity.

Management in practice | Disney's 'production' of cartoons

At the age of 21, Walter Elias 'Walt' Disney left the midwest, moved to Hollywood and opened his own movie studio. In *The Magic Kingdom* Steven Watts (2001) describes Walt Disney's attempts to apply the techniques of mass production to the art of making cartoons. Disney had great admiration for Henry Ford and his achievements, and introduced an assembly line at the Disney studio. Like all production lines this system employed a rigorous division of labour. Instead of drawing entire scenes, artists were given narrowly defined tasks, meticulously sketching and inking characters while supervisors looked on with stopwatches timing how long it took to complete each activity. During the 1930s this 'production' system resembled that of an automobile plant. Hundreds of young people were trained and fitted into the machine for 'manufacturing' entertainment. While this was labelled the 'Fun Factory' the working conditions on the assembly line were not always fun for the workers, with operations management methods leading to employee dissatisfaction and strikes.

Before Taylor, work was based on the **craft system** where individuals controlled the work process because their skill and knowledge told them what to do and how to do it. However, this left managers and owners who were trying to implement **factory production** with a level of control over the process of manufacture similar to that which a beekeeper has over the productive capacity of a hive of bees. To take full advantage of the possibilities of mechanisation and the factory system, all of the activities within a particular transformation process had to be fully understood by those who controlled the organisation.

Although Taylor carried out the experiments that resulted in his five principles almost exclusively in the steel industry, his ideas have endured to become the basis of operations management today. These ideas were initially developed by Henry Ford into the production line system that came to dominate manufacturing, and have since spread to the service sector.

While the principles of Taylor had a profound and positive effect on efficiency, they also had some negative effects which are worth considering in the context of operations management. The separation of the conception of the work, the planning and organising, from the

Factory production is a process-based system that breaks down the integrated nature of the craft worker's approach and makes it possible to increase the supply of goods by dividing tasks into simple and repetitive processes and sequences which could be done by unskilled workers and machinery on a single site.

execution, or doing, of the work coupled with the implementation of detailed process for the worker to follow with no task-related discretion had the effect of deskilling the worker and disrupting the craft system. In Taylor's system the worker was reduced to little more than a pair of hands trained in a very limited way to carry out a small set of repetitive tasks.

This deskilling effect meant that the worker no longer had the knowledge or skill to ensure the manufacture of a quality product. This depended more on the quality of the process of manufacture than on the skill of the workman. With this system the design of the process was paramount as a poorly designed process would produce a poor product.

Activity 18.2   Taylor's processes

- Look around at the organisations that you come into contact with in your daily life. Try to identify the processes that they use. Can you find any that are not under-pinned in some way by Taylor's principles?

Management in practice   Seeking the best www.sunseeker.com

From modest beginnings in a shed, to a workforce of 2,500, modern shipyards and world-beating technology, Sunseeker is the iconic brand in the supply of super-yachts to the super-rich. While the products are at the cutting edge of quailty and technology, the company remains committed to craftsmanship. Although much of the work in design and manufacturing is done by computers and machinery, Sunseeker claims the basis of its success is the skill of the artisans who form and polish the woods, metals and glass, that produce the work of art that is a Sunseekeer yacht.

The production process is a subtle blend of machine-produced fabication using the best that process management can offer, and hand-assembly and detail finishing where the human influence on product quality cannot be matched.

Sunseeker admits that you can build a quality boat without the traditonal craftsmanship they rely on – but, they say, it wouldn't be Sunseeker . . .

Source: Company website.

Activity 18.3   Craft versus factory

- Consider the manufacture of high-quality products such as a Sunseeker yacht, a Rolls-Royce motor car or a Rolex watch. In each of these products consider which parts of the manufacturing process are best done by machines and which parts are best done by hand.

Operations strategy

Chapter 8 looks at managing strategy as the process of setting an organisation's future direction. As operations is the means by which the company creates and delivers products, a company also needs an **operations strategy**. Slack *et al.* (2007) define operations strategy as the pattern of decisions that shapes the long-term capability of an operation – which is intended to support the corporate strategy. It clarifies the primary purposes and characteristics of the operations processes, and designs the systems to achieve these.

Operations strategy is the pattern of decisions that shapes the long-term capability of the operation.

Management in practice Linn Products www.linn.co.uk

Linn Products was established in 1972 by Ivor Tiefenbrun. Born in Glasgow, he was passionate about two things – engineering and listening to music. When he couldn't buy a hi-fi good enough to satisfy his needs he decided to make one himself.

In 1972 Linn introduced the Sondek LP12 turntable, the longest-lived hi-fi product still in production anywhere in the world and still the benchmark by which all turntables are judged. The Linn Sondek LP12 turntable revolutionised the hi-fi industry, proving categorically that the source of the music is the most important component in the hi-fi chain. Linn then set out to make the other components in the hi-fi chain as revolutionary as the first, setting new standards for performance over the years with each new product.

Today, Linn is an independent, precision-engineering company uniquely focused on the design, manufacture and sale of complete music and home theatre systems for customers who want the best. Linn systems can be found throughout the world in royal residences and on-board super-yachts.

At Linn operations is an integrated process, from product development through to after-sales service. All aspects of Linn's products are designed in-house and all the key processes are controlled by Linn people. Linn believe that everything can be improved by human interest and attention to detail. So the same person builds, tests and packs a complete product from start to finish. He/she takes all the time necessary to ensure that every detail is correct.

Only then will the person responsible for building the product sign his/her name and pack it for despatch. Every product can be tracked all the way from that individual to the customer, anywhere in the world. Linn systems are sold only by selected specialist retailers which have a similar commitment to quality products and service.

Source: Company website.

Activity 18.4 Searching for excellence

- While most organisations strive for excellence in some way or other, consider the operational challenges in actually becoming and remaining a world leader.

Case study Zara – the case continues: operations strategy: react rather than predict

What sets Zara apart from many of its competitors is what it has done with its business information and operations processes. Rather than trying to forecast demand and producing to meet that (possible) demand, it concentrates on reacting swiftly to (actual) demand. A typical clothes supplier may take three months to develop the styles for a season's range and the same again to set up the supply chain and manufacturing processes: six months pass before the garments are in the stores. Zara does this in weeks by:

- making decisions faster with better information;
- running design and production processes concurrently;
- holding stocks of fabric that can be used in several lines;
- distributing products more efficiently.

Some criticise Zara for copying designs from more prestigious brands. Customers do not seem to mind, as they buy Zara's affordable garments when they are in fashion. The company's operations strategy is clearly directed at speed – ensuring the shortest time between the design idea and the garment in the stores.

Case question 18.3

- Investigate the operational strategy of another large clothing retailer such as Marks and Spencer. Can you identify any differences?

The 4 Vs of operations

Although all operations systems transform input resources into output products, they differ on four dimensions:

- Volume: how many units are produced of a given type of product. Consumer goods are examples of high-volume production, supported by investment in specialised facilities, equipment and process planning.
- Variety: how many types (or versions) of a product have to be manufactured by the same facility. Fashion houses and custom car makers use more hand tools and highly skilled staff to enable the flexibility required to make a variety of unique products.
- Variation in demand: how the volume of production varies with time. Facilities at holiday resorts have to cope with vast differences in throughput depending on the time of year.
- Visibility: the extent to which customers see manufacturing or delivery process. This applies mainly to the service sector where the presence of the customer is vital to the process.

Management in practice   Bidding for success www.ebay.co.uk

Founded in 1995, eBay connects a diverse and passionate community of individual buyers and sellers, as well as small businesses. Its collective impact on e-commerce is staggering, in 2008, the total worth of goods sold on eBay was $60 billion–$2,000 every second.

With more than 88 million active users globally, eBay is the world's largest online marketplace, where anyone can buy and sell almost anything. The website is part car-boot sale, part auction house, part local market, part high street store, with the cost determined by how much people are prepared to pay.

eBay's strategy in recent years has been to move from a bid-only auction site to a site that also sells fixed price goods from other retailers much like other internet-based sellers such as Amazon. However, during the strategic shift this aspiration has not always been matched by eBay's operational capability to deliver. In 2009 the site experienced technical difficulties due to the inabilty of its operational processes and systems to cope with the increased volume and variety of orders that were the result of this strategic move. These difficulties resulted in the site being unavailable for periods of time and a consequent loss of revenue.

Sources: *Financial Times,* 23 November 2009; company website.

18.4   Operations processes

The 4 V's are key considerations in defining operations strategy. Before designing the detailed processes, managers decide on the type of operation it will be: what volume, how much variation, how will volume vary with time, and how visible?

Production systems

For production operations these decisions translate into two main considerations: volume of product and flexibility of the operations system – its ability to cope with changes in volume and/or variety. Hayes and Wheelwright (1979) propose that a single manufacturing system cannot efficiently produce different volumes of a variety of products. If a high volume is required consistently and reliably, then the manufacturing system must be arranged to produce only one product. If several products are required then a more flexible system is required to cope with their multiple requirements. Hayes and Wheelwright categorise four types of production operation (see Figure 18.4).

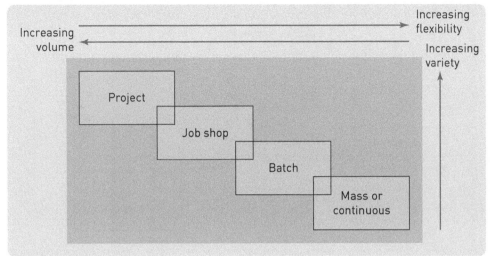

Figure 18.4
The product–process matrix

Project systems

These exist at the low-volume end of the spectrum and deal with the manufacture of very small numbers of product – often only single units. This entails many interdependent parallel operations of long duration to achieve an output. Examples include construction projects such as oil rigs, dams and skyscrapers, in which thousands of operations accumulate to complete one product over several years. The defining feature of this system is that the product is built in one place with all the resources brought to it and all the activities going on around it. The product will not move until it is complete, and sometimes not at all.

Job-shop systems

These are also relatively low-volume producing special products or services to customer specifications with little likelihood that any product will be repeated often. In a manufacturing context a tool room that makes special tools and fixtures is a classic example, as is a tailor who makes made-to-measure clothes to customer requirements. Such low-volume systems tend to use general-purpose equipment manned by highly skilled personnel. They exhibit a high degree of flexibility but have high unit costs.

Batch operations

These are possibly the most common systems in use today. Many different products are produced at regular or irregular intervals. One of the distinctive features of such systems in comparison to job-shop systems is that, since orders are repeated from time to time, it becomes worthwhile to spend time planning and documenting the sequence of processing operations, employing work study techniques, providing special tooling and perhaps some automation. There will be a mix of skilled, semi-skilled and unskilled labour in this type of system.

Mass production and continuous flow manufacturing

This type is used where demand for a single product is sufficiently high to warrant the installation of specialised automatic production lines. With their high rates of output and low manning levels, unit costs are typically very low. Such systems generally have little flexibility. Where the entities produced are discrete items such as cars or mobile phones, the term 'mass production' is used, where the entity is not discrete such as chemicals like petroleum or other substances such as cement then the term 'continuous production' is used.

Service systems

In service delivery operations, the product–process matrix does not adequately cater for the fourth V – visibility: the presence of the customer in the process and the potential for

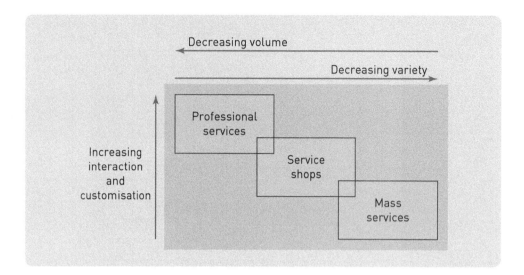

Figure 18.5
Service process
types

diversity and randomness this brings will defeat the best-designed processes. Figure 18.5 shows a similar model which helps in categorising service processes.

Professional services

These are high-contact operations where customers may spend a lot of time in the process. These services provide high levels of customisation and are adaptable to individual customer's needs. As a result the operational system relies on skilled and knowledgeable people rather than high levels of automation. Typical examples of these may be legal services or healthcare.

Service shops

These offer lower levels of customer contact and less customisation to deal with larger volumes of customers with similar needs. Examples include most restaurants and hotels, high street banks and many public services. Essentially the customer is buying a fairly standardised service which maybe slightly customised to the customers' needs. While people are still an integral part of the process they will tend to have limited skills and knowledge and have less discretion while working within a more rigid process.

Mass services

These provide standardised customer transactions, very limited contact time and little or no customisation: the emphasis is on automation and repetition. Staff will be low skilled and follow set procedures much like the staff on a production line, and the processes may be highly automated. Typical mass services include supermarkets, call centres and mass transport systems. For example, in a railway station, staff can sell tickets but have no discretion to offer customised journeys or make decisions beyond the scope of the process.

Activity 18.5   **Cutting up craft skills**

Consider a service such as a surgical operation. Do you think that routine surgery could be carried out by more scientifically managed methods where, for example, the person that performs the operation is not a qualified surgeon, but is trained to carry out a single procedure?

It is important to note that in the service sector 'interaction' (how much the customer can intervene in the process) is not the same as 'contact time'. A lecture to a large number of students is high in 'contact' but comparatively low in 'interaction': so high duration of contact does not always mean a more interactive service.

'Customisation' reflects the degree to which the service provided is tailored to the needs of the customer. Organisations which have a high degree of both interaction and customisation are categorised as professional services, e.g. legal practices. Conversely, organisations which have a low degree of both interaction and customisation are categorised as mass services, e.g. schools. The purpose of such classification of systems is to allow operations managers to decide how systems should be set up to deliver the type of process required.

These classifications exist as a continuum. Using education as an example, most state schools would be positioned near the bottom right-hand corner of the matrix. However a fee-paying school could be positioned more to the top-left due to its lower class sizes, greater provision of support staff and additional extra-curricular activities. Another example would be a specialist clinic dealing with rare and difficult to diagnose and treat conditions, which may operate as a professional service while a hospital that deals with standard operations such as cataracts or hip replacements may be set up more as a service shop. The type of service operation is therefore less about what the service is and more about how it might be provided.

18.5 | Process design

Span of processes: make or buy?

When Henry Ford developed his moving assembly-line method of producing the Model T car, he chose to 'own' all stages of production, i.e. the widest possible span of processes. Ford's company owned the rubber plantations that supplied the raw materials for the tyres; the forests that supplied the wood for the wheels; and the iron mines, steel plants, foundries, forges, rolling mills and machine shops that manufactured the engine and other components. Its ownership of the complete span of processes even extended to a shipping line and a railroad to transport materials and product.

Today no car manufacturer tries to manage such a wide **span of processes**, as specialism is the key to efficient operations. Parts require a different set of skills and machinery to produce than those required to assemble them into the car itself – so it is more efficient for a dedicated supplier to make them. Direct control of the operation has been replaced to a great extent by contractual control of the supplier.

The span of processes is the variety of processes that a company chooses to carry out in-house.

This is equally true in the service sector, where in a service such as airline travel, a company may decide to focus on the long-haul flights between hub airports, leaving the feeder flights to and from the hubs to be provided by other airlines. Likewise, the catering service and maintenance activity might be outsourced to specialist suppliers.

Activity 18.6 | The supply chain

- Consider a consumer product such as a bicycle – choose a popular model from one of the larger more famous brands and investigate its manufacturing process drawing a supply chain map that includes all of the companies that are involved in the manufacture of this one item.

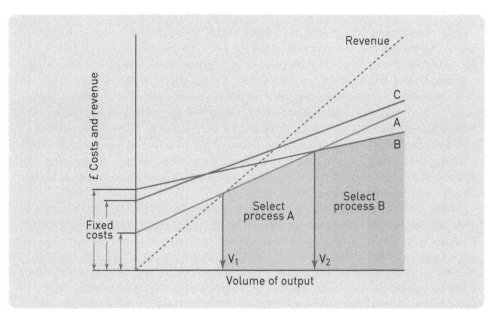

Figure 18.6
Break-even analysis

Process selection

Having identified strategically which type of operation you want to create in relation to the 4Vs, what you want to do within your operation and what you want to buy-in from a specialist supplier, the question then to be answered is what process configuration to implement.

The first thing to consider is the amount of automation to be used in comparison to manpower. Automation, while expensive, is generally very efficient therefore more investment in automation (fixed cost) will result in less need for manpower and therefore lower the variable costs of production. In this case a simple **break-even analysis** may help in making the choice. For each of the process sequences to be compared, the fixed and variable costs are determined. Fixed costs are those, such as special tooling costs, which are required to set up the processes and are independent of the volume of output. Variable costs are those, such as direct labour and material costs, which vary in direct proportion to the volume of output. Figure 18.6 shows how the total costs of three process sequences (A, B and C) change with volume of output, alongside the associated revenue.

The figure shows that, for quantities below V_1, none of the process sequences recover their costs; for quantities between V_1 and V_2, process sequence A is the most economical; for quantities greater than V_2, process B becomes the least costly. In this example process sequence C is uncompetitive at all levels of output.

A break-even analysis is a comparison of fixed versus variable costs that will indicate at which point in volume of output it is financially beneficial to invest in a higher level of infrastructure.

| Case study | Zara – the case continues: the design centre |

Zara designs all its products in-house – about 40,000 items per year from which 10,000 are selected for production. The firm encourages a collegial atmosphere among its designers, who seek inspiration from many sources such as trade fairs, discotheques, catwalks and magazines. Extensive feedback from the stores also contributes to the design process.

The designers for women's, men's and children's wear sit in different halls in a modern building attached to the headquarters. In each of these open spaces the designers occupy one side, the market specialists the middle and the buyers (procurement and production planners) occupy the other side. Designers first draw design sketches by hand and then discuss them with colleagues – not only other designers but also the market specialists and planning and procurement people. This process is crucial in retaining an overall 'Zara style'.

The sketches are then redrawn where further changes and adjustments, for better matching of weaves, textures and colours, are made. Critical decisions are made at this stage, especially regarding the selection of fabric. Before moving further through the process, it is necessary to determine whether the new design could be produced and sold at a profit.

The next step is to make a sample, a step often completed manually by skilled tailors located in the small pattern and sample-making shops co-located with the designers. If there are any questions or problems, the tailors can just walk over to the designers and discuss and resolve them on the spot.

The final decision on what, when and how much to produce is normally made by agreement between the relevant designer, market specialist, and procurement and production planner.

Facility layout

In addition to the sequence of the processes, consideration must also be given to their physical layout in relation with each other. **Layout planning** is an important issue because operational efficiency will be affected by the chosen layout's effects on the following factors:

- amount of inter-process movement of materials and/or customers;
- health and safety of staff and customers;
- levels of congestion and numbers of bottlenecks;
- utilisation of space, labour and equipment;
- levels of work-in-progress inventory required.

> **Layout planning** is the activity that determines the best configuration of resources such as equipment, infrastructure and people that will produce the most efficient process.

In the layout of service operations there may be other factors to consider, as a result of the customers' participation in the processes:

- Maximum product exposure – in the layout of retail stores, basic purchases and check-out stations are often positioned remote from the shop entrance, obliging the customer to walk past displays of other more-profitable products, which they may be enticed to buy.
- The 'ambience' of the physical surroundings – décor, noise levels, music, temperature and lighting may affect the customers' judgement of the service, how long they stay and how much they spend.
- The customers' perception of waiting times.

The reason for the inclusion of the word 'perception' in this last point is best illustrated by an example. An airline operating at Houston airport experienced a high level of complaints from its passengers about the waiting time in the baggage-reclaim area. The airline's solution was to re-direct baggage to the carousel furthest from the arrival gates. Although passengers had to walk further, and the baggage took just as long to arrive, the customers' perceptions were that the waiting time had been reduced.

Layout planning occurs at three levels of detail:

- Layout of departments on the site. For example, in a public house this would concern the sizing and positioning of the public bar, the lounge bar, toilets, kitchen and storeroom within the confines of the building used.
- Layout within departments. Continuing with the bar example, this would address the sizing and positioning of customer seating areas, the drinks counter, the food counter, slot machines, public telephone, passageways, etc.
- Layout of workplaces. For the bar counter this would determine the detailed layout of pumps for draught beers and other drinks, cash registers, sinks, shelves for bottled beers, spirits, wines and soft drinks, etc.

There are four well-established forms of facility layout: fixed-position, process, product and cell.

Fixed-position layout

This configuration is typically used for low-volume, project-type operations where the product being produced is massive, and movement of the material from process to process is impossible or impractical. Bridges, oil rigs and office buildings fall into this category, so the processes required come to the site.

In the service sector, football stadiums, theatres, cinemas and lecture rooms are all examples of fixed-position layouts, where the service that is the performance is presented in one place for communal attendance.

Process layout

This form of layout is used when there is no dominant flow pattern, and is particularly appropriate for job shop and small-batch operations. Figure 18.7 is a schematic representation of a process layout, showing three (of many) job process sequences.

By bringing similar process types together in departments, the advantages of flexibility and concentration of process expertise are gained. The disadvantages are: long delivery times; high levels of materials handling and transport; relatively high levels of work-in-progress inventory; low equipment utilisation; and consequent high unit costs. Scheduling of many jobs with different process routes through a process layout while monitoring their progress are among the most challenging tasks for operations managers.

Many service operations adopt the process layout but, instead of material movements, customers move from department to department; common examples include supermarkets, department stores, museums, art galleries and libraries.

Product layout

Where the demand for a single product is sufficiently high to warrant truly continuous operation mass production for discrete items such as, cars mobile phones, ball-point pens and confectionery; and process systems for 'fluids' such as oil products, sugar and cement. It is possible to have an automatic production line specially designed to incorporate not only the sequence of processes, but also an automatic transport system to move the product from process to process, in unison. With such a system there is no need for expensive work-in-progress

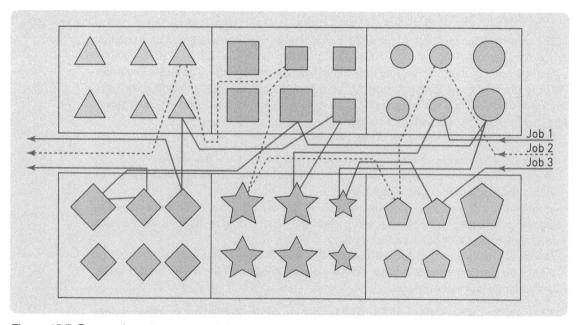

Figure 18.7 Process layout

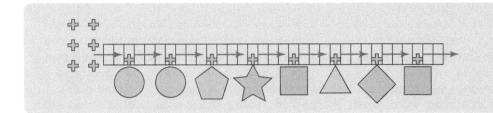

Figure 18.8
Product layout

between processes, less floor space is required, and throughput time for a particular item is very short.

However, although such systems deliver very low unit costs, they are vulnerable because of the absence of work-in-progress buffers: if one process fails, very quickly the whole line comes to a halt. Since only a single product type is produced, the challenge for the operations manager is to balance the level of output with the anticipated level of customer demand. When an imbalance occurs it is often reported in the business press; for example, computer components, such as memory chips, seem to be in a perpetual flux of over-supply and shortage. Automobile companies also are guilty of overproducing then storing cars until they are sold. As a car buyer this is an important consideration as the 'new' car that you buy may not be new at all but may have been 'stored' in a car park for a year or more before it is sold. Applications of the product layout are less common in service operations, but the following display some of its characteristics: self-service cafeteria, student registration, automatic mail sorting and some hospital diagnostic procedures.

Cell or group layout

Cell or group layout is suitable for many small- to medium-batch operations, and is a modified form of product layout. The difference is that whereas the products manufactured in a product layout have identical process sequencing requirements, and are obviously members of a family (e.g. different sizes and colours of a particular style of shoe), the products produced in a cell layout have similar process sequencing requirements, but may otherwise be dissimilar in appearance.

In order to convert a process layout to a cell layout, a study must first be made of the process sequences of all the products made, with a view to identifying clusters that are similar. Service operations which exhibit some of the cell layout's attributes include car tyre/exhaust/battery replacement outlets, and island-layout self-service cafeterias.

Case study   **Zara – the case continues: production process**

Zara manufactures approximately 50 per cent of its products in its own network of Spanish factories and uses subcontractors for all sewing operations. The other half of its products are procured from outside suppliers. With its relatively large and stable orders, Zara is a preferred customer for almost all its suppliers. This is important as suppliers will therefore prioritise Zara orders and generally be more responsive.

The make/buy decisions are usually made by the procurement and production planners. The key criteria for making these decisions are required levels of speed and expertise, cost-effectiveness and availability of sufficient capacity. Such decisions are made carefully, paying great attention to minimising the risks associated with achieving the correct workmanship and speed of supply.

For its in-house production, half of all fabrics are purchased un-dyed to allow faster response to mid-season colour changes.

The purchased fabric is then cut by machine. A typical factory has three or four cutting machines with long tables, where typically 30 to 50 layers of fabric are laid out under a top paper layer. The cutting pattern is generated by the CAD system (which automatically minimises fabric waste), checked by skilled operators, and then drawn by the machine onto the top layer (so that cut pieces can be identified later).

After a final visual check by the operator, the machine then cuts the multiple layers into hundreds of different small pieces. Operators then pack each piece into a separate clear plastic bag to be sent to sewing subcontractors.

Zara uses subcontractors for all sewing operations. Subcontractors themselves often collect the bagged-up cut pieces, along with appropriate components (such as buttons and zippers) in small trucks. There are some 500 sewing subcontractors in close proximity to La Coruña and most work exclusively for Zara. Zara closely monitors their operations to ensure quality, compliance with labour laws and adherence to the production schedule. Zara believes that outsourcing a highly labour-intensive operation,

such as sewing, allows its own factories to remain more focused and provides more flexibility to change production volumes quickly. Subcontractors then bring back the sewn items to the same factory, where each piece is inspected. Finished products are then placed in plastic bags, labelled and sent to the distribution centre.

Completed products procured from outside suppliers are also sent directly to the distribution centre and Zara control their quality by sampling batches of these.

Case questions 18.4

- Is Zara a craft or a factory system?
- Review the information about the manufacturing system Zara uses, then list its advantages and disadvantages.

18.6   The main activities of operations

Providing goods and services to a customer depends on five key operations activities, and these provide a useful way of describing and analysing an organisation's operations system (Sprague, 1990). These activities are:

- capacity
- standards
- materials
- scheduling
- control.

None of these activities operate alone but combine to form an operations system.

Capacity

Capacity is the ability to yield an output – it is a statement of the ability of the numerous resources within an organisation to deliver to the customer. Defining capacity depends on identifying the main resources required to deliver a saleable output – staff, machinery, materials and finance. Capacity is limited by whichever resource is in shortest supply – a hospital's capacity to conduct an operation will be determined by some minimum number of specifically competent surgeons, nurses and related professionals. In service organisations all aspects of capacity may be visible to the customer – they can see the quality of staff, and the state of the physical equipment and resources.

Standards

Standards relate to either quality or work performance. Quality standards are embedded in the specification of the product or service delivered to the customer. Work performance standards enable managers to estimate and plan capacity by providing information on the time it takes to do something. One of the advantages which low-cost airlines have established is that the time it takes them to turn around an aircraft between landing and take-off is much lower than for conventional airlines. This enables them to fly more journeys with each aircraft – significantly increasing capacity at little cost.

Materials

A vital aspect of the operations function is to ensure an adequate supply of the many material resources needed to deliver an output. One of the dilemmas is that holding stocks of materials, called inventory, is expensive – it ties up working capital, incurs storage costs and in changing markets there is a risk that stocks become outdated because of a change in model. Too much material can be as problematic as too little. Materials management is particularly important in manufacturing systems where all labour costs are invested in the product itself. In service settings most material is simple and is usually consumed by the customer during the service process.

Scheduling

This is the function of co-ordinating the available resources by time or place – specifying which resources need to be available and when, in order to meet demand. It begins with incoming information about demand and its likely impact on capacity. Service, productivity and profitability depend on matching supply with demand. Capacity management generates supply; scheduling links demand with capacity. It can be carried out over several time periods. Aggregate scheduling is done for the medium term, and is closely associated with planned levels of capacity: as airlines plan their future fleets, which they need to do several years ahead, they make judgements about both their capacity and the likely demand (translated into frequency of flights on particular routes). Master scheduling deals with likely demand (firm or prospective orders) over the next few months, while dispatching is concerned with immediate decisions, for example about which rooms to allocate to which guests in a hotel.

Control

Control is intended to check whether the plans for capacity, scheduling and inventory are actually working. Without control, there is little point in planning, as there is no mechanism then to learn from the experience. There are generally four steps in the control process:

- setting objectives – setting direction and standards;
- measuring – seeing what is happening;
- comparing – relating what is happening to what was expected to happen;
- acting – taking short-term or long-term actions to correct significant deviations.

Only through control can immediate operations be kept moving towards objectives, and lessons learned for future improvements.

Management in practice   **Computing speed** www.dell.com

By redesigning its whole supply chain, Dell has made a virtue out of speed and response to customers in a way that repays the company by efficient use of money. Customers buy online and pay for their product in advance. Dell also tries to manage the elective choices customers make by offering discounts for inventory that is moving too slowly. Its operational control system is such that customers can call into Dell to check progress in the manufacture of their order. By then Dell has the use of their money and some time later will pay its suppliers' bills for the materials they have provided. This system is so responsive that Dell is able to change its pricing structure daily to take advantage of material price fluctuations and to price aggressively for certain markets in ways that its less flexible competitors find difficult to match.

Source: Company website.

18.7 Quality

What is quality?

In addition to the factors that govern the design of effective and efficient operations systems, features of the product or service that is being delivered must also be considered – especially price and quality.

For undifferentiated products, such as transport, consumer goods such as cleaning products, or services, such as fast food, the price will be paramount as many customers will reason that cheapest is best. The price the customer is charged is governed largely by the cost the company incurs in producing the product or service. That in turn is largely driven by the efficiency of the operation. Therefore, if low cost is important, the operational processes – how they are sequenced, the automation and tooling, and the people who work within them – must all be designed with low cost in mind. This may mean compromising on the quality of the product by offering a basic service or product as opposed to a more comprehensive or functional one.

Quality appears difficult to quantify as it depends on the product, the application and the subjective views of the person making the assessment. As Crosby (1979) wrote:

> The first erroneous assumption is that quality means goodness, or luxury or shine, or weight. The word 'quality' is used to signify the relative worth of things in such phrases as 'good quality', bad quality . . . Each listener assumes the speaker means what he or she, the listener, means by the phrase . . . This is precisely the reason we must define quality as conformance to requirements if we are to manage it. If a Cadillac conforms to the requirements of a Cadillac then it is a quality car, if a Pinto conforms to the requirements of a Pinto then it is a quality car. Don't talk about poor quality or high quality talk about conformance and non-conformance. (p. 14)

Crosby's proposal moves the definition of quality from a term that is nebulous and difficult to define to a set of more tangible measures.

Key ideas | **Product quality**

The quality of products and services is not absolute but is based on the requirements of the customer. Therefore any product, as long as it does what the customer wants of it, can be considered a quality product. The most important activity is therefore to define and understand precisely what the customer is expecting and set-up operations to deliver exactly that.

Six features help to define quality in terms of what customers expect:

- Functionality – what the product does. Where price is less of a consideration, products that do more may be more attractive. This is especially true with technology-based products such as the iPhone where functionality is the prime consideration in choice: users see a product that does more as being of higher quality than one that does less.
- Performance – how well it does what it is meant to do. This element will feature more strongly in higher value 'statement' products such as a Porsche car, where top-speed and acceleration are considered important. A product that is faster, more economical, stronger or easier to use will be seen as higher quality than others which are not. A higher performance product is seen as a higher quality product.
- Reliability – the consistency of performance over time. Are the promises made to the customer honoured correctly and in the same way over many occasions? A more reliable product is seen as a higher-quality product.

- Durability – how robust it is. This may feature more on products that are used a lot such as tools and equipment or products that operate in a harsh environment. Climbing equipment needs to be resistant to breakage. A more durable product is seen as a higher-quality product.
- Customisation – how well the product fits the need. This is more relevant in products where additional features may be added to the core functions in products, such as a mobile phone or in financial services. The more a product or service fits exactly to a customer's need the higher quality it is seen to be.
- Appearance – how the product looks. This is important not only to convey the correct image such as a well-decorated house or a highly polished car but also where appearance affects the utility of the product such as a website: a clear layout will be a major factor in how easy it is to use. A product that looks good is considered a higher-quality product.

The customer's perception of quality will combine some or all of these factors: each of which can contribute to the quality standard the customer desires.

Case study   **Zara – the case continues: cost and quality**

The middle-aged mother buys clothes at Zara because they are cheap, while her teenage daughter buys there because they are in fashion. The matching of both low cost and acceptable quality is a winning combination. Like any other industry low cost in the clothing industry is obtained by having efficient and streamlined operational processes. Quality is more subjective; with garments, quality is defined more by the design or 'look' that the customer wants to be seen wearing rather than the quality of the construction. Most of these garments are destined to have a short life, as they will be discarded or relegated to the back of the wardrobe when fashion changes. This means certain aspects of manufacturing quality such as durability and robustness will be of little importance to the customer so long as a certain standard is reached.

Case question 18.5

- Consider the concept of fashion, what does quality actually mean? Think of specific factors that define the quality of fashion.

Additional dimensions of service quality

All of the elements mentioned apply to both products and services and are commonly labelled the 'tangibles'. In service operations intangible features affect perceptions of quality:

- Responsiveness – willingness to help a customer and provide prompt service. While applicable to all service encounters, this element is most powerful in a less structured service environment where there is more opportunity for the customer to request something at random that may be outwith the normal scope of the operation. A high-class restaurant may be expected to be more responsive than a fast-food outlet where the customer would not think to request an alteration to the meal on offer.
- Assurance – ability of the operation to inspire confidence. This element is most easily illustrated in provision of professional services: in a dental surgery the ambience of the surroundings, the equipment, and the knowledge and expertise of the staff make the customer feel secure.
- Empathy – understanding and attentiveness shown to customers. Here the focus is mainly on the skills of the staff, their awareness of others and ability to communicate effectively. This is most easily seen in relation to the emergency services where empathising with the victim is both a key feature of the service experience and a critical factor in the effective performance of the task.

Order-winning and order-qualifying criteria

A good way to determine the relative importance of each quality element is to distinguish between order winning criteria and order qualifying criteria (Hill, 1993).

- Order-winning criteria are features that the customer regards as the reason to buy the product or service. Improving these will win business.
- Order-qualifying criteria will not win business but may lose it – if they are not met they will disqualify the product or service from consideration.

Quality management

Quality depends on operational systems in place. Theory and techniques about managing quality were developed first in the manufacturing sector, but are now also used in the service sector.

In manufacturing, craftspeople tend to have pride in their work and continuously strive to improve their mastery of the craft. During the evolution of the factory system, the craft system suffered as management subdivided the work process into smaller tasks performed by different people. This had two detrimental effects on quality. First, no single person was responsible for the whole process, so the pride in work that was evident in the craft system and was the basis of quality was removed. Second, craft skills were eroded and the consequence of this was that the capability of the individual to build quality into a product was lost. In essence, process management removed quality assurance from the remit of production staff, in effect taking the responsibility for producing quality products away from manufacturing workers. To remedy this situation attempts were made to 'build' quality into the process with more and more detailed and comprehensive processes used for the manufacture of each product. This, however, had only limited success.

The problem of production quality was not fully grasped until the mid to late twentieth century with pioneers such as Juran (1974), Deming (1988) and Feigenbaum (1993), working to develop philosophies and methods. Although developed initially in the West it was the Japanese who had most success as they applied the lessons widely and conscientiously. They also recognised the fundamental truth of craft production, which is the person who performs the transformation is the best person to ensure quality. The Japanese quality revolution was therefore based on placing the responsibility for quality with the worker. History has thus come full circle, with individuals taking pride in doing quality work and striving to make regular improvements in the production process.

Key ideas   **Principles of total quality management (TQM)**

- **Philosophy**: waste reduction through continuous improvement.
- **Leadership**: committed and visible from top to bottom of the organisation.
- **Measurement**: costs involved in quality failures – the cost of quality.
- **Scope**: everyone, everywhere across whole supply chain.
- **Methods**: simple control and improvement techniques implemented by teams.

Total quality management (TQM) is a philosophy of management that is driven by customer needs and expectations and focuses on continually improving work processes.

Although there were many people involved in the search for quality and many systems developed, the principles are best encapsulated in the system of **total quality management** (TQM). This advocates that a constant effort to remove waste adds value. Some of these wastes are obvious – scrapped material and lost time through equipment failure – but other wastes come through bad systems or poor communications, and may be more difficult to find and measure. Progressive, small improvements reduce costs as the operational process uses resources more effectively. Crosby (1979) introduced the idea that 'quality is free': it is getting it wrong that costs money.

In contrast with the scientific management approach, modern writers propose that quality management should not be separated from production: everyone is responsible for contributing to quality. Methods used include team working, brainstorming techniques and simple statistical process controls (Oakland, 1994).

Thinking about quality at the design stage brings important benefits. Choices here should incorporate ideas and information from as many insiders, customers and suppliers as is sensible. Such processes capture the prevention and 'right first time' ideals and create opportunities to save cost and time. Waste minimisation is the goal – waste being the use of resources that does not add value for the customer. Note that customers are not the only stakeholders. Management may be able to justify an activity not directly required by a direct customer – such as environmental and legal obligations.

Quality systems and procedures

While it is relatively simple to understand the elements that make up quality and the philosophy behind it, operationalising it by implementing a system to embed quality into all that the organisation does is a different matter. A quality management system consists of the organisational structure, responsibilities, procedures, processes and resources for implementing quality management. Dale (2007) proposes that:

> The purpose of a quality management system is to establish a framework of reference points to ensure every time a process is performed the same information, methods, skills and controls are used and applied in consistent manner. (p. 280)

The documentation which makes up the quality system has three levels:

1 Company quality manual – a basic document that provides a concise summary of the quality management policy, strategy and system together with how it supports the company objectives and organisational structure.
2 Procedures manual that describes the function, structure and responsibilities of each department.
3 Detail work instructions, specifications, standards and methods which support the processes.

While setting up a quality system is relatively straightforward, achieving its effective implementation requires some additional elements:

- A clear quality strategy that supports the company strategic objectives – this is necessary to provide the direction that keeps the company quality programme in line with operational strategy.
- Top management support – the top management must understand and believe in the benefits of doing things right, promote these at all times, communicate the principles of quality development and maintain a clear idea of what quality means for the operation.
- Team-based approach – these days everyone must work together to achieve the quality goals.
- Investment in training – changes in attitudes, work practice and skills are key, therefore the achievement of quality throughout the organisation is very much reliant on the development of quality people.

18.8 | **Integrating themes**

Sustainable performance

All pollution is caused in some way by an operational failure. Whether it is a poorly designed process producing more waste than necessary or the result of an accident, the cause is an inadequate operations process. Hawken *et al.* (1999) describe the planet Earth in operational terms as a transformation process where resources are constantly input to biological, chemical and geological processes which transform them into other states. They claim that human beings, through production and consumption, have created an industrial metabolism that exists beside, and disrupting, the Earth's natural processes.

The Earth, however, is a closed system: resources cannot be added or taken away, they can only be changed. As the finite resources of the planet are transformed through industrial activity into increasing amounts of waste, the Earth's capacity to sustain life will be compromised. Although operations managers are continually striving to increase the efficiency of industrial processes and reduce waste, on a planetary scale, levels of waste are enormous. Every product has a 'hidden history' of waste: producing 1 ton of paper consumes 98 tons of resources. The point is that while waste at the factory level is being addressed, waste on a planetary scale is only beginning to be understood. Today legislation is being introduced that requires organisations to work in a more sustainable manner. Operations managers need to design and operate the processes of transformation by considering the entire external supply chain and its effect on the planet, not just the internal processes of the factory.

Governance and control

Safety and quality standards are now more prevalent than ever. In addition to umbrella organisations such as the International Standards Organisation (ISO) and the British Standards Institute (BSI) all industries have specific bodies such as the Civil Aviation Authority (CAA) for airline safety and the Food Standards Agency (FSA) which is concerned with food and how it is sold and labelled.

As more standards are introduced and business becomes more highly regulated, it is the responsibility of the operations staff to design processes that are compliant in how they operate. There have been many high-profile cases where industrial accidents such as the Cyanide gas leak in Bhopal caused by Union Carbide or the radiation leak at the Three Mile Island Nuclear Generating facility operated by Metropolitan Edison have led to serious disasters. These examples were the result of process failure. Operations personnel must become aware of the governance regulating all operational activity, as any contravention, while probably not newsworthy, will have some detrimental effect on the business, the customer or the environment.

Internationalisation

Advances in technology and telecommunications mean that few major organisations operate locally – most buy and sell internationally. This expanded context provides both opportunities and challenges. The main challenge is increased competition as geographical barriers are removed and companies from other countries enter global markets. From an operational perspective, the world market for goods and services is not a level paying field, differentials in labour, power and utility costs and availability of natural resources provide some, what could be called 'unfair', advantages. The corresponding opportunity is that all companies have better access to a larger supplier network. Puig *et al.* (2009), from their study of the textiles industry, propose that this means that companies must become more aggressive in their adoption of the appropriate operations strategy, focusing on higher value-adding activities, not relying solely on price as a competitive advantage but also on quality and customer support.

Summary

1 **Define the term operations management**

- Operations management is the activities, decisions and responsibilities of managing the production and delivery of products and services.
- This includes responsibility for people and process and product.

2 **Describe the transformation process model of operations management**

- Transformation process is the organisational system that takes inputs:
  - facilities
  - staff
  - finance
  - raw materials
  - information

and transforms these into output products – either tangible goods or intangible services – that can be sold in the market.

3 **Show how operations management can contribute to the competitiveness of the organisation**

- By designing and implementing systems and processes that are repeatable, consistent, reliable, efficient and compliant with the legislation that governs the overall environment.
- By creating an operations system that is aligned with the goals of the organisation in terms of volume of output, variety of product, variation in demand and visibility of process.

4 **Identify different forms of operational activity**

- Managing the capacity of the transformation process.
- Setting process and product standards to be adhered to within the transformation process.
- Managing the materials pipeline into and through the transformation process.
- Scheduling of the required resources to be used in the transformation process.
- Controlling the activities within the transformation process.

5 **Define the term quality and describe features that can be used to quantify it**

- Quality means conformance to the requirements of the customer.
- Product or service quality can be described in relation to functionality, performance, reliability, durability, customisation and appearance.

6 **Show how ideas from the chapter add to your understanding of the integrating themes**

- All waste is the result of an operations failure, so performance depends on changes to operations to reduce waste not just within the immediate process but across the supply chain.
- Operations staff work in an increasingly regulated environment, so need to focus on designing processes that are not only efficient and sustainable, but which also comply with regulatory and control systems.
- The growth of international trade brings challenges for operations managers as they seek to satisfy geographically dispersed customers in conjunction with equally dispersed suppliers.

Review questions

1 Review some consumer goods such as mobile phones, cars and kitchen appliances. Identify the service elements attached to the purchase of these products.

2 Discuss why variation in the inputs to the transformation process is a bad thing. Which of the five inputs is likely to be subject to most variation and which to least?

3 Why is control over quality at source so important?

4 How does service quality differ from manufacturing quality?

5 Why is delivery reliability more important than delivery speed?

6 Describe and discuss the importance of the demand/supply balance.

7 Discuss why it is impossible to have a single production system that is equally efficient at all volumes of throughput.

8 Describe the differences between product, process and cell layouts.

9 Discuss the concepts of order winners and order qualifiers.

10 Summarise an idea from the chapter that adds to your understanding of the integrating themes.

Concluding critical reflection

Think about the ways in which a company you are familiar with deals with operational issues such as capacity, scheduling, quality or cost. Then make notes on the following questions:

- What ideas discussed in this chapter struck you as being relevant to practice in this company?

- To what extent does this company experience external pressures from customers or competitors for increased operational performance?

- Identify the main inputs, outputs and feedback mechanisms used in the company's transformation process.

- Identify the main processes that the company uses and analyse how well they work.

- Describe the relationship between operations and other parts of the organisation.

- Identify the features that are used to define the quality of the product or service that this company provides.

Further reading

Crosby, P. (1979) *Quality is Free*, McGraw Hill, New York.

> A classic text detailing the basics of quality management and showing how it all started.

Lowson, R.H. (2002) *Strategic Operations Management the New Competitive Advantage,* Routledge, London.

> An established comprehensive and authoritative text specialising in operations strategy and its philosophies and techniques.

Slack, N., Chambers, S. and Johnston, R. (2009) *Operations Management,* Prentice Hall, Harlow.

> A large buffet-style bible which covers all of the main topics in operations management today.

Sprague, L. (2007) 'Evolution of the field of operations management,' *Journal of Operations Management*, 25, 219–238.

> A brief but comprehensive summary of the field of operations a management from a historical perspective.

Weblinks

These are the websites that have appeared in this chapter:

www.zara.com
www.sunseeker.com
www.linn.co.uk
www.ebay.co.uk
www.dell.com

Visit two of the websites in the list (or any other company that interests you) and navigate to the pages dealing with the products and services they offer. This is usually the first one you see, but in some it may be further back.

- What messages do they give about the nature of the goods and services they offer? What challenges are they likely to raise for operations in terms of their emphasis on, for example, quality, delivery or cost? What implications might that have for people working in the company?
- See if you can find any information on the site about the operating systems, or how they link with their suppliers.

 For video case studies, audio summaries, flashcards, exercises and annotated weblinks related to this chapter, visit **www.pearsoned.co.uk/mymanagementlab**

GLOSSARY

Administrative management is the use of institutions and order rather than relying on personal qualities to get things done.

The **administrative model of decision making** describes how people make decisions in uncertain, ambiguous situations.

Ambiguity is when people are uncertain about their goals and how best to achieve them.

Arbitrariness (of corruption) is the degree of ambiguity associated with corrupt transactions.

Assessment centres are multi-exercise processes designed to identify the recruitment and promotion potential of personnel.

Assets are the property, plant and equipment, vehicles, stocks of goods for trading, money owed by customers and cash: in other words, the physical resources of the business.

The **balanced scorecard** is a performance measurement tool that looks at four areas: financial, customer satisfaction, internal processes and innovation, which contribute to organisational performance.

A **balance sheet** shows the assets of the business and the sources from which finance has been raised.

Behaviour is something a person does that can be directly observed.

Behaviour modification is a general label for attempts to change behaviour by using appropriate and timely reinforcement.

The **big five** refers to trait clusters that appear consistently to capture main personality traits: openness, conscientiousness, extraversion, agreeableness and neuroticism.

A **blog** is a weblog that allows individuals to post opinions and ideas.

Bounded rationality is behaviour that is rational within a decision process which is limited (bounded) by an individual's ability to process information.

A **break-even analysis** is a comparison of fixed versus variable costs that will indicate at which point in volume of output it is financially beneficial to invest in a higher level of infrastructure.

Bureaucracy is a system in which people are expected to follow precisely defined rules and procedures rather than to use personal judgement.

A **business plan** is a document that sets out the markets the business intends to serve, how it will do so and what finance is required.

The **capital market** comprises all the individuals and institutions that have money to invest, including banks, life assurance companies and pension funds and, as users of capital, business organisations, individuals and governments.

A **cash flow statement** shows the sources from which cash has been generated and how it has been spent during a period of time.

Centralisation is when a relatively large number of decisions are taken by management at the top of the organisation.

Certainty describes the situation when all the information the decision maker needs is available.

A **channel** is the medium of communication between a sender and a receiver.

Co-creation is product or service development that makes intensive use of the contributions of customers.

Collectivism 'describes societies in which people, from birth onwards, are integrated into strong, cohesive in-groups which . . . protect them in exchange for unquestioning loyalty' (Hofstede, 1991, p. 51).

Communication is the exchange of information through written or spoken words, symbols and actions to reach a common understanding.

Competences are the skills and abilities by which resources are deployed effectively – systems, procedures and ways of working.

Competencies (in HRM) refer to knowledge, skills, ability and other personal characteristics required to perform a job well.

A **competitive environment (or context)** is the industry-specific environment comprising the organisation's customers, suppliers and competitors.

Competitive strategy explains how an organisation (or unit within it) intends to achieve competitive advantage in its market.

Complexity theory is concerned with complex dynamic systems that have the capacity to organise themselves spontaneously.

Concertive control is when workers reach a negotiated consensus on how to shape their behaviour according to a set of core values.

Consideration is a pattern of leadership behaviour that demonstrates sensitivity to relationships and to the social needs of employees.

Content is the specific substantive task that the group is undertaking.

Contingencies are factors such as uncertainty, interdependence and size that reflect the situation of the organisation.

Contingency approaches propose that the performance of an organisation depends on having a structure that is appropriate to its environment.

Control is the process of monitoring activities to ensure that results are in line with the plan and acting to correct significant deviations.

The **control process** is the generic activity of setting performance standards, measuring actual performance, comparing actual performance with the standards, and acting to correct deviations or modify standards.

A **control system** is the way the elements in the control process are designed and combined in a specific situation.

Core competences are the activities and processes through which resources are deployed to achieve competitive advantage in ways that others cannot imitate or obtain.

Corporate governance refers to the rules and processes intended to control those responsible for managing an organisation.

Corporate responsibility refers to the awareness, acceptance and management of the wider implications of corporate decisions.

Corrective action aims to correct problems to get performance back on track.

A **cost breakdown structure** is a system for categorising and collecting costs, which allows cost to be attributed and analysed by activity rather than unit.

A **cost leadership strategy** is one in which a firm uses low price as the main competitive weapon.

The **craft system** refers to a system in which the craft producers do everything. With or without customer involvement, they design, source materials, manufacture, sell and perhaps service.

Creativity is the ability to combine ideas in a unique way or to make unusual associations between ideas.

Critical success factors are those aspects of a strategy that *must* be achieved to secure competitive advantage.

Critical thinking identifies the assumptions behind ideas, relates them to their context, imagines alternatives and recognises limitations.

Culture is a pattern of shared basic assumptions that was learned by a group as it solved its problems of external adaptation and internal integration, and that has worked well enough to be considered valid and transmitted to new members (Schein, 2004, p. 17).

Current assets can be expected to be cash or to be converted to cash within a year.

A **customer-centred organisation** is focused upon, and structured around, identifying and satisfying the demands of its consumers.

Customer relationship management (CRM) is a process of creating and maintaining long-term relationships with customers.

Customer satisfaction is the extent a customer perceives that a product matches their expectations.

Customers are individuals, households, organisations, institutions, resellers and governments that purchase products from other organisations.

Data are raw, unanalysed facts, figures and events.

Decentralisation is when a relatively large number of decisions are taken lower down the organisation in the operating units.

A **decision** is a specific commitment to action (usually a commitment of resources).

Decision criteria define the factors that are relevant in making a decision.

Decision making is the process of identifying problems and opportunities and then resolving them.

Decision support systems help people to calculate the consequences of alternatives before they decide which to choose.

A **decision tree** helps someone to make a choice by progressively eliminating options as additional criteria or events are added to the tree.

Decoding is the interpretation of a message into a form with meaning.

Delegation occurs when one person gives another the authority to undertake specific activities or decisions.

Demands are human wants backed by the ability to buy.

Determinism is the view that the business environment determines an organisation's structure.

Differentiation The state of segmentation of the organisation into subsystems, each of which tends to develop particular attributes in response to the particular demands posed by its relevant external environment.

Differentiation strategy consists of offering a product or service that is perceived as unique or distinctive on a basis other than price.

Disintermediation Removing intermediaries such as distributors or brokers that formerly linked a company to its customers.

A **divisional structure** is when tasks are grouped in relation to their outputs, such as products or the needs of different types of customer.

Dynamic capabilities are an organisation's abilities to renew and recreate its strategic capabilities to meet the needs of a changing environment.

e-business refers to the integration, through the internet, of all an organisation's processes from its suppliers through to its customers.

e-commerce refers to the activity of selling goods or service over the internet.

Economies of scale are achieved when producing something in large quantities reduces the cost of each unit.

Effectiveness is a measure of how well an activity contributes to achieving organisational goals.

Efficiency is a measure of the inputs required for each unit of output.

Emergent strategies are those that result from actions taken one by one that converge in time in some sort of consistency pattern.

Encoding is translating information into symbols for communication.

Enlightened self-interest is the practice of acting in a way that is costly or inconvenient at present, but which is believed to be in one's best interest in the long term.

Enterprise resource planning (ERP) is a computer-based planning system which links separate databases to plan the use of all resources within the enterprise.

An **Entrepreneur** is someone with a new venture, project or activity, and is usually associated with creative thinking, driving innovation and championing change.

Equity theory argues that perception of unfairness leads to tension, which then motivates the individual to resolve that unfairness.

Escalating commitment is a bias which leads to increased commitment to a previous decision despite evidence that it may have been wrong.

Ethical audits are the practice of systematically reviewing the extent to which an organisation's actions are consistent with its stated ethical intentions.

Ethical consumers are those who take ethical issues into account in deciding what to purchase.

Ethical decision-making models examine the influence of individual characteristics and organisational policies on ethical decisions.

Ethical investors are people who only invest in businesses that meet specified criteria of ethical behaviour.

Ethical relativism is the principle that ethical judgements cannot be made independently of the culture in which the issue arises.

Exchange is the act of obtaining a desired object from someone by offering something in return.

An **executive information system** provides those at the top of the organisation with easy access to timely and relevant information.

Existence needs reflect a person's requirement for material and energy.

Expectancy theory argues that motivation depends on a person's belief in the probability that effort will lead to good performance, and that good performance will lead to them receiving an outcome they value (valence).

The **external environment (or context)** consists of elements beyond the organisation – it combines the competitive and general environments.

External fit is when there is a close and consistent relationship between an organisation's competitive strategy and its HRM strategy.

An **extranet** is a version of the internet that is restricted to specified people in specified companies – usually customers or suppliers.

Extrinsic rewards are valued outcomes or benefits provided by others, such as promotion, a pay increase or a bigger car.

Factory production is a process-based system that breaks down the integrated nature of the craft worker's approach and makes it possible to increase the supply of goods by dividing tasks into simple and repetitive processes and sequences which could be done by unskilled workers and machinery on a single site.

Feedback (in communication) occurs as the receiver expresses his or her reaction to the sender's message.

Feedback (in systems theory) refers to the provision of information about the effects of an activity.

Femininity pertains to societies in which social gender roles overlap.

Five forces analysis is a technique for identifying and listing those aspects of the five forces most relevant to the profitability of an organisation at that time.

Fixed (long-term) assets are the physical properties that the company possesses – such as land, buildings, production equipment – which are likely to have a useful life of more than one year. There may also be intangible assets such as patent rights or copyrights.

A **focus strategy** is when a company competes by targeting very specific segments of the market.

Foreign direct investment (FDI) is the practice of investing shareholder funds directly in another country, by building or buying physical facilities, or by buying a company.

Formal authority is the right that a person in a specified role has to make decisions, allocate resources or give instructions.

Formalisation is the practice of using written or electronic documents to direct and control employees.

Formal structure consists of guidelines, documents or procedures setting out how the organisation's activities are divided and co-ordinated.

A **formal team** is one that management has deliberately created to perform specific tasks to help meet organisational goals.

Franchising is the practice of extending a business by giving other organisations, in return for a fee, the right to use your brand name, technology or product specifications.

Functional managers are responsible for the performance of an area of technical or professional work.

A **functional structure** is when tasks are grouped into departments based on similar skills and expertise.

The **general environment (or context)** (sometimes known as the macro-environment) includes political, economic, social technological, (natural) environmental and legal factors that affect all organisations.

General managers are responsible for the performance of a distinct unit of the organisation.

Global companies work in many countries, securing resources and finding markets in whichever country is most suitable.

Globalisation refers to the increasing integration of internationally dispersed economic activities.

A **goal (or objective)** is a desired future state for an activity or organisational unit.

Goal-setting theory argues that motivation is influenced by goal difficulty, goal specificity and knowledge of results.

Groupthink is 'a mode of thinking that people engage in when they are deeply involved in a cohesive ingroup, when the members' striving for unanimity overrides their motivation to realistically appraise alternative courses of action' (Janis, 1972).

Growth needs are those that impel people to be creative or to produce an effect on themselves or their environment.

Heuristics Simple rules or mental short cuts that simplify making decisions.

High-context cultures are those in which information is implicit and can only be fully understood by those with shared experiences in the culture.

Horizontal specialisation is the degree to which tasks are divided among separate people or departments.

Human relations approach is a school of management which emphasises the importance of social processes at work.

Human resource management refers to all those activities associated with the management of work and people in organisations.

Hygiene (or maintenance) factors are those aspects surrounding the task which can prevent discontent and dissatisfaction but will not in themselves contribute to psychological growth and hence motivation.

An **ideology** is a set of integrated beliefs, theories and doctrines that helps to direct the actions of a society.

The **illusion of control** is a source of bias resulting from the tendency to overestimate one's ability to control activities and events.

Incremental innovations are small changes in a current product or process which brings a minor improvement.

People use an **incremental model** of decision making when they are uncertain about the consequences. They search for a limited range of options, and policy unfolds from a series of cumulative small decisions.

Individualism pertains to societies in which the ties between individuals are loose.

Influence is the process by which one party attempts to modify the behaviour of others by mobilising power resources.

An **informal group** is one that emerges when people come together and interact regularly.

Informal structure is the undocumented relationships between members of the organisation that emerge as people adapt systems to new conditions, and satisfy personal and group needs.

Information comes from data that have been processed so that they have meaning for the person receiving it.

Information overload arises when the amount of information a person has to deal with exceeds his/her capacity to process it.

Information richness refers to the amount of information that a communication channel can carry, and the extent to which it enables sender and receiver to achieve common understanding.

Information systems management is the planning, acquisition, development and use of these systems.

Initiating structure is a pattern of leadership behaviour that emphasises the performance of the work in hand and the achievement of production or service goals.

Innovation is usually concerned with product or service development.

An **input measure** is an element of resource that is measured as it is put in to the transformation process.

Instrumentality is the perceived probability that good performance will lead to valued rewards, measured on a scale from 0 (no chance) to 1 (certainty).

Intangible resources are non-physical assets such as information, reputation and knowledge.

Integration is the process of achieving unity of effort among the various subsystems in the accomplishment of the organisation's task.

The **interaction model** is a theory of change that stresses the continuing interaction between the internal and external contexts of an organisation, making the outcomes of change hard to predict.

Internal fit is when the various components of the HRM strategy support each other and consistently encourage certain attitudes and behaviour.

International management is the practice of managing business operations in more than one country.

The **internet** is a web of hundreds of thousands of computer networks linked together by telephone lines and satellite links through which data can be carried.

An **intranet** is a version of the internet that only specified people within an organisation can use.

Intrinsic rewards are valued outcomes or benefits that come from the individual, such as feelings of satisfaction, achievement and competence.

Job analysis is the process of determining the characteristics of an area of work according to a prescribed set of dimensions.

Job characteristics theory predicts that the design of a job will affect internal motivation and work outcomes, with the effects being mediated by individual and contextual factors.

A **joint venture** is an alliance in which the partners agree to form a separate, independent organisation for a specific business purpose.

Key performance indicators (KPIs) are a summarised set of the most important measures of performance that inform managers how well an operation is achieving organisational goals.

Knowledge builds on information and embodies a person's prior understanding, experience and learning.

Knowledge management systems are a type of IS intended to support people as they create, store, transfer and apply knowledge.

Layout planning is the activity that determines the best configuration of resources such as equipment, infrastructure and people that will produce the most efficient process.

Leadership refers to the process of influencing the activities of others towards high levels of goal setting and achievement.

A **learning organisation** is one that has developed the capacity to continuously learn, adapt and change.

Liabilities of a business as reported in the balance sheet are the debts and financial obligations of the business to all those people and institutions that are not shareholders, e.g. a bank or suppliers.

Licensing is when one firm gives another firm the right to use assets such as patents or technology in exchange for a fee.

Lifecycle models of change are those that view change as an activity which follows a logical, orderly sequence of activities that can be planned in advance.

A **limited liability company** has an identity and existence in its own right as distinct from its owners (shareholders in Europe, stockholders in North America). A shareholder has an ownership right in the company in which the shares are held.

Line managers are responsible for the performance of activities that directly meet customers' needs.

Low-context cultures are those where people are more psychologically distant so that information needs to be explicit if members are to understand it.

Management is the activity of getting things done with the aid of people and other resources.

Management as a distinct role develops when activities previously embedded in the work itself become the responsibility not of the employee but of owners or their agents.

Management as a universal human activity occurs whenever people take responsibility for an activity and consciously try to shape its progress and outcome.

Management by objectives is a system in which managers and staff agree their objectives, and then measure progress towards them periodically.

A **management information system** provides information and support for managerial decision making.

Management tasks are those of planning, organising, leading and controlling the use of resources to add value to them.

A **manager** is someone who gets things done with the aid of people and other resources.

A **market offering** is the combination of products, services, information or experiences that an enterprise offers to a market to satisfy a need or want.

Market segmentation is the process of dividing markets comprising the heterogeneous needs of many consumers into segments comprising the homogeneous needs of smaller groups.

Marketing is the process by which organisations create value for customers in order to receive value from them in return.

The **marketing environment** consists of the actors and forces outside marketing that affect the marketing manager's ability to develop and maintain successful relationships with its target consumers.

A **marketing information system** is the systematic process for the collection, analysis and distribution of marketing information.

Marketing intelligence is information about developments in the marketing environment.

The **marketing mix** is the set of marketing tools – product, price, promotion and place – that an organisation uses to satisfy consumers' needs.

Marketing orientation refers to an organisational culture that encourages people to behave in ways that offer high-value goods and services to customers.

Masculinity pertains to societies in which social gender roles are clearly distinct.

A **matrix structure** is when those doing a task report both to a functional and a project or divisional boss.

A **mechanistic structure** means there is a high degree of task specialisation, people's responsibility and authority are closely defined and decision making is centralised.

The **message** is what the sender communicates.

A **metaphor** is an image used to signify the essential characteristics of a phenomenon.

Metcalfe's law states that the value of a network increases with the square of the number of users connected to the network.

A **mission statement** is a broad statement of an organisation's scope and purpose, aiming to distinguish it from similar organisations.

A **model (or theory)** represents a complex phenomenon by identifying the major elements and relationships.

Motivation refers to the forces within or beyond a person that arouse and sustain their commitment to a course of action.

Motivator factors are those aspects of the work itself that Herzberg found influenced people to superior performance and effort.

Multinational companies are managed from one country, but have significant production and marketing operations in many others.

Needs are states of felt deprivation, reflecting biological and social influences.

A **network structure** is when tasks required by one company are performed by other companies with expertise in those areas.

Networking refers to behaviours that aim to build, maintain and use informal relationships (internal and external) that may help work-related activities.

Noise is anything that confuses, diminishes or interferes with communication.

Non-linear systems are those in which small changes are amplified through many interactions with other variables so that the eventual effect is unpredictable.

A **non-programmed (unstructured) decision** is a unique decision that requires a custom-made solution when information is lacking or unclear.

Non-receptive contexts are those where the combined effects of features of the organisation (such as culture or technology) appear likely to hinder change.

Non-verbal communication is the process of coding meaning through behaviours such as facial expression, gestures and body postures.

Observation is the activity of concentrating on how a team works rather than taking part in the activity itself.

An **office automation system** uses several systems to create, process, store and distribute information.

An **open system** is one that interacts with its environment.

Operational plans detail how the overall objectives are to be achieved, by specifying what senior management expects from specific departments or functions.

Operational research is a scientific method of providing (managers) with a quantitative basis for decisions regarding the operations under their control.

Operations management is all of the activities, decisions and responsibilities of managing the production and delivery of products and services.

Operations strategy is the pattern of decisions that shapes the long-term capability of the operation.

An **opportunity** is the chance to do something not previously expected.

Optimism bias is a human tendency to see the future in a more positive light than is warranted by experience.

An **organic structure** is one where people are expected to work together and use their initiative to solve problems; job descriptions and rules are few and imprecise.

An **organisation** is a social arrangement for achieving controlled performance towards goals that create value.

An **organisation chart** shows the main departments and senior positions in an organisation and the reporting relations between them.

Organisation structure 'The structure of an organisation [is] the sum total of the ways in which it divides its labour into distinct tasks and then achieves co-ordination among them' (Mintzberg, 1979).

Organisational change is a deliberate attempt to improve organisational performance by changing one or more aspects of the organisation, such as its technology, structure or business processes.

Organisational performance is the accumulated results of all the organisation's work processes and activities.

Organisational readiness refers to the extent to which staff are able to specify objectives, tasks and resource requirements of a plan appropriately, leading to acceptance.

An **output measure** is a measurement taken after an operational process is complete.

Outsourcing (offshoring) is the practice of contracting out defined functions or activities to companies in other countries that can do the work more cost-effectively.

The **participative model** is the belief that if people are able to take part in planning a change they will be more willing to accept and implement the change.

A **perceived performance gap** arises when people believe that the actual performance of a unit or business is out of line with the level they desire.

Perception is the active psychological process in which stimuli are selected and organised into meaningful patterns.

Performance imperatives are aspects of performance that are especially important for an organisation to do well, such as flexibility and innovation.

Performance-related pay involves the explicit link of financial reward to performance and contributions to the achievement of organisational objectives.

A **person culture** is one in which activity is strongly influenced by the wishes of the individuals who are part of the organisation.

A **personality test** is a sample of attributes obtained under standardised conditions that applies specific scoring rules to obtain quantitative information for those attributes that the test is designed to measure.

Pervasiveness (of corruption) represents the extent to which a firm is likely to encounter corruption in the course of normal transactions with state officials.

PESTEL analysis is a technique for identifying and listing the political, economic, social, technological, environmental and legal factors in the general environment most relevant to an organisation.

Philanthropy is the practice of contributing personal wealth to charitable or similar causes.

Planning is the iterative task of setting goals, specifying how to achieve them, implementing the plan and evaluating the results.

A **planning system** refers to the processes by which the members of an organisation produce plans, including their frequency and who takes part in the process.

A **policy** is a guideline that establishes some general principles for making a decision.

Political behaviour is 'the practical domain of power in action, worked out through the use of techniques of influence and other (more or less extreme) tactics' (Buchanan and Badham, 1999).

Political models reflect the view that organisations are made up from groups with separate interests, goals and values, and that these affect how they respond to change.

Political risk is the risk of losing assets, earning power or managerial control due to political events or the actions of host governments.

Power is 'the capacity of individuals to exert their will over others' (Buchanan and Badham, 1999).

A **power culture** is one in which people's activities are strongly influenced by a dominant central figure.

Power distance is the extent to which the less powerful members of organisations within a country expect and accept that power is distributed unevenly.

Preferred team roles are the types of behaviour that people display relatively frequently when they are part of a team.

Prior hypothesis bias results from a tendency to base decisions on strong prior beliefs, even if the evidence shows that they are wrong.

A problem is a gap between an existing and a desired state of affairs.

A procedure is a series of related steps to deal with a structured problem.

A process control system monitors and controls variables describing the state of a physical process.

A process measure is a measurement taken during an operational process that provides data on how the process is performing.

The product lifecycle suggests that products pass through the stages of introduction, growth, maturity and decline.

A profit and loss statement reflects the benefits derived from the trading activities of the business during a period of time.

A programmed (or structured) decision is a repetitive decision that can be handled by a routine approach.

Project managers are responsible for managing a project, usually intended to change some element of an organisation or its context.

A psychological contract is the set of understandings people have regarding the commitments made between themselves and their organisation.

Radical innovations are large game changing developments that alter the competitive landscape.

The range of variation sets the acceptable limits within which performance can vary from standard without requiring remedial action.

The rational model of decision making assumes that people make consistent choices to maximise economic value within specified constraints.

Real goals are those to which people give most attention.

Receptive contexts are those where features of the organisation (such as culture or technology) appear likely to help change.

Reintermediation Creating intermediaries between customers and suppliers, providing services such as supplier search and product evaluation.

Relatedness needs involve a desire for relationships with significant other people.

Representativeness bias results from a tendency to generalise inappropriately from a small sample or a single vivid event.

Responsibility refers to a person's duty to meet the expectations others have of them in their role.

Risk refers to situations in which the decision maker is able to estimate the likelihood of the alternative outcomes.

A role is the sum of the expectations that other people have of a person occupying a position.

A role culture is one in which people's activities are strongly influenced by clear and detailed job descriptions and other formal signals as to what is expected from them.

A rule sets out what someone can or cannot do in a given situation.

Satisficing is the acceptance by decision makers of the first solution that is 'good enough'.

Scenario planning is an attempt to create coherent and credible alternative stories about the future.

Scientific management: the school of management called 'scientific' attempted to create a science of factory production.

Selective attention is the ability, often unconscious, to choose from the stream of signals in the environment, concentrating on some and ignoring others.

A self-managing team operates without an internal manager and is responsible for a complete area of work.

A sensitivity analysis tests the effect on a plan of several alternative values of the key variables.

Shareholders are the principal risk takers in a company. They contribute the long-term capital for which they expect to be rewarded in the form of dividends – a distribution from the profit of the business.

Shareholders' funds are the capital contributed by the shareholders plus profits that have not been distributed to the shareholders.

Situational (contingency) models of leadership attempt to identify the contextual factors that affect when one style will be more effective than another.

The social contract consists of the mutual obligations that society and business recognise they have to each other.

Social networking sites use internet technologies which enable people to interact within an online community to share information and ideas.

A socio-technical system is one in which outcomes depend on the interaction of both the technical and social subsystems.

A span of control is the number of subordinates reporting directly to the person above them in the hierarchy.

The span of processes is the variety of processes that a company chooses to carry out in-house.

Staff managers are responsible for the performance of activities that support line managers.

Stakeholders are individuals, groups or organisations with an interest in, or who are affected by, what the organisation does.

Standard of performance is the defined level of performance to be achieved against which an operations actual performance is compared.

Stated goals are those which are prominent in company publications and websites.

Stereotyping is the practice of consigning a person to a category or personality type on the basis of his/her membership of some known group.

A **strategic business unit** consists of a number of closely related products for which it is meaningful to formulate a separate strategy.

Strategic misrepresentation is where competition for resources leads planners to underestimate costs and overestimate benefits, to increase the likelihood that their project gains approval.

A **strategic plan** sets out the overall direction for the business, is broad in scope and covers all the major activities.

Strategy is about how people decide to organise major resources to enhance performance of an enterprise.

Structural choice emphasises the scope which management has to decide the form of structure, irrespective of environmental conditions.

Structure is the regularity in the way a unit or group is organised, such as the roles that are specified.

Subjective probability (in expectancy theory) is a person's estimate of the likelihood that a certain level of effort (E) will produce a level of performance (P) which will then lead to an expected outcome (O).

Subsystems are the separate but related parts that make up the total system.

Sustainable performance refers to economic activities that meet the needs of the present population while preserving the environment for the needs of future generations.

A **SWOT analysis** is a way of summarising the organisation's strengths and weaknesses relative to external opportunities and threats.

A **system** is a set of interrelated parts designed to achieve a purpose.

A **system boundary** separates the system from its environment.

Tangible resources are the physical assets of an organisation such as plant, people and finance.

A **target market** is the segment of the market selected by the organisation as the focus of its activities.

A **task culture** is one in which the focus of activity is towards completing a task or project using whatever means are appropriate.

A **team** is 'a small number of people with complementary skills who are committed to a common purpose, performance goals, and approach for which they hold themselves mutually accountable' (Katzenbach and Smith, 1993).

Team-based rewards are payments or non-financial incentives provided to members of a formally established team that are linked to the performance of the group.

Technology is the knowledge, equipment and activities used to transform inputs into outputs.

The **theory of absolute advantage** is a trade theory which proposes that by specialising in the production of goods and services which they can produce more efficiently than others, nations will increase their economic well-being.

Total quality management (TQM) is a philosophy of management that is driven by customer needs and expectations and focuses on continually improving work processes.

A **trait** is a relatively stable aspect of an individual's personality that influences behaviour in a particular direction.

A **transaction** occurs when two parties exchange things of value to each at a specified time and place.

A **transaction processing system (TPS)** records and processes data from routine transactions such as payroll, sales or purchases.

A **transactional leader** is one who treats leadership as an exchange, giving followers what they want if they do what the leader desires.

The **transformation process** the operational system that takes all of the inputs; raw materials, information, facilities, capital and people and converts them into an output product to be delivered to the market.

A **transformational leader** is a leader who treats leadership as a matter of motivation and commitment, inspiring followers by appealing to higher ideals and moral values.

Transnational companies operate in many countries and delegate many decisions to local managers.

Uncertainty is when people are clear about their goals, but have little information about which course of action is most likely to succeed.

Uncertainty avoidance is the extent to which members of a culture feel threatened by uncertain or unknown situations.

Unique resources are resources that are vital to competitive advantage and which others cannot obtain.

User generated content (UGC) is text, visual or audio material which users create and place on a website for others to view.

Valence is the perceived value or preference that an individual has for a particular outcome.

Validity occurs when there is a statistically significant relationship between a predictor (such as a selection test score) and measures of on-the-job performance.

Value is added to resources when they are transformed into goods or services that are worth more than their original cost plus the cost of transformation.

A **value chain** 'divides a firm into the discrete activities it performs in designing, producing, marketing and distributing its product. It is the basic tool for diagnosing competitive advantage and finding ways to enhance it' (Porter, 1985).

Vertical specialisation refers to the extent to which responsibilities at different levels are defined.

Virtual teams are those in which the members are physically separated, using communications technologies to collaborate across space and time to accomplish their common task.

Wants are the form which human needs take as they are shaped by local culture and individual personality.

Wikinomics describes a business culture in which customers are no longer only consumers but also co-creators and co-producers of the service.

A **work breakdown structure** is a system for categorising work activity based on phases or packages of work rather than the unit that is performing the work.

A **working group** is a collection of individuals who work mainly on their own but interact socially and share information and best practices.